# LIBRARY OF HEBREW BIBLE/
# OLD TESTAMENT STUDIES

# 424

*Formerly Journal for the Study of the Old Testament Supplement Series*

# THE STORIES ABOUT NABOTH THE JEZREELITE

A Source, Composition, and Redaction Investigation
of 1 Kings 21 and Passages in 2 Kings 9

Patrick T. Cronauer, O.S.B

t&t clark

NEW YORK • LONDON

T & T Clark International, Madison Square Park, 15 East 26th Street, New York, NY 10010

T & T Clark International, The Tower Building, 11 York Road, London SE1 7NX

*T & T Clark International is a Continuum imprint.*

Unless otherwise indicated, all texts of the Hebrew Bible cited in this work are from the *BHS* [or WTT] - *Biblia Hebraica Stuttgartensia* (*BHS*) (Hebrew Bible, Masoretic Text or Hebrew Old Testament), edited by K. Elliger and W. Rudolph of the Deutsche Bibelgesellschaft, Stuttgart, Fourth Corrected Edition, Copyright © 1966, 1977, 1983, 1990 by the Deutsche Bibelgesellschaft (German Bible Society), Stuttgart. Used by permission.

Unless otherwise indicated, all texts of the Greek Bible cited in this work are from the LXT - LXX *Septuaginta* (LXT) (Old Greek Jewish Scriptures) edited by Alfred Rahlfs, Copyright © 1935 by the Württembergische Bibelanstalt / Deutsche Bibelgesellschaft (German Bible Society), Stuttgart. Used by permission.

Unless otherwise indicated, all texts of the Bible in English cited in this work are from the *Revised Standard Version of the Bible* (RSV), copyright © 1946, 1952, and 1971 by the Division of Christian Education of the National Council of the Churches of Christ in the USA. Used by permission. All rights reserved.

BWHEBB, BWHEBL [Hebrew]; BWGRKL, BWGRKN, and BWGRKI [Greek] Postscript® Type 1 and TrueType™ fonts Copyright © 1994-2002 BibleWorks, LLC. All rights reserved. These Biblical Greek and Hebrew fonts are used with permission and are from BibleWorks, software for Biblical exegesis and research.

Library of Congress Cataloging-in-Publication Data

Cronauer, Patrick T.
The Stories about Naboth the Jezreelite: A Source, Composition, and Redaction Investigation of 1 Kings 21 and Passages in 2 Kings 9 / Patrick T. Cronauer.
        p. cm. — (Journal for the Study of the Old Testament. Supplement Series; 424)
Includes bibliographical references and index.
        ISBN 0-567-02940-9 (hardcover)
        1. Bible. O.T. Kings, 1st, XXI-XXII--Criticism, interpretation, etc. 2. Bible. O.T. Kings, 2nd, IX—Criticism, interpretation, etc. 3. Naboth (Biblical figure) 4. Jezebel, Queen, consort of Ahab, King of Israel. I. Title. II. Series.
        BS1335.52.C76 2005
        222'.53066—dc22
             2005006785

Typeset and edited for Continuum by Forthcoming Publications Ltd
www.forthcomingpublications.com

Printed in the United States of America

ISBN 0-567-02940-9 (hardback)

# CONTENTS

Part III
THE STORY OF THE ACQUISITION OF NABOTH'S VINEYARD:
1 KINGS 21:1-16

Part IV
THE SOURCES AND ORIGINS OF THE STORY
OF NABOTH'S VINEYARD IN 1 KINGS 21:1-16: AN HYPOTHESIS

# ACKNOWLEDGMENTS

The present text is a revision of large portions of my doctoral dissertation, "The Stories about Naboth: A Search for Sources and Origins," which I defended on April 29, 1999, at l'École Biblique et Archéologique Française de Jérusalem. The thesis was directed by Reverend Dr Francolino Gonçalves, OP, my teacher, mentor, and friend for whose direction, wisdom, and insightful guidance I am truly grateful. I also wish to express my deep appreciation and gratitude for the administration, faculty, staff, and fellow students who assisted, encouraged, and journeyed with me both at the Pontifical Biblical Institute in Rome and at l'École Biblique in Jerusalem.

I am profoundly grateful to my Archabbot, Douglas R. Nowicki, OSB, and my Benedictine confreres at St Vincent Archabbey in Latrobe, Pennsylvania for their constant support, prayers, and encouragement throughout the years of my doctoral work and those in preparing this volume. Their faith in me has been the fuel which drove my work. In particular, I want to express my gratitude to my confrere and friend, the Reverend Stanley Markiewicz, OSB, who was the first to instill in me a great love and respect for the Word of God and for the Holy Land, and who has mentored me in both for the past 35 years.

In true gratitude, I also acknowledge the Reverend David Turner, OSB, of St Precopius Abbey in Lisle, IL, who graciously read the text of my manuscript and made editorial suggestions. His insights were accurate, careful, and wise. I am truly grateful for his encouragement, his efforts, and the time he spent to help make my manuscript more readable and clear.

Finally I want to thank my family, and in particular my dear mother and father, for their unceasing prayers, love, and sacrifice on my behalf over the years as I pursued my vocation and my studies. Their unwavering support and encouragement kept me going and empowered me to persevere through all, and they still do today. It is my honor to dedicate this book to my family, and in particular to my mother, Marion, who continues to be one of my shining lights here on Earth, and to my father, Harold, who now shines with the Eternal Light in heaven. May he rest in peace.

# ABBREVIATIONS

| | |
|---|---|
| BDB | F. Brown, S. R. Driver, and C. A. Briggs, *The New Brown-Driver Briggs-Gesenius Hebrew and English Lexicon*. Peabody, MA: Hendrickson, 1979. |
| Dtr | Both the Deuteronomist and Deuteronomistic |
| DtrH | Deuteronomistic History |
| DtrN | Deuteronomistic redactor with nomistic/legal interests |
| DtrP | Deuteronomistic redactor with prophetic interests |
| fasc. | fascicle |
| *GK* | W. Gesenius, *Hebrew Grammar*. Edited by E. Kautzsch. Translated by A. E. Cowley. 2d ed.; Oxford: Oxford University Press, 1910. |
| LXX | Septuagint |
| LXX[A] | Codex Alexandrinus |
| LXX[B] | Codex Vaticanus |
| LXX[L] | The Lucianic Version/s |
| MT | Masoretic Text |
| *NK-B* | L. Koehler and W. Baumgartner, *The Hebrew and Aramaic Lexicon of the Old Testament: The New Koehler-Baumgartner in English*. Edited and translated by M. E. J. Richardson. Revised by Walter Baumgartner and Johann Jakob Stamm. Leiden: Brill, 1994. |
| Rd | redactor |
| RSV | Revised Standard Version |

# LIST OF TABLES

# INTRODUCTION

Most people, when they hear the name "Naboth" from the Bible, rightfully recall the story of Naboth's Vineyard in 1 Kgs 21. This is by far the primary and the largest text concerning Naboth, but it is not the only text. We also find reference to Naboth, to what we might call the "Naboth Affair," in 2 Kgs 9:21, 25–26. These two texts represent the only material in the Bible concerning Naboth and neither is without its difficulties.

The sources and origins of the texts about Naboth and his death have long been an object of scholarly and non-scholarly interest. The story of Naboth's Vineyard in 1 Kgs 21 (MT) is one of the best known and most popular stories of the Old Testament. It is a story that speaks to the heart and soul of anyone who has ever suffered injustice at the hands of those in authority or power. The story teaches that injustice, racism, hatred, and murder (whether physical, psychological or spiritual) will not be allowed to go unpunished. The story speaks of political and judicial corruption and of collusion at the highest levels of government and religious institutions. It is a story that speaks of the basic human and religious rights of people being totally disregarded by others who are greedy and unscrupulous. As such, it is no surprise that it is so popular. I believe that its universal applicability is part and parcel with the intention of its author. It is this very "universality" which indicates that what we are dealing with in this story is not an "historical account" of an actual crime, but rather, an account whose purpose was to teach moral, ethical, and religious lessons; it is a *didactic parable*.[1]

Perhaps because of mention by name in this parable of the historical characters, Ahab and Jezebel, some scholars have succumbed to the temptation to find the historical locus for the sources and origins of the story in the actual period of the Ahabite dynasty (873–842 B.C.E.) or the period of their usurper Jehu's dynasty (842–745 B.C.E.).[2] The fact that the story also mentions Elijah

---

1.   This is not to say that this story was not, perhaps, based upon some actual event concerning the murder of a certain Naboth, but, in my opinion, this actual event was then taken by a gifted artist and created into a story which offers strong warnings to all those who might be tempted or "seduced" by foreign "women" (i.e. foreign gods, or power, or greed) to misuse their authority and power against the innocent and faithful people under their "care."

2.   See, among others: O. H. Steck, *Überlieferungs und Zeitgeschichte in den Elia-Erzählungen* (Neukirchen–Vluyn: Neukirchener Verlag, 1968), 40–53; P. Welten, "Naboth's Weinberg (I Könige 21)," *EvTh* 33 (1973): 18–32 (31); S. DeVries, *Prophet Against Prophet: The Role of the Micaiah Narrative (I Kings 22) in the Development of Early Prophetic Tradition* (Grand Rapids: Eerdmans, 1978), 116, 131–32; B. P. Robinson, *Israel's Mysterious God: An Analysis of some Old Testament Narratives* (Newcastle upon Tyne: Grevatt & Grevatt, 1986), 52. See also the presentation of the scholarly opinion of the question of the oldest layer of the tradition in Appendix 1.

(vv. 17–20a) has bolstered this attempt to date the story to the time of Elijah, whose tenure as prophet in the Bible matches the reigns of Ahab and his first son and successor, Ahaziah.

The search for the historical "locus" of this story is further complicated by the fact that it is also found within the so-called "Deuteronomistic History" (DtrH). More specifically, because a substantial portion of 1 Kgs 21 (vv. 20b–26) is comprised of recognizable Deuteronomistic terminology, many scholars consider the story as a whole to have come into being during the composition of this DtrH.[3]

First Kings 21:1–20a has also caused a great deal of scholarly debate concerning its sources and origins, since it contains very little, if any, recognizably Deuteronomistic language. Alongside this fact, there is also a great imbalance between the two halves of the story in 1 Kgs 21 in terms of responsibility for the crime committed. In vv. 1–16 Jezebel is the main mover; it is she who arranges the death of Naboth and the taking of his vineyard for Ahab. Ahab, meanwhile, was in his bed. In vv. 17–26, however, it is Ahab who receives the "lion's share" of the accusations and condemnations. Jezebel is never directly accused for the murder of Naboth. In fact, in many ways, the two halves of the chapter appear to have precious little in common.

The central problem in the history of scholarly interpretation of 1 Kgs 21 has to do, therefore, with the sources and origins of the account as it is currently found in the Bible and with the complex history of its composition. The present work contributes to this ongoing search, debate, and conversation. The main thesis of this work is that there is sufficient textual, thematic, and linguistic "evidence" which would allow us to hypothesize a much later dating for the origins of the story in 1 Kgs 21:1–16 than is normally attributed to it, namely, to postexilic, Persian-period Jehud. I maintain that a Persian-period Jehud writer took a text which was already found in the DtrH (1 Kgs 21:17–29), which contained both an account of a crime committed by Ahab against Naboth—what I call an "Elijah–Naboth Fragment" (vv. 17–19a, 20a)—and Deuteronomistic accusations and condemnations of Ahab and his dynasty, supposedly for this same crime (vv. 20b–26), and expanded and filled out this composite text with the addition of a parable of his own creation (1 Kgs 21:1–16, 23, 25bα).

In this new story the author created a fictional account, a didactic parable, in which he described in detail the crime against Naboth, and in which he shifted the blame for this crime from Ahab to Jezebel. By means of his interventions, this author changed the entire focus and purpose of the older and shorter Dtr text.

---

3.    See, among others: S. R. Driver, *An Introduction to the Literature of the Old Testament* (5th ed.; Edinburgh: T. & T. Clark, 1894), 196; C. F. Burney, *Notes on the Hebrew Text of the Books of Kings* (Oxford: Oxford University Press, 1903; repr., New York: Ktav, 1970), 207; M. Noth, *Überlieferungsgeschichtliche Studien*, vol. 1, *Die sammelnden und bearbeiten Geschichtswerke im Alten Testament* (Schriften der Königsberger gelehrten Gesellschaft. Geistewissenschaftliche Klasse; 18 Jahrgang, Heft 2; Halle [Saale]: Max Niemeyer, 1943), 120-21 (78–79) (note: there are two sets of page numbers found in this text); T. Veijola, *Das Königtum in der Beurteilung der deuteronomistischen Historiographie: Eine redaktionsgeschichtliche Untersuchung* (AASF 198; Helsinki: Suomalainen Tiedeakatemia, 1977), 91–92.

The presentation of my research into the text and history of 1 Kgs 21 will proceed in a certain "chronological" order. In Part I, I will first discuss the oldest layer of the tradition concerning Naboth, namely, the Elijah–Naboth Fragment. I will then investigate what I call the "Jehu-Apologetic Redaction" of the account of Jehu's overthrow of the Ahabite dynasty found in 2 Kgs 9–10. This is then followed by a consideration of yet another layer of redaction which I call the "Anti-Jezebel Redaction." All of this will call for the need to analyze the use of the "prophecy-fulfillment" pattern in these texts.

In Part II, I will consider the accusations and condemnations made against Ahab and Jezebel now found in 1 Kgs 21:20b–29. I will then present an analysis of the Deuteronomistic composition of 1 Kgs 21:17–29 and its relationship to the Jehu-Apologetic Redaction in 2 Kgs 9.

Having studied 1 Kgs 21:17–29 and its relationship to 2 Kgs 9, in Part III I turn my attention to the story of the acquisition of Naboth's vineyard found in 1 Kgs 21:1–16. In this part, I will present what I have called an "expository reading" of the text in which I will engage scholarly opinion on a wide range of issues in each act and scene of the narrative drama found in this text.

In the final section of the book, Part IV, I present my hypothesis concerning the sources and origins of the story of Naboth's Vineyard in 1 Kgs 21:1–16. Here I propose answers to the questions of when, where, why, how, and by whom the story of Naboth's Vineyard was written.

# Part I

AN OLD "ELIJAH–NABOTH FRAGMENT"
AND THE "JEHU-APOLOGETIC REDACTION":
1 KINGS 21:17–29

# Chapter 1

## 1 KINGS 21:17Aα–19Aβ AND 20Aα–Bα: AN OLD "ELIJAH–NABOTH FRAGMENT"

In 1 Kgs 21:17–19aβ and 20aα–bα is found what I maintain is an old "Elijah–Naboth Fragment." I designate the Elijah–Naboth Fragment in this way since it forms a separate layer of tradition within 1 Kgs 21 which might well be the oldest element of that chapter.[1] This fragment is obviously not a complete story in itself, but appears to be merely the ending of an earlier story that had been either excised from a no-longer extant text, or that had somehow survived the loss of its original context and was now being reused by a later author. This fragment, together with the remainder of its original context, was probably a part of the ancient oral tradition of the books of Kings by the time the Deuteronomistic historian compiled his history, or at least it was a part of a pre-Dtr edition of the tradition. The same is probably true in the case of a similar, but independent, tradition found in what I refer to as the "Jehu-Apologetic Redaction" in 2 Kgs 9:21bγ, 25–26.

These two old and originally independent fragments are now linked together by means of the Deuteronomistic "oracle of transferal" found in 1 Kgs 21:27–29. Because of the very strong Deuteronomistic "dynastic" emphasis found in the accusations and condemnations in 1 Kgs 21:20b–22, 24–26, there was a need on the part of the compiler to facilitate the "transfer" of the clearly individual and personal punishment designated for Ahab, found in the Elijah–Naboth Fragment, to a punishment that would include the whole of Ahab's dynasty. The Deuteronomist was able to accomplish this by transferring the "accomplishment" or fulfillment of the oracle in the Elijah–Naboth Fragment to Ahab's last son, Joram, in 2 Kgs 9. This was achieved by the addition of the "oracle of transferal" found in 1 Kgs 21:27–29.

---

1. Steck (*Überlieferung und Zeitgeschichte*) maintains that vv. 17–18a and 19–20bα form the oldest layer in 1 Kgs 21, what he calls "den Grundstock der prophetischen Nabothsüberlieferung" which he claims is the "ältesten Elia-Naboth-Überlieferung" (p. 52). Steck maintains that 1 Kgs 21:27–29 come from around the same time as the Jehu story—namely, from the beginning of Jehu's reign (p. 45). R. Bohlen, *Der Fall Nabot* (TTS 35; Trier: Paulinus-Verlag, 1978), 172–87, also refers to vv. 17a–19d as a "Fragment." He maintains "dass 17a–20d die früheste literarisches Schicht des Nabotkapitels" and he claims that the earliest time for it was towards the end of the reign of Jeroboam II—namely, 784/83–753/52 (p. 302). He assigns 21:27–29 to a post-Dtr hand (pp. 304–9).

## 1. *The Oracle of 1 Kings 21:19b and its "Fulfillment Notices"*

I maintain that the oracle of 1 Kgs 21:19b is a secondary insertion into the old Elijah–Naboth Fragment, probably even by the hand of the Dtr editor.[2] The purpose of this insertion was to create and impose a prophecy–fulfillment relationship between these two texts. It is possible that this insertion replaced an older oracle of punishment or doom which formed a part of the original Elijah–Naboth Fragment, either at the present location, or after v. 20bα. First Kings 21:17–19aβ, 20aα–bα (the Elijah–Naboth Fragment), represent a commissioning of the prophet to go down and confront Ahab, the king of Israel, who himself had gone down to take possession of Naboth's vineyard; a vineyard which was obtained by unjust

---

2.   With the following: A. Jepsen, who holds that v. 19b is a later insertion and that the original oracle spoken against Ahab has been lost (A. Jepsen, *Nabi, Soziologische Studien zur alttestamentlichen Literatur und Religionsgeschichte* [Munich: Beck, 1934], 58–59 and n. 1). J. M. Miller and H.-C. Schmitt see v. 19b as a gloss whose purpose is to introduce into the text the prophecy supposedly fulfilled by the death of Ahab in 22:38 (J. M. Miller, "The Fall of the House of Ahab," *VT* 17 [1967]: 307–24 [313]; H.-C. Schmitt, *Elisa: Traditionsgeschichtliche Untersuchungen zur vorklassischen nordisraelitischen Prophetie* [Gütersloh: Gütersloher Verlagshaus Gerd Mohn, 1972], 122–23 n. 2). W. Dietrich holds that there is a disruption between 19a and 19b. Verse 19b represents for him "a supplement identifiable by means of the doublet. The doublet itself in 19b is translated by the LXX as if the Hebrew was לְכֵן, therefore this is clearly a smoothing over of the text" (W. Dietrich, *Prophetie und Geschichte: Eine redaktionsgeschichtliche Untersuchung zum deuteronomistischen Geschichtswerk* [FRLANT 108; Göttingen: Vandenhoeck & Ruprecht, 1972], 48–49). E. Würthwein argues that there are many indications that 19a and 19b are not from the same hand: "In 19b is a prophecy which is said to be fulfilled in 22:38. This characteristic schema of prophecy–fulfillment shows that 19b and 22:38 are to be recognized as Dtr, more specifically, as DtrP." He also maintains that "the repetition of the introductory clauses from 19a in 19b forms a 'wiederaufnahmen' and that normally, the text between the two elements of a 'wiederaufnahmen' is considered to be interpolation" (E. Würthwein, "Naboth-Novelle und Elia-Wort," *ZThK* 75 [1978]: 375–97 [380–82]). R. Bohlen maintains that "the very repetition of the commissioning and messenger formulas in 19b prevents judging the oracle in 19b to be a part of the accusation in 19a" (Bohlen, *Der Fall Nabot*, 188, 192). G. H. Jones considers 19b to have been added to the text as a result of the misidentification of the king who was murdered in Samaria in the Syrian war accounts. He maintains that 22:38 and 19b are meant to link the Syrian wars with the Elijah–Ahab tradition (G. H. Jones, *1 and 2 Kings*, vol. 2, *1 Kings 17:1–2 Kings 25:30* [New Century Bible Commentary; Grand Rapids: Eerdmans, 1984], 358). H. Schmoldt holds that "one can, without difficulty, believe that 17–19aα(β) is a continuation of vv. 1–16. This is not, however, the case for 19bβ for this word of threat is in no way prepared for by the previous account and it must, therefore, be seen as a later addition" (H. Schmoldt, "Elijas Botschaft an Ahab: Überlegungen zum Werdegang von 1 Kön 21," *BN* 28 [1985]: 39–52 [43]). M. Oeming maintains that "due to the presence of the suspicious double כֹּה אָמַר יְהוָה, the invective against Ahab must be considered a later addition, but certainly not of Dtr origin" (M. Oeming, "Naboth, der Jesreeliter: Untersuchung zu den theolog-ischen Motiven der Überlieferungsgeschichte von 1 Reg 21," *ZAW* 98 [1986]: 363–82 [368]). S. L. McKenzie holds that vv. 17, 18, and 19a and perhaps 20abβ are the oldest remaining segments of ch. 21. These verses introduce an individual condemnation of Ahab. The original content of this condemnation has been supplanted by the insertions of vv. 19b and 20bβ–29 (S. L. McKenzie, *The Trouble with Kings: The Composition of the Book of Kings in the Deuteronomistic History* [VTSup 42: Leiden: Brill, 1991], 67). McKenzie considers the relative clause אֲשֶׁר בְּשֹׁמְרוֹן in v. 18 and all of v. 19b to be post-Dtr glosses added to the Elijah oracles. In v. 19b he believes the sign of its secondary nature is the repetition of the command וְדִבַּרְתָּ אֵלָיו לֵאמֹר כֹּה אָמַר יְהוָה, which in his view is meant to set the stage for 1 Kgs 22.38 (*The Trouble with Kings*, 69).

means. Elijah is to pronounce both the Lord's accusations and his condemnation for this deed (vv. 17–19a). The accusations and condemnation found in these verses apply to Ahab, and to Ahab alone. They include neither Jezebel nor Ahab's sons.

The oracle of 21:19b reads as follows:

כֹּה אָמַר יְהוָה בִּמְקוֹם אֲשֶׁר לָקְקוּ הַכְּלָבִים אֶת־דַּם נָבוֹת יָלֹקּוּ הַכְּלָבִים אֶת־דָּמְךָ
גַּם־אָתָּה:

This oracle follows upon the accusation in v. 19a in which Ahab is charged with having murdered and taken illegal possession of the vineyard of the murdered Naboth. In this oracle, Elijah (speaking on behalf of YHWH) informs Ahab that "*in the very place* (בִּמְקוֹם) where the dogs have licked up the blood of Naboth, *there* the dogs will also lick up your very own blood." The primary focus of this oracle is a type of equivalent justice which is specifically linked to a precise location, a type of equivalence also emphasized in the *Lex Talionis*. The punishment is to take place *in the precise location* where the crime took place and it is to consist of blood-for-blood; a life for a life.

This oracle is not without its problems. Unlike v. 19a, where the accusations made against Ahab match perfectly with, and in fact summarize, the story found in vv. 1–16, v. 19b's links with the content of those same verses are very superficial and indirect. Verse 19b is linked to vv. 1–16 only by the mention of the name of Naboth and by the indirect reference to his death, "the dogs have licked up the blood of Naboth." The first difficulty with v. 19b is that the location is not specified, but rather is left very vague and imprecise. A second problem is the reference to the dogs licking up Naboth's blood; not only is there no mention of dogs licking up blood in vv. 1–16, but also, in fact, there is no mention of dogs. In the end we are left with an oracle that is only very loosely connected with the account of the actual crime and which also introduces a new element of information not found in the account of the actual crime. This encounter between Elijah and Ahab took place privately. There is absolutely no information given which would indicate the presence of other people with Elijah and Ahab during the course of their conversation, people who might then act as witnesses to the events.

A consideration of the fulfillment notices for the oracle of v. 19b must also deal with the presence of vv. 27–29, which "postpone" the personal punishment of Ahab "to his son's day." This so-called "postponement" raises several difficulties. First of all, it is suggested by many scholars that vv. 27–29 were added by someone who knew that, in fact, Ahab did not die on the same spot where Naboth died and that he died a peaceful death and was buried "with his fathers" (1 Kgs 22:40). In order to maintain the belief in the absolute power and irreversibility of YHWH's word, it was then necessary to postpone the personal punishment of v. 19b from Ahab to one of his descendants, and thus the insertion of vv. 27–29 was made. I believe that this was done by the Dtr Historian.[3]

---

3.   See the discussion of the prophecy–fulfillment pattern beginning on p. 14.

A second difficulty is caused by the postponement notice in vv. 27–29, namely, that this notice is also very general. The postponement merely says that the punishment is postponed "to his son's day." However, Ahab had at least two sons who ruled after him, Ahaziah and Joram. Which of Ahab's sons is to suffer the punishment of the oracle in v. 19b? It is nearly universally accepted that the prophecy is "fulfilled" in Jehu's murder of Joram, Ahab's second son, at the beginning of his revolution (2 Kgs 9–10).[4] But what about his eldest son, Ahaziah (2 Kgs 1)? He dies after having fallen from his upper room and having suffered severe injuries. He sends to Baalzebub, the god of Ekron, to inquire as to whether he will recover. The Lord dispatches Elijah to intercept Ahaziah's messengers and to send them back to the king with a message from God, namely, that the king would surely die. Elijah himself eventually confronts the injured king and pronounces the same message, and the king dies. Why was the death of Ahaziah not considered to have been the fulfillment of the oracle of Elijah in 21:19b? Perhaps because it occurred in Samaria or perhaps because there was no mention of dogs licking up his blood. Yet there is no mention in the account of Joram's death of dogs licking up his blood.

A third difficulty is the fact that though there are two accounts that present themselves as the fulfillment of the oracle, 1 Kgs 22:37–38 and 2 Kgs 9:25–26, neither account literally fulfills the oracle in every regard. They are, in fact, only very loosely or very generally related to the oracle, and only in a secondary manner. When we consider these texts, we discover many difficulties and questions regarding their precise relationship to, and fulfillment of, the oracle of 21:19b. It is to an analysis of these that I now turn.

## 2. The Fulfillment Notices for the Oracle of 1 Kings 21:19b

### a. The Fulfillment Notice in 1 Kings 22:37–38

The first of the fulfillment notices is found in 1 Kgs 22:37–38. In these verses we also encounter the first "problem" with the fulfillment of the oracle of 1 Kgs 21:19b.[5] These verses form a part of the account of the battle at Ramoth-Gilead

---

4.   See, for example, J. Skinner, *Kings* (The Century Bible: A Modern Commentary; London: Caxton, n.d., ca. 1893), 259; I. Benzinger, *Die Bücher der Könige* (KHAT 9; Freiburg: J.C.B. Mohr [Paul Siebeck], 1899), 116; P. N. Schlögl, *Die Bücher der Könige, Die Bücher der Chronik* (WKAT I, 3, II; Vienna: Verlag von Mayer, 1911), 245; A. Šanda, *Die Bücher der Könige*, vol. 1, *Das erste Buch der Könige* (EHAT 9/1; Münster: Aschendorff, 1911), 65–66; J. A. Montgomery and H. S. Gehman, *A Critical and Exegetical Commentary on the Books of Kings* (ICC; Edinburgh: T. & T. Clark, 1951), 332; B. D. Napier, "The Omrides of Jezreel," *VT* 9 (1959): 366–78 (374–77); K. D. Fricke, *Das zweite Buch von den Königen* (BAT 12/2; Stuttgart: Calwer, 1972), 114; E. Würthwein, *Die Bücher der Könige, I. Kön. 17–2 Kön. 25* (ATD 11, 2; Göttingen: Vandenhoeck & Ruprecht, 1984), 251; R. D. Nelson, *First and Second Kings* (Interpretations; Atlanta: John Knox Press, 1987), 144.

5.   Scholarly opinion with regard to the precise relationship between 21:19b and 22:38 varies widely. The majority of scholars note the prophecy–fulfillment relationship between these two verses; others merely state that 22:38 fulfills 21:19b without further comment: so J. Wellhausen, *Prolegomena zur Geschichte Israels* (3d ed.; Berlin: Georg Reimer, 1886), 283 n. 2; Burney, *Notes*, 210;

in which Ahab is mortally wounded and eventually dies. We are then told that his body was brought *to Samaria* (v. 37) and that there, at the pool where they washed the blood from his chariot, "the dogs licked up his blood and the whores washed themselves in it." It is then solemnly declared that this was "according to the word of the Lord which he had spoken," explicitly relating the event to a prophecy. The problems here are twofold: first, in this account the dogs do not lick up Ahab's blood in "the exact spot where the dogs licked up the blood of Naboth the Jezreelite" (1 Kgs 21:19b). One has the distinct sense that the author of this account of Ahab's death, or at least its redactor, went to great lengths to attempt *to create* a connection or allusion to 1 Kgs 21:19b.[6] The second problem with the account of Ahab's death found in 1 Kgs 22:37–38, in which he dies violently in battle, is the fact that it is immediately followed by a second account of his death in 22:40 in which it is said that Ahab "slept with his fathers." This formulary is traditionally used by the Dtr editors only for those kings who die of natural causes.[7] So, in 1 Kgs 22:37–38 we have conflicting reports of Ahab's

F. I. Anderson, "The Socio-Juridical Background of the Naboth Incident," *JBL* 85 (1966): 46–57 (46); Fricke, *Das zweite Buch von den Königen*, 114; Dietrich, *Prophetie und Geschichte*, 27; M. Rehm, *Das erste Buch der Könige: Ein Kommentar* (Würzburg: Echter Verlag, 1979), 211; Nelson, *First and Second Kings*, 144. Others maintain that 21:19b is fulfilled by 22:38, but also note that the relationship is secondarily or artificially imposed and that one or both of the verses are secondary insertions: Benzinger, *Die Bücher der Könige*, 115; R. Kittel, *Die Bücher der Könige* (HKAT I/5; Göttingen: Vandenhoeck & Ruprecht, 1900), 178; H. Gressmann, *Die älteste Geschichtsschreibung, und Prophetie Israels [von Samuel bis Amos und Hosea]* (Göttingen: Vandenhoeck & Ruprecht, 1910), 272, 277 n. *; Noth, *Überlieferungsgeschichtliche Studien* 1:125 (83) n. 3; G. Fohrer, *Elia* (AThANT 31; Zurich: Zwingli Verlag, 1957), 63; Miller, "The Fall of the House of Ahab," 313; M. Weinfeld, *Deuteronomy and the Deuteronomic School* (Winona Lake, Ind.: Eisenbrauns, 1992), 19; Schmitt, *Elisa*, 43 n. 42; G. Hentschel, *Die Elijaerzählungen: Zum Verhältnis von historischen Geschehen und geschichtlicher Erfahrung* (ETS 33; Leipzig : St.-Benno-Verlag, 1977), 26–28; Jones, *1–2 Kings* 2:349, 352; Y. Zakovitch, "The Tale of Naboth's Vineyard: I Kings 21," in M. Weiss, *The Bible From Within: The Method of Total Interpretation* (Jerusalem: Magnes, 1984), 379–405 (38 n. 5); Würthwein, *Die Bücher der Könige, I. Kön. 17–2 Kön. 25*, 246 n. 12, 247, 252; Oeming, "Naboth, der Jesreeliter," 367–68; M. A. O'Brien, *The Deuteronomistic History Hypothesis: A Reassessment* (OBO 92; Göttingen: Vandenhoeck & Ruprecht, 1989), 201–2.

6. See the second group of scholars mentioned in the previous footnote.

7. With, among others: G. Hölscher, "Das Buch der Könige, seine Quellen und seine Redaktion," in *Eucharisterion: Studien zur Religion und Literatur des Alten und Neuen Testaments; Hermann Gunkel zum 60. Geburtstage. Am 23. Mai 1922 dargebracht von seinen Schülern und Freunden* (ed. H. Schmidt; 2 vols.; FRLANT 36; Göttingen: Vandenhoeck & Ruprecht, 1923), 1:158–213 (185); B. Alfrink, "L'Expression וַיִּשְׁכַּב עִם־אֲבֹתָיו," *OTS* 2 (1943): 106–18 (111–12); Dietrich (*Prophetie und Geschichte*, 135) maintains that the author of 22:40 was DtrG (Dietrich's early designation for DtrH) and that he was not the author of 22:38. In n. 100 on p. 135, Dietrich notes that this is the typical closing formula for those kings who die a natural death: Israelite kings (1 Kgs 14:20; 16:6, 28; 2 Kgs 13:9, 13; 14:16, 29; 15:22; and for Judean Kings: 1 Kgs 2:10; 11:43; 14:31; 15:8, 24; 22:51; 2 Kgs 8:24; 15:7, 38; 16:20; 20:21; 21:18; 24:6). When a king dies violently, in a coup, or a battle, etc., the formula of "sleeping with his fathers" is not found—see Dietrich, *Prophetie und Geschichte*, 135 n. 101 (Israelite kings: 1 Kgs 15:27–31; 16:10–14, 18–20; 2 Kgs 9:24–26; 15:10–11, 14–15, 25–26, 30–31; 17:4; Judean kings: 2 Kgs 9:27–28; 12:22; 14:9–10; 21:23–26; 23:28–30, 31–34; 24:12; 25:7;) DeVries, *Prophet against Prophet*, 97–99; H. Weippert, "Ahab el campeador?

manner of death and we have a tenuous and artificial connection regarding the location in the first of these accounts with the oracle found in 1 Kgs 21:19b.

Also problematic is the fact that in the fulfillment account the event takes place in "the pool at Samaria," whereas, in the oracle as found in the MT, it is apparently to take place outside the walls of Jezreel. Either the author of the fulfillment account was unaware of the location of the crime (according to the MT), or an exact correlation between oracle and fulfillment was unimportant for him.[8] But this point raises a further problem, namely, that at least in the application of the prophecy–fulfillment pattern by the Dtr, the two elements normally match perfectly.[9] In addition, the author of the fulfillment account in 1 Kgs 22:37–38 appears to be totally unaware of the existence of 1 Kgs 21:27–29 (and vice versa), in which, because of Ahab's repentance, the punishment is "postponed" until his son's generations. Therefore, these two passages cannot be from the same author.

Another area of confusion that comes to the fore in 1 Kgs 21 has to do with the references to dogs. In v. 19b the oracle is that on the very spot where the dogs licked up the blood of Naboth (i.e. outside the gates of Jezreel according to the MT) there the dogs would also *lick up the blood* of Ahab. We have seen the problems in this regard relative to the supposed fulfillment of this oracle in 1 Kgs 22:37–39. But a further confusion has entered the text of 1 Kgs 21 with regard to the dogs. Except for the names of Ahab and Jezebel, the only other thing that obviously connects the two major parts of 1 Kgs 21 (vv. 1–20bα with vv. 20bβ–29) is the mention of the "dogs" (vv. 19b, 23, 24). Unless one is cautious in reading the text of this chapter, the mere repetition of the term "dogs" will be enough for one to think that the various oracles in which this term occurs are all the same. This is indeed *not* the case. Verse 19b is an oracle of doom spoken to Ahab alone for his role in the death of Naboth and the appropriation of his vineyard. In this oracle the intent is that Ahab is to die on the very spot where Naboth died (implied by the logic of the oracle, though not specifically stated), and there, in that very same spot, the dogs would also lick up Ahab's blood after he has been killed. This oracle by no means implies that Ahab's body (nor that of Naboth)

Redaktions-geschichtliche Untersuchungen zu 1 Kön 22," *Bib* 69 (1988): 457–79 (465); M. White, *The Elijah Legends and Jehu's Coup* (BJS 311; Atlanta: Scholars Press, 1997), 22.

8.   The other possibility is that the redactor was working from a tradition similar to that found in Vaticanus, where the confusion over the locations is not found and everything takes place in Samaria.

9.   Many scholars argue for the particular Dtr usage of prophecy–fulfillment. See among others: Benzinger, *Die Bücher der Könige*, 152; G. von Rad, "Die deuteronomistische Geschichtstheologie in den Königsbüchern," in *Gesammelte Studien zum Alten Testament* (Munich: Chr. Kaiser Verlag, 1971 [originally published 1947]), 189–204 (52–64) (note: there are two sets of page numbers found in this text); K.-H. Bernhardt, "Prophetie und Geschichte," in *Congress Volume: Uppsala, 1971* (VTSup 22; Leiden: Brill, 1972), 20–46 (22); Weinfeld, *Deuteronomy and the Deuteronomic School*, 15; H.-D. Hoffmann, *Reform und Reformen: Untersuchungen zu einem Grundthema der deuteronomistischen Geschichtsschreibung* (AThANT 66; Zurich: Theologischer Verlag, 1980), 99; B. Peckham, *The Composition of the Deuteronomistic History* (HSM 35; Atlanta: Scholars Press, 1985), 66; J. Van Seters, *In Search of History: Historiography in the Ancient World and the Origins of Biblical History* (Winona Lake, Ind.: Eisenbrauns, 1997 [originally published 1983 by Yale University Press]), 315–16.

would go without burial. This oracle says nothing at all about the dogs "*eating the corpse*" of the deceased. When, however, we focus our attention on those oracles found in vv. 23 and 24, we find a totally different meaning and intent. In these oracles the mention of the dogs *eating* the bodies is deliberately meant to indicate the fact of non-burial. Here the dogs do not merely lick up spilled blood, they literally devour the bodies. What we have between v. 19b and vv. 23 and 24 are in fact two very distinct and very different types of oracles. These oracles are not references to 1 Kgs 21:19b, but rather they are related to the oracles found in 1 Kgs 21:23 and 24.

We can draw several conclusions thus far in our analysis. First, the Dtr editor who created or imposed the prophecy–fulfillment pattern upon 1 Kgs 21:19b and 1 Kgs 22:37–38 was not the same editor who saw the same type of relationship between 1 Kgs 21:27–29 and 2 Kgs 9:25–26. Secondly, 1 Kgs 21:19b and 1 Kgs 21:27–29 are not from the same hand. Thirdly, the authors of 1 Kgs 22:37–38 and 2 Kgs 9:25–26 are not the same person. Finally, the role of the dogs mentioned in the oracle found in 19b *is not the same* as that found in the oracles in vv. 23 and 24. These two oracles are, in fact, unrelated.

### b. *The Fulfillment Notice in 2 Kings 9:25–26 (Part of the "Jehu-Apologetic Redaction")*

Second Kings 9:25–26 of the Jehu-Apologetic Redaction[10] are presented in the Dtr version of Kings as one of the fulfillment notices of an oracle of the Lord supposedly spoken by Elijah to Ahab in 1 Kgs 21:19b. According to 1 Kgs 21:27–29, because of Ahab's repentance, his personal punishment decreed by the oracle of 21:19b appears to be "postponed" and transferred to "his son's day." In 2 Kgs 9:25–26, Jehu declares that his murder of King Joram is in fulfillment of an oracle of YHWH spoken in Ahab's day. But it is not certain that the oracle to which Jehu is referring is specifically the oracle found in 1 Kgs 21:19b.[11] Also, it might *not* be appropriate to speak of the events recounted in 1 Kgs 21:27–29 as a "postponement." I will argue below that this term is both insufficient and potentially misleading.

When we focus our attention on the Jehu-Apologetic Redaction in 2 Kgs 9:21bγ, 25–26, which I maintain is a separate and independent tradition from that of the Elijah–Naboth Fragment found in 1 Kgs 21, we see that the relationship between these verses and 1 Kgs 21 is indeed very loose. In the Jehu-Apologetic

---

10. See the fuller discussion of this layer of redaction in Chapter 2.

11. Several scholars have noted that 9:25–26 and 21:19b do not belong to the same traditions. O. Eissfeldt, *Das erste Buch der Könige*. Vol. 1 in E. Kautzsch, *Die Heilige Schrift des Alten Testaments* (ed. A. Bertholet; Tübingen: J. C. B. Mohr, 1922), 557 n. a; R. de Vaux, "Le Cycle d'Élie dans les Livres des Rois," in *Élie le prophète*, vol. 1 (Études Carmélitaines; Desclée de Brouwer, 1956), 157 n. b; Bohlen, *Der Fall Nabot*, 287; M. Rehm, *Das zweite Buch der Könige: Ein Kommentar* (Würzburg: Echter Verlag, 1982), 96; Jones, *1 and 2 Kings* 2:460; S. Olyan, "*Hāšālôm*: Some Literary Considerations of 2 Kings 9," *CBQ* 46 (1984): 652–68 (658); Oeming, "Naboth, der Jesreeliter," 370 n. 32; Nelson, *First and Second Kings*, 144; A. Rofé, "The Vineyard of Naboth: The Origin and the Message of the Story," *VT* 38 (1988): 89–104 (95–96); White, *The Elijah Legends and Jehu's Coup*, 38.

Redaction, the author is using the reference to the Naboth tradition as a means of justification—specifically for the murder of Joram and the command to cast his body on Naboth's field, and, in general, for Jehu's coup as a whole. By linking Jehu's actions with the case of a past and evidently well-known execution of a prominent citizen of Jezreel, the author hopes to win the sympathy of the reader for Jehu. The author of these verses presents Jehu's actions as both fulfilling and being justified by an oracle supposedly uttered years before when Jehu and his adjutant Bidkar were charioteers behind Ahab. In the present text the oracle recounted in 2 Kgs 9:25–26 is presented as both the restatement and the fulfillment of the oracle uttered in 1 Kgs 21:27–29, which itself is supposedly in reference to 21:19b.

Several problems exist in this "relationship." First, the Dtr author who imposed this prophecy–fulfillment pattern upon these verses was apparently unaware that the same type of pattern existed between 1 Kgs 21:19b and 1 Kgs 22:37–38.[12] Secondly, the quotation of the oracle found in 2 Kgs 9:26 is very different from those found in 1 Kgs 21:27–29 and 21:19b. In fact, nowhere in 1 Kgs 21 do we find *the exact oracle* found in 2 Kgs 9:26. The first part of the oracle in 9:26 refers to the fact that YHWH witnessed the murder of Naboth "and his sons," which took place "the night before." In 1 Kgs 21, there is no mention of the murder having taken place *at night*; rather, we are simply told that it was during a fast day. Also, in 1 Kgs 21 there is never any mention of Naboth's sons or of their being killed with him.

Other difficulties are found when we compare the oracle of 1 Kgs 21:19b with that of 2 Kgs 9:26b. First, there is a major difference between the *type of action* that YHWH promises to take. In 21:19b, the oracle is stated in a form reminiscent of the *Lex Talionis*. In 2 Kgs 9:26, it is stated as a vengeance on the part of YHWH, using the phrase: וְשִׁלַּמְתִּי לְךָ בַּחֶלְקָה הַזֹּאת. The use of the term וְשִׁלַּמְתִּי is most likely a late feature. It is only found in six passages in the Old Testament and always with YHWH as the subject (2 Kgs 9:26; Isa 65:6; Jer 16:18; 25:14; 52:24; Joel 2:25). This particular usage does not occur in 1 Kgs 21 where we find no sense of YHWH seeking vengeance for the murder of Naboth; rather, in 1 Kgs 21 we find a YHWH who is merely seeking retributive justice based upon the *Lex Talionis*.

Another important difficulty and confusion between these texts is that the oracle supposedly being quoted by Jehu in 2 Kgs 9:26b is presented as the fulfillment of 1 Kgs 21:27–29, which recount the "postponement" or transfer of the personal punishment of Ahab (21:19b) to his son's generation. However when we compare the actual oracles we find major differences:

כֹּה אָמַר יְהוָה בִּמְקוֹם אֲשֶׁר לָקְקוּ הַכְּלָבִים אֶת־דַּם נָבוֹת יָלֹקּוּ הַכְּלָבִים
אֶת־דָּמְךָ גַּם־אָתָּה:
(1 Kgs 21:19b)

---

12. Either he was simply unaware of this other pattern, or he chose to ignore the previous relationship, or he was writing prior to the addition of the other pattern. We cannot be certain which was the actual case.

הֲרָאִיתָ כִּי־נִכְנַע אַחְאָב מִלְּפָנַי יַעַן כִּי־נִכְנַע מִפָּנַי לֹא־(אָבִי) [אָבִיא] הָרָעָה בְּיָמָיו
בִּימֵי בְנוֹ אָבִיא הָרָעָה עַל־בֵּיתוֹ׃
(1 Kgs 21:29)

וְשִׁלַּמְתִּי לְךָ בַּחֶלְקָה הַזֹּאת נְאֻם־יְהוָה
(2 Kgs 9:26bα)

The shortest of the oracles is that found in 2 Kgs 9:26bα. In this oracle, the Lord simply promises to avenge the deaths of Naboth and his sons on the same plot of land where he witnessed their spilled blood. There is no mention of either the "evil" (הָרָעָה) which he promised in 1 Kgs 21:21a and 29b, nor of the dogs licking up the blood of the deceased as in 1 Kgs 21:19b. Verses 21:27–29 are presented as supposedly referring back to 21:19b and as referring forward to 9:25–26. Verse 21:29 presents the oracle/punishment simply as "the evil," with no further specification. This manner of representation is both ambiguous and imprecise. There is no specific mention in 21:29b of the central elements of the oracle of 21:19b, namely, the dogs and the fact that the punishment will take place on the exact spot where the crime occurred. Yet the ambiguity of הָרָעָה in 21:29b allows for its insertion into the text and for its being able to be read and understood as *both* a "postponement" of 21:19b and as a "prediction" of 9:25–26. The Dtr editor of the books of Kings did this.

The personal oracle of punishment of Ahab in 21:19b is *not* postponed per-se, but rather, *it is essentially changed*, being transformed from an oracle pronounced upon a single person—Ahab, for his personal crime of murder and taking possession of property belonging to another—to an oracle supposedly spoken against an entire dynasty. The so-called "dynastic character" of vv. 27–29 happens to be far more in accord with, and of the same character as, the oracles found in 1 Kgs 21:20bβ–22, 24 (all of which are from the Dtr), than with that presented in 21:19b.

This very characterization of 21:27–29 as "dynastic," however, is itself not without difficulty. When read through the lens of the Jehu story in 2 Kgs 9–10, one is deliberately led to believe that this is the purpose and intent of 1 Kgs 21:27–29. However, if we look closely at the wording of 21:29, "the evil" which YHWH promises is transferred to "*his son's* (sing.) *day*." If the clear intent of this passage was to express the transfer *to the entire dynasty*, then instead of the singular, בְנוֹ, it would need to read in the plural, בָּנָיו. This leads to the possibility that 21:29 does *not* intend *the entire dynasty*. This is supported by the story about Ahab's eldest son and direct successor, Ahaziah, in 2 Kgs 1. Though Ahaziah does die after an encounter with Elijah and after having had an oracle spoken to him by Elijah, nowhere is there any reference to his death being interpreted as a fulfillment of the oracle spoken in 1 Kgs 21:29. If Elijah himself had spoken the oracle of 21:29 and intended it to mean the entire dynasty of Ahab, and the same Elijah was involved in the circumstances of the death of Ahaziah, then it would only seem logical that Elijah would have linked Ahaziah's death with the oracle of 21:29. Yet, as we see, Ahaziah's death is conveniently "skipped over" in this regard. His death is never said to be a fulfillment of 21:29. In my view, this fact argues for the position that 21:27–29 were inserted by a redactor who wanted to make a deliberate connection between 1 Kgs 21:27–29 and the Jehu-Apologetic Redaction in 2 Kgs 9:21bγ, 25–26.[13] This author/redactor saw the events surrounding the death of Ahab's second son, Joram, as *the unique fulfillment* of *the unique oracle* of 21:29.

I conclude, therefore, that 21:27–29 *do not* represent a "postponement" of Ahab's punishment; rather, these verses represent *a change* of the punishment/oracle from one spoken against Ahab personally, to one spoken against one of his sons—Joram.[14] Also, 21:27–29 do not represent an oracle of "dynastic destruction"; rather, they are an oracle spoken against only one of Ahab's sons—Joram. The "dynastic destruction" theme does not come from 21:27–29; rather, it comes first from the fact that the son to whom it was applied, Joram, was in fact the last of Ahab's sons, and secondly, from the fact that Jehu's "purge" included all of Joram's sons, family, and retainers—in effect, anyone who might possibly have made a dynastic claim to the throne which Jehu was attempting to capture for himself. Therefore, I maintain that 9:21bγ, 25–26 were inserted into the story of Jehu's revolution in order to justify his murder of the king, and that at the same time, 21:27–29 were added by the same author to give a "prophetic oracle" which was meant to justify Jehu's actions theologically.

When we compare 1 Kgs 21:19b and 2 Kgs 9:26b, we find that the only similarity between the two oracles is the emphasis upon the punishment occurring *in the same place* as the crime. Otherwise, the two oracles are very different. In 21:19b, the dogs lick up the blood; in 9:26b, YHWH will avenge. These two oracles are not equivocal. Even though the only explicit connection between these two oracles is the emphasis on *the place* of the crime and punishment, this very emphasis raises a further difficulty. The "place" being referred to in the individual oracles is not necessarily in the same location. In 21:19b, the referent is to the place where Naboth was stoned to death—outside the city walls of Jezreel (in the MT). The precise location of this place is not made explicit. It is, however, unlikely that it was so far outside the city that the people would have had to drive there in chariots. In the so-called "fulfillment notice" in 9:26b, the place is a plot of land previously owned by the dead Naboth—a plot of land which is still known and referred to as "Naboth's plot" and which is a chariot's drive away from the city. Obviously, it is not the exact same place where Naboth was stoned to death, and therefore this fulfillment notice does not specifically match the oracle of 21:19b—neither in terms of the specific punishment, nor in terms of the specific location of the punishment.

A further difference between 21:19b and 9:26b has to do with the "context" within which each of the two oracles was spoken. The context of the oracle in

---

13. With Wellhausen (*Prolegomena zur Geschichte Israels*, 281) and Hentschel (*Die Elijaerzählungen*, 36) who maintain that 21:27–29 and 9:25–26 were only secondarily brought together.

14. *Contra* Benzinger (*Die Bücher der Könige*, 116) and S. J. DeVries (*I Kings* [WBC 12; Waco, Tex.: Word Books, 1985], 255), who both maintain that these verses represent the postponement of 21:19b.

21:19b is a private encounter between Ahab and Elijah the Tishbite in which Elijah utters the oracle that is presented as a just punishment for the death of Naboth and the appropriation of his vineyard by the crown. Implying that Ahab is to die on the same place where Naboth died, the oracle states that just as the dogs licked up Naboth's blood, so too in the very same place, the dogs will lick up the blood of Ahab.

In 2 Kgs 9:25–26, the context in which we find the oracle being applied is very different. Here the context is that of the explanation for Jehu's command to Bidkar, for the non-burial of Joram's body ("cast his body on the plot of Naboth"). This is neither the connotation nor the implied context of 21:19b. There, the mention of the dogs "licking up the blood" of Naboth in no way implies that Naboth's body was not buried and that the dogs "ate his flesh." They merely licked up his blood where it fell when Naboth was stoned to death. In this sense, also, the oracle against Ahab in 21:19b does not imply that his body would not, or should not, receive proper burial. It merely means that he would die on the same spot as did Naboth. In 2 Kgs 9:25–26, however, the rationalization which Jehu gives for his command of non-burial is that it was a fulfillment of the oracle of the Lord spoken against Ahab years before. His clear wish and intent is that Bidkar understands that the supposed oracle meant not only the death of Joram, but that it also meant, and therefore justified, the act of non-burial/desecration of the dead king's body.

When we consider the scholarly opinion with a specific focus on 2 Kgs 9:25–26 and the question of "fulfillment," we encounter a variety of opinions. The largest number of scholars maintain that 9:25–26 are the fulfillment (to a greater or lesser degree) of all, or part, of 1 Kgs 17–19.[15] L. Barré, maintains that the Dtr redactor, using an older oracle (v. 26a), which probably belonged to the narrative of 1 Kgs 21:1–20a, 27–29, added the introduction found in 2 Kgs 9:22b [*sic*; 21bγ?] and 25 when he inserted it into 2 Kgs 9–10. This resulted in the oracle being applied to Ahab instead of Joram, and appears, then, to be a fulfillment of 1 Kgs 21:21–24. He also notes that the actual oracle found in 9:26 itself has no fulfillment notice.[16] B. O. Long sees 9:25–26 as fulfilling 2 Kgs 9:7–10, the prophetic commissioning of Jehu by the son of the prophets.[17] S. Timm maintains

---

15. A. Klostermann, *Die Bücher Samuelis und der Könige* (KHANT 3; Nördlingen: Verlag der C. H. Beck'schen Buchhandlung, 1887), 419; Skinner, *Kings*, 259; Benzinger, *Die Bücher der Könige*, 151; Schlögl, *Die Bücher der Könige, Die Bücher der Chronik*, 245; H. Gunkel, *Geschichten von Elisa* (Meisterwerke hebräischer Erzählungskunst 1; Berlin: Verlag Karl Curtius, 1913), 81; Montgomery and Gehman, *A Critical and Exegetical Commentary*, 402; Fohrer, *Elia*, 64; J. Gray, *I & II Kings: A Commentary* (OTL; Philadelphia: Westminster, 1964 [3d ed. 1970]), 435–36 (only v. 19b and generally); Steck, *Überlieferung und Zeitgeschichte*, 33–34; Weinfeld, *Deuteronomy and the Deuteronomic School*, 18–19; DeVries, *I Kings*, 255; McKenzie, *The Trouble with Kings*, 74 (only 21:17–19a).

16. L. Barré, *The Rhetoric of Political Persuasion* (CBQMS 20; Washington: Catholic Biblical Association of America, 1988), 110–11.

17. B. O. Long, *II Kings, with an Introduction to Historical Literature* (FOTL 10; Grand Rapids: Eerdmans, 1991), 127.

simply that 9:25–26 fulfill 1 Kgs 21.[18] Several other scholars, recognizing the imprecise relationship between 9:25–26 and any of the proposed oracles, maintain that either there is no specific fulfillment of those oracles or that the fulfillment is in no way "literal." Scholars taking this line include J. Skinner, C. F. Burney, R. de Vaux, and L. Barré.[19]

When we consider the question of the origins or sources of 9:25–26, again the opinion of the scholars is diverse. O. Eissfeldt, R. de Vaux, R. Bohlen, M. Rehm, G. H. Jones, S. Olyan, A. Rofé, and M. White all recognize the fact that 9:25–26 and 21:19b are from different traditions, and the majority of these scholars maintain that 9:25–26 is the older of the two traditions.[20] Other scholars attempt to identify the particular period, source, or tradition from which 9:25–26 comes. These include: I. Benzinger (post-Dtr); O. H. Steck (pre-Dtr); H.-C. Schmitt (apologetic redaction); R. Bohlen (9:25 and 26b belong to an apologetic redaction from the time of Jehu's dynasty, while 9:26a belongs to the oldest layer of the Naboth tradition); S. Timm (post-Dtr); M. Oeming (probably a post-Dtr gloss); and Y. Minokami (v. 26b is an early chronicalistic notice which was added to 9:25–26a and which are part of the "Vengeance Theology Redaction").[21] All the above-mentioned opinions highlight both the difficulty of achieving certitude and the complexity of discerning the relationships and origins of these verses and their actual role in any prophecy–fulfillment pattern.

The problems and difficulties caused by the imposition of a prophecy–fulfillment pattern upon the texts we have considered thus far highlight the artificiality of this relationship and the looseness of its construction. These difficulties argue for the fact that this pattern was imposed secondarily. In fact, the oracle in 1 Kgs 21:19b is not "literally fulfilled" by any of the so-called fulfillment notices, nor anywhere else.[22] I maintain, therefore, that on the level of the original layer of the texts themselves, there is no direct relationship of dependence between the three texts found in 1 Kgs 21:19b, 22:38 and 2 Kgs 9:25–26. None of these texts can be considered to be "quotes" or direct references to each other. Neither of the so-called fulfillment notices is a precise fulfillment of the oracle in any of the forms in which it occurs. The secondary and very loose redactional relationship imposed

18. S. Timm, *Die Dynastie Omri* (FRLANT 124; Göttingen: Vandenhoeck & Ruprecht, 1982), 120.

19. Skinner, *Kings*, 259; Burney, *Notes*, 211; R. de Vaux, *Les livres des Rois* (traduite en français sous la direction de l' École Biblique de Jérusalem; La Sainte Bible 9; Paris: Cerf, 1949), 157 n. b; Barré, *The Rhetoric of Political Persuasion*, 111.

20. Eissfeldt, *Das erste Buch der Könige*, 557 n. a; de Vaux, *Les livres des Rois*, 157 n. b; Bohlen, *Der Fall Nabot*, 287; Rehm, *Das zweite Buch der Könige*, 96; Jones, *1 and 2 Kings* 2:460; Olyan, "*Hăšālôm*," 658; Rofé, "The Vineyard of Naboth," 95–96; White, *The Elijah Legends and Jehu's Coup*, 38.

21. Benzinger, *Die Bücher der Könige*, 149; Steck, *Überlieferung und Zeitgeschichte*, 33–34; Schmitt, *Elisa*, 27; Bohlen, *Der Fall Nabot*, 288; Timm, *Die Dynastie Omri*, 140–42; Oeming, "Naboth, der Jesreeliter," 370 n. 32; Y. Minokami, *Die Revolution des Jehu* (GTA 38; Göttingen: Vandenhoeck & Ruprecht, 1989), 37–39.

22. With Skinner, *Kings*, 259.

upon these texts by the Dtr explains the near total confusion and, at times, the diametrically opposed positions held by the scholars regarding the relationships between these verses.[23]

23. Some maintain that 21:19b is secondary: Šanda (*Das erste Buch der Könige*, 465–66) and Jones (*1 and 2 Kings* 2:352) argue that 21:19b comes from 22:38 while others merely maintain that 21:19b is secondary: Jepsen, *Nabi*, 93; Miller, "The Fall of the House of Ahab," 313; Steck, *Überlieferung und Zeitgeschichte*, 38 (Dtr); Oeming, "Naboth, der Jesreeliter," 367–68 (Dtr); O'Brien, *The Deuteronomistic History Hypothesis*, 202. Still others maintain that 22:38 is a secondary and late gloss: Benzinger, *Die Bücher der Könige*, 125; Gressmann, *Die älteste Geschichtsschreibung*, 277 n. *; Noth, *Überlieferungsgeschichtliche Studien* 1:125 (83) n. 3; de Vaux, *Les livres des Rois*, 122 n. a, and "Rois," in *La Bible de Jérusalem* (Paris: Cerf, 1973), 375–435 (404) n. k; Fohrer, *Elia*, 63; Napier, "The Omrides of Jezreel," 377; Weinfeld, *Deuteronomy and the Deuteronomic School*, 19; Hentschel, *Die Elijaerzählungen*, 26–29; Würthwein, *Die Bücher der Könige I. Kön. 17– 2 Kön. 25*, 246 n. 12; Zakovitch, "The Tale of Naboth's Vineyard," 380 n. 5; Oeming, "Naboth, der Jesreeliter," 367–68; O'Brien, *The Deuteronomistic History Hypothesis*, 202. Regarding the sources of the oracles and fulfillments: Benzinger, *Die Bücher der Könige*, 149 (21:19b and 9:25–26 are not from the same hand); Gressmann, *Die älteste Geschichtsschreibung*, 272 (21:19b and 22:38 are from different hands); 277 n. * (23:38 is based upon 21:19b); Noth, *Überlieferungsgeschichtliche Studien* 1:125 (83) n. 3 (22:38 is from Dtr); N. H. Snaith, "The First and Second Book of Kings: Introduction and Exegesis," *IB* 3:3–338 (184) (21:19 and 22:38 are from the same hand); Miller, "The Fall of the House of Ahab," 314–16 (21:19b was constructed based upon 9:25–26); Bohlen, *Der Fall Nabot*, 302 (9:25–26 were totally unknown to the author of 21:17a–20d); Oeming, "Naboth, der Jesreeliter," 367–68 (22:38 is probably best understood as a Dtr harmonization with the older oracle in 21:19b); A. F. Campbell, *Of Prophets and Kings: A Late Ninth-Century Document (I Samuel 1–2 Kings 10)* (CBQMS 17; Washington: Catholic Biblical Association of America, 1986), 97 n. 80 (there was a collection of early [independent?—P.T.C.] sayings circulating concerning Ahab's and Elijah's confrontation; included were 21:19a, 19b, 20abα and 9:26a). Scholarly opinion regarding locus of the fulfillment of 21:19b varies greatly: Montgomery and Gehman, *A Critical and Exegetical Commentary*, 332, maintained that 21:17–19 was fulfilled in 22:38 for Ahab; in 9:36–37 for Jezebel; and in 9:25–26 for Joram (possibly); Gray, *I & II Kings*, 436, maintained that 21:19b was generally fulfilled in 9:24–26 and literally fulfilled in 22:38. Those who maintain that it is literally fulfilled in 22:38 include: Wellhausen, *Prolegomena zur Geschichte Israels*, 283 n. 2; F. I. Anderson, "The Socio-Juridical Background," 46; Dietrich, *Prophetie und Geschichte*, 27; Rehm, *Das erste Buch der Könige*, 211; Würthwein *Die Bücher der Könige I. Kön. 17–2 Kön. 25*, 246 n. 12; 252; Jones, *1 and 2 Kings* 2:349; Nelson, *First and Second Kings*, 144. Finally, those who consider 1 Kgs 21:19b to be literally fulfilled in 2 Kgs 9:25–26 include: Šanda, *Das erste Buch der Könige*, 465–66; Schlögl, *Die Bücher der Könige, Die Bücher der Chronik*, 245; Gunkel, *Geschichten von Elisa*, 81; Napier, "The Omrides of Jezreel," 374–77; Weinfeld, *Deuteronomy and the Deuteronomic School*, 19; de Vaux, "Rois," 403; DeVries, *I Kings*, 255.

# Chapter 2

## THE "JEHU-APOLOGETIC REDACTION" IN 2 KINGS 9.21Bγ, 25–26

Outside of 1 Kgs 21, the only other place in the Bible where we find reference to Naboth is within the context of the so-called "historical narrative" of the coup-d'etat of Jehu in 2 Kgs 9–10. Within this narrative, we find Naboth material in three verses: 2 Kgs 9:21bγ, 25–26. These verses represent a secondary editing of the narrative in 2 Kgs 9–10, and I refer to these as the "Jehu-Apologetic Redaction."

When the scholarship concerning these verses is consulted, no scholar from A. Klostermann (1887) to H.-C. Schmitt (1972) can be seen to have considered 2 Kgs 9:25–26 as redactional.[1] These scholars either made no comment at all concerning the sources of these two verses, taking it for granted that they were part of the original (historical) layer of the story;[2] or, they considered them to be

---

1. Only one author within these dates considered a small part of these verses to be secondary, namely, C. F. Whitley, "The Deuteronomic Presentation of the House of Omri," *VT* 2 (1952): 137–52 (149). In his opinion, v. 25b is "obviously an interpolation to connect this incident with the circumstances of Ahab's death told in 1 Kgs." There is, however a possible problem with his supporting "evidence." Whitley refers to Wellhausen, *Prolegomena zur Geschichte Israels*, 290—where he claims that Wellhausen says that: "who does not see in this an attempt to harmonise conflicting narratives." I presume that he is referring to the English translation of Wellhausen's work that was translated by J. S. Black and A. Menzies in 1885, but this volume is unavailable to me. In the 1886 third edition of Wellhausen's German work, however, on p. 302 Wellhausen's remark, "aber wer merkt hier nicht die Harmonistik," is in fact in reference to 1 Kgs 21:27–29 and *not* to 2 Kgs 9:25. Wellhausen seems to maintain that it is 1 Kgs 21:27–29 that are the interpolation based upon 2 Kgs 9:25. This would appear to be contrary to the way in which Whitley has understood the remark.

2. Klostermann, *Die Bücher Samuelis und der Könige*, 25–26; J. Wellhausen, *Die Composition des Hexateuchs und der historischen Bücher des Alten Testaments* (3d ed.; Berlin: Georg Reimer, 1899), 286–87; Skinner, *Kings*, 325; Benzinger, *Die Bücher der Könige*, 151; Kittel, *Die Bücher der Könige*, 233; Burney, *Notes*, 300; B. Stade and F. Schwally, *The Book of Kings: Critical Edition of the Hebrew Text* (Leipzig: J. C. Hinrichs, 1904), 39, 224; Gressmann, *Die älteste Geschichtsschreibung*, 305–6; Schlögl, *Die Bücher der Könige, Die Bücher der Chronik*, 245; A. Šanda, *Die Bücher der Könige*, vol. 2, *Das zweite Buch der Könige* (EHAT 9/2; Münster: Aschendorff 1912), 98–99; Gunkel, *Geschichten von Elisa*, 81; Eissfeldt, *Das erste Buch der Könige*, 557; Noth, *Überlieferungsgeschichtliche Studien* 1:126 (84); Montgomery and Gehman, *A Critical and Exegetical Commentary*, 399 (who comment that these verses are "absolutely original"); G. Hölscher, *Geschichtsschreibung in Israel: Untersuchungen zum Jahvisten und Elohisten* (Lund: C. W. K. Gleerup, 1952), 398; A. Jepsen, *Die Quellen des Königsbuches* (Halle: Max Niemeyer, 1953), 8, 103; A. Jepsen, "Ahabs Buße: Ein kleiner Beitrag zur Methode literar-historischer Einordnung," in *Archäologie und Altes Testament. Festschrift für Kurt Galling zum 8. Januar 1970* (ed. A. Kuschke and E. Kutsch; Tübingen: J. C. B. Mohr, 1970), 145–55; de Vaux, "Le Cycle d'Élie," 157; Gray,

original to the sources used by the Dtr Historian.[3] The fact that they considered these verses as original to the account indicates that they either appreciated the role that these verses played in the account of Jehu's coup and accession to the throne, or, they respected and recognized the artistic license of the author who had created the account.

There are reasons, however, for considering these verses to be secondary to the text. This is, in fact, the opinion of the majority of scholars since 1972. The first reason, though by no means the most significant or substantial reason, is that if we look carefully at the immediate context of vv. 25–26—at the verse which precedes and the one which follows our verses—it becomes obvious that if one were to eliminate our two verses and read directly from v. 24 to v. 27, the text would make absolutely perfect sense and one would detect no break or roughness in the text:[4]

> And Jehu drew his bow with his full strength, and shot Joram between the shoulders, so that the arrow pierced his heart, and he sank in his chariot . . . . When Ahaziah the king of Judah saw this, he fled in the direction of Bethhaggan. And Jehu pursued him, and said, 'Shoot him also'; and they shot him in the chariot at the ascent of Gur, which is by Ibleam. And he fled to Megiddo, and died there. (2 Kgs 9:24, 27 RSV)

The fact that the elimination of these two verses from the text causes no roughness in the flow of the text, nor in the sense of the text, is not, in and of itself, sufficient grounds for judging them to be secondary, but it is a small hint that this might be the case.

A second question that can be asked concerning these verses has to do with their content. What do these verses add to the story of Jehu's coup? These verses actually add to the text information concerning two related themes: the "Naboth the Jezreelite" theme and the theme of "Divine Vengeance." These themes will be discussed in the context of our analysis of the content of the verses which form what I have called the "Jehu-Apologetic Redaction," 2 Kgs 9:21bγ, 25–26.

### 1. 2 Kings 9:21bγ

In v. 21bγ the reference to Naboth serves the purpose of situating precisely the location of the encounter of Joram and Ahaziah with Jehu. Here again, the secondary nature of this reference could be indicated by the superfluous nature of the statement. One senses its superfluity when one looks at v. 16a where we are told that Jehu mounted his chariot and went to meet Joram at Jezreel. This is followed by the account of the watchmen spotting Jehu, and then of Joram sending out messengers. Throughout this entire account, no mention is made of any specific

---

*I & II Kings*, 539 (but on pp. 537–38 he is questioning); Fricke, *Das zweite Buch von den Königen*, 124–25; Dietrich, *Prophetie und Geschichte*, 50–51; Weinfeld, *Deuteronomy and the Deuteronomic School*, 20.

3. Steck, *Überlieferung und Zeitgeschichte*, 33–34, 43–46.

4. Bohlen, *Der Fall Nabot*, p. 284; Barré, *The Rhetoric of Political Persuasion*, 14. This can basically be seen as the understanding of all those who maintain that these verses are secondary.

location or piece of property where Jehu is to be found. It is merely indicated that he is within view from the tower of the city. Finally we are told that Joram and Ahaziah mount up: וַיֵּצְאוּ לִקְרַאת יֵהוּא. The sentence could end with this statement and would make perfect sense. Further precision, though not necessary to the story, was added by someone who was definitely interested in linking the events of this account with Naboth the Jezreelite. This addition, which situates the encounter on the specific plot of Naboth the Jezreelite, בְּחֶלְקַת נָבוֹת הַיִּזְרְעֵאלִי, does, in fact, serve a purpose, namely, the setting of the stage for the second and main part of the same Jehu-Apologetic Redaction—vv. 25–26.

### 2. 2 Kings 9:25a

The first thing we notice is that v. 25 begins with a command from Jehu to his adjutant, Bidkar. This command follows upon Jehu's murder of Joram, the king of Israel—Ahab's son and Jehu's king and commander. Jehu then commands Bidkar to take up the body of Joram and cast it upon the land owned by Naboth the Jezreelite. Several things should be noticed from this command. First, this is the only time that this officer or aide, Bidkar, is ever mentioned in the Old Testament. Who was he? What role does he play in the overall story and in history? To this point in the story, we know absolutely nothing about him. We might imagine that he was one of the officers present with Jehu when the son of the prophet arrived secretly to anoint Jehu (vv. 5, 11–13).

The second element of this first part of v. 25 is the command: "Take him up, and cast him on the plot of ground belonging to Naboth the Jezreelite." There is a potential problem of interpretation with this command. It becomes visible only when we compare this command with v. 21:

וַיֹּאמֶר יְהוֹרָם אֱסֹר וַיֶּאְסֹר רִכְבּוֹ וַיֵּצֵא יְהוֹרָם מֶלֶךְ־יִשְׂרָאֵל וַאֲחַזְיָהוּ מֶלֶךְ־יְהוּדָה
אִישׁ בְּרִכְבּוֹ וַיֵּצְאוּ לִקְרַאת יֵהוּא וַיִּמְצָאֻהוּ בְּחֶלְקַת נָבוֹת הַיִּזְרְעֵאלִי׃
(2 Kgs 9:21)

שָׂא הַשְׁלִכֵהוּ בְּחֶלְקַת שְׂדֵה נָבוֹת הַיִּזְרְעֵאלִי
(2 Kgs 9:25aβ)

At the end of v. 21 we hear that Joram and Ahaziah met Jehu, בְּחֶלְקַת נָבוֹת הַיִּזְרְעֵאלִי ("at the property [portion] of Naboth the Jezreelite"). This would seem to indicate that they are in fact on the property of Naboth when they do meet. But this does not appear to be the obvious case when in v. 25 Jehu commands Bidkar to take up Joram's body and "cast him on the property of Naboth the Jezreelite."[5] If they were already on the property of Naboth (v. 21), why would he give such a command? The simple solution to this potential problem of interpretation is to

---

5.    The verb √שׁלך in conjunction with the locative בּ and with reference to dead bodies occurs some eight times in the Old Testament: Gen 37:20 (where it is used in the conversation of Joseph's brothers regarding their plan to kill Joseph); 1 Kgs 13:24, 25, 28 (all with regard to the Man of God from Judah whose body was cast in the road); 2 Kgs 9:25, 26 (regarding the casting of Joram's body upon/in Naboth's property); 2 Kgs 13:21 (regarding the casting of a dead man into Elisha's grave); Amos 8:3 (regarding the casting out of the dead bodies in silence).

say that the encounter between the two kings and Joram and his soldiers took place on a roadway that traversed the property of Naboth. This would be the logical solution if one were to imagine that low walls built from fieldstones marked out the fields' boundaries.

Another approach that may shed some light upon this problem would be to do a detailed study of the term used—בְּחֶלְקַה. The verbal root חלק means "to divide, share, measure off, apportion," usually in terms of property. The noun occurs in both the masculine form חֵלֶק and in the feminine form חֶלְקָה, both of which mean "a portion, tract or territory."[6] In 2 Kgs 9 we find the use of the feminine form of the term three times—vv. 21, 25, 26. In v. 21, the term occurs in the construct form: בְּחֶלְקַת נָבוֹת הַיִּזְרְעֵאלִי. Here, in the construct form, the property is specifically identified as "the property of Naboth the Jezreelite." That the location of this property is generally known and recognized is obvious from the text. The kings in v. 21 are driving to "the property of Naboth the Jezreelite." The sense in this particular usage, however, is still very general. The phrase can legitimately be understood as referring to *all* the property which Naboth owned in a specific region and that this property could be comprised of various sub-sections of land (i.e. different fields). Since in 2 Kgs 9 the people have to ride by chariots to get to the "property of Naboth," it can also be argued that this property, this חֶלְקָה, was located some distance from the city.

An analysis of the usage of חֶלְקָה in the Old Testament would support the argument that the term, when used by itself, the majority of times refers to "property in general" (×9), often in the sense of referring to an inheritance.[7] This is perhaps the best way to understand the use of the term in 2 Kgs 9:21. The term חֶלְקָה is also used in reference to a portion or representation of a group of people in 2 Chr 35:5. Six times the word is used for a specific piece of land or a specific field.[8] Of these six occurrences, three of them are direct references to the immediately preceding verse in which the form שָׂדֶה or חֶלְקַת שָׂדֶה occurs (2 Sam 23:11–12; 2 Kgs 9:25a; 1 Chr 11:13–14). The results of this survey allow us to say that when this word occurs by itself, the majority of the occurrences are in reference to "property in general."

This brings us to the construct form of the term, חֶלְקַת שָׂדֶה, as found in 2 Kgs 9:25a. This form occurs a total of eight times in the Old Testament, and in each case I maintain that this construct form of the term is a reference to a specific piece of property.[9] When we consider 2 Kgs 9:25, I would argue that the command given by Jehu to Bidkar is in reference to a *specific* part of the whole property of Naboth referred to in 2 Kgs 9:21, namely, the part within which Jehu and his soldiers are presently located. The reference to חֶלְקָה found in v. 26a is special in the sense that it has been removed from its original context in which it

---

6. BDB, 323–24.

7. See Deut 33:21 (the Gadite territory); 2 Kgs 3:19, 25 (good properties—possibly fields); Job 24:1 (inherited portions); Jer 12:10 (×2 = the Lord's inherited portion = the whole earth in v. 11); Amos 4:6 (×2 = property in general, maybe fields in general); 2 Kgs 9:21.

8. See 2 Sam 14:30–31 (×3); 23:12; 2 Kgs 9:26; 1 Chr 11:14.

9. See Gen 33:19; Josh 24:32; Ruth 2:3 (×2); 4:3; 2 Sam 23:11; 2 Kgs 9:25; 1 Chr 11:13.

probably referred to a specific location and even more probably to a specific field. This original context, however, is missing and therefore it is not possible to make a firm judgment about it. The reference in v. 26b is a reference to the same piece of property as that of v. 25a.

Thus, (1) when חֶלְקָה is used alone it is most often a reference to property in general. When the term is used with שָׂדֶה it always refers to a specific field that is usually affiliated with agriculture. (2) Thus חֶלְקַת שָׂדֶה *does not equal*, nor encompass the whole, of the owner's property. It is always a reference to a specific part of one's property.[10]

If we now return to the apparent problem caused by the references in 2 Kgs 9:21 and 25, I would suggest the following interpretation. In v. 21 the kings depart from the city of Jezreel and drive to the property of Naboth (property in the general sense of the term). In v. 25, Jehu who has just murdered Joram *on Naboth's property* (property in general; probably upon the roadway which traversed the property of Naboth), now commands Bidkar to take the body and cast it *upon a specific field*, namely, the part on either side of the roadway upon which they are located. In the end, what is most important for the overall story is the fact that Joram's body *had* to end up on the murdered Naboth's property in order to be interpreted as "fulfilling" the supposed oracle referred to in v. 26b.

A second bit of information that we learn from Jehu's command is the specific identity of the plot of land where Joram's body is to be cast—the property of Naboth the Jezreelite. What can we infer from this bit of information? First of all, we can infer that this property of Naboth the Jezreelite was a piece of property that was "known" by people. This could be for any number of reasons. Perhaps Naboth was a famous "landlord" whose land holdings were known and recognized by the general populous, even after his death that took place years before. If this were the case, however, why cast a dead body upon his property? Perhaps because of the fact that Naboth was said to have been put to death, having been accused and condemned for having "cursed both God and King" (1 Kgs 21), and his previous good name was now and forever cursed. In this case, to cast a corpse on his property could have been a sign of hatred toward Naboth. Though the text does not explicitly tell us the reason, we the readers of the story already know the reason. We already know what happened in 1 Kgs 21. But, if we focus our attention strictly upon our two verses alone, we would have to conclude that we would have *no idea* why Jehu commanded Bidkar to cast Joram's body specifically upon Naboth's property.

There is a second and perhaps far more important inference that can be drawn from Jehu's command: the fact that what this command refers to is an act of non-burial of the king's body. While there is no direct or explicit command *not* to

---

10. This is evident in several passages, such as Gen 33:19 where we are told that Jacob buys a field upon which he had pitched his tent, while in v. 33:17 we are told that he built his home in Succoth. The field is both separate from and apart from the place where he built his home. Another example is found in Ruth 2:3 where twice there is reference to the חֶלְקַת שָׂדֶה, which is not the same place where Boaz lives (in Bethlehem).

bury the body, the command to cast it on the ground *implies* this practice and alludes to curses and oracles that explicitly expound this practice.

### a. *Oracles of Non-Burial*

The oracles which intend the non-burial of the victims are usually expressed in rather fixed forms or stereotypical ways. According to D. R. Hillers, this form normally contains three elements: "1) the body will be unburied; 2) it will be food for bird and beast; and 3) it will be like refuse on the face of the earth."[11] It is more often the case, however, that all three elements are not found together (although this does occur on some occasions—e.g. Jer 16:4). In fact, I would even expand Hillers' list of three elements to include the specific sayings concerning the dogs eating the body, over against the category about the birds and the beasts eating the bodies. I make this distinction based upon the fact that the two categories are not equivalent in the biblical texts. A scan of the Old Testament for these elements results in the following breakdown:

Table 1. *Oracles of Non-Burial*

| | Non-Burial | Dogs will Eat | Birds and Beasts will Eat | Will be as Dung on the Ground |
|---|---|---|---|---|
| Gen | | | 40:19 | |
| Deut | | | 28:26 | |
| 1 Sam | | | 17:44, 46 | |
| 2 Sam | | | 21:10 (negative) | |
| 1 Kgs | 14:13 | 14:11; 16:4; 21:23, 24 | 14:11; 16:4; 21:24 | |
| 2 Kgs | 9:10 | 9:10, 36 | | 9:37 |
| Pss | 79:3 | | 79:2–3 | 83:11 |
| Isa | 14:19 | | | 5:25 (offal on the streets—כַּסּוּחָה) |
| Jer | 7:33; 8:1–2; 14:16; 16:4, 6; 22:19; 25:33; 36:30 | 15:3 | 15:3; 16:4 | 8:1–2; 9:21; 16:4; 25:33 |
| Ezek | | | 32:4; 39:17–20 | |

This sample of occurrences makes no claims to completeness, for 2 Kgs 9:25 does not appear on this chart. The reason is that in this verse we are dealing with an *allusion* to the curse of non-burial, what I call an "indirect" oracle of non-burial, and not with the stereotypical form of the curse. This allusion, however, carries just as strong a message as the original curse.

Second, though the various elements of these curses are found scattered throughout the whole of the Old Testament, the strongest concentration of these

---

11. D. R. Hillers, *Treaty-Curses and the Old Testament Prophets* (BibOr 16; Rome: Pontifical Biblical Institute, 1964), 68–69. Concerning curses, see also: S. H. Blank, "The Curse, Blasphemy, the Spell, and the Oath," *HUCA* 23/I (1950/51): 73–95; H. J. Boecker, *Redeformen des Rechtslebens im Alten Testament* (WMANT 14; Neukirchen–Vluyn: Neukirchener Verlag, 1964); M. R. Lehmann, "Biblical Oaths," *ZAW* 81 (1969): 74–92.

elements occurs in 1 and 2 Kings and in the prophet Jeremiah. According to M. Weinfeld's analysis, twelve of the fourteen references in 1 and 2 Kings and 10 of the 15 references found in Jeremiah (on the above chart), are attributed to the Deuteronomistic hand.[12] This does not, however, mean that the Deuteronomistic writer created these curses. They were actually a common part of ancient Near Eastern treaties. What he did do was to use them to stress his own particular theological perspective in his judgments concerning the kings of Israel.

Scholars have highlighted the fact that curses of the type we are discussing were a standard part of treaty and covenant formulas throughout the ancient Near East. Some samples are instructive. The following curse is found at least three times in a treaty of Esarhaddon of Assyria with Baal of Tyre that was concluded in 677 B.C.E. This curse says that the one who breaks this treaty will not receive a proper burial, but instead, will be eaten by animals:

> '[May Ninurta, chief of the gods], fill you with his swift arrow; [may he fill] the plain [with your corpses;] may he feed your flesh to the eagle (and) jackal' (col. vi; lines 425–27); and, 'May dogs and swine drag them (your corpses) to and fro in the squares of Asshur; may the earth not receive your corpses (in burial); may you be food in the belly of a dog or a pig' (col. vi; lines 483–84—see also line 451 for reference to the dogs and swine eating your flesh).[13]

This type of curse is also found in Babylonian records. A *kudurru* from the time of Nabû-Mukîn-Apli contains the following curse:

> 'May Ninib, the lord of boundary-stones, tear out his (the breaker of the treaty) boundary-stone, and his name, and his seed, and his offspring (lines 14ff) . . . and may Gula, the great lady, cause there to be a wasting sickness in his body . . . and [his corpse] may she de[prive] of burial . . .' (lines 20ff).[14]

These curses and treaty formularies not only deal with the element of non-burial, but they often connect or develop this curse with the description of the beasts (usually dogs and pigs or eagles/vultures) eating the corpses. Both of these elements have been found also in the biblical texts. With H. N. Wallace, I conclude, based upon the similarities between the biblical curses/oaths and those found in surrounding cultures, that the Deuteronomistic author/editor "has either adopted an ancient curse for the oracles, or, composed one using typical patterns, rhythms and images found in other ancient Near Eastern curse formulae."[15]

Thus, Jehu's command to his aide Bidkar is an allusion to, and can best be understood as, a command concerning the non-burial of the corpse. It can be further understood as emphasizing the fact that what Jehu saw himself doing by this action was, indeed, the fulfillment of a curse of non-burial which had been

---

12. Weinfeld, *Deuteronomy and the Deuteronomic School*. For the specific reference and location, see his index of Scripture References in "Appendix A: Deuteronomic Phraseology," 320–65.

13. D. J. Wiseman, "The Vassal Treaties of Esarhaddon," *Iraq* 20 (1958): 1–99 (62, 64, 66).

14. L. W. King, ed., *Babylonian Boundary-Stones and Memorial-Tablets in the British Museum* (2 vols; London: The British Museum, 1912), 2:62, col. II, ll. 14–16, 24–25.

15. H. N. Wallace, "The Oracles against the Israelite Dynasties in 1 and 2 Kings," *Bib* 67 (1986): 21–40 (35).

uttered either against Joram or against his father Ahab. The remainder of vv. 25 and 26 further substantiates this interpretation.

### 3. 2 Kings 9:25b

After Jehu commands Bidkar to take up Joram's body and to cast him upon the property of Naboth (v. 25a), he then gives what appears to be the supporting rationale for his command: "for I remember and you (we both remember) riding (chariots) as teams (pairs) behind Ahab, his father, when the Lord raised up upon him this very oracle . . . ." This is a difficult passage from the point of view of syntax and textual criticism,[16] but it is not impossible.[17]

16. Regarding כִּי־זְכֹר אֲנִי וָאַתָּה, some scholars prefer to change the imperative to a participle. According to Burney (*Notes*, 300), the LXX, Lucianic texts, Vulgate and the Peshitta presuppose the phrase: . . . כִּי זֹכֵר אֲנִי כִּי אֲנִי וָאַתָּה ("for I remember that I and thou . . ."). Burney's judgment is that this is probably correct and that the MT resulted from homoioteleuton in which the כִּי אֲנִי dropped out. Stade and Schwally concur saying that the phrase . . . כִּי זֹכֵר אֲנִי כִּי אֲנִי gives the reason for Jehu's order. All the versions rightly interpret the clause in this way, viz., that Jehu remembers the incident referred to in what follows." They go on to explain that both Vaticanus (ὅτι μνημονεύω) and the Targum (אֲרֵי דְכִיר) read אֶזְכֹּר or זֹכֵר. If we read אֶזְכֹּר then we must add כִּי after it; and if we adopt the second reading, זֹכֵר, we must add אֲנִי כִּי. LXX^L reads: δι ὅτι μνημνημαι ἐγὼ ὅτε ἐγὼ καὶ σύ. The Syriac either reads or supplies אֲנִי כִּי. It is an obvious conjecture that the two words dropped out in the MT through homoioteleuton (Stade and Schwally, *The Book of Kings*, 224). See also the critical apparatuses of *BHK* and *BHS*; Gunkel, *Geschichten von Elia*, 81, 99 n. 30 (no date given—but this article was previously published as: "Der Aufstand des Jehu, II König 9:1–10:27," *Deutsche Rundshau* 40 [1913]). See also: Klostermann, *Die Bücher Samuelis und der Könige*, 422; Burney, *Notes*, 300; Schlögl, *Die Bücher der Könige, Die Bücher der Chronik*, 245; Eissfeldt, *Das erste Buch der Könige*, 577; Schmitt, *Elisa*, 228 n. 197. T. Muraoka (*Emphatic Words and Structures in Biblical Hebrew* [Jerusalem: Magnes, 1985], 157) lists this particular passage among those that he says "must be judged as hopelessly corrupt." The above-proposed solution, however, is not unanimously accepted. Some prefer to keep the MT and the imperative זְכֹר which would refer to Bidkar, Jehu's aide, instead of Jehu himself (see Montgomery and Gehman, *A Critical and Exegetical Commentary*, 406, Šanda, *Das zweite Buch der Könige*, 89; Schmitt, *Elisa*, 228 n. 197). In both interpretations, the basic sense of the story remains unaffected. Either way, the phrase is meant to set the stage for the oracle that follows in v. 26.

Regarding the phrase אֵת רֹכְבִים צְמָדִים אַחֲרֵי אַחְאָב, the object of the recollection is an event in the past when Bidkar and Jehu were supposedly riding as chariot teams behind Ahab. The object-marker, אֵת, is missing in many manuscripts and versions. However, since it is the direct object marker connoting that which follows as the object of the recollection, there is no need to delete it, as is recommended by the critical apparatus of the *BHS*. The next two terms, רֹכְבִים צְמָדִים, are of interest in that they modify each other—Bidkar and Jehu were both riding (charioteering) in teams. Since the second of the pair of terms, צְמָדִים, is a plural form of the noun, it appears that the sense of the phrase implies that though Bidkar and Jehu were riding in the same location and at the same time. They were evidently *not* riding together in the same chariot, nor were they riding in Ahab's chariot (with O. Thenius, *Die Bücher der Könige* [KHAT 9; Leipzig: Weidmann, 1849 (2nd ed. 1873)], 311). If they had been in the same chariot as part of the same team, then the noun would have had to have been in the singular, צֶמֶד—"when we were riding together as *a team*." This appears to be the interpretation found in the Lucianics and the Targums that have the singular form. There is no need to rewrite the term, changing it into a participle as does P. Haupt. This change is merely an attempt to find a way of placing Bidkar and Jehu in the *same* chariot as Ahab, presumably so that they could better have overheard the supposed oracle. What this change causes, however, is an awkwardness of having two

The first bit of information to be gathered from this phrase has to do with the question of justification. Why does Jehu feel justified for issuing the proceeding command, which, as I have argued, represents a deliberate act of non-burial? The author, through Jehu, informs both Bidkar and the reader of the justification for the command by means of the statement introduced with the particle כִּי. The data supplied by this phrase give Bidkar, and ourselves, not only the *rationale* for the action, but also the *authority* for the action—"for I remember and you (we both remember) ... when the Lord raised up upon him this very oracle." In other words, it is because *YHWH* spoke an oracle against him that Bidkar is justified in obeying the command to cast Joram's body on Naboth's field. It is by this same authority, in fact, that Jehu feels justified in having murdered Joram. The sense is, "Take him up and cast him upon the plot of Naboth the Jezreelite, *because* God has uttered an oracle *against* him." It is because God is against Joram that his murder and the non-burial of his body are justified. Jehu is merely fulfilling God's will. It is in this sense that this justification can be interpreted as paralleling the above-mentioned Assyrian and Babylonian curses/oracles of non-burial in which it is actually a god (by means of the reigning king) who is portrayed as the one who will fulfill the oracle. In both cases, the act is portrayed as being done in accordance with the divine will.

If we look at the first part of v. 25, we find the two imperatives, שָׂא הַשְׁלִכֵהוּ. The clear object of both of these imperatives is Joram's body. Bidkar is the subject, the one who is to carry out the imperatives. The imperative שָׂא is a qal masculine singular form. The form, הַשְׁלִכֵהוּ, is a hiphil masculine singular imperative with a 3d masc. sing. suffix. These imperatives are in an asyndetic construction in which one verb follows immediately upon the other with no *waw*-conjunctive. This is a common feature in Biblical Hebrew, especially when the first verb denotes a physical movement.[18] In this relationship, the pronominal suffix added to the end of the second imperative, suffices for, and applies to, the first imperative as well. In other words, the object of both imperatives is "him" (referring to Joram's body)—Joram is never mentioned directly in these two verses. This pronominal reference serves as the redactional link between these verses and the previous v. 24 in which Jehu murdered Joram.

---

participles in a row and then leads to the conclusion that רֹכְבִים is to be deleted as an "explanatory gloss" (see P. Haupt, "The Hebrew term שָׁלִישׁ," *BASS* 4 [1902]: 583–87 [587]). There is no need for such manipulation of the text.

Regarding, וַיהוה נָשָׂא עָלָיו אֶת־הַמַּשָּׂא הַזֶּה, the word מַשָּׂא can mean either "a burden" or "an oracle." It is as "an oracle" that it is used in our verse and with this meaning; it occurs a total of twenty-eight times in the Old Testament. It is found only in the following texts: 2 Kgs 9:25; Isa 13:1; 14:28; 15:1; 17:1; 19:1; 21:1, 11, 13; 22:1; 23:1; 30:6; Jer 23:33, 34, 36, 38 (×3); Ezek 12:10; Nah 1:1; Hab 1:1; Zech 9:1; 12:1; Mal 1:1; Lam 2:14.

17. With M. Cogan and H. Tadmor, *II Kings* (AB 11; New York: Doubleday, 1988), 110; see also Šanda, *Das zweite Buch der Könige*, 98; Montgomery and Gehman, *A Critical and Exegetical Commentary*, 402, 406.

18. P. Joüon, *A Grammar of Biblical Hebrew* (trans. and rev. T. Muraoka; 2 vols.; SubBib 14/I–II; Rome: Editrice Pontificio Istituto Biblico, 1991), §177e, 650–51.

The second bit of data that we glean from this phrase is that at some point in the past Jehu and Bidkar were riding together, as a team, behind Ahab, Joram's father. This information is crucial for any understanding of the *intended* "historical setting" of both the oracle and of the events mentioned in it, as well as the events taking place in the "present time" in the actual narrative. There are several other bits of information that we glean from this phrase. First, we learn that the oracle of the Lord that Jehu sees as justifying both his murder of Joram, and his command to Bidkar, was uttered against *Ahab*. This utterance was made at a time when Jehu and Bidkar were still in the service of the former king. This would situate the utterance of the oracle several years earlier than the present events in the narrative.[19] A second important fact is that we are not informed, and therefore do not know, the original circumstances of this oracle. Thirdly, we are dealing with texts which were written long after the events they wish to portray and which have subsequently undergone a great deal of redaction.

The very phrase שָׂא הַשְׁלִכֵהוּ raises another question about the final phrase in v. 25—וַיהוָה נָשָׂא עָלָיו אֶת־הַמַּשָׂא הַזֶּה. To whom does the term עָלָיו refer? Grammatically, its referent could be either Joram or Ahab. Did YHWH raise up an oracle against Ahab himself; or, was the oracle, from the time it was first uttered when Jehu and Bidkar were riding behind Ahab, always against Joram (or Ahab's descendant)? Grammatically speaking, it could be either. This עָלָיו is a compound of the preposition עַל and the 3d masc. sing. pronominal suffix.

Nearly all the scholars and commentators take the position that the reference is to Ahab. This is understandable, especially since they interpret the following "oracle" in v. 26a to be a reference to one or more of the oracles in 1 Kgs 21:17–29. I would argue that it is just as likely that it could refer to Joram, as does the other 3d masc. sing. suffix in this same sentence. This can be argued on the same basis as the positions of those who hold that it refers to Ahab. We could argue that this is a reference to 1 Kgs 21:29 in which YHWH speaks to Elijah and tells him that the oracle against Ahab will be transferred to one of his sons. This would seem to imply that we accept that 1 Kgs 21:29 and 2 Kgs 9:25 are related, which, though a distinct possibility, is a totally different question. The fact remains that עָלָיו is ambiguous and it is my contention that this ambiguity serves the purpose of the redactor. If, as I maintain, this verse together with vv. 26 and 21bγ are secondary to the text, then it is by means of this particular, though ambiguous, preposition that the redactor was able to make a connection with the context into which he inserted this material.

### 4. *2 Kings 9:26aα*

Jehu's rationale and justification for his own actions, and for his command to Bidkar, are next clarified and concretized by appeal to the oracle(s) supposedly spoken by the Lord on an occasion years before when Jehu and Bidkar had ridden behind Ahab:

---

19. Gray, *I & II Kings*, 548, holds that the time was "some 20 years before."

אִם־לֹא אֶת־דְּמֵי נָבוֹת וְאֶת־דְּמֵי בָנָיו רָאִיתִי אֶמֶשׁ נְאֻם־יְהוָה וְשִׁלַּמְתִּי לְךָ
בַּחֶלְקָה הַזֹּאת נְאֻם־יְהוָה
(2 Kgs 9:26a)

The first bit of data that we find in v. 26α has to do precisely with what it was that YHWH witnessed that night. Here the text reads: אֶת־דְּמֵי נָבוֹת וְאֶת־
דְּמֵי בָנָיו רָאִיתִי אֶמֶשׁ נְאֻם־יְהוָה. What do we learn from this statement? Literally, that *the Lord saw blood.*[20] We are neither told *how* it was that the blood was spilled nor *who* was responsible for spilling it.[21] We are not specifically told that

---

20. Regarding אֶת־דְּמֵי, the term דְּמֵי is used rather infrequently in the Old Testament. It is found some twenty-three times in the whole of the Old Testament (Gen 4:10, 11; Lev 12:4, 5; 1 Sam 26:20; 2 Sam 16:8; 1 Kgs 2:5 (×2), 31; 2 Kgs 9:7 (×2), 26 (×2); 2 Chr 24:25; Job 16:18; Ps 30:9; Isa 4:4; Jer 51:35; Ezek 16:36; Hos 1.4; 2:8, 17), and of these, seven of the occurrences are found in the context of an oracle, Gen 4:11; 2 Kgs 9:7 (×2), 26 (×2); Isa 4:4; Hos 1:4. Four of these seven oracular occurrences are found in 2 Kgs 9. We find it twice in 9:7, which is an oracle spoken against Jezebel for having spilled the "blood of my servants the prophets and the blood of all the servants of the Lord." We also find it twice in 9:26, which is in reference to the supposed murder in which the blood of Naboth and the blood of his sons was spilled. Out of the total of seven oracular occurrences, five are related to the events concerning Naboth and Jehu (2 Kgs 9:7 [×2], 26 [×2]; Hos 1:4). The occurrence found in Hos 1:4 predicts punishment upon the house of Jehu for his having spilt the blood of Jezreel (a reference to the murder of the *entire* "house of Ahab" in Jezreel). There is an interesting extra-biblical parallel to this phrase. In his article, "Die Inschriften Asarhaddons Königs von Assyrien: Nachträge und Verbesserungen" (*AfO* 18 [1957–58]: 113–18), R. Borger presents some comments and improvements upon his earlier work on the inscriptions of Asarhaddon (*Die Inschriften Asarhaddons Königs von Assyrien* [*AfO*B 9; Graz: Im Selbstverlage des Herausgebers, 1956]). He remarks that in the Vienna Museum, Professor von Soden found a small fragment of an eight-sided prism whose left column contained a duplicate of the Nineveh A prism, col. III, ll. 60–75. Its right column contains a parallel text to the same part of the "Annals of Sennacherib." In his transcription of the text of this right column (115) he transcribes the Akkadian of l. 2 as follows: *hab-ba-tum šar-ra-qu a-mir* [∓ 8 spaces]. This he translates as, "Räuber, Diebe, [Blut]befleckte [ . . . ]" ("robber, thief, [blood]stained [ . . . ]"). In his notes on this transcription/translation he comments that this text coincides rather exactly to the text of the Asarhaddon's "Letter to God," I, l. 2 (British Museum: K 7599) which reads: *hab-ba-tú šar-ra-gu lu šá . . . da-mi it-bu-ku*, the last phrase of which he translates as "wer Blut vergossen hatte" ("who had spilled blood"). He then remarks that for the phrase at the end of this line, *šá . . . da-mi it-bu-ku*, another prism, Taylor V II, col. 5, l. 2, which dates from ca. 691 B.C.E., according to D. D. Luckenbill, reads, "der Blut gesehen hat" ("who has seen blood") (*Ancient Records of Assyria and Babylonia*, vol. 2, *Historical Records of Assyria, from Sargon to the End* [Chicago: The University of Chicago Press, 1927]), 115. The Taylor Prism text, in place of the phrase *šá . . . da-mi it-bu-ku*, reads *a-mir da-me*, which according to the *The Assyrian Dictionary of the Oriental Institute of the University of Chicago* (University of Chicago Oriental Institute, 1968), vol. 1, A, pt. 2:63, is an idiom or fixed phrase meaning: "experienced in bloodshed; a murderer." A literal translation is "one seeing blood." Even the Oriental Institute prism published by Luckenbill at col. V, l. 22 (the end) reads *a-mir da-me*, but he translates it as "the run-away." What we have in these texts, then, is an idiomatic use of the phrase *a-mir da-me* (lit. "the one seeing blood"). It is normally used in reference to the one who has committed the crime or caused the bloodshed and in this sense is the same in meaning as *da-mi it-bu-ku* (lit. "the one who spills blood"). In our biblical text of 2 Kgs 9:26, the one who sees the blood is the Lord. In this case he is not the murderer, but rather, he observed the results of the crime. The biblical author has used the phrase literally, in juxtaposition to the Akkadian usage which is much more metaphoric or idiomatic.

21. *Contra* the conclusions drawn by Rofé, "The Vineyard of Naboth," 96, and M. White, "Naboth's Vineyard and Jehu's Coup: The Legitimization of a Dynastic Extermination," *VT* 44, no. 1 (1994): 66–76 (68).

the Lord personally or physically witnessed *the commission of the murder*, nor are we told that anyone else may have witnessed *the actual act of the murder*—all details which would normally be supplied by the author. We cannot even say that Naboth's blood was spilled by violent means until we look at the second part of the passage. All we can deduce from the first statement itself is that the Lord says that he saw the blood of Naboth and his sons last night—literally that, he saw only the blood, that is, the *results* of the crime.

The lack of specificity and detail regarding the performance of the crime should not take us totally by surprise. In Gen 4:10, in a similar type of metaphoric reference to the role of blood as a "witness" to a crime, the implication is that the Lord "heard" the "blood of your brother (Cain's) crying out to me from the earth." The blood was witnessing, as if of its own volition, to the fact of the crime. The act of the blood "crying out" obviously occurred after the fact of the crime, after the crime had already taken place.

We find another example in Exod 12:23, where we read that when the Lord "sees" the blood on the lintels and doorposts of the Hebrews' homes in Egypt, he will pass over them. Also, in Ezek 9, the Lord shows the prophet Ezekiel a vision in which he sends forth destroyers to the city of Jerusalem because of its great guilt. This city and the land "was full of blood and injustice" and the people have accused the Lord of "forsaking the land and of *not seeing*" (9:9). Interestingly, the Lord responds by saying, "As for me, *my eye* will not spare, nor will I have pity, but *I will requite* their deeds upon their heads" (RSV). In this verse we find a similar combination of the Lord both seeing and avenging as is found in 2 Kgs 9:26. The verbs used in both cases are synonyms. In 9:26 we have the verb שׁלם√ ("to avenge"), whereas in this verse from Ezekiel we have the two roots חוס√ and חמל√, both of which mean "to spare" or "to have compassion upon," and both of which are used in the negative.

In none of the above examples, including 2 Kgs 9:26, are we ever informed, on the narrative level of the texts, that the Lord actually witnessed the particular criminal acts. In all three examples, however, we are told specifically that the Lord has definitely seen the results of the crimes—the blood. For the purpose of these narratives, this is apparently sufficient. When we are told that YHWH "saw the blood" it is to be understood as a metaphoric indication that the blood itself is a witness to the fact of a crime before God.

R. J. Tournay, O.P., argued a similar position in a recension he wrote[22] concerning a commentary on Job written by D. Wolfers.[23] In his commentary, Wolfers identifies the גּאֵל in Job 19:23 as YHWH. This would imply that it is God, himself, who is the adversary of Job (19:11b); the one with whom Job discusses or disputes.[24] As such, he could not at the same time be Job's defender or advocate.[25] Tournay contends that this identification of YHWH as Job's opponent or

---

22. R. J. Tournay, recension of D. Wolfers, *Deep Things out of Darkness: The Book of Job and a New English Translation*, RB 104, no. 3 (July 1997): 416–19.
23. D. Wolfers, *Deep Things Out of Darkness: The Book of Job* (Grand Rapids: Eerdmans, 1995).
24. See the discussion in Wolfers, *Deep Things Out of Darkness*, 485–91.
25. Tournay, Recension of Wolfers, 417–18.

adversary is mistaken. In Tournay's mind, the advocate for Job can be none other than the personified cry of the blood. The blood cries out to God from the ground where it had been spilled and where it remains visible (Job 16:18a). It is this "blood which cries out" that will become the "avenger of blood—the גֹּאֵל," when it rises up from the dust where it was spilled (19:25b).[26] In Tournay's interpretation it is this same "blood which cries out" that is the witness/ avenger/גֹּאֵל for Job in the heavenly court in 16:18–21. He points out that this personification of blood is not unique to the book of Job, but is also found in Gen 4:10; 37:26; Pss 79:11; 88:3; 102:2; Isa 26:21; Lam 3:41; and Ezek 24:7–8. In all these cases the personification of the blood is that of the דָּבָר or the קוֹל. In the same way Tournay believes that the word גֹּאֵל, meaning "the avenger of blood," applies to the text of Job 19:25 as a strong poetic metaphor referring to the spilled blood. At the end of time, this spilled blood will arise from the dust and witness in the heavenly court, where God will be the judge, against those who spilled it.[27]

In 1 Kgs 9:26, however, the blood appears as a silent and passive witness that is observed by YHWH, who then himself promises to avenge the murders. In this case, it might appear that Tournay's interpretation of the Job passages does not apply. In the Job passages, the blood cries out actively and seeks justice/vengeance before the heavenly court. But even in this case, the vengeance or justice can only take place *after* the divine judge has decreed it. In this sense, though the active role of the blood in the case of Job might be understood as that of a גֹּאֵל, it still is powerless to seek vengeance until it receives a favorable "hearing" from YHWH. In the case of 2 Kgs 9:26, the blood is totally passive. The blood is not said to "cry out." Its role is that of a "silent witness." YHWH is the active character in this scene; he is the one who both sees the blood, and who promises vengeance. I maintain, however, that the blood is still *the witness* (the one who gives the testimony) whether that be actively as in Job or passively as in 2 Kgs 9:26 and that YHWH is the judge who decrees the punishment (vengeance) in both cases.

This understanding of the role of blood is very similar to that found in those texts that present YHWH as the one who "consults," "seeks out" or, "requires" the blood of those who have killed. This is expressed in the concept of דָּרַשׁ דָּמִים. D. Daube defines this phrase as "to require the blood," and describes it as being used in those cases where God requires the murdered person's blood from the murderer. He believes that this concept could only have come into existence in a culture and time when there was a belief that the blood of a murdered person was somehow "taken under the control of the murderer." It is only in this sense that people would understand vengeance as a demanding back, a "requiring' of the blood that was spilled. The way in which God "requires" the blood of the one who was killed, is invariably by means of killing, or having killed, the murderer. In all of this, Daube maintains that the Old Testament language has preserved a

---

26. Tournay, Recension of Wolfers, 418.
27. Tournay, Recension of Wolfers, 418–19.

term that distinctly implies the notion that the soul of one who is murdered is taken into the control of the murderer. The way that the Old Testament authors use the term reflects the same idea as that found in the *Lex Talionis*, namely, that the killing of the murderer is the way of taking back (control of/over) that which had been lost.[28] Texts that use one form or another of this phrase include Gen 9:5; 42:22; Ezek 33:6; Ps 9:13.

A second element of 2 Kgs 9:26 that requires our attention is the term אֶמֶשׁ. This term is rare in the Old Testament and its precise meaning is debated. The term itself is found only five times (Gen 19:34; 31:29, 42; 2 Kgs 9:26; and Job 30:3—which is dubious). Of these five occurrences, three are found in Genesis. In every one of these occurrences in Genesis, the term is found in close proximity to and in reference to the term לַיְלָה ("night"). All three cases are referring to a vision, a dream or an event that occurred either during the previous night, or to a night in the immediate past (19:34 refers to 19:33; both 31:29 and 42 refer to 31:24). There is little doubt, in my opinion, that in these cases the term אֶמֶשׁ means specifically "last evening" or "last night" and is not referring to "yesterday" in a less specific or more general sort of way. This is the position held by some of the more recent scholars.[29] Other scholars, however, have or still do translate the term more generally as "yesterday."[30] In 2 Kgs 9:26, then, we have a reference to an oracle of the Lord which is spoken by Jehu after his execution of Joram, king of Israel. In the context of this quote, we find the term אֶמֶשׁ with reference to *when* it was that "*the Lord saw* the blood of Naboth and the blood of his sons."

Several difficulties arise in reference to the way the term is used in our text. One difficulty is that the quoted oracle has obviously been taken out of its *original context* (whatever that might have been), whereas I argue that, based upon the usage of the term in the Old Testament, it was probably also found in reference to the term לַיְלָה which would have given it the specification of "last night" (as in all the other undisputed occurrences). The term in our passage was meant to express the specific time when the murder of Naboth took place *in the original oracle and in its original context*. But, this is *not* where we find the

28. D. Daube, "Lex Talionis," in *Studies in Biblical Law* (Cambridge: Cambridge University Press, 1947), 102–53 (123–24).

29. L. Koehler and W. Baumgartner, *Lexicon in Veteris Testamenti Libros* (Leiden: Brill, 1953), 66; W. Gesenius, *Hebräisches und Aramäisches Handwörterbuch* (17th ed.; Berlin: Springer, 1962), 52; F. Zorell, *Lexicon Hebraicum Veteris Testamenti* (Rome: Pontifical Biblical Institute, 1984), 67; BDB, 57; I. L. Seeligmann, "Die Auffassung von der Prophetie in der deuteronomistischen und chronistischen Geschichtsschreibung (mit einem Exkurs über das Buch Jeremia)," *Congress Volume: Göttingen, 1977* (VTSup 29; Leiden: Brill, 1978), 254–84 (260); Rofé, "The Vineyard of Naboth," 96 n. 3; Cogan and Tadmor, *II Kings*, 102, 111; White, "Naboth's Vineyard and Jehu's Coup," 68.

30. See, among others: Šanda, *Das zweite Buch der Könige*, 99; Gunkel, *Geschichten von Elisa*, 81; Kittel, *Die Bücher der Könige*, 133; Montgomery and Gehman, *A Critical and Exegetical Commentary*, 399; Whitley, "The Deuteronomic Presentation of the House of Omri," 149; Gray, *I & II Kings*, 546; Miller, "The Fall of the House of Ahab," 308; Bohlen, *Der Fall Nabot*, 281; Schmitt, *Elisa*, 229; McKenzie, *The Trouble with Kings*, 73; T. R. Hobbs, *2 Kings* (WBC 13; Waco, Tex.: Word Books, 1985), 108; P. D. Miscall, "Elijah, Ahab, and Jehu: A Prophecy Fulfilled," *Prooftexts* 9, no. 1 (1989): 73–83 (79).

oracle in our text. Despite the fact that it has lost its immediate connection with the term לַיְלָה, it should still be translated as "last night" or "last evening."

M. White correctly defines the term as "last night" but then appears to infer that because the crime happened at night, it was done "secretly."[31] This is the same conclusion that has been drawn by A. Rofé. Rofé goes so far as to say that "2 Kings ix, 26 mentions the Lord seeing the blood of Naboth and his sons at night. He swears that he saw it; he is the sole witness of a hidden murder, perpetrated at night, seen by nobody else."[32] I do agree that the murder is said to have occurred in the evening or night (probably the evening or night *before* in its original context), but I hesitate to infer from this that it was *necessarily done in secret or hiding*. There is no implicit or explicit reference in our text to any hidden or secret nature to the crime. We are dealing with an old and unrelated oracle that, in the context of vv. 25–26, is secondarily reused and applied to Ahab for the specific reason of justifying the murder and non-burial of Ahab's son, Joram. In my opinion, it leads to false conclusions if we read into an oracle of this type that which we think might have been the circumstances in its original context.

Another interpretation that I find difficult to accept is that of C. F. Whitley. Whitley compares the deaths of Ahab and Joram and says:

> Here the crime of *Joram* is that he slew Naboth and his sons *on the previous day*; because, *as Jehu said*, 'surely I have seen yesterday the blood of Naboth and the blood of his sons saith Yahweh,' the immediate half verse, 'for remember how that I and thou rode together after Ahab, his father, the Lord laid this burden upon him,' being obviously an interpolation to connect this incident with the circumstances of Ahab's death as told in I Kgs.[33]

Whitley, apparently based upon a literal interpretation of אֶמֶשׁ as the previous day, understands that it was *Joram* who murdered Naboth and his sons, and not *Ahab*. This then forces him to interpret the first occurrence of נְאֻם־יְהוָה as יֵהוּא —Jehu. This in turn makes Jehu the witness to the murders of Naboth and his sons. But this would have been highly unlikely since, as we are told, Jehu was at Ramoth-Gilead, whereas the murders supposedly took place at Jezreel or Samaria.

A second important difficulty which the use of the term אֶמֶשׁ in our passage raises has to do not with the "specific time," which the term in an abstract (non-contextualized) sense might imply, but rather with its meaning in its "contextual" sense. This is an important distinction upon which theories and interpretations concerning our verses, and more specifically the oracle (or reference to an oracle) found in v. 26a, have been based. Simply put, did the murder of Naboth and his sons take place "last night" (specifically) or at some time in the more distant past (generally)? If we understand the term אֶמֶשׁ literally or specifically, we would have to say that the murder took place during the immediate night before. This,

31. White, "Naboth's Vineyard and Jehu's Coup," 68.
32. Rofé, "The Vineyard of Naboth," 96.
33. Whitley, "The Deuteronomic Presentation of the House of Omri," 148–49 (my emphasis).

however, would imply that Ahab could not have committed the murders, since he is already dead. The immediate context of this story is that of the coup of Jehu against Ahab's son Joram, and not that of the time when Jehu and Bidkar were riding behind Ahab the king (v. 25b). Instead, the murders would have had to have been committed by someone in the immediate time and context, namely, Joram or Jezebel or even by Jehu himself. The author of the present text attempts to smooth over this technical difficulty by having Jehu specifically clarify that it was Ahab who committed the crime and that it took place several years ago in the "remembered past." This is accomplished by introducing the "oracle" with v. 25b in which Jehu recalled (or asks Bidkar to recall) an event which occurred while he and Bidkar had been riding behind Ahab, Joram's father. The reflective mood of this passage is somewhat discordant with the intensity of the activity in the surrounding scene. This has been interpreted by some scholars as a sign that vv. 25–26 are intrusive and, therefore, that they are not original to the story.

The immediate context in which the term is found in the oracle is that of *the Lord* recalling an event which occurred אֶמֶשׁ, upon which *he* is about to utter an oracle. It would be a mistake to attempt to make an argument, based upon an overly literal interpretation of the term אֶמֶשׁ (regardless of whether we translate it as "yesterday" or "last evening"),[34] that the events which the Lord says he witnessed occurred "yesterday" in *real time*, that is, that they occurred the day before *Joram* was killed.[35] To do so would be to ignore both the secondary nature of the oracle itself, and its present context.

Third is the fact that in 2 Kgs 9:26a we find that the statement that YHWH saw the results of the crime (the blood) is also "solemnized" and given added authority by the statement, נְאֻם־יְהוָה. This phrase occurs twice in our so-called "oracle" and is variously translated as "oracle of the Lord," "thus says the Lord," "says Yahweh," and so on. The term נְאֻם is a masculine noun that in the older lexicons was explained as a passive participle. It means an "utterance, declaration or revelation."[36] A lexical and concordance analysis of this term is helpful in understanding its double usage in our passage. The word נְאֻם occurs in some 357 verses in the Old Testament. Of these, 267 occurrences are in the form of the syntagma, נְאֻם־יְהוָה. Of these 267 having YHWH as subject, the phrase occurs twice in the same verse on only eight occasions (2 Sam 2:30; 2 Kgs 9:26; Isa 14:22; 52:5; Jer 3:6; 23:9; 29:14, 19), and it occurs three times in the same verse on only two occasions (Hag 2:4, 23). These double and triple occurrences in the same verse serve the literary purpose of adding very strong emphasis and solemnity to the oracle being spoken.

The utterance, declaration, or revelation which is emphasized by the double occurrence of נְאֻם־יְהוָה in 2 Kgs 9:26 is reinforced and highlighted by its having

---

34. With, for example, Olyan, "*Ḥăšālôm*," 665 n. 46.

35. *Contra*: Whitley, "The Deuteronomic Presentation of the House of Omri," 148–49; Miller, "The Fall of the House of Ahab," 308 (text and n. 2), who holds that vv. 25–26 "imply that the Naboth affair took place the day before Jehoram's death rather than during Ahab's reign"; and J. M. Miller and J. H. Hayes, *A History of Ancient Israel and Judah* (Philadelphia: Westminster, 1986), 254–55.

36. BDB, 610,

been introduced as a מַשָּׂא at the end of v. 25. The occurrences of נְאֻם־יְהוָה together with the term מַשָּׂא in very close proximity, referring to one another and meaning an "oracle or an utterance of the Lord," is very rare—occurring only in our verse and in Zech 12:1. It also occurs in Prov 30:1, which is difficult and apparently which does not have YHWH as the subject. As a genre, מַשָּׂא "is found in the Old Testament only in the prophetic movement where it is presented as a response to a question concerning a lack of clarity in the relationship between divine intention and human reality."[37] The question remains as to why the author or editors chose to use this emphatic double usage of נְאֻם־יְהוָה in our story. Obviously, we cannot know the precise reason, but we can surmise that it was for the purpose of adding strong emphasis. This is precisely what Jehu was trying to convey, he was attempting to justify emphatically his actions by stating that he was acting strictly in accord with the word of the Lord spoken against Ahab and his family.

The phrase נְאֻם־יְהוָה also brings to a close the "reason" ("*Begründung*") for the oracle of doom that is to follow. The reason is a necessary part of this type of oracle and is found either following the oracle, or preceding the oracle proper, as in our case.[38] The information gained from this initial part of v. 26 sets the stage, and gives the legitimizing rationale, for the utterance of the oracle proper which follows. This reason for the oracle is solemnized by the use of the phrase נְאֻם־יְהוָה. This phrase serves as part of the linkage with the "oracle proper"[39] and, together with the second occurrence of the same phrase at the end of the oracle, forms a part of a "frame" or "bookend" around the oracle.

A fourth point to consider in 2 Kgs 9:26 is the anonymous character of the phrase.[40] T. R. Hobbs points out that "the oracle which Jehu recalls in vv. 25b–26 is unusual for a prophetic oracle. It bears little resemblance to classic prophetic oracles, save for the use of שׁלם√ ('to requite') with יְהוָה ('Yahweh' [as its subject—P.T.C.]). Its form is that of an oath."[41] I would add to this description the fact that what we essentially have in v. 26b is only a remnant, or a part, of an original oracle, namely, only the promise of divine retribution—וְשִׁלַּמְתִּי לְךָ בַּחֶלְקָה הַזֹּאת נְאֻם־יְהוָה. This remnant of an oracle, taken completely out of its original context (whatever that may have been), is now, in the context of this "Naboth Redaction" of 2 Kgs 9, applied to a totally different set of circumstances.

The disassociation of the oracle from its original context with its immediate referent has caused its present anonymous character. It is attributed to the Lord

---

37. R. D. Weis, "Oracle," in *ABD* 5:28.

38. For a very clear discussion of this type of oracle and of its necessary elements, see H. W. Wolff, " 'Die Begründungen,' der prophetischen Heils- und Unheilssprüche," *ZAW* 52 (1934): 1–22. See also, C. Westermann, *Grundformen prophetischer Rede* (BETh 31; Munich: Chr. Kaiser, 1960), 92–119, esp. 94 n. 2.

39. Wolff, "Die Begründungen," 1–2.

40. With, for example, G. Hölscher, *Die Profeten* (Leipzig: J. C. Hinrichs, 1914), 177; Bohlen, *Der Fall Nabot*, 283; M. Mulzer, *Jehu schlägt Joram: Text-, literar- und struckturkritische Untersuchung zu 2 Kön 8,25–10,36* (ATSAT 37; St. Ottilien: EOS Verlag, 1992), 234–35 and n. 66.

41. Hobbs, *2 Kings*, 113.

in a generic way, but it is very rare that the Lord speaks in oracles without the use of an explicitly named intermediary, a prophet, priest, or some other human mediator. This lack of an explicitly named intermediary might also be explained by the fact that the present oracle has been removed from its original context. Verse 25b supplies us with an "indication" of its original setting; the oracle was uttered several years earlier and under different circumstances about which we have *not* been specifically informed. This "indication" is also redactional and, therefore, is highly suspicious as well. There is also the fact that no prophet is directly linked with this prophecy. In the context of 2 Kgs 9, it might be tempting for us to surmise that it was the "son of the prophet" whom Elisha sent to anoint Jehu (vv. 1–3). But this does not fit well with the introduction to the oracle found immediately before in v. 25. We might then consider it to have been Elijah, since the introduction in v. 25 refers to the time when Jehu and Bidkar were riding behind Ahab, Joram's father, with whom Elijah had many encounters. This solution, however, is problematic since Jehu specifically says that "the Lord" raised up the oracle—not "Elijah," and not "through Elijah." The phrase in v. 25, וַיהוָה נָשָׂא עָלָיו אֶת־הַמַּשָּׂא הַזֶּה, is in fact, a *hapax*. The fact remains, therefore, that as the oracle is recounted in v. 26, it is an "anonymous" oracle, in the sense of there being no explicit mention of the prophetic intermediary. Instead, the oracle is directly attributed to YHWH himself. But this would appear then to indicate that the recipients of the oracle from YHWH were, in fact, Jehu and Bidkar. However, even the redactor of this passage appears to be hesitant to make this specific claim. The "anonymous" quality regarding the human agent of this oracle indicates that vv. 25–26 are a secondary addition to the text.

### 5. 2 Kings 9:26aβ

The second part of v. 26a recalls the "reaction" of the Lord to having seen the blood of Naboth and his sons and it constitutes the oracle proper: וְשִׁלַּמְתִּי לְךָ בַּחֶלְקָה הַזֹּאת נְאֻם־יְהוָה. Here the theme of "divine vengeance" is introduced. Because of having seen the blood, the Lord will require and seek retributive justice; he will require the blood of the one, or ones, responsible for having spilled the blood of Naboth and his sons. This oath is made solemn and is emphasized by the addition of the second occurrence of נְאֻם־יְהוָה. Focusing our attention upon the data we can glean from this passage, we see that the oracle is comprised of two bits of information: first, *what* the Lord will do; and second, *where* he is going to do it. The issue of what the Lord will do, that is, of divine vengeance, will be discussed in the following chapter.

The second part of the oracle in v. 26aβ highlights the "place" or location where the Lord's vengeance will occur, namely, "on this plot" (בַּחֶלְקָה הַזֹּאת).[42] This phrase actually localizes three separate events in one and the same place: (1) the location where the murder of Naboth and his sons took place; (2) the

---

42. See the above discussion regarding v. 21bγ, pp. 21–22.

location where the Lord saw the blood of Naboth and his sons; and (3) the location where the Lord will requite those murders. From this information, we may conclude that the place where the retributive justice of the Lord will occur is the same place where the crime against Naboth took place. In other words, this justice is not only associated with a specific crime, but in this case it is also apparently associated with the specific locale of the crime.

## 6. *2 Kings 9:26b*

The final part of v. 26 is not part of the actual oracle, but rather, it presents us with the *conclusion* to the dialogue between Jehu and Bidkar: וְעַתָּה שָׂא הַשְׁלִכֵהוּ בַּחֶלְקָה כִּדְבַר יְהוָה. It is a conclusion on two different levels. First, it concludes the encounter and discussion between Jehu and Bidkar. Second, and more importantly, it serves as the conclusion of Jehu's argument for his own justification of his actions. It is as if he were arguing his case before a tribunal, and now that he has done so, he gives his forensic summation introduced by וְעַתָּה.

The first part of this summation is a reiteration of Jehu's initial command to Bidkar found in v. 25aβ, to take up Joram's body and cast it upon the plot of ground. In v. 26b, however, we notice that the plot of land is no longer specifically identified as that belonging to Naboth the Jezreelite, as it had been identified in the original command. It is merely generically identified. The reason for this is that in the present form of the text, it is meant to refer for its specification back to the end of v. 25bβ where we find reference to a specific plot of land. Therefore, in v. 26b there is no need to be repetitive. It also forms a bookend with the first occurrence of the command in v. 25aβ.

The second part of this summation is a final appeal to the basis of the authority for the whole of the argument and for the justification that Jehu sought by means of the entire argument throughout the two verses. Everything is based upon, and justified by, the fact that it is all done "in accordance with the word of the Lord." The final two words of this summation, כִּדְבַר יְהוָה, emphasize and further strengthen the double usage of נְאֻם־יְהוָה in v. 26. The use of this particular phrase as a description of the authority upon which something was done, appears particularly frequently in the books of Kings—seventeen out of a total number of twenty-six occurrences in the Old Testament.[43] Interestingly, of the nine occurrences outside the books of Kings, none make any direct reference to a prophet being the channel through which the Lord spoke. Instead, it is usually the Lord himself, who communicates the message. In the books of Kings, on the other hand, of the seventeen occurrences of the phrase, it is directly connected to a specifically named prophet or Man of God in at least thirteen cases. It is quite possible, then, that at least in the books of Kings, the use of the phrase כִּדְבַר יְהוָה is part of a Dtr redactional system whose purpose is to confirm that the

---

43. See Josh 8:8, 27; 1 Kgs 12:24; 13:26; 14:18; 15:29; 16:12, 34; 17:5, 16; 22:38; 2 Kgs 1:17; 4:44; 7:16; 9:26; 10:17; 14:25; 23:16; 24:2; 1 Chr 11:3, 10; 15:15; 2 Chr 35:6; Jer 13:2; 32:8; Jonah 3:3.

Lord's words to his prophets are in fact always fulfilled. Many scholars consider this theme of prophecy–fulfillment to be a typical part of the Dtr style.[44] The fulfillment of the prophecies concerning Ahab and his dynasty are presented in the texts of 1 and 2 Kings as expressions of divine vengeance.

44. With Benzinger, *Die Bücher der Könige*, 153; Gunkel, *Geschichten von Elisa*, 87 and nn. 51–52; Noth, *Überlieferungsgeschichtliche Studien* 1:126 (84); Steck, *Überlieferung und Zeitgeschichte*, 34 n. 5, 40 n. 4; Schmitt, *Elisa*, 22 n. 24, 23; M. Sekine, "Literatursoziologische Beobachtungen zu den Elisaerzählungen," in *The Annual of the Japanese Biblical Institute* (ed. M. Sekine and A. Satake, Tokyo: Yamamoto Shoten, 1975), 39–62 (55); Timm, *Die Dynastie Omri*, 138; Rehm, *Das zweite Buch der Könige*, 106; Würthwein *Die Bücher der Könige, 1. Kön. 17–2 Kön. 25*, 337; J. C. Trebolle Barrera, *Jehú y Joás, Texto y composición literaria de 2 Reyes 9–11* (ISJ 17; Valencia: Institución San Jerónimo, 1984), 62–63; G. Hentschel, *2 Könige* (Die Neue Echter Bibel; Würzburg: Echter Verlag, 1985), 46; Peckham, *The Composition of the Deuteronomistic History*, 139, fig. 7; Campbell, *Of Prophets and Kings*, 92 n. 61; Barré, *The Rhetoric of Political Persuasion*, 17–18; McKenzie, *The Trouble with Kings*, 76–78.

# Chapter 3

## THE THEME OF DIVINE VENGEANCE/JUSTICE
## AND THE PRINCIPLE OF THE *LEX TALIONIS*

### 1. *The Theme of Divine Vengeance/Justice*

In the first part of the oracle of the Lord in 2 Kgs 9:26aα, the Lord says: וְשִׁלַּמְתִּי לְךָ ("I will requite/avenge you"). The verb in this case is a piel perfect, 1st com. sing. of the root שׁלם√. In the piel form, the semantic range of this verb includes: "to complete or finish; to make safe; to make whole, good, or to restore; to make good one's word, or vows; to requite, recompense or reward for either good or evil."[1] This word, in all its forms and usage in the Old Testament, is extremely rich. In 2 Kgs 9:26b, however, we find a rather rare usage of this term, in that we have one of only a few occurrences in which it is spoken against an individual person.[2] In most occurrences the oracle is spoken against an entire people, either Israel or Babylon.[3] In 2 Kgs 9:26a, the use of this particular form of the verb, applied to a single individual, might be an indication that the oracle has been taken out of its original setting. In that original setting it might be assumed to have applied to a whole nation, whereas here in our context it is secondarily applied to a single individual.

S. Olyan has strongly emphasized the richness of this term.[4] Approaching the text of 2 Kgs 9 from the perspective of narrative and literary analysis, Olyan argues that the root שׁלם√ (*šlm*) is in fact the *Leitwort* of the passage and that "the key to interpreting the *šlm* motif in 2 Kgs 9 lies in Yahweh's oracle in v. 26."[5] He maintains that the literary unity in 2 Kgs 9 is centered upon this term.

---

1. BDB, 1022.
2. See also Deut 7:10; 32:41; Judg 1:7; 2 Sam 3:39.
3. See Isa 65:6; Jer 16:18; 25:14; 51:24—the only other cases where the exact form of the verb וְשִׁלַּמְתִּי occurs. Isaiah 65:6–7 is spoken against Israel, following upon chs. 63:7–64:12 which are considered to be a "psalm of intercession," in which the Lord responds in ch. 65. The first part of the response is a recollection of Israel's sinfulness—especially that of having abandoned YHWH for other gods. In this context the Lord refers to a written record which he has before him and in which he has promised retributive justice. This scene represents a litigious atmosphere—a courtroom scene. Jeremiah 16:18 is spoken against Israel. In ch. 16, Jeremiah's own life is presented as a symbol. In this context, Israel is accused of having abandoned YHWH and of practicing idol worship. The divine judgment is that the Lord will requite them doubly for their iniquity. Jeremiah 25:14 is an oracle spoken against Babylon. After the Exile has ended, the Lord will then requite Babylon for its sins and deeds. Jeremiah 51:24 is an oath against Babylon for its evil deeds.
4. Olyan, "*Hăšālôm*," 652–88.
5. Olyan, "*Hăšālôm*," 653.

According to Olyan, the situation in the story is that through the murder of Naboth and the "harlotries and sorceries" of Jezebel, the divinely established order, unity, or fullness of life and creation has been disrupted. YHWH intervenes through his chosen instrument, Jehu, to re-establish this original order and unity, this שָׁלוֹם.[6] In v. 26, Olyan holds that the oracle was probably originally an anonymous and independent oracle that was taken by the original author of 2 Kgs 9 and used to supply the focus of the story. The function of the oracle in our story is that "it explains in a subtle manner, through the use of the piel *šlm*, why the state of *šālôm* did not exist in Israel."[7] Verses 25–26 reveal the true motivation for Jehu's actions. They are the same motivations that move YHWH to pronounce the oracle in the first place.[8]

Olyan's arguments for the centrality of the verb שׁלם√ in the literary unity of the chapter appear logical. Jehu has just murdered the legitimate king of Israel in a dramatic coup which included military maneuvering, deceit, and trickery, and a certain amount of incertitude concerning how the people would view or accept these developments. The use of this oracle appears to be an attempt at self-justification on Jehu's part. It is as if he were trying to convince Bidkar that YHWH commanded him to murder Joram, and that YHWH has just commanded Bidkar to deal with the body of the dead king. The difficulty with Olyan's position, however, is that if vv. 25–26 are in fact secondary to the account, and not an "independent oracle which was taken by the original author of 2 Kgs 9 and used to supply the basic focus of the story," then his theory must be reworked. If, indeed, vv. 25–26 are secondary to the story of Jehu's coup, then it would imply that their secondary insertion into the text was the deliberate attempt on the part of a *later redactor* to change or adjust the focus of the original story, and not an attempt of the original author to give a particular focus to his original work. The debate over the origin and function of these two verses in the context of 2 Kgs 9 has led some scholars to see in vv. 25–26 a deliberate "apologetic" attempt to justify or whitewash both Jehu himself and his actions.[9] In recent years scholars have been divided on how precisely to perceive Jehu in this story. Some, like Olyan, see Jehu in a very positive light—"Jehu is presented as Yahweh's instrument of restoration of *šālôm*."[10] Others view Jehu and his actions in a less positive view. W. Eisenbeis, for example, sees Jehu as a cold-hearted and "bloody murderer."[11]

---

6. Olyan, "*Hăšālôm*," 654; also 661–62, where Olyan argues that recognizing this underlying intellectual framework is key to understanding 2 Kgs 9.

7. Olyan, "*Hăšālôm*," 667.

8. Olyan, "*Hăšālôm*," 667.

9. See, among others, Schmitt, *Elisa*, 23; Sekine, "Literatursoziologische Beobachtungen zu den Elisaerzählungen," 56.

10. Olyan, "*Hăšālôm*," 654. See also, for example, Gray, *I & II Kings*, 538, where he claims the author of the Jehu account preserves his sense of historical perspective in avoiding the temptation to make vengeance for Naboth and the fulfillment of Elijah's prophecy in 1 Kgs 21:19 the main motive for Jehu. Rather, he claims, the primary influence of Jezebel was what the resurgents opposed (v. 22).

11. W. Eisenbeis, *Die Wurzel שלם im Alten Testament* (BZAW 113; Berlin: de Gruyter, 1969), 110. "The suspicion is near the surface, that in the account, the representative of the house of Ahab is

Perhaps another approach to an understanding of the verb שׁלבם in our particular oracle is to see the use of this verb, and this oracle, as an expression of
retributive justice. This type of justice would obviously be governed by the
principle of the *Lex Talionis*.[12] Olyan does not directly address this aspect of the
story in his analysis.

## 2. *The Principle of* Lex Talionis

The principle of *talionis* can be understood from both a positive and a negative
perspective. To put it simply, if one is just and obedient to the law, one will be
rewarded, but, if one is unjust and disobedient of the law, one will be punished *in
equal measure* to the crime. The original principle appears to have been established not so much to "impose" punishment, but rather to "limit" vengeance and
punishment to an equal and reasonable measure. The famous *Lex Talionis*, as a
principle of Israelite law, is found in Exod 21:22–25.[13]

The traditional school of thought regarding the *Lex Talionis* held that this
principle was a very ancient, in fact "primitive," element of Israelite law. It was
understood to imply *a literal application* of the principle in all cases. It had come
to be interpreted as an early remedy to prevent excessive vengeance from being
exacted by a wronged individual or his or her survivors against the wrongdoer or
his family. In more recent years, with the greater ability to do comparative analysis with other ancient law codes, this general interpretation has changed.

In 1952, G. R. Driver and J. C. Miles still maintained that the similarities
found when comparing the various ancient Near Eastern systems of law (biblical,
Babylonian, Hittite, Assyrian, etc.) "were neither close or numerous enough to
prove direct borrowing by the later from the older law." Driver and Miles maintained that there was a certain logical or "expected" similarity of practice in law
that could be expected "among different peoples in similar stages of civilization."
These scholars maintained that the "natural remedy for an assault is retaliation
and that *talion* was a fundamental principle of early law and was only gradually
replaced by a system of fixed compensation."[14] In 1957, however, A. S. Diamond
argued just the opposite position. He maintained that despite the fact that the *Lex
Talionis* is found in the ancient law code in the Book of the Covenant, "it is one
of the plainest interpolations in the Pentateuch, *prima facie* it represents a late
development in the law."[15] Similarly, W. F. Albright wrote in 1964 that

portrayed as the peace-maker, whereas Jehu, although he refers (calls upon) to the word of God with
regard to the retaliation, in the end, remains the bloody murderer" (654 [my translation]). Olyan's
evaluation of Jehu is in total disagreement with that of Eisenbeis.

12. See also the study by Daube, "Lex Talionis," 102–53, especially the discussion of this root on
pp. 133–47.

13. Especially in vv. 23–25; Lev 24:17–20; Deut 19:21; 24:16; 2 Kgs 14:6; and many other
places.

14. G. R. Driver and J. C. Miles, *The Babylonian Laws*, vol. 1, *Legal Commentary* (Oxford:
Clarendon, 1952), 408.

15. A. S. Diamond, "An Eye for an Eye," *Iraq* 19 (1957): 151–55 (153).

one of the most remarkable generalizations in Old Testament law, compared to slightly earlier Ancient Oriental law, is the use of the principle known as 'lex talionis' . . . . This principle may seem and is often said to be extraordinarily primitive. But it is actually not in the least primitive. Whereas the beginnings of 'lex talionis' are found before Israel, the principle was now extended by analogy until it dominated all punishment of injuries or homicides.[16]

This being the case, however, the Mosaic principle of *Lex Talionis* does show refinement over similar principles found in other cultures. In non-Israelite cultures, the extent of the application of the principle apparently depended upon the social class to which one belonged, usually applying only to the upper class. In the Mosaic application, however, "for the first time in any legislation the principle of *equal justice for all*, regardless of class or wealth, is enunciated."[17] This was a tremendous advance. The one exception in its "universal" application in Israelite culture was in the case of slaves.[18] That there were also developments in this direction in other non-Israelite legal traditions is indicated by J. J. Finkelstein who wrote concerning the principle of *talionis* found in the Code of Hammurabi:

> In short, what the talionic rules of the Laws of Hammurabi actually herald is the enlargement of the scope of criminal law beyond the spheres of God and king (i.e., blasphemy and sedition) which had long before constituted the sole realm of criminal action, to embrace for the first time—albeit in a crudely formulated fashion . . . a class of derelicts that had previously been treated purely as civil torts.[19]

P. Doron, discussing the various changes in the formulation of the law as it is found in the Old Testament, argues that there was a development in the way in which the law was understood and applied in the Bible. He maintains that in the biblical tradition and application of the law, it was *not applied literally*, but rather that there was a system of monetary compensation that stood behind the application of the law in all cases except intentional homicide.[20] S. Paul, on the other hand, agreeing with Finkelstein and others, wrote that, "the 'lex talionis', far from being a primitive residuum, is actually an important advance in the history of jurisprudence."[21] According to Paul, "the common view that talion is 'a fundamental principle of early law and was only gradually replaced by a system of fixed composition'[22] is no longer tenable."[23] Paul, much like Albright, notes that in biblical tradition and practice, the application of the law was *nearly universal* in terms of the people, the only exception being slaves:

16. W. F. Albright, *History, Archaeology and Christian Humanism* (New York: McGraw-Hill, 1964), 74.

17. Albright, *History, Archaeology*, 98–99.

18. Albright, *History, Archaeology*, 98–99.

19. J. J. Finkelstein, "Ammiṣadqa's Edict and the Babylonian 'Law Codes,'" *JCS* 15 (1961): 98–104 (98).

20. P. Doron, "A New Look at an Old Lex," *JANES* 1, no. 2 (1969): 21–27.

21. S. Paul, *Studies in the Book of the Covenant in the Light of Cuneiform and Biblical Law* (VTSup 18; Leiden: Brill, 1970), 76.

22. Driver and Miles, *The Babylonian Laws* 1:408, and above p. 42.

23. Paul, *Studies in the Book of the Covenant*, 76 n. 2.

> Talion is equitable: the rich receive the same punishment as the poor—a punishment which is limited to the exact measure of the injury and is restricted to the culprit himself. Talion, furthermore, serves as a deterrent: the rich, who could otherwise afford to pay for injuries inflicted, would now 'pay' with the same limb as the injured one of the other party.[24]

Similar positions, with various refinements, have been put forward more recently. The debate over when the principle precisely entered into Israelite law continues. B. S. Jackson argues for a late development of the *Lex* as found in Exod 21:22–25. He finally attributes it to the hands of several different individuals. For him, 21:24 is neither original (i.e. early) nor very late since v. 25 is later still. This fact, together with what he argues to be its "aristocratic" origins, bring him to suggest that it comes from the hand of the Deuteronomist. Verse 25 is from an even later hand.[25] Against Jackson, S. E. Loewenstamm maintains that:

> if the formula, 'eye for an eye etc.' had been a Deuteronomic innovation, it would have appeared in rulings on corporeal damages. In its actual context, however, it is patently intended to call to mind a commonly known principle, generally accepted at this time. Deuteronomy then provides us with a clear *terminus ante quem*. No *terminus post quem* is evident.[26]

M. Gilbert, similar to J. J. Finkelstein, notes the presence of principle of *talion* found in the Code of Hammurabi from ca. 1750 B.C.E.[27] According to Gilbert, the fact is that in this Babylonian law code it came to be applied only to the upper class, and especially in cases of quarrels that developed into criminal acts. It did not apply to the lower class of "freedmen" or to the slaves. In the case of the lower class, there was a system of monetary (or property) fines. In Gilbert's mind, this application of the *Lex Talionis* to the upper class in Babylon was probably motivated by a concern for safeguarding the public order.[28] The novelty of the principle of *talion* in the code of Hammurabi is suggested by the fact that it is not found in two older law codes from the ancient Near East, that of *Our-Nammou* (ca. 2100 B.C.E.) and *Lipit-Ishtar* (ca. 1930 B.C.E.). In these law codes there is only found evidence of a system of monetary compensation. This, according to Gilbert, argues for the fact that the principle of the *Lex Talionis* is not as primitive as is often thought.[29]

After discussing the presentation of the *Lex Talionis* in the biblical record, Gilbert then focuses his attention upon the meaning and the applications of the principle in the Old Testament. He argues that it is necessary to distinguish between the *Lex Talionis* and other similar principles that existed together with it. At the base of the *Lex Talionis* is the principle that "those who are guilty should

---

24. Paul, *Studies in the Book of the Covenant*, 76.
25. B. S. Jackson, "The Problem of Exod. XXI 22–25 (*Ius Talionis*)," *VT* 23 (1973): 273–304 (303–4).
26. S. E. Loewenstamm, "Exodus XXI 22–25," *VT* 27 (1977): 352–60 (356).
27. M. Gilbert, "La loi du talion," in *Il a parlé par les Prophètes: Thèmes et Figures Bibliques* (Brussels: Lessius, 1998), 145–55; repr. from *Christus* 31, Fasc. 121 (1984): 73–82.
28. Gilbert, *Il a parlé par les Prophètes*, 145–46.
29. Gilbert, *Il a parlé par les Prophètes*, 146.

be punished and in a measure proportional to the crime." In this sense, it is speaking of retribution. Certainly, like many biblical principles, the *Lex* insists upon the proportionality that must exist between the crime and the punishment. It is in this way that it intends to place limits upon uncontrolled vengeance.[30] The *Lex* "affirms the personal responsibility of the one who commits a crime and in this it recognizes the equality of all before the law."[31]

Gilbert, however, also insists upon the recognition of the precise application of this *Lex Talion*:

> It deals with a legal disposition that is not left to the free judgment of everyone, and, if one understands it well, the application of this principle supposes the intervention of a jurisdiction (a judge) who is capable of judging between the victim and the guilty one, and who also has the power to execute the sentence.[32]

In this sense, the application of the *Lex* removes the judgment of a crime from the private sphere and places it squarely in the public sphere where there would be judgment made by an impartial, and uninvolved, judge. In this way, Gilbert argues that the intent of the *Lex Talionis* is to protect and maintain the peace between citizens.[33]

This being the case, one would expect to find plenty of clear documentation of the application of this principle in the Bible. However, as Gilbert points out, one is struck by the near-total absence of any clear-cut examples. This leads him to conclude that, "in effect the talionic formulations of the Old Testament appear to be stereotyped and without tight connections with the cases they were supposedly meant to clarify. They appear to be general principles, while cases of their strict and literal application are lacking."[34] In the end, Gilbert concludes that when confronted with the above-mentioned realities, the *Lex Talionis* appears, in Israelite tradition, to be a principle whose purpose was to affirm: (1) the personal responsibility of an individual for his/her own acts; (2) equality before the law, in opposition to an unlimited vengeance; and (3) the just proportion between punishment to be applied and the crime committed.[35]

Another scholar, R. Westbrook, appears at first to lean more toward Jackson's position than toward that of Loewenstamm. However, he then rejects them both saying:

> We shall not enter into a detailed discussion of the relative sophistication or clumsiness of the biblical draftsman since in our view all theories that assume changes in the text are on an unsound basis as long as two key words in the text remain unclear—'*swn* and *plym*.[36]

In Westbrook's opinion, the law in Exod 21:22–25 deals with a case in which an innocent person is injured in a situation in which it is impossible to determine

30. Gilbert, *Il a parlé par les Prophètes*, 151.
31. Gilbert, *Il a parlé par les Prophètes*, 152.
32. Gilbert, *Il a parlé par les Prophètes*, 152 (my translation).
33. Gilbert, *Il a parlé par les Prophètes*, 152.
34. Gilbert, *Il a parlé par les Prophètes*, 152 (my translation).
35. Gilbert, *Il a parlé par les Prophètes*, 153.
36. R. Westbrook, "Lex Talionis and Exodus 21:22–25," *RB* 93 (1986): 52–69 (54–55).

who actually struck the person. In this case, the responsibility for paying the "ransom-money" which, in the case of a known assailant would fall to the victim or his/her family, would fall to the community. Based upon the similar practice in Ugarit, this monetary penalty would most likely have been lower than the ransom-money that could have been demanded from a known perpetrator. For this reason, the author argues that this passage "provides no information as to the existence of a talionic principle for physical injuries in biblical law."[37]

The above brief review of some of the recent scholarly opinion concerning the *Lex Talionis* as found in the Bible and ancient Near East gives a clear picture of the fact that it remains uncertain exactly when or how the principle came into effect in the Israelite legal tradition.[38] The position that I will maintain here is that it is most probably a later development and refinement of the older laws regulating vengeance and retribution. How "literally" or "strictly," in the legal sense of the term, this principle was applied is open to great debate.

However, the influence of this law can be found in the story of the accession of Jehu, particularly in the oracular passages. We can especially see it in 2 Kgs 9:7–10a where the whole purpose of the striking down of the house of Ahab is presented as vengeance upon Jezebel for the blood of the Lord's servants, the prophets, and the blood of all the servants of the Lord. Verses 7–10a are almost universally recognized as secondary.[39] When we consider vv. 25–26, this same

37. Westbrook, "Lex Talionis," 67 and n. 69.

38. See the further discussion of this issue in Daube, "Lex Talionis," (1947), 102–53, and the above discussion of the role of blood as witness in connection to God's vengeance in Chapter 2, pp. 29-33.

39. The secondary nature of some or all of the verses between 7–10a is commonly recognized, though opinion varies as to whom specifically to attribute these additions. See A. Klostermann, *Die Bücher Samuelis und der Könige*, 419 (7b–end is gloss); Wellhausen, *Die Composition des Hexateuchs und der historischen Bücher*, 287; Skinner, *Kings*, 320; Benzinger, *Die Bücher der Könige*, 150; Kittel, *Die Bücher der Könige*, 229–30; Burney, *Notes*, 297; Stade and Schwally, *The Book of Kings*, 39; Gressmann, *Die älteste Geschichtsschreibung*, 305; Schlögl, *Die Bücher der Könige, Die Bücher der Chronik*, 242 (7bβ–8aα); Šanda, *Das zweite Buch der Könige*, 94, 121; Gunkel, *Geschichten von Elisa*, 73; Eissfeldt, *Das erste Buch der Könige*, 555; Hölscher, "Das Buch der Könige," 192, and *Geschichtsschreibung in Israel*, 145, 398; Noth, *Überlieferungsgeschichtliche Studien* 1:126 (84) (8b–10a); Jepsen, *Nabi*, 74 n. 1, and *Die Quellen des Königsbuches*, 80, 120 (chart); Montgomery and Gehman, *A Critical and Exegetical Commentary*, 400; de Vaux, *Les livres des Rois*, 155 n. a; Gray, *I & II Kings*, 539; Steck, *Überlieferung und Zeitgeschichte*, 38–39; Fricke, *Das zweite Buch von den Königen*, 114; Dietrich, *Prophetie und Geschichte*, 47–48; Weinfeld, *Deuteronomy and the Deuteronomic School*, 20; Schmitt, *Elisa*, 20–23; Sekine, "Literatursoziologische Beobachtungen zu den Elisaerzählungen," 55; DeVries, *Prophet against Prophet*, 90 (8a–9a); Bohlen, *Der Fall Nabot*, 291–95; Timm, *Die Dynastie Omri*, 137; Rehm, *Das zweite Buch der Könige*, 95; Würthwein *Die Bücher der Könige, 1. Kön. 17– 2 Kön. 25*, 329; Trebolle Barrera, *Jehú y Joás*, 162; Olyan, "*Ḥāšālôm*," 655–56; Hentschel, *2 Könige*, 41–42; Campbell, *Of Prophets and Kings*, 37 n. 41 (maybe 7b, 9b, 10a); Cogan, and Tadmor, *II Kings*, 118; A. Rofé, *The Prophetical Stories: The Narratives about the Prophets in the Hebrew Bible, their Literary Types and History* (Jerusalem: Magnes, 1988), 86; Barré, *The Rhetoric of Political Persuasion*, 9–11; Minokami, *Die Revolution des Jehu*, 53–55, 60; Long, *II Kings*, 115; McKenzie, *The Trouble with Kings*, 70–71; W. Gugler, *Jehu und seine Revolution: Voraussetzungen, Verlauf, Folgen* (Kampen: Kok, 1996), 166; White, *The Elijah Legends and Jehu's Coup*, 37–38 (7b–10a).

emphasis on a *Lex Talionis* understanding of justice can also be seen, whether directly or indirectly. The oracle found in v. 26a states that "the Lord will requite (avenge)" because he has "surely seen the blood of Naboth and his sons." The vengeance will be in equal measure; blood for blood; life for life. In the present form of the text, Jehu is proposing this notion of vengeance-justice, of retributive justice, as the justification for both his murder of Joram and for his command of non-burial of the body.

However, in vv. 7–10a the verb used is not the same as that found in v. 26. In 9:7 we find the verb וְנִקַּמְתִּי,[40] which is synonymous in meaning and form with the verb found in the oracle of 9:26—וְשִׁלַּמְתִּי. The use of the verb נקם√ in the Old Testament is much more frequent (×52) than that of שלם√ with the meaning of "avenge" (×30). The majority of the occurrences of the verb נקם√ have YHWH as the subject of the action—at least 30 times. Many more occurrences are found when one considers the substantival forms of the term. Fully half of the occurrences of this verb with YHWH as subject occur in the prophets Isaiah[41] and Jeremiah[42] where virtually every time this verbal root is used in these two books, the subject is YHWH.

Besides the similar meaning of these two terms for vengeance, they are also used in a similar grouping of words in 2 Kgs 9.

וְנִקַמְתִּי דְּמֵי עֲבָדַי הַנְּבִיאִים וּדְמֵי כָּל־עַבְדֵי יְהוָה

(2 Kgs 9:7)

אִם־לֹא אֶת־דְּמֵי נָבוֹת וְאֶת־דְּמֵי בָנָיו רָאִיתִי . . . וְשִׁלַּמְתִּי לְךָ

(2 Kgs 9:26)

Second Kings 9 is the only place where this particular pattern of a verb for YHWH's vengeance (וְנִקַמְתִּי) occurs with the double usage of the direct object, דְּמֵי. In both cases in this chapter, I suggest that the usage is secondary to the text of 2 Kgs 9–10, but not from the same hand. In the case of v. 7, it pertains to a late "Anti-Jezebel Redaction,"[43] and in v. 26, it pertains to the Jehu-Apologetic Redaction.

---

40. See H. G. L. Peels, *The Vengeance of God: The Meaning of NQM and the Function of the NQM-Texts in the Context of Divine Revelation in the Old Testament* (OTS 31; Leiden: Brill, 1995).
41. Seven times: Isa 1:2; 34:8; 35:4; 47:3; 59:17; 61:2; 63:4.
42. Eight times: Jer 5:9, 29; 9:8; 15:15; 46:10; 50:15 (×2); 51:36.
43. The "Anti-Jezebel Redaction" is found in parts of 1 Kgs 21 and in 2 Kgs 9:7, 10a, 22b, 30–37. It is my opinion that this is a very late layer of redaction and was done by the author of 1 Kgs 21.1–16. This author had a particular dislike for the danger that Jezebel represented for himself and his listeners, and this dislike is visible in every place where his hand is found. This type of redaction has also been postulated by Steck, *Überlieferung und Zeitgeschichte*, 40–43, 50–52; Hentschel, *I Könige* (Die Neue Echter Bibel; Würzburg: Echter Verlag, 1984), 127; Würthwein, *Die Bücher der Könige 1. Kön. 17–2 Kön. 25*, 332–33; Campbell, *Of Prophets and Kings*, 97 n. 77; Oeming, "Naboth, der Jesreeliter," 366; Barré, *The Rhetoric of Political Persuasion*, 10; Minokami, *Die Revolution des Jehu*, 59–60; O'Brien, *The Deuteronomistic History Hypothesis*, 99 n. 85; 198–200; McKenzie, *The Trouble with Kings*, 76. For a fuller discussion of this layer of redaction, see Chapter 4 and the whole of Part IV of the present work.

The concept of retributive justice or vengeance apparently only became an "early" element of Israelite law when it was retrojected to that time, perhaps by the Dtr.[44] The Deuteronomist uses it as an important part of the theology and editorial framework. W. Eisenbeis, in discussing the use of the intensifying piel form of the verb √שלם, notes that particularly in Dtr texts, this form of the verb has the meaning: "to avenge," "to punish," "to retaliate," and so on. In his opinion, "this particular usage is related to the legal sphere and probably has its origins in the lex talionis." He also notes that, "Dtr uses it in a theological way which gives it a particularly Israelite flavor."[45] This being the case, however, he also shows that the use of this term based upon legal systems is neither unique to Israel nor to the Hebrew language.[46]

Eisenbeis conjectures a case in which a violation of divine law resulted in the expulsion of the law-breaker from the community:

> The law-breaker must answer for himself before God. If he remains within the community, he would endanger the community itself. Just such a case is found in Joshua 7. It is through the expulsion from the community of the law-breaker that the breach caused by the crime in the community's relationship with God is repaired. At the same time, this action allows for God's just punishment/vengeance of the guilty individual.[47]

In Eisenbeis' opinion, "it is this Dtr theological concept of divine vengeance which stands behind the texts of Deut 7:10; 32:41; Judg 1:7; 2 Sam 3:39 and 2 Kgs 9:26, all cases in which God's vengeance is expressed towards individuals using the verb √שלם in the Piel."[48] This is the same "theological interpretation" that many scholars have made concerning the reasons for calling the public fast in 1 Kgs 21. I will discuss this further below.

J. A. Soggin has arrived at a similar opinion to that of Eisenbeis. In his discussion of the Deuteronomistic editing found in the book of Judges, he remarks that the schematized form of the introductions found repeatedly in this book are "the product of a later organic rethinking which sets out to use an ancient episode to instruct audience or readers."[49] He identifies the authors of this "later organic thinking" as the Deuteronomists. He goes on to say: "Now these introductions prove to be Deuteronomistic in both style and content: among other things, the formulation of the doctrine of retribution and the criteria for judgment, inspired by Deuteronomy, seem to be typical."[50] In his discussion of the books of Kings, and given the historical realities of that period in Israel's history, Soggin suggests that "it was easy to interpret the history of the two peoples (Israel and Judah) in categories like that of divine retribution."[51]

---

44. See Jackson, "The Problem of Exod. XXI 22–25," 303–4.
45. Eisenbeis, "*Die Wurzel* שלם, " 309.
46. Eisenbeis, "*Die Wurzel* שלם, " 309–10.
47. Eisenbeis, "*Die Wurzel* שלם, " 310.
48. Eisenbeis, "*Die Wurzel* שלם, " 310.
49. J. A. Soggin, *Introduction to the Old Testament* (trans. J. Bowden; 3d ed.; London: SCM Press, 1989), 200.
50. Soggin, *Introduction to the Old Testament*, 200.
51. Soggin, *Introduction to the Old Testament*, 232.

I maintain that in 2 Kgs 9:25–26, whether one might agree or disagree with the various positions regarding the presence or absence of Dtr editing, the oracle comes out of a tradition of retributive justice. From this perspective, the requital of Naboth's and his sons' blood is justified according to this tradition. This is not to say that Jehu is justified in his murders, but merely that in the oracle which he recalls in order to *attempt* to justify his own actions and those he has commanded of Bidkar, in this particular oracle, *the Lord* is justified in his promised requiting of Naboth's and his sons' blood.

The Lord's vengeance upon Ahab and Jezebel is portrayed in both 2 Kgs 9 and in 1 Kgs 21 as the punishment for having an innocent Israelite falsely accused, condemned, and stoned to death, and for the crown taking his property. As a result of the false accusations made against Naboth, instigated by Jezebel and under Ahab's seal, Ahab and Jezebel will in turn be accused and condemned to death by the Lord. The Lord's vengeance for the unjust killing of Naboth and the taking of his ancestral inheritance will eventually be fulfilled.

# Chapter 4

## THE "ANTI-JEZEBEL REDACTION" AND THE USE OF THE PROPHECY–FULFILLMENT PATTERN IN THE NABOTH MATERIALS IN 1 AND 2 KINGS

The "Anti-Jezebel Redaction" I propose employs, among other things, the literary pattern of prophecy–fulfillment. Within 2 Kgs 9–10, this redaction is comprised of 2 Kgs 9:7, 10a, 22b, 30–37. These verses are presented as relating to, and "fulfilling," the condemnation and accusation made against Jezebel in 1 Kgs 21:23, 25a. One would immediately think, therefore, that the accusation and condemnation of Jezebel in 21:23, 25a was for her wicked role in the murder of Naboth as portrayed in 1 Kgs 21:1–16. This is not, however, the case. In fact, the condemnation and accusation of Jezebel in 1 Kgs 21:23, 25a have absolutely nothing at all to do with her role in the death of Naboth. Rather, the accusation and condemnation are for Jezebel's role in the other stories of the Elijah Cycle found in chs. 17–19 of 1 Kings. They are for her supposed promotion and support of the Baal cult and for her role in the murder of the servants of YHWH. This is clear in all the insertions placed into the text of 2 Kgs 9–10 that I maintain belong to the Anti-Jezebel Redaction. When we consider these "anti-Jezebel" redactions from the perspective of the prophecy–fulfillment pattern, we find that, in fact, they cause a great deal of confusion in the text. In the story found in 2 Kgs 9–10, these redactions are presented as being the fulfillment of the oracle spoken in 1 Kgs 21:23, which is itself presented as the punishment for Jezebel's having "seduced" Ahab into going after other gods (21:25a).

In its present form, the whole story of the Jehu coup in 2 Kgs 9–10 is presented as being the fulfillment of the oracles spoken against the Ahabite dynasty in 1 Kgs 21:20bβ–29. In their present setting in 1 Kgs 21, however, vv. 20bβ–26 are themselves presented as the accusations and punishments for the crime of having had Naboth killed in order to take possession of his vineyard (vv. 1–16). We have seen how, textually and literarily, vv. 20bβ–26 have nothing to do with the crime of 1 Kgs 21:1–16. Rather, the accusations and punishments in 1 Kgs 21:20bβ–26 are concerned with the crimes of apostasy and murder found in the other sections of the Elijah Cycle in 1 Kgs 17–19. Within 1 Kgs 21:20bβ–26, v. 23 is spoken against Jezebel and is a loose repetition of the same oracle found in 2 Kgs 10:10a and 36b. First Kings 21:23 also interrupts the chain of condemnations being spoken against Ahab and thus does cause a certain roughness in the text. We must now consider the relationship between the three oracles spoken against Jezebel that are found in the Elijah Cycle.

1. *The Oracle (Oracles) against Jezebel in 2 Kings 9 and 1 Kings 21*

When we consider more closely the three occurrences of an oracle against Jezebel, it is clear that though all three are similar, none is an exact duplicate of the others. Second Kings 9:10a and 9:36–37 are fuller and more explicit forms of the oracle than that which is found in 1 Kgs 21:23.[1] The three oracles are as follows:

וְגַם־לְאִיזֶבֶל דִּבֶּר יְהוָה לֵאמֹר הַכְּלָבִים יֹאכְלוּ אֶת־אִיזֶבֶל בְּחֵל יִזְרְעֶאל:
(1 Kgs 21:23)

וְאֶת־אִיזֶבֶל יֹאכְלוּ הַכְּלָבִים בְּחֵלֶק יִזְרְעֶאל וְאֵין קֹבֵר
(2 Kgs 9:10a)

וַיָּשֻׁבוּ וַיַּגִּידוּ לוֹ וַיֹּאמֶר דְּבַר־יְהוָה הוּא אֲשֶׁר דִּבֶּר בְּיַד־עַבְדּוֹ אֵלִיָּהוּ הַתִּשְׁבִּי
לֵאמֹר בְּחֵלֶק יִזְרְעֶאל יֹאכְלוּ הַכְּלָבִים אֶת־בְּשַׂר אִיזֶבֶל: (וְהָיָת) [וְהָיְתָה]
נִבְלַת אִיזֶבֶל כְּדֹמֶן עַל־פְּנֵי הַשָּׂדֶה בְּחֵלֶק יִזְרְעֶאל אֲשֶׁר לֹא־יֹאמְרוּ זֹאת אִיזֶבֶל:
(2 Kgs 9:36–37)

The common feature of these three oracles is that they all share the same oracular element, the statement that the dogs shall eat the flesh of Jezebel. As they now appear, the oracle of 1 Kgs 21:23 looks to be the simplest form of the oracle since the other two oracles have additional elements in them. In 2 Kgs 9:10a, we find the additional element of וְאֵין קֹבֵר. This is the unique occurrence in the Old Testament of this phrase and of the particular form of קֹבֵר, the qal participle, masculine singular of the verb קבר√. This phrase, though, adds nothing new to the oracle. It merely restates in a more explicit manner that which is already implicitly stated by the original oracle, namely, that if "the dogs shall eat the body of Jezebel in the ramparts/plot of Jezreel," then obviously her body would not have received a proper burial. In the oracle as it occurs in 2 Kgs 9:36, we also find an additional element vis-à-vis the form of the oracle found in 1 Kgs 21:23. In this case the additional element is comprised of the phrase אֶת־בְּשַׂר. This phrase occurs a total of eight times in the Old Testament.[2] In Gen 17 it occurs four times in connection with the covenantal sign of the "circumcision *of the flesh* of the foreskin." In Exod 29:32 the phrase occurs in the context of the ordination of Aaron and his sons as priests for the Lord. Aaron and his sons are to eat *of the flesh* of the ram of ordination and of the bread in the basket at the door of the tent of meeting. In the remaining occurrences of the phrase it is found only within the context of oracles.[3] In both Jer 19:9 and Zech 11:9, it is in an oracle of the Lord being spoken against Israel/Jerusalem. In both these instances the Lord is rejecting Israel and says that those remaining of Israel shall "eat the flesh" of one another (cannibalism). It is precisely here that the differences become clear between these two oracles and the one found in 2 Kgs 9:36. First, the oracles in Jer 19:9 and Zech 11:9 are spoken to and against large numbers of

---

1.  The Greek Versions follow the Hebrew closely. The only exceptions are in the case of 2 Kgs 9:10 where Vaticanus and Alexandrinus have ἐν τῇ μερίδι Ιορανλ instead of ἐν τῇ μερίδι Ιεζραελ and the Lucianics read τοῦ ἀγροῦ Ιεζρανλ.
2.  See Gen 17:11, 14, 23, 25; Exod 29:32; 2 Kgs 9:36; Jer 19:9; Zech 11:9.
3.  See 2 Kgs 9:36; Jer 19:9; Zech 11:9.

Israelites, whereas the oracle in 2 Kgs 9:36 is spoken uniquely to and against Jezebel. Second, whereas in Jer 19:9 and Zech 11:9 the *people* are condemned to eat one another, in 2 Kgs 9:36 it is the *dogs* who will eat Jezebel. For these reasons I conclude that there is no direct link between the oracles found in Jer 19:9 and Zech 11:9, and the one found in 2 Kgs 9:36. I conclude as well, that despite the fact that the phrase אֶת־בְּשַׂר is found in all of the eight verses mentioned above, its usage in 2 Kgs 9:36 is unique and refers specifically to the body of Jezebel.

The usage of אֶת־בְּשַׂר in 2 Kgs 9:36 also raises the same question as did the additional phrase in 2 Kgs 9:10a, namely: What does it add to the oracle? Here again we discover that this additional phrase adds nothing substantially new to the oracle. It too is redundant, repeating information that is already implied by the main oracle—the statement that "the dogs shall eat Jezebel" means that the dogs will eat "the flesh and bones" of Jezebel.

In 1 Kgs 21, the main focus of the Dtr collection of oracles into which the oracle in v. 23 was inserted is upon Ahab's sinfulness and the punishments he was to receive. His sins are presented in standardized Dtr formulas that were used for the sins of all the kings of Israel. Verse 24 contains a standard oracle of non-burial which is also used for Jeroboam, the first of the northern kings (1 Kgs 14:11), and for Baasha (1 Kgs 16:4). Because of the close proximity and all-inclusive nature of this oracle in 1 Kgs 21:24, I suggest that the anti-Jezebel author/redactor who was inserting v. 23 into this context felt that the specific mention of the exact same punishment for Jezebel, who is already necessarily included under the oracle of v. 24, would have been overly redundant and awkward.

If we were to "eliminate" the two unique but redundant statements found in 2 Kgs 9:10a and 36, then we would be left with the same oracle in all three verses. However, there are no literary grounds for such elimination. There is no internal evidence that these elements are not original to these redactions. The whole purpose for the Anti-Jezebel Redaction of these texts appears to have been to make it specifically and emphatically clear that the downfall of Ahab and his dynasty was due to the great wickedness and "apostasy"[4] *of his foreign wife, Jezebel*. Her punishment would therefore also be to the extreme.

The account of the military coup by Jehu in 2 Kgs 9–10 supplied the anti-Jezebel author/redactor with the perfect setting within which to weave his

---

4. Let me clarify my use of the term "apostasy" when referring to Jezebel. Jezebel was a Phoenician princess, and as such, a non-Israelite. The fact is that Baalism was her native religion. As such, in her practice and promotion of Baalism it cannot be said that she was an "apostate." When I use this term it is used strictly as an evaluative summary for the whole of the presentation of Jezebel by the anti-Jezebel editor. As the protector and promoter of Baalism, Jezebel becomes the symbol of any and all who would seduce a faithful Israelite (see 1 Kgs 21:25a and Deut 13) away from faith in YHWH alone and towards the Baalim or any other non-Israelite gods or religions. In this sense, in the mind of the anti-Jezebel redactor, she becomes the epitome of "The Great Apostate." It is in this sense, and from this perspective, that I refer to her actions as "apostasy" and to her person as an "apostate." It is the perspective of the symbolic biblical presentation of Jezebel.

anti-Jezebel bias in the strongest possible terms. By his additions concerning the negative effects, and the disastrous end of Jezebel within this context, he was able to "round out" his presentation of Jezebel's character as it was presented in 1 Kgs 21 and throughout the rest of the Elijah Cycle. Thus, considering the evidence, we can see the oracles in 2 Kgs 9:10a, 36–37, and the shorter version found in 1 Kgs 21:23, are all from the same hand. Together they form a part of a prophecy–fulfillment schema imposed upon these texts by the anti-Jezebel author/editor.

### a. *2 Kings 9:7, 10a, 22b*
In 2 Kgs 9:1–6 a "son of the prophets" is sent by Elisha to anoint and commission Jehu to become king. The original message of the commission that the "son of the prophets" was to announce, has been secondarily expanded by vv. 7–10a:[5]

> So he arose, and went into the house; and the young man poured the oil on his head, saying to him, 'Thus says the LORD the God of Israel, I anoint you king over the people of the LORD, over Israel. *And you shall strike down the house of Ahab your master, that I may avenge on Jezebel the blood of my servants the prophets, and the blood of all the servants of the LORD.* For the whole house of Ahab shall perish; and I will cut off from Ahab every male, bond or free, in Israel. And I will make the house of Ahab like the house of Jeroboam the son of Nebat, and like the house of Baasha the son of Ahijah. *And the dogs shall eat Jezebel in the territory of Jezreel, and none shall bury her.'* Then he opened the door, and fled. (2 Kgs 9:6–10 RSV)

There are a couple of salient features in this short expansionary speech. First, in its present location following the announcement of in whose name the anointing of Jehu is taking place (v. 6b), the expansion to the son of the prophet's speech opens and closes with reference to Jezebel. The first reason presented by the "son of the prophet" for anointing Jehu as king, and thus also for the annihilation of the Ahabite dynasty, is found in v. 7. Here we read, "*that I may avenge on Jezebel* the blood of my servants the prophets and the blood of all the servants of the Lord." For this reason the whole house of Ahab will perish (vv. 7a and 8a). Ahab, as king and individual, is never specifically mentioned nor held responsible in this regard. What follows in vv. 8–9 is an explication of all that the Lord will do to Ahab's house, *not* because of Ahab himself, but, *because of Jezebel's murder of the prophets of YHWH* (see 1 Kgs 18:4, which I maintain is also a secondary expansion). Then, at the end of the speech, just before the "son of the prophets" flees, he mentions the punishment that will be specifically applied to Jezebel—"the dogs will eat her in the territory/ramparts of Jezreel." In this short speech, then, we do not have Ahab directly accused of anything, but rather, *it is Jezebel* who is presented as the one responsible for the annihilation of Ahab's dynasty.

This is how the story now appears. I maintain, however, that this is the end result of two distinct layers of redaction. In the first, a Dtr redactor added vv. 8–9 to the end of v. 6. Verses 8–9 contain oracles with typical Dtr language. When

---

5. See p. 46 n. 39.

these were inserted after v. 6, they served to explain why it was that YHWH had decided to replace Ahab and his dynasty with Jehu and his dynasty—it was YHWH's punishment of Ahab. Then, at a later time, the anti-Jezebel redactor inserted vv. 7 and 10a, forming bookends around the Dtr redaction and breaking its connection with v. 6. By so doing, the anti-Jezebel redactor shifted the entire focus of vv. 7–10a. Now, instead of giving the rational for the replacement of Ahab's dynasty with Jehu's dynasty as punishment upon *Ahab*, the passage shifts the blame from Ahab to Jezebel. In this redactor's mind, and in the form of the text as we now have it, Jezebel is the one to be blamed for the downfall of the Ahabite dynasty.[6]

Verses 7 and 10a are nearly verbatim repetitions of material found in 1 Kgs 21:21b–23. One of the expansions to these texts found in 2 Kgs 9:10a, which betrays the anti-Jezebel editor's own hand and sentiments, is the statement that Jezebel is not to be buried—וְאֵין קֹבֵר. The act of non-burial (also found in 2 Kgs 9:25–26 for Joram and 9:36–37 for Jezebel) is very significant from the religious and theological perspective. It is the ultimate expression of disrespect, humiliation, and "excommunication" for the deceased. This anti-Jezebel editor is also the one responsible for the comment about the "harlotries and sorceries" of Jezebel in 2 Kgs 9:22b, an indirect reference to her support for Baal and his cult —to her apostasy.[7] The oracles against Jezebel and against Ahab's dynasty found in these verses are also situated within the prophecy–fulfillment schema imposed by the redactor. They are presented as being fulfilled by Jehu's actions throughout the remainder of 2 Kgs 9–10.[8]

---

6.    A few scholars make specific note of the "target/s" of these verses. Steck (*Überlieferung und Zeitgeschichte*, 36 n. 1) and Würthwein (*Die Bücher der Könige, 1. Kön. 17–2 Kön. 25*, 330) note that vv. 7 and 10 are against Jezebel; Cogan and Tadmor (*II Kings*, 107) note that v. 10 is against Jezebel and O'Brien (*The Deuteronomistic History Hypothesis*, 199–200) notes simply that vv. 7–10a are against Jezebel. A few others ignore Jezebel's place in these verses or focus only upon Ahab and his dynasty. These include Benzinger (*Die Bücher der Könige*, 149) who sees vv. 7–10a as being against Ahab; de Vaux (*Les livres des Rois*, 155 n. a and 0) maintains that they are against "Ahab's family"; Barré (*The Rhetoric of Political Persuasion*, 109–10) sees vv. 7–9* as being against "Ahab and his sons"; and McKenzie (*The Trouble with Kings*, 71) notes that vv. 7a, 8–9 are against "the Royal house."

7.    O'Brien, *The Deuteronomistic History Hypothesis*, 199–200, also maintains that these verses belong to an Anti-Jezebel Redaction. Other scholars recognize the Dtr character of parts of these verses and assign some or all of them to the Dtr redactor: Skinner, *Kings*, 320; Noth, *Überlieferungsgeschichtliche Studien* 1:126 (84); Fohrer, *Elia*, 26–27; Steck, *Überlieferung und Zeitgeschichte*, 36 n. 1; Schmitt, *Elisa*, 23; Bohlen, *Der Fall Nabot*, 301; Jones, *1–2 Kings* 2:454; Barré, *The Rhetoric of Political Persuasion*, 109–10; O'Brien, *The Deuteronomistic History Hypothesis*, 199–200; McKenzie, *The Trouble with Kings*, 71; White, *The Elijah Legends and Jehu's Coup*, 37.

8.    With Long, *II Kings*, 127, who says that they are fulfilled re. Jezebel in 9:36–37; re. Joram in 9:25–26; re. Joram's family in 10:1–11, 12–14; and re. the Baal cult in 10:15–27. A group of other scholars highlight only the fulfillment of these verses against Jezebel in 9:36–37: Burney, *Notes*, 250; Steck, *Überlieferung und Zeitgeschichte*, 36 n. 1; Weinfeld, *Deuteronomy and the Deuteronomic School*, 20–21; Olyan, "*Hăšālôm*," 656; Jones, *1–2 Kings* 2:454; Hobbs, *2 Kings*, 113; O'Brien, *The Deuteronomistic History Hypothesis*, 199–200.

### b. *2 Kings 9:30–37*

The oracle of 2 Kgs 9.10a against Jezebel is ultimately "fulfilled" in the account of her death at the command of Jehu in 2 Kgs 9:30–37. This account is another original construction from the hand of the anti-Jezebel redactor (more precisely, vv. 30b–33, 34b–37). In this story, Jezebel is thrown from the window and trampled by horses (v. 33). Afterwards, Jehu orders that she be buried because "she was a king's daughter" (v. 34b). We are then told that "they went to bury her" (v. 35a), however, they could not find enough of her to bury (v. 35), and so they return and inform Jehu of that fact (v. 36aα). Upon hearing their report, Jehu proclaims that this is indeed the fulfillment of the oracle spoken by Elijah (v. 36aβ); he then he gives an indirect oracle of non-burial (v. 36b) referring to the oracles found in 2 Kgs 9:10 and 1 Kgs 21:23. This oracle is then expanded by the addition of v. 37, an oracle about her body being like dung upon the surface of the field (v. 37). When we look closely at the text of this account, we find several indicators of its late creation and its secondary insertion into the story of Jehu's coup.

I suggest that the original sequence of the story ran in the following manner:

> (2 Kgs 9:27) When Ahaziah the king of Judah saw this, he fled in the direction of Bethhaggan. And Jehu pursued him, and said, 'Shoot him also'; and they shot him in the chariot at the ascent of Gur, which is by Ibleam. And he fled to Megiddo, and died there. (28) His servants carried him in a chariot to Jerusalem, and buried him in his tomb with his fathers in the city of David. [*29*] (30a) When Jehu came to Jezreel, [*30b–33*] (34a) he went in and ate and drank; [*34b–37*] (10:1) Then Jehu wrote letters, and sent them to Samaria, to the rulers of the city, to the elders, and to the guardians of the sons of Ahab, saying . . .[9] (RSV translation)

This sequence of events is perfectly logical and flows smoothly from a narrative point of view. After the death of Joram and Ahaziah, we can surmise that the city of Jezreel capitulated to Jehu. Jezreel probably only had minimal military forces and palace guards to protect it since the majority of its fighting force was either at Ramoth-Gilead with the rest of the army or with Jehu himself. In light of the fact that Jehu had just killed the king in what was an obvious coup within view of the city itself, the people of the city would most likely have submitted and opened its gates to Jehu. Verse 28, the burial notice for Ahaziah, is picked up again and continued in 2 Kgs 11:1, with the account of Athalia's actions upon seeing that her son Ahaziah was dead. Intervening between these two parts of that particular story is the whole of 2 Kgs 10, the continuation of the story of Jehu's coup, a chapter that I maintain is also very heavily redacted.

A further argument for the secondary nature of vv. 30b–33, 34b–37 is to be found in the philological evidence. In what follows I will present and discuss each bit of this evidence; evidence which is found in every verse of this addition.

(1) *Verse 30b*. When Jehu entered the city we are told that Jezebel heard about it and that, וַתָּשֶׂם בַּפּוּךְ עֵינֶיהָ ("she put eye-shadow on her eyes"). The noun, פּוּךְ, is

---

9. The square bracketed and italicized numbers are those which I consider to be the secondary insertions—namely, vv. 29, 30b–33, 34b–37.

defined as "antimony, stibium, black paint, eye-shadow." It is a very rare term in the Old Testament, occurring only five times, and it is considered to be a Late Biblical Hebrew term.[10] In 1 Chr 29:2 and Isa 54:11 it appears with the meaning of antimony or stibium, that is, a type of dark or black precious stones. In Job 42:14 it is found as part of a proper name, קֶרֶן הַפּוּךְ. In its remaining two occurrences—in our verse, 2 Kgs 9:30b, and in Jer 4:30—it appears with the meaning of "eye shadow."

A second rare usage is found in the phrase, וַתֵּיטֶב אֶת־רֹאשָׁהּ. Though not necessarily a "late" usage, this phrase, as such, is a *hapax* in the Old Testament. The particular form of the verb in this phrase, a hiphil converted imperfect, 3d fem. sing. of √יטב, is only found four times in the Old Testament. In 2 Kgs 9:30b, "Jezebel makes her head pleasing"; in Ps 69:32, praise and thanksgiving "will please the Lord"; and in Esth 2:4, 9, Esther is "pleasing to the eyes" of the king. Only in 2 Kgs 9:30b is the term used specifically in regard to making one's "head" pleasing in appearance. Again, though the term itself is not necessarily late, this particular form of the verb is found only in texts that are thought to be late (Esth 2:4, 9; Ps 69) and in our text, which I maintain is also from the late Anti-Jezebel Redaction.

A third rare phrase is found in v. 30b, וַתַּשְׁקֵף בְּעַד הַחַלּוֹן. The phrase בְּעַד הַחַלּוֹן, occurs only seven times in the Old Testament, five times in conjunction with the verb √שקף ("to lean out, to look down from"), and twice with the verb √תרר ("to lower, to let down", Josh 2:15; 1 Sam 9:12). Of the five occurrences construed with √שקף, it is found three times in the niphal (Judg 5:28; 2 Sam 6:16 and its parallel in 2 Chr 15:29) and twice in the hiphil (Gen 26:8; 2 Kgs 9:30b).

In v. 30b, then, we find one term which is most probably from the stage of Late Biblical Hebrew, one term which is rare and possibly of late usage, and a third phrase that is very rare.

(2) *Verse 31.* In v. 31 we find the question, הֲשָׁלוֹם. The form הֲשָׁלוֹם is found a total of eighteen times in the Old Testament. It is construed with the articular *he* in four texts.[11] Construed with the interrogative *he*, it is found fourteen times. These usages can be subdivided into two senses of the question: (a) as a greeting —"Is it well?" or "How is it going?" (×9);[12] and (b) as a challenge—"Have you come in peace (or in war, *understood*)?" (×5). Of the five times it occurs as a challenge, it is found once in 1 Kgs 2:13 (Bathsheba to Adonijah), and four times in 2 Kgs 9 (vv. 17, 18, 22, 31). Of the occurrences found in 2 Kgs 9, twice it is a

---

10. See BDB, 806 (NH = New [late] Biblical Hebrew); *NK-B* 3:918 (MHb = Middle Hebrew). For this designation they refer the reader to E. Kutscher's article on Middle Hebrew in which he defines two different layers of Middle Hebrew, mhe1 and mhe2. These were his early designations for Late Biblical or Mishnaic Hebrew (see E. Kutscher, "Mittelhebräische und Jüdaisch-Aramäisch im Neuen Köhler-Baumgartner," in *Hebräische Wortforschung: Festschrift zum 80. Geburtstag von Walter Baumgartner* [ed. B. Hartmann et al.; VTSup 16; Leiden: Brill, 1967], 158–75; see also R. Polzin, *Late Biblical Hebrew: Toward an Historical Typology of Biblical Hebrew Prose* [HMS 12; Missoula, Mont.: Scholars Press, 1976], xi).

11. See 2 Kgs 9:22 (the second occurrence of the form); Jer 25:37; 33:9; Zech 8:2.

12. See Gen 29:6; 43:27; 2 Sam 18:32; 20:9; 2 Kgs 4:26 (×3); 5:21; 9:11.

challenge to Jehu on the part of Joram, via his messengers (vv. 17, 18), and once directly from Joram to Jehu in v. 22. In 9:31, however, it has nothing to do with the incident between Joram and Jehu, but rather is found in totally different circumstances. In 9:31 we find it in a statement from Jezebel, addressed to Jehu in which she refers to Jehu as "Zimri, the murderer of your master." The phrase הֲרֹג אֲדֹנָיו is a *hapax*. Most interpreters see in this statement a contemptuous comparison of Jehu to Zimri who "conspired against" (= overthrew by means of a coup) his king, Elah, the son of Baasha, then killed him and took his throne (1 Kgs 16:8–10). In this context, they interpret the statement as a sarcastic insult against Jehu.[13] However, if, as I maintain, vv. 30b–33, 34b–37 are in fact from the hand of the late anti-Jezebel redactor, there may be another possible way of interpreting this particular reference to Zimri. It is true that according to the text of 1 Kgs 16:9–20, Zimri murdered and took the throne from Elah. It is also true that he is said to have wiped out all the male line of Baasha, indicating the destruction of Baasha's dynasty (16:11). It is also true that these actions received *a positive evaluation* from the hand of the Dtr editor:

> Thus Zimri destroyed all the house of Baasha, according to the word of the LORD, which he spoke against Baasha by Jehu the prophet. (1 Kgs 16:12 RSV)

It might also be possible that the anti-Jezebel redactor has Jezebel make specific reference to this account for its "ironic value." On the one level of interpretation, Zimri was indeed known as a usurper and murderer. By having Jezebel refer to Jehu as Zimri, the statement would certainly imply the same thing about Jehu. However, it could be that the editor also wanted to imply, on another level, that Jehu was in fact "fulfilling the word of the Lord" by means of his murder of Joram, and, by means of the soon-to-occur murder of Jezebel. The reference to Zimri, in the anti-Jezebel redactor's mind, could quite intentionally be meant to create a link with the "positive role" of Zimri in the fulfillment of *Jehu the prophet's* words in 1 Kgs 16:12. On this level, the positive role of Zimri is directly linked to the name Jehu, albeit to a different Jehu. For the anti-Jezebel editor this difference did not matter. The fact is that in 16:12 both Zimri and Jehu the prophet perform positive acts that are in accordance with the word of YHWH, just as Jehu the usurper will fulfill a positive role in his murder of Jezebel.

(3) *Verse 32.* After Jezebel's remark to Jehu, he is said to have asked the question, מִי אִתִּי. Though this might sound like a common enough question, it is actually very rare in the Old Testament. It only is found in our verse and in Isa 44:24, which is a Qere–Ketiv and which is considered to be a late text.

---

13. See, e.g., Benzinger, *Die Bücher der Könige*, 152; Kittel, *Die Bücher der Könige*, 233–34; Gressmann, *Die älteste Geschichtsschreibung*, 311–12; Šanda, *Das zweite Buch der Könige*, 101; Montgomery and Gehman, *A Critical and Exegetical Commentary*, 403; Gray, *I & II Kings*, 551; Steck, *Überlieferung und Zeitgeschichte*, 58 n. 1; Fricke, *Das zweite Buch von den Königen*, 126; Würthwein, *Die Bücher der Könige, 1. Kön. 17– 2 Kön. 25*, 334; Cogan and Tadmor, *II Kings*, 111–12. *Contra* S. B. Parker ("Jezebel's Reception of Jehu," *MAARAV* 1, no. 1 [1978]: 67–78 [69]), and Barré (*The Rhetoric of Political Persuasion*, 78) who see in Jezebel's actions a sexual attempt to seduce Jehu.

A second term is סָרִיסִים. This term has two interpretations: (1) a type of official or officer, and (2) a eunuch. It is not always clear which meaning is intended in a given text. In our verse, it is almost universally translated as eunuch. In the non-prefixed plural form found in our verse, the term only occurs three times (2 Kgs 9:32; 20:18 = Isa 39:7 where the term refers to the Babylonian court). A search of the root form of the term reveals that it is only found in late texts (×10 in the singular and ×15 in the plural).[14] It is possible that this term might be a loan-word and it could be considered a Late Biblical Hebrew term.[15]

(4) *Verse 33*. In v. 33 Jehu orders the eunuchs to throw or drop Jezebel from the window. They obey and we are told that the horses then trampled her to death. In the process of this gruesome death, the text says that: וַיִּז מִדָּמָהּ אֶל־הַקִּיר וְאֶל־ הַסּוּסִים. The verbal root, √נזה, is found only twenty-four times in the Old Testament. In twenty-two of these instances, it refers to the sprinkling or spattering of blood, oil, or water in a liturgical or ritual setting. In the two remaining cases, it refers to the spattering of human blood as a result of violence. In 2 Kgs 9:33 it is in reference to Jezebel's blood spattering upon the wall and the horses, and in Isa 63:3 it is in reference to the blood of the Edomites which spattered upon YHWH's garments when he took revenge upon them. There is also one occurrence found in Isa 52:15, but there it has the meaning of "to startle" the nations, or to "cause the nations to jump up." Once again, according to the lexicons, this term can be considered to be a late term.[16]

A second term in v. 33 to consider is √רמס ("to trample"). This root occurs only nineteen times in the Old Testament[17] and of these it is only used in reference to human beings being trampled by animals in 2 Kgs 9:33 and in Ps 7:6. This term can also be considered to be of Late Biblical Hebrew provenance.[18]

(5) *Verse 34*. The first phrase to consider in v. 34 is פִּקְדוּ־נָא. This qal imperative from the root √פקד means "to attend to, to care for, to visit; to gather, muster, to count or appoint." In the exact imperative, masculine plural form as it is found in our verse, the term occurs only four times in the Old Testament—in 1 Sam 14:7 and 2 Sam 24:2 meaning "to count or number," in 2 Kgs 9:34 meaning "to attend to, take care of," and in Jer 51:27 meaning "to appoint." It is found with the preposition of exhortation or supplication, נָא, only in 1 Sam 14:7 and 2 Kgs 9:34. The term פָּקַד might also be considered to be from Late Biblical Hebrew.[19]

Another term in v. 34 which is very rare is the feminine form, אֲרוּרָה, which is a qal passive participle, feminine singular of √ארר ("to curse"). The term is

---

14. Singular: 2 Kgs 23:11; Esth 2:3, 14, 15, 21; 4:4, 5; 6:2, 14; Isa 56:3; plural: 2 Kgs 9:32; 20:18; Esth 1:10, 12, 15; 7:9; Isa 39:7; 56:4; Jer 29:2; Dan 1:7, 8, 9, 10, 11, 18.

15. BDB, 710; *NK-B* 2:769–70, who interpret the term in our passage as meaning "officials."

16. BDB, 633; Gesenius, *Hebräisches und Aramäisches Handwörterbuch*, 494; *NK-B* 2:683.

17. 2 Kgs 7:17, 20; 9:33; 14:9; 2 Chr 25:18; Pss 7:6; 91:13; Isa 1:12; 16:4; 26:6; 28:3; 41:25; 63:3; Ezek 26:11; 34:18; Dan 8:7.10; Mic 5:7; Nah 3:4.

18. BDB, 942; *NK-B* 3:1245.

19. BDB, 823; *NK-B* 3:955.

found only twice in this form in the Old Testament. In Gen 3:17 it is in reference to the state of the ground/earth after God had cursed it (הָאֲדָמָה אֲרוּרָה),[20] and in our verse where it is applied to Jezebel's person. This term could also be considered to be a Late Biblical Hebrew usage.[21]

A third term in this verse to consider is בַּת־מֶלֶךְ ("princess; the daughter of the/a king"; also found as בַּת־הַמֶּלֶךְ). In the singular, this form occurs six times.[22] It is also found in the plural on four occasions: as בְּנוֹת־הַמֶּלֶךְ in 2 Sam 13:18; Jer 41:10; 43:6; and as מְלָכִים בְּנוֹת in Ps 45:10. Nearly all of these texts can be considered to be of late provenance.

(6) *Verse 35.* The term הַגֻּלְגֹּלֶת means "the skull." The lemma, גֻּלְגֹּלֶת, occurs twelve times in the Old Testament. This is another Late Biblical Hebrew term that might even be an Aramaism.[23] The root can also mean, "a census, poll, count, a shekel," and these are the senses found in the majority of the cases.[24] It is only found three times as the object of a verb—in Judg 9:35; 2 Kgs 9:35 and 1 Chr 10:10. It is only in these three cases that it also has the meaning of skull. In Judg 9:35 it refers to "the skull" of Abimelech whose head was crushed by a millstone dropped from above. In both 2 Kgs 9:35 (Jezebel) and 1 Chr 10:10 (Saul) the term refers to heads which have been detached from the rest of the body. That this is probably a late usage is seen by the fact that in the older parallel account to the story of Saul's death and dismemberment in 1 Sam 31:10, the text does not speak of dismemberment of the head and of its being attached to the city wall, but rather, it speaks of his entire body being stuck to the wall.

A second phrase to consider is וְכַפּוֹת הַיָּדַיִם. The plural form כַּפּוֹת occurs a total of nineteen times. Of these, it is in reference to a ritual utensil ten times (see Num 7:84, 86, etc.). It is used in reference to the "soles" of the feet, six times,[25] and it is found three times with reference to the "palms" of the hands (1 Sam 5:4; 2 Kgs 9:35; Dan 10:10). Only twice does it occur in the sense of hands, or palms of the hands, which have been cut off—in 1 Sam 5:4 re. Dagon, and 2 Kgs 9:35 re. Jezebel. In Dan 10:10, the context is Daniel's vision of the last days, and, when he passed out, a hand touched him and his "shoulders and the palms of his hands trembled." In my estimation, the fact that the only two texts that recount the palms of the hands being dismembered from the body are texts dealing with "foreigners" is significant. In 2 Sam 9:35 it happens to Dagon, one of the gods of the Philistines, and in 2 Kgs 9:35 to Jezebel, the daughter of Ethbaal, king of the Sidonians. In the mind of the anti-Jezebel redactor, the issue of Jezebel's "foreignness" is crucial, and he alludes to it throughout his redaction.

---

20. For another reference to the earth which the Lord cursed, but in the piel, see Gen 5:29.
21. *NK-B* 1:91.
22. See 2 Kgs 9:34; 11:2; and its parallel in 2 Chr 22:11; Ps 45:14; and Dan 11:6.
23. BDB, 166; *NK-B* 1:191. BDB notes that it is found only in "P" texts, late texts, and in Aramaic.
24. See Exod 16:16; 38:26; Num 1:2, 18, 20, 22; 3:47; 1 Chr 23:3, 24.
25. See Josh 3:13; 4:18; 1 Kgs 5:7; Isa 60:14; Ezek 43:7; Mal 3:21.

(7) *Verse 36.* Of the four occurrences of the exact phrase וַיַּגִּידוּ לוֹ,[26] this is the
only occurrence where the statement is *not* immediately followed by a direct
object phrase indicating precisely what it was that "they said to him." In 2 Kgs
9:36aβ-b we find, instead, Jehu's response concerning the fulfillment of Elijah's
oracle. This is uncharacteristic and indicative of the fact that the material following וַיַּגִּידוּ לוֹ may be of a secondary origin, replacing that which originally had
been said.

The exact phrase, דְּבַר־יְהוָה הוּא, only occurs three times in the Old Testament—in 2 Kgs 9:36aβ;[27] Jer 32:28 (with כִּדְבַר יְהוָה); and in Zech 11:11. In the
last two of these references the phrase is preceded by the preposition כְּ + a form
of the verb ידע√. In these two cases the phrases are statements in which either the
speaker, or the one(s) being spoken about, have come to know that something
which had taken place was in fact in accord with a previously spoken word of
YHWH. In both cases it is a reflective sentiment—"then I (they) knew that it was
the word of YHWH." This, however, is not the same context in which we find the
statement in 2 Kgs 9:36aβ. Here we have no reflective sentiment acknowledging
something as having taken place according to YHWH's word; rather, we have a
public proclamation of justification on Jehu's part. He is proclaiming that it was
because "it was the word of the Lord" (דְּבַר־יְהוָה הוּא), that there was not enough
of Jezebel's body left to bury. Though the function of the statement in 9:36aβ
might be somewhat similar to that of Jer 32:8 and Zech 11:11, it is not exactly so.
In 9:36aβ we find no כִּי and no form of the verb ידע√, both of which together
would give it the reflective quality found in the other texts. This reflective quality
also serves to add a certain emphasis to the situation being referred to in these
verses. This is seen by the location in which the statement is found in both Jer
32:8 and Zech 11:11, where the phrase is situated at *the very end of the verse.* In
this position, it serves as both a reflective and emphatic explanation of the events
that have transpired. As such, the phrase does not require any further expansion.

In 2 Kgs 9:36, however, this is not the case. First of all, in 9:36aβ the phrase
דְּבַר־יְהוָה הוּא occurs at the very *beginning* of the statement of Jehu. It is then
further explained by the addition of a relative clause which serves as the direct
object of the statement: אֲשֶׁר דִּבֶּר בְּיַד־עַבְדּוֹ אֵלִיָּהוּ הַתִּשְׁבִּי (v. 36aγ). This phrase
is even further developed by the addition of a supposed quote of the precise oracle made against Jezebel by Elijah the Tishbite (36aδ–b). This is then expanded
even further by the addition of v. 37 which explains and elaborates the oracle of
v. 36aγ–b.

Additionally, the form of the combined statement, דְּבַר־יְהוָה הוּא אֲשֶׁר דִּבֶּר
בְּיַד־עַבְדּוֹ אֵלִיָּהוּ הַתִּשְׁבִּי, is not exactly one of the typical Dtr phrases. One characteristic of Dtr usage is that it normally is found with the initial statement, כִּדְבַר
יְהוָה, or one of its parallel forms, prior to the relative clause.[28]

26.   See Gen 42:29; 1 Kgs 20:17; 2 Kgs 9.36; Isa 36:22.
27.   Verse 36 is divided in the following manner: aα—וַיֹּאמֶר דְּבַר־יְהוָה הוּא; aβ—וַיָּשֻׁבוּ וַיַּגִּידוּ לוֹ;
aγ—בְּחֵלֶק יִזְרְעֶאל יֹאכְלוּ הַכְּלָבִים אֶת־בְּשַׂר אִיזָבֶל; aδ—לֵאמֹר; b—אֲשֶׁר דִּבֶּר בְּיַד־עַבְדּוֹ אֵלִיָּהוּ הַתִּשְׁבִּי.
28.   See 1 Kgs 14:18; 15:29; 16:34; 17:16; 2 Kgs 10:10b; 14:25; 24:2.

In my opinion, at least in the historical and prophetic texts of the Old Testament, the phrase כִּדְבַר יְהוָה, followed by a variety of other fixed phrases, should be considered to be a Dtr usage.[29] According to W. H. Schmidt, "the fulfillment of the word of God proclaimed by the prophet is frequently affirmed by the phrase: "כִּדְבַר יְהוָה אֲשֶׁר דִּבֶּר בְּיַד עֲבָדָיו הַנְּבִיאִים"[30] In my analysis of the occurrences of this phrase, I would categorize its usage according the following "types" which use the phrase כִּדְבַר יְהוָה. The individual "types" are categorized in the following presentation according to their contexts. There are four basic types, some of which show several variations-on-the-theme of the basic type:

1. כִּדְבַר יְהוָה—In the *Context of a Command*:
   This is the simplest form of the phrase, occurring as a simple statement of authority. In this context the phrase כִּדְבַר יְהוָה is cited as the motivation for following the given command (Josh 8:8; 1 Chr 15:15).

2. כִּדְבַר יְהוָה אֲשֶׁר צִוָּה אֶת־—In the *Context of a Command*:
   This form is more developed and is more emphatic. It indicates that that which the Lord spoke was given in a command to a specific person (Josh 8:27; see also Judg 3:4; 1 Chr 16:40).

3. כִּדְבַר יְהוָה—In the *Context of a Statement of the Fulfillment of God's Word or Command*:
   This is the simplest form of this category and indicates that God's word was, in fact, obeyed (1 Kgs 12:24; 17:5; 2 Kgs 4:44; 7:16; 9:26; Jer 13:2; 32:8; Jonah 3:3). There are three slightly developed forms of this statement:

   a. כִּדְבַר יְהוָה עַל־יִשְׂרָאֵל (1 Chr 11:10).
   b. כִּדְבַר יְהוָה בְּיַד־ + *the name of the prophet* (1 Chr 11:3; 2 Chr 35:6—these texts present the fulfillment of a command spoken by God to Samuel or Moses).
   c. כִּדְבַר יְהוָה אֲשֶׁר קָרָא אִישׁ הָאֱלֹהִים אֲשֶׁר קָרָא אֶת־הַדְּבָרִים הָאֵלֶּה (2 Kgs 23:16), a much more fully developed and emphatic statement of fulfillment of God's word.

4. כִּדְבַר יְהוָה אֲשֶׁר דִּבֶּר—In the *Context of the Fulfillment of Prophecy*:
   a. כִּדְבַר יְהוָה אֲשֶׁר דִּבֶּר־לוֹ—in this form the name of the prophet who made the prophecy is not specifically mentioned, though it may have occurred earlier in the verse or context (1 Kgs 12:24; 22:28).

29. With Benzinger, *Die Bücher der Könige*, 153; Gunkel, *Geschichten von Elisa*, 87 and nn. 51–52; Noth, *Überlieferungsgeschichtliche Studien* 1:126 (84); Steck, *Überlieferung und Zeitgeschichte*, 34 n. 5, 40 n. 4; Schmitt, *Elisa*, 22 n. 24, 23; Sekine, "Literatursoziologische Beobachtungen zu den Elisaerzählungen," 55; Timm, *Die Dynastie Omri*, 138; Rehm, *Das zweite Buch der Könige*, 106; Würthwein, *Die Bücher der Könige, 1. Kön. 17–2 Kön. 25*, 337; Treholle Barrera, *Jehú y Joás*, 62–63; Hentschel, *2 Könige*, 46; Peckham, *The Composition of the Deuteronomistic History*, 139 fig. 7; Campbell, *Of Prophets and Kings*, 92 n. 61; Barré, *The Rhetoric of Political Persuasion*, 17–18; McKenzie, *The Trouble with Kings*, 76–78.

30. See 2 Kgs 24:2; see also 1 Kgs 14:18; 15:29; 16:12, 34, etc. W. H. Schmidt, "דבר," in *TDOT* 3:114.

b. כִּדְבַר יְהוָה אֲשֶׁר דִּבֶּר + *the prophet's name*—a statement of the fulfillment of God's word spoken through a specific prophet (2 Kgs 1:17).

c. כִּדְבַר יְהוָה אֲשֶׁר דִּבֶּר בְּיַד־עַבְדּוֹ + *the prophet's name*—this is the most common of this form (1 Kgs 14:18; 15:29; 16:12 with slight variation; 2 Kgs 14:25 with slight variation; 24:2 in the plural with הַנְּבִיאִים as the subject).

(1) כִּדְבַר יְהוָה אֲשֶׁר דִּבֶּר בְּיַד + *the prophet's name*—this form is found only in 1 Kgs 16:34 and 17:16.

d. כִּדְבַר יְהוָה אֲשֶׁר דִּבֶּר אֶל־ + *the prophet's name*—this form is only found in 2 Kgs 10:17b.

In none of these Dtr cases do we find a quote of the referred-to oracle immediately following the introductory statement. In 2 Kgs 9:36, however, we do find a quote of the supposed oracle. I maintain that the material found in 9:36aα–γ, which forms a part of the overall account of the death of Jezebel (vv. 30–37), was created as part of the comprehensive Anti-Jezebel Redaction. The redactor added the statement of fulfillment in v. 36aβ–aγ (ending with הַתִּשְׁבִּי) drawing upon or imitating Dtr's Elijah material and the themes of the efficacy of the Lord's word and "zeal for the Lord." He then expanded this statement with the "quote" of the oracle Elijah had supposedly spoken (v. 36b; see 2 Kgs 9:10 and 1 Kgs 21:23).

In 2 Chr 10:15 and Jer 37:2, both later texts, we also find a typical Dtr relative clause, but a different type of non-typical preliminary statement preceding it.[31] In neither 2 Chronicles nor Jeremiah is there found any quote of an oracle following the statement. *Only* in 2 Kgs 9:36aβ–aγ do we find an "irregular" initial statement concerning the origins of the words דְּבַר־יְהוָה הוּא,[32] plus a typical Dtr relative clause naming the prophetic speaker of YHWH's words, which is then followed by a quote of the oracle. This particular combination of elements is found nowhere else. It therefore appears to be a secondary and imperfect imitation of a Dtr formula. I assign this to the hand of the anti-Jezebel redactor.

A third phrase to consider in this verse is יֹאכְלוּ הַכְּלָבִים. The plural form of the noun, כְּלָבִים, is found thirteen times in the Old Testament. Dogs are assigned a variety of different roles. They lick up blood (Naboth's in 1 Kgs 21:19; and Ahab's in 21:19 and 22:38), they surround in a threatening manner (Ps 22:17), they are dumb or mute and have insatiable appetites (Isa 56:10, 11), and they are sent by YHWH as destroyers (as "ones who tear," Jer 15:3). But the most frequent reference is to dogs that eat flesh. In this usage it only occurs in oracular formulae. It is found in the typically Dtr formulae spoken against the "people of Jeroboam" (1 Kgs 14:11), the "people of Baasha" (1 Kgs 16:4), and the "people of Ahab" (1 Kgs 21:24). It is found on three other occasions with reference to Jezebel (1 Kgs 21:23; 2 Kgs 9:10, 36). Here it would appear to be the hand of the anti-Jezebel redactor at work. That the "quotation" of the oracle in 2 Kgs 9:36b is

---

31. See 2 Chr 10:15: לְמַעַן הָקִים יְהוָה אֶת־דְּבָרוֹ; and Jer 37:2: וְלֹא שָׁמַע הוּא וַעֲבָדָיו וְעַם הָאָרֶץ אֶל־דִּבְרֵי יְהוָה.

32. Only found in this verse, Jer 32:8 and Zech 11:11.

not an original version of the Dtr oracle supposedly spoken by Elijah, is seen by the fact that in all cases where the idiom (כ)דְּבַר־יְהוָה אֲשֶׁר דִּבֶּר) appears, it is *never followed* by a quote of the oracle itself.[33] Verse 36, however, reads:

וַיָּשֻׁבוּ וַיַּגִּידוּ לוֹ וַיֹּאמֶר דְּבַר־יְהוָה הוּא אֲשֶׁר דִּבֶּר בְּיַד־עַבְדּוֹ אֵלִיָּהוּ הַתִּשְׁבִּי
לֵאמֹר בְּחֵלֶק יִזְרְעֶאל יֹאכְלוּ הַכְּלָבִים אֶת־בְּשַׂר אִיזָבֶל׃

Another sign of the secondary nature of this oracle and of its placement into the mouth of Jehu is the fact that the report of Jezebel's death in v. 33 makes no mention of any dogs eating her corpse, as is specifically mentioned in this prophecy supposedly uttered by Jehu. We are told only that she was trampled by the horses to such a point that very little of her body remained. The details of the report of Jezebel's death do not, therefore, technically fulfill the oracles supposedly spoken about her death. Evidently this "minor" detail did not prevent the anti-Jezebel redactor from having Jehu declare her death to be a fulfillment of the oracle(s) (v. 36). As we have seen, this redactor shows other signs of "inconsistency" or "artistic license." For example, in 1 Kgs 21:23 he reverses the word order of the oracle—instead of the usual form of יֹאכְלוּ הַכְּלָבִים, we find the only instance of the emphatic word order, הַכְּלָבִים יֹאכְלוּ. This manner of death implies the fact of the non-burial of Jezebel's body. This is explicitly made clear in the only direct reference to non-burial of Jezebel in 2 Kgs 9:10. There, as has already been discussed, the same editor's hand adds the phrase וְאֵין קֹבֵר to the oracle "quoted" about the dogs eating her corpse.

A final phrase to be considered in this verse is אֶת־בְּשַׂר אִיזָבֶל. The use of the phrase אֶת־בְּשַׂר in contexts such as the present one is very rare. The phrase itself occurs eight times in the Old Testament. Of these occurrences, it refers to circumcision (×4 in Gen 17:11, 14, 23, 25), to the flesh of the ram of sacrifice (Exod 29:32), and to the flesh of human beings which is eaten (×3 in 2 Kgs 9:36; Jer 19:9 re. sons and daughters; and Zech 11:9 re. those who remain when YHWH annuls his covenant—they shall eat each others' flesh). Of the three occurrences relating to the eating of human flesh, the fact that two of them are found in later texts (Jeremiah and Zechariah) might be an indication of a late usage in our text as well.

(8) *Verse 37.* Another peculiarity of the use of the oracle in 9:36 is that it is also followed in v. 37 by a second oracle that expands and emphasizes the results of the non-burial:

(וְהָיָת) [וְהָיְתָה] נִבְלַת[34] אִיזֶבֶל כְּדֹמֶן עַל־פְּנֵי הַשָּׂדֶה בְּחֵלֶק
יִזְרְעֶאל אֲשֶׁר לֹא־יֹאמְרוּ זֹאת אִיזָבֶל׃
(2 Kgs 9:37)

---

33. See 1 Kgs 14:18; 15:29; 2 Kgs 10:10b; 14:25, all of which are references to an oracle or "word" spoken shortly *before* the statement. The only exception to this is found in our verse where the oracle follows the idiom.

34. According to *NK-B* 2:664, the use of this term for corpse or cadaver is Late Biblical Hebrew (MHb).

The particular combination of an oracle of non-burial with an oracle that the body will be "like dung upon the surface of the field" is rare and is found elsewhere only in Jeremiah (8:2; 9:21; 16:4; 25:33). There are, however, some differences between the way the oracles are found in Jeremiah and that found in 2 Kgs 9:36–37. First of all, in 2 Kgs 9:36–37 we have the only occurrence of the oracle of being like dung upon the field coupled with an "indirect" oracle of non-burial. Linked to this is the fact that in three of the four cases found in Jeremiah, the explicitness of the oracle of non-burial is made emphatic by either the presence of at least two (and in one case three) direct statements of non-burial, or by reference to the fact that there will be no one mourning their deaths. This feature is not found in 2 Kgs 9:36–37:

לֹא יֵאָסְפוּ וְלֹא יִקָּבֵרוּ לְדֹמֶן עַל־פְּנֵי הָאֲדָמָה יִהְיוּ׃

(Jer 8:2)

לֹא יִסָּפְדוּ וְלֹא יִקָּבֵרוּ לְדֹמֶן עַל־פְּנֵי הָאֲדָמָה יִהְיוּ

(Jer 16:4)

לֹא יִסָּפְדוּ וְלֹא יֵאָסְפוּ וְלֹא יִקָּבֵרוּ לְדֹמֶן עַל־פְּנֵי הָאֲדָמָה יִהְיוּ׃

(Jer 25:33)

וְנָפְלָה נִבְלַת הָאָדָם כְּדֹמֶן עַל־פְּנֵי הַשָּׂדֶה וּכְעָמִיר מֵאַחֲרֵי הַקֹּצֵר וְאֵין מְאַסֵּף׃

(Jer 9:21)

In 2 Kgs 9:36b–37 we find only the indirect oracle of non-burial (v. 36b) and none of the explicit and emphatic statements as found in the verses of Jeremiah. Verse 21 is the closest parallel in Jeremiah to 2 Kgs 9:37,[35] but it is not exact. Both verses have the same statement כְּדֹמֶן עַל־פְּנֵי הַשָּׂדֶה, not הָאֲדָמָה ("the earth")—as in the other Jeremiah statements. Both are also similar in that the statement about the dung is followed by *two* other statements, but these statements vary from one verse to the other. The best way to see the differences is to compare the two statements:

Table 2. *A Diagrammatic Comparison of Oracles of Non-Burial in 2 Kings 9:37 and Jeremiah 9:21*

---

35. Verse 37 is divided in the following manner: (וְהָיָת) [וְהָיְתָה] נִבְלַת אִיזֶבֶל—aα; כְּדֹמֶן—aβ; עַל־פְּנֵי הַשָּׂדֶה—ay; בְּחֵלֶק יִזְרְעֶאל—b; אֲשֶׁר לֹא־יֹאמְרוּ זֹאת אִיזֶבֶל.

In 2 Kgs 9:37 we have a main statement concerning the corpse of Jezebel, {וְהָיְתָ}‏ [וְהָיְתָה] נִבְלַת אִיזֶבֶל, which is then modified by one appositive statement, כְּדֹמֶן עַל־פְּנֵי הַשָּׂדֶה. This appositive statement is itself modified by two further statements. First, כְּדֹמֶן is modified by the relative clause, אֲשֶׁר לֹא־יֹאמְרוּ זֹאת אִיזָבֶל (as the dotted lines indicate, it could also modify the "body"). Secondly, the location of the dung, עַל־פְּנֵי הַשָּׂדֶה, is further modified by the phrase, בְּחֵלֶק יִזְרְעֶאל.

In Jer 9:21, however, we find a totally different structure. In this case, the main statement, וְנָפְלָה נִבְלַת הָאָדָם, is modified, not by one appositive as in 2 Kgs 9:37, but by two appositive statements: (1) כְּדֹמֶן עַל־פְּנֵי הַשָּׂדֶה; (2) וּכְעָמִיר מֵאַחֲרֵי הַקֹּצֵר. The final statement of Jer 9:21, וְאֵין מְאַסֵף ("and there shall be no gathering"), is another indirect statement of non-burial and follows in sequence with the verb וְנָפְלָה. Just as the grains and shafts of the harvest which are left upon the field after the harvest are not gathered up, so too the dead bodies "shall not be gathered (to their ancestors)," that is, "shall not be buried."

Second Kings 9:37 differs from this in that the indirect statement of non-burial comes *before* the statement about being dung upon the field (9:36b), and not afterwards as in Jer 9:21. Another difference between the Jeremiah texts and 2 Kgs 9:37 is that in Jer 8:2; 16:4 and 25:33 there appears to be an "idiomatic" repetition of the exact same phrase: לְדֹמֶן עַל־פְּנֵי הָאֲדָמָה יִהְיוּ. The form found in 2 Kgs 9:37, similar to that found in Jer 9:21—כְּדֹמֶן עַל־פְּנֵי הַשָּׂדֶה—appears to be an exception to this idiom. In my mind, the differences between 2 Kgs 9:36b–37 and Jer 9:21 outweigh the similarities. It is unlikely that they could have come from the same hand. It is more probable that the anti-Jezebel author/redactor of 2 Kgs 9:36b–37 might have been merely attempting to imitate, though not very precisely, the idiom and the style of the text of Jer 9:21.

The particular oracle found in 2 Kgs 9:37, connected with an oracle of non-burial, is also similar to the Jeremiah passages in that together they form a part of what is a rare pronouncement of YHWH's wrath and punishment for the sins of apostasy.[36] Unlike 2 Kgs 9:37, however, in all the occurrences of the combination of these two oracular curses in Jeremiah, there is also found the *stated reason* for these curses, namely, the abandonment of sole reliance and faith in YHWH and the worshipping of other gods—that is, apostasy.[37] In 2 Kgs 9:35b–37, we find no

---

36. In Isa 5:25 there is a similar combination of non-burial with the body being compared to a different, but perhaps synonymous, word—כַּסּוּחָה, meaning "offal."

37. Jeremiah 8:2 (RSV): Because of Judah's disobedience, the bones of her kings, nobles, priests, prophets, and all the inhabitants of Jerusalem are to be brought out of their tombs and thrown upon the surface of the ground "*before the sun and the moon and all the host of heaven, which they loved, and served; which they have gone after and which they sought and worshipped; and they shall not be gathered or buried, but they shall be as dung upon the surface of the ground.*"; Jer 9:22 (RSV): mentions the punishment for the sins mentioned in 9:13–14: forsaking YHWH's laws; not obeying his voice or walking in his ways; stubbornly following their own hearts; and going after the Baals as their fathers taught; therefore, "*the dead bodies of their men shall fall like dung upon the field . . . and none shall gather them.*"; Jer 16:4 (RSV): YHWH commands Jeremiah not to take a wife and have children because all the children born in Judah will die of diseases: "*They shall not be lamented, nor shall they be buried; they shall be as dung upon the earth . . . and their dead bodies shall be food for the birds*"

stated reason as to why this combined oracle is "spoken" against Jezebel. In this case, I would argue that the explanation for the absence of the reason is that the author of these verses simply borrowed the combined oracle from one of his sources (i.e. Jeremiah). He then inserted it here in order to express his own extreme dislike for, and condemnation of, Jezebel. The fact is that his entire work of redaction in these texts expresses his reason(s) for this oracle.

Given the thematic and linguistic peculiarities of 2 Kgs 9:30–37, it is possible to conclude that it is most probable that this account is an independent creation of the anti-Jezebel redactor which was inserted into the account of Jehu's coup at the time of this redaction. The linguistic evidence could point to a relatively late period in the development of the language. The purpose of this insertion was to highlight and explicate how Jezebel's death was both a fulfillment of prophecy and a just reward for her "foreign," pagan, and criminal activities. The anti-Jezebel author of 1 Kgs 21:23 needed to create an appropriate "conclusion" for Jezebel that would match his oracle concerning her death—the dogs would eat her corpse (i.e. there would be no burial). In the story of the death of Jezebel in 2 Kgs 9:30–37, we find this "conclusion."

Technically speaking, the account of Jezebel's death could have ended at 2 Kgs 9:34 where Jehu, after Jezebel's death, goes in to eat and orders his men to see to the burial of the body, since, after all, "she was a king's daughter." However, in the mind of the anti-Jezebel redactor it was considered insufficient punishment to have Jezebel simply die and be buried. This editor, therefore, compiled vv. 35–37. Verse 35 tells us that when his men went to fulfil Jehu's command all they could find of Jezebel's body after the horses had trampled her to death (v. 33) was her skull, her feet, and the palms of her hands. When they return and announce this to Jehu, our redactor has Jehu make the public proclamation of prophetic completion in vv. 36–37.

This proclamation of completion, however, reveals the confusion brought about by the artificial imposition of the prophecy–fulfillment pattern. There are several difficulties with this proclamation. The first problem is that technically it does not match the actual account of Jezebel's death in v. 33. In the account of her death, we are told that Jezebel was thrown from a window and trampled to death *by horses*. In both the oracle (1 Kgs 21:23; 2 Kgs 9:10a) and the fulfillment of the supposed oracle (2 Kgs 9:30–37, specifically in 36–37) we are told that the dogs were to eat her body, and that they did so. Yet there is no mention at all of any dogs in the actual account of her death in vv. 33–35. Though it is possible to surmise that there might have been dogs around when Jezebel was killed, this is nowhere indicated in the text.

*of the air and for the beasts of the field*." The reason for this judgment is given in vv. 11–12: "Because your fathers have forsaken me, says the Lord, and gone after other gods and have served and worshipped them . . ."; Jer 25:33 (RSV): "And those slain by the LORD on that day shall extend from one end of the earth to the other. *They shall not be lamented, or gathered, or buried; they shall be dung on the surface of the ground*." This verse forms part of the oracles against the nations. It follows upon the accusations found in vv. 3–7: "you have not listened to all that the Lord has said . . . do not go after other gods to serve and worship them . . ."

A second problem is found in the fact that in the oracle of 2 Kgs 9:10a it is explicitly stated that Jezebel was not to be buried. In the announcement of completion in 2 Kgs 9:36–37, the fulfillment of this part of the oracle is only *implied* through the mention of the dogs eating her flesh, and the mention that her corpse was to be as dung upon the surface of the ground (2 Kgs 9:37). Finally, in 2 Kgs 9:34 we find Jehu, who was supposedly the recipient of the specific oracle of 2 Kgs 9:10a and in which he was informed that Jezebel *was not to be buried*, ordering his men *to bury her body* since "she was a king's daughter." This statement might best be understood as the author recalling, and perhaps wanting to emphasize, the fact that Jezebel was Ahab's *foreign wife*, the daughter of a foreign king, Ethbaal (see the proleptic summary in 1 Kgs 16:31). However, by emphasizing this point, the editor caused confusion within his own account. Recognizing this difficulty, he then added 2 Kgs 9:35, which gives a seeming "explanation" or "rationale" as to why there could not be any burial of Jezebel's body, namely, there wasn't enough of her left for burial.

## Part II

THE ACCUSATIONS AND CONDEMNATIONS
OF AHAB AND JEZEBEL: 1 KINGS 21:20B–29

# Chapter 5

## THE ACCUSATIONS AND CONDEMNATIONS OF AHAB AND JEZEBEL
## IN 1 KINGS 21:20Bβ–22Bβ, 24Aα–25Aβ, 26Aα–Bβ

This scene within the overall drama of 1 Kgs 21 begins with a jolt. In the previous scene, vv. 17–20a, YHWH commissioned Elijah to go and confront Ahab in Naboth's vineyard and now, with no forewarning, we suddenly find ourselves in the middle of this encounter. Not only this, but we are also surprised that the first voice we hear in this scene is *not* the spokesperson of God, the prophet, but rather the perpetrator of the crime—Ahab. This situation is perhaps part of the deliberate style of the author.

After a brief narrative introduction in v. 20aα, וַיֹּאמֶר אַחְאָב אֶל־אֵלִיָּהוּ, Ahab's words are in the form of a question: הַמְצָאתַנִי אֹיְבִי. This question is followed by Elijah's brief one-word response: מָצָאתִי (v. 20bα—also with a narrative introduction: וַיֹּאמֶר).[1] This is then followed by an accusation which is presented as the rationale for Elijah's having come to seek out Ahab: יַעַן הִתְמַכֶּרְךָ לַעֲשׂוֹת הָרַע בְּעֵינֵי יְהוָה. This short dialogue between Ahab and Elijah is straight and to the point. In its style and brevity it reminds us of another encounter between Ahab and Elijah in which we find a similar type of dialogue, namely, 18:17.[2] There, Elijah comes to meet Ahab and Ahab also takes the initiative and speaks first.

---

1. For many scholars this is considered to be the point at which the original layer of the story ends. Among those scholars who hold that vv. 1–20a form the basic story and that vv. 20bβ–29 derive from various later sources, are: Kittel (*Die Bücher der Könige*, 158; Kittel is unsure whether v. 27 is late or whether it belongs to the original layer of the tradition—in the end, with this reservation, he says that vv. 27–29 should be considered as later additions); Gressmann, *Die älteste Geschichtsschreibung*, 272; Hölscher, "Das Buch der Könige," 190; Jepsen, *Nabi*, 93–94 (in n. 1 p. 59 he specifies that v. 19b is also late); Montgomery and Gehman, *A Critical and Exegetical Commentary*, 332–33; Fohrer, *Elia*, 26; Weinfeld, *Deuteronomy and the Deuteronomic School*, 24 (Weinfeld holds that vv. 20bβ–26 and 28–29 are from Dtr and that v. 27 might be original [pp. 18–19]); Schmitt, *Elisa*, 134–35; Welten, "Naboth's Weinberg," 26–27; H. Seebass, "Der Fall Naboth in 1 Reg. XXI," *VT* 24 (1974): 474–88 (482–83); Hentschel, *Die Elijaerzählungen*, 14–42; Oeming, "Naboth, der Jesreeliter," 363–82 (see p. 369; Oeming believes that vv. 1–16 and vv. 17–20 were originally two separate traditions which were eventually combined into the unit they now form); Rofé, "The Vineyard of Naboth," 89. For these scholars the main reason for locating the end of the basic unit at v. 20a is that from 20bβ onward they identify various later redactional additions, most of which they attribute to various Dtr or pre-Dtr redactions.

2. Other accounts of prophets appearing on the scene suddenly and/or unexpectedly are found regarding Samuel in 1 Sam 13:10; Nathan in 2 Sam 12:1; a Man of God in 1 Kgs 13:1; and Elijah in 1 Kgs 17:1.

There also Ahab's words are in the form of a challenging question: הַאַתָּה זֶה
עֹכֵר יִשְׂרָאֵל ("Is that you, O troubler of Israel?"). Elijah responds: לֹא עָכַרְתִּי
אֶת־יִשְׂרָאֵל כִּי אִם־אַתָּה וּבֵית אָבִיךָ. This is then followed in v. 18b by Elijah's
rationale for the charge against Ahab and his father's house, בַּעֲזָבְכֶם אֶת־מִצְוֹת
יְהוָה וַתֵּלֶךְ אַחֲרֵי הַבְּעָלִים ("In [because/by means of] your forsaking of the
commandments of the Lord and because you follow after the baalim").

In 2 Sam 12 there is a similar situation, but with different circumstances. Here,
Nathan suddenly appears to David and presents to him a parable which arouses
David's anger and judgment against the supposed perpetrator of the crime. At
that point Nathan simply states: אַתָּה הָאִישׁ. In this brief response, Nathan con-
demns David by his own words and then proceeds to announce YHWH's punishment. Similarly in both cases mentioned above concerning Ahab and Elijah,
Ahab's initial words to Elijah are reversed and turned back against Ahab himself
as a charge. In all three cases the accused condemn themselves with their own
words. Why does Ahab speak first in 1 Kgs 21:20? Perhaps the simplest answer
is that the mere appearance of the prophet before him is enough to cause him to
realize that he has been found out. He knows that he will not be able to avoid the
truth or to escape the inevitable punishment. This appears to be the case, as at the
end of our present scene we are told that Ahab humbles himself and does
penance. This same element is also found in the Nathan and David story (2 Sam
12:13, 16).

The only other case in which I have found a report of the Lord sending a
prophet to accuse and condemn a king, and in which, at the sudden appearance
of the prophet, the king takes the initiative and speaks first, is 1 Sam 15. This
chapter recounts an encounter between Samuel and Saul. Saul was to conquer the
Amalekites and dedicate every one of them and all their possessions to *herem*.[3]
He conquered them, but kept the king alive and the people took as loot the best of
the belongings of the Amalekites. In this case, Saul's words are in the form of
both a greeting and a justification. He says: בָּרוּךְ אַתָּה לַיהוָה הֲקִימֹתִי אֶת־דְּבַר
יְהוָה. The second half of this statement can be interpreted as a type of self-justification on Saul's part. As in the above-mentioned cases, the sudden appearance
of the prophet was probably interpreted by Saul as a sure sign of trouble. He
knew that he was guilty of breaking the ban of *herem* and his first reaction upon
seeing Samuel was to make the claim that he had fulfilled the Lord's command.
This is precisely what the prophet will accuse him of *not* doing. Similar also to
our story in 1 Kgs 21 and to that of Nathan and David (2 Sam 12), Saul eventually admits his guilt and repents (1 Sam 24–25).

---

3.   *Herem* is here understood to be "dedicated booty." The term basically means dedicated,
restricted or reserved. When used in the context of ancient Israelite warfare, it is understood to be a
part of the so-called, "holy-war" terminology, theology, and practice. In these cases, God is seen as
the divine warrior and the war is held to be a holy-war only when it is commanded specifically by
God. When this is the case, the war itself is often referred to as a *herem* and all the booty (people,
materiel, and animals) obtained in this war is considered to be absolutely "dedicated" to God.
According to the "rules" or customs of this type of warfare, the booty is normally "given" to God as
his rightful due by means of its utter destruction and immolation. See Deut 20:1–20 for an exposition
of the rules for this type of warfare.

The question–answer duplex in 1 Kgs 21:20 appears to be straight-forward: וַיֹּאמֶר אַחְאָב אֶל־אֵלִיָּהוּ הַמְצָאתַנִי אֹיְבִי וַיֹּאמֶר מָצָאתִי. This is the only time in the Old Testament in which this particular question is asked. The verb הַמְצָאתַנִי is a qal perfect, 2d masc. sing. + 1st sing. suffix + the *he* interrogative prefix of √מצא, meaning "to attain," "to find." The response is from the same root and is a qal perfect, 1st com. sing. The question for us at this point is: "What does Ahab's question mean?"

On the level of the logic of the text, it appears that Ahab is both asking a question and making a statement. The question in this sense is rhetorical and calls for a positive answer. Ahab is not stupid; he knows precisely what the sudden appearance of Elijah means—it means that he and his actions are going to be challenged by the prophet. This raises the important issue of the relationship between prophet and king.

When we consider the story found in 1 Kgs 21:1–16, though there was deceit, injustice, and probably "criminal activity" on the part of Jezebel and the false witnesses—at least as far as the story of the actual testifying against, judging, and execution of Naboth was concerned—everything appears and is presented as having been done "according to the law." Everything appears to have been "legal." If this is the case, then we must question the reason for the confrontation between Ahab and Elijah. It is precisely here that the issue of the relationship between king and prophet comes to the fore. The prophets of the Old Testament are often cast in the role of speaking out against the unjust laws which where promulgated by kings, or against the unjust application of laws. These laws may have carried with them the weight of civil law, but when the prophets felt that they went against the laws of YHWH or infringed upon either the divine rights of YHWH or the rights of his people, they vigorously opposed both the kings and these laws (see Amos 4:4–13). Among some recent scholars who study this issue, the prophetic role is described as the "loyal opposition" to the kings;[4] they were the "watchmen"[5] or "watchdogs"[6] vis-à-vis the royalty and royal actions.

G. von Rad held that the Naboth's Vineyard story illustrated the contrast between two different concepts of law: "the arbitrary interpretation of the rights and privileges of a king which was characteristic of Canaanite city-states," as opposed to that which existed in Israel; a type which was more "democratic" but which also had more stringent demands. According to this law, a person's rights and property, especially his life, were regarded to be under divine protection.[7] Based upon comparative analysis with the Alalakh tablets, von Rad maintains that new light is shed upon the story in 1 Kgs 21. According to these tablets, the whole of the economic life of a country was under the control of the king who

---

4. D. C. Benjamin, "An Anthropology of Prophecy," *BTB* 21, no. 4 (1991): 135–44 (137).

5. B. Lang, *Monotheism and the Prophetic Minority* (SWBA 1; Sheffield: Almond Press, 1983), 68–69.

6. V. H. Matthews and D. C. Benjamin, *The Social World of Ancient Israel: 1250–587* (Peabody, Mass.: Hendrickson, 1993), 213.

7. G. von Rad, *Old Testament Theology*, vol. 2, *The Theology of Israel's Prophetic Traditions* (trans. D. M. G. Stalker; London: SCM Press, 1965), 23.

was constantly trying to expand his own personal holdings. The Alalakh tablets record frequent instances of "excambion." Apparently the kings of Israel and Judah increasingly adopted these practices to which the prophets stood in strong opposition. Instead, the prophets advocated the form of economy which had developed in early Israel.[8]

Another approach to the problem places the conflict between king and prophet in the broader context of a conflict between YHWH and Baal. According to B. Lang, Elijah's opposition to Ahab and Jezebel is to be considered against the backdrop of the larger battle for an absolute faith in YHWH in ninth-century Israel.[9] He maintains that the social function of some of the prophets was "conceived as 'creative outsiders'" who enjoyed "at a charismatic distance the freedom to express new, alternative and opposing ideas."[10] It is in this role that he sees Elijah's opposition to Ahab. He was the "protector" of the rights of both YHWH and of the citizen against the actions of the king. Elijah, like his contemporary Micaiah ben Imlah, was functioning in the role of a "watchdog" similar to Samuel (1 Sam 12:14–15), Hosea (Hos 11:1), and Amos (Amos 5:15).[11] In the view of D. C. Benjamin, classical prophecy in Israel opposed both the royal policies which attempted to centralize the economy in an attempt to create a surplus, and the negotiation of treaties with foreign powers for the sake of military security. The position of the prophets was that these policies were direct challenges to YHWH's power to provide for the needs of his chosen people and to protect them (see Ezek 16 and 23).[12]

Von Rad, Lang, and Benjamin all use the situation presented in 1 Kgs 21 as the basis upon which to conjecture what the actual relationship between Ahab, as king, and Elijah, as prophet, might have been in ninth to eighth-century Israel. Though it may indeed be the case that in that period of time the prophets saw themselves, or were seen by others, as the opponents of the kings and their policies, it is perhaps not so wise to base these theories upon the situations described in what I would call the "didactic parable" found in 1 Kgs 21. As this didactic parable is not "historical" in the literal sense of the term (though it may be based upon some recollection of an historical event), it is dubious evidence upon which to base theories concerning the historical period of the ninth to eighth centuries B.C.E.

The various nuances of this brief interrogative dialogue between Ahab and Elijah in 1 Kgs 21:17–20a come across clearly when we consider the ways in which the question and response have been translated and interpreted by the scholars. Since it is an issue of debate as to whether or not the response belongs to the oldest layer of the tradition, I will consider the question and the response separately.

---

8.  Von Rad, *Old Testament Theology*, 23 n. 35.
9.  Lang, *Monotheism and the Prophetic Minority*, 26–30.
10.  Lang, *Monotheism and the Prophetic Minority*, 68–69.
11.  Matthews and Benjamin, *The Social World of Ancient Israel*, 213.
12.  Benjamin, "An Anthropology of Prophecy," 132.

Keil and Delitzsch translated the question as: "Hast du mich gefunden (getroffen), mein Feind?" It is specifically stated that it should not be translated as in the Vulgate and Luther Bible—"Has du mich je deinen Feind erfunden?" Keil and Delitzsch interpret this translation as meaning: "Have you, my enemy, come against me again?" They comment further that Ahab calls Elijah his "enemy" as if the oracles of Elijah were understood to be an expression of the personal animosity which existed between Ahab and Elijah.[13] A. Klostermann translates the question as: "Has du mich je als seinen Feind erfunden?" He argues that אֹיְבִי should be rewritten as אֹיְבוֹ, since Ahab is not an accessory in the crime and, in fact, he was never known to have been hostile against Naboth. According to Klostermann, one cannot conclude that he was the culprit or instigator of the crime. Klostermann claims that the MT reading of אֹיְבִי is very unfitting ("unpassend").[14] R. Kittel translates it as: "Hast du mich gefunden, mein Feind?" He indicates that the sense of the question is "Have you found something against me, my enemy?"[15]

Like Kittel, H. Gressmann translates the question in his text of 1 Kgs 21 as, "Hast du mich gefunden, mein Feind?" In his commentary section he interprets it as "Hast du mich endlich ertappt?"—"Have you finally caught me, my enemy?"[16] With A. Šanda we find the same verb used in the translation. He translates the question as: "Da hast du mich also ertappt, mein Feind?" Instead of the verb "finden" ("to find" or "to discover") these scholars use "ertappen" (to "catch" or "surprise"). Šanda comments that the question Ahab asks sounds similar to 1 Kgs 18:17—as if it were motivated, half out of unnatural derisiveness/mocking, and half out of embarrassment (to mask his embarrassment in front of Jehu and Bidkar who were riding with him—see 2 Kgs 9:25).[17] N. Schlögl translates the question as "Hast du mich denn als *deinen* Feind befunden?" "Have you then found me to be *your* enemy?" [my emphasis]). He interprets this to be a proclamation of innocence on Ahab's part.[18] Similarly, O. Eissfeldt translates the question as, "hast du mich gefunden, mein Feind?," and then explains that this means,

---

13. C. F. Keil and F. Delitzsch, eds., *Das Alte Testament, Das Alte Testament*, vol. 2, *Prophetische Geschichtsbücher*, pt. 3, *Die Bücher der Könige* (Leipzig: Dörffling & Franke, 1876), 226.

14. Klostermann, *Die Bücher Samuelis und der Könige*, 384–85. Benzinger does not offer a translation or explanation of his own, except to refer the reader to 1 Kgs 18:17 and to note that Klostermann considers it "unpassend" (Benzinger, *Die Bücher der Könige*, 115).

15. Kittel, *Die Bücher der Könige*, 158. See also the more recent studies by Welten, "Naboth's Weinberg," 24; Timm, *Die Dynastie Omri*, 129 n. 15; Jones, *1–2 Kings* 2:359; Zakovitch, "The Tale of Naboth's Vineyard," 399; and DeVries, *I Kings*, 253.

16. Gressmann, *Die älteste Geschichtsschreibung*, 271–72. See also the more recent studies by Seebass, "Der Fall Naboth in 1 Reg. XXI," 483; and Bohlen, *Der Fall Nabot*, 449, Taffel 2.

17. Šanda, *Das erste Buch der Könige*, 466.

18. P. N. Schlögl, *Die Bücher der Könige, Die Bücher der Chronik*, 176. There appears to be some confusion in Schlögl's commentary. In v. 20 of his commentary section instead of the text found in his translation ("als *seinen* Feind", "as his enemy") he has "als *deinen* Feind" ("as your enemy"). The appearance of the pronoun "deinen" must be a typographical error since in the commentary which follows he states that the text should not be read with the MT, but rather with Klostermann as, "als *seinen* (Naboth's) Feind."

"Have you caught me *in the act of an offense/crime, my enemy?*" ("bei einem Vergehen ertappt?").[19]

J. A. Montgomery and H. S. Gehman note that Ahab's question was prompted by "angry terror" and that he asked, "Have you found me, my enemy?"[20] They also observe that some manuscripts of the Vulgate have "num invenisti me inimicum tibi?," which reads the Hebrew as אֹיְבֶךָ (in pause).[21] É. Dhorme translates it as, "Tu m'as donc retrouvé, ô mon ennemi?" He notes that Ahab had hoped not to see the prophet Elijah, the "censeur de sa conduite," ever again.[22] J. Gray translates the question as, "Have you caught up with me, O mine enemy?"[23] He later states that one finds this sense of √מצא as "to overtake in pursuit of" in 1 Kgs 13:14 and Josh 2:22. He goes on to surmise that Ahab apparently considered Elijah to be an "avenger of blood" who constantly pursues the perpetrator of a crime.[24] The majority of the remaining scholars consulted translate the MT literally as, "Hast du mich gefunden, mein Feind? / Have you found me, my enemy?"

In the MT, Elijah's answer to the question of Ahab is one word, מָצָאתִי (1 Kgs 21:20bα), followed by a secondary explanatory expansion. This one-word answer has caused some difficulties in interpretation. It translates literally as "I have found/discovered." The crux of the problem focuses upon whether or not this verbal answer should imply the object-pronoun "you." The question becomes even more complicated when it is addressed within the context of the debate over where precisely the "end" of the oldest layer of the tradition is to be found.[25]

When we consult the scholars with regard to this verbal answer we find that they are split roughly in half. Several of the older commentators have interpreted מָצָאתִי to mean simply "Yes." These include A. Klostermann, R. Kittel, N. Schlögl, and R. de Vaux.[26] When attempts are made to translate the verb more literally we begin to find the introduction of the pronoun, apparently in order to avoid an awkwardness which is felt without its presence. Keil and Delitzsch translate it as "Gefunden hab ich (dich)."[27] H. Gressmann translates it with a

---

19. Eissfeldt, *Das erste Buch der Könige*, 539. De Vaux, *Les livres des Rois*, 71, follows Eissfeldt's interpretation, translating the question as: "Tu m'as donc pris sur le fait, ô mon ennemi." Fohrer, *Elia*, 26, translates the MT as, "Hast du mich gefunden," and interprets it similarly to Eissfeldt, "hast du mich endlich bei einem Verbrechen ertappt?"

20. Montgomery and Gehman, *A Critical and Exegetical Commentary*, 332.

21. Montgomery and Gehman, *A Critical and Exegetical Commentary*, 335. According to Montgomery and Gehman this interpretation is accepted by some commentators. P. Joüon also accepts it on the basis that Ahab was excusing himself from ever having been Naboth's enemy (P. Joüon, *Notes de critique textuelle* (Mél 5, fasc. 2 [n.p.: 1912], 473–74). Montgomery and Gehman critique this position as having no basis in the text.

22. É. Dhorme, *La Bible*, vol. 1, *L'Ancien Testament de la Bibliothèque de la Pléiade* (Bruge: Gallimard, 1956), 1126–27.

23. Gray, *I & II Kings*, 438.

24. Gray, *I & II Kings*, 442.

25. See Appendix 1.

26. Klostermann, *Die Bücher Samuelis und der Könige*, 384; Kittel, *Die Bücher der Könige*, 158; Schlögl, *Die Bücher der Könige, Die Bücher der Chronik*, 176; de Vaux, "Le Cycle d'Élie," 71.

27. Keil and Delitzsch, *Das Alte Testament*, 226.

combination of both the older position and that of Keil and Delitzsch, "Ja. Ich habe dich gefunden."[28] O. Eissfeldt translates it as "Ich habe (dich) gefunden."[29] Montgomery amd Gehman write "I have found," which they say equals "I have."[30] It is similarly translated by É. Dhorme, G. Fohrer, J. Gray, Y. Zakovitch, G. H. Jones, and S. DeVries.[31]

Some more recent scholars have entered into a debate over the issue of the insertion of the personal pronoun. As we have seen some of the older scholars recognized the awkwardness of translating the phrase without the pronoun and included it in parentheses.[32] More recently, P. Welten, when discussing the oldest layer of the tradition, takes the position that the oldest layer ends with Ahab's question, and that the response, and that which follows it, are from later hands.[33] He notes that the observation that it must/should be read as מְצָאתִיךָ leads one to suppose that the answer of Elijah is to be taken as the reported completion of the dialogue and that together they constitute a combination of key terms (*Stichtwortverknüpfung*). He does not agree with those authors who tacitly enlarge the verbal response, מָצָאתִי, with the missing suffix.[34] In a similar way, S. Timm argues that the personal pronoun ("dich/you") is not found in the text and represents a false expansion. He maintains, similar to those who simply translated it as "Yes," that מָצָאתִי is meant simply as an affirmative answer to the question.[35] Finally, R. Bohlen argues that the answer which Elijah gives is a typical type of answer to questions found throughout the Old Testament (for example Num 10:29–30 and 1 Sam 3:5–6). He sees the syntactic function of the response מָצָאתִי as an emphatic affirmative answer, "Jawohl." Bohlen takes issue with what he presents as Welten's position that v. 20d should mean מְצָאתִיךָ and that thereby it should be a part of a combination of fixed terms (*Stichtwortverknüpfung*). Bohlen argues that this position ignores the fact that the positive answer repeats the verb without an object.[36] Though Bohlen's opinion regarding the syntactic function of the verb may be correct, his interpretation of Welten's position is evidently mistaken. First of all, Welten does not include Elijah's response to Ahab's question as a part of the oldest layer, and secondly, Welten is also critiquing those who argue that the verb should be taken as מְצָאתִיךָ.[37] Welten is *not* arguing for this interpretation, contrary to the way Bohlen appears to have interpreted his

---

28. Gressmann, *Die älteste Geschichtsschreibung*, 271.

29. Eissfeldt, *Das erste Buch der Könige*, 539.

30. Montgomery and Gehman, *A Critical and Exegetical Commentary*, 332.

31. Dhorme, *La Bible*, 1127; Fohrer, *Elia*, 26; Gray, *I & II Kings*, 438; Zakovitch, "The Tale of Naboth's Vineyard," 319; Jones, *1–2 Kings* 2:359; DeVries, *I Kings*, 253.

32. Keil and Delitzsch, *Das Alte Testament*, 226; Eissfeldt, *Das erste Buch der Könige*, 539.

33. Welten, "Naboth's Weinberg," 24.

34. Welten, "Naboth's Weinberg," 21 n. 7.

35. Timm, *Die Dynastie Omri*, 129 n. 15. He refers also to G/K §150, 3. J. T. Walsh "I Kings," in *Berit Olam: Studies in Hebrew Narrative and Poetry* (ed. D. W. Cotter; Collegeville: Liturgical Press, 1996), 33, holds the same opinion, though he translates it with the pronoun. He still comments that it is equivalent to "Yes."

36. Bohlen, *Der Fall Nabot*, 193–94 n. 74.

37. Welten, "Naboth's Weinberg," 21 n. 7.

remarks. As both Timm and Bohlen correctly point out, and as many of the older scholars rightly recognized by their translations, the answer which Elijah gives to Ahab's question is a very common way of answering a question in the affirmative found in the Old Testament. There are abundant examples throughout the Old Testament of this particular usage.[38] In all these cases the repetition of the main verb of the question as the response represents either a positive or negative answer to the question and does not necessarily imply any further expansion. In most cases, this method of answering a question is used for emphasis. In our particular case of 1 Kgs 21:20bα, Elijah's answer to Ahab's question is, therefore, an emphatic, "Yes."

After Elijah's affirmative answer in v. 20bα, we find what appears to be the first "accusation" made by Elijah to Ahab in v. 20bβ, יַעַן הִתְמַכֶּרְךָ לַעֲשׂוֹת הָרַע בְּעֵינֵי יהוה.[39] The position of this statement in the text deserves comment. One must ask whether this phrase is meant to be read with v. 20bα, in which case it would be read as, "I have found (you) *because* you have sold yourself to do evil in the eyes of YHWH." In this case v. 20bβ explains the reason why Elijah found Ahab. However, if we read v. 20aβ–bα as a sentence in itself and read the statement in 20bβ, יַעַן הִתְמַכֶּרְךָ לַעֲשׂוֹת הָרַע בְּעֵינֵי יהוה, as the beginning of the next verse (sentence), then this statement becomes the motivation for the subsequent pronouncement of the oracles against Ahab and his entire dynasty.[40]

Another important fact to notice is that the pronouncement that Elijah makes in v. 20bβ is not that which YHWH told him to speak in v. 19. Given the formal structure of the two parts of v. 19 in which the Lord tells Elijah exactly what to say to Ahab, we would expect a precise repetition of the charge and the judgment. However, in vv. 20–29, we find no such thing. Perhaps one explanation is that a "scene" has dropped out of the tradition which recounted the initial confrontation between Elijah and Ahab and in which Elijah conveyed precisely the oracle of YHWH. However, since we have no hard evidence to substantiate this possibility, we find ourselves back at the text as we have it. In this text, as we have already indicated, v. 19b has no connection whatsoever with vv. 1–19a, nor does it have any direct connection with the remainder of the chapter. Verse 20a–bα recounts the actual confrontation between Ahab and Elijah, and appears to be a natural and actual part of vv. 1–19a. In v. 20bβ, on the other hand, we have a statement that finds no support in vv. 1–19a. Nowhere in vv. 1–19a is there any reference to Ahab, himself, doing anything "evil," at least in comparison to Jezebel. In fact, the opposite appears to be the case. Ahab is presented in

38. To mention just a few examples: Gen 18:28; 24:58; 29:5, 6; Exod 2:7–8; 1 Sam 9:11–12; 23:11–12; 2 Sam 5:19; 12:19; 1 Kgs 2:13; 2 Kgs 3:7; 5:21–22, etc.

39. One should recall that it is generally maintained that the material from vv. 20bβ–26 is comprised of late redactional additions. This does not, however, affect a synchronic reading of the text. Regarding יַעַן הִתְמַכֶּרְךָ, the term יַעַן is technically a substantive which connotes "purpose" or "intention." However, it is only very rarely found in this function. Its normal usage is as an adverb or conjunction meaning, "because" or "on account of" (BDB, 774, and N. H. Snaith, *Notes on the Hebrew Text of I Kings, XVII–XIX and XXI–XXII* [London: Epworth Press, 1954; repr. 1965], 78).

40. This reading would appear to support the argument that the end of the original layer is to be placed immediately after Elijah's one-word response to Ahab.

vv. 2–4 as having no option in the face of Naboth's refusal to sell or trade his vineyard, and therefore, he returns to his home, albeit in a dejected mood. The next time we hear of Ahab is after the death of Naboth when Jezebel commands him to get up and go to take possession of the vineyard. Ahab is taking possession of a vineyard for which, according to the story, we can presume there is no owner. This would not be a crime. So we are faced in v. 20bβ with a statement, similar to that of v. 19b, which has nothing to base itself upon in the story of vv. 1–19a.

The specifics of the crime for which Ahab is to be condemned are another element of the text to note. In vv. 19–24 we find two different accusations of crimes and two different punishments. When YHWH informs Elijah of the condemnation which he is to communicate to Ahab, we read: כֹּה אָמַר יְהוָה הֲרָצַחְתָּ וְגַם־יָרָשְׁתָּ (v. 19a). According to this information, the crime for which Ahab has incurred the wrath of YHWH is that of murder and the illegal taking possession of property. For this he is to be condemned. This accusation appears to be well founded in the story of vv. 1–16, though Ahab's actual role in the commission of the crime may legitimately be questioned. The fact remains that it is to Ahab alone that Elijah is sent and it is he alone whom Elijah accuses in vv. 17–19. When we come to vv. 20bβ–26, however, we find that the accusations that are made and the condemnations pronounced by Elijah are not for the crimes mentioned in v. 19a. In fact, the accusations and condemnations in vv. 20bβ–26 have absolutely no connections with the story as recounted in vv. 1–19a. It is to an investigation of these that I now turn.

## 1. *The Accusations and Condemnations against Ahab in 1 Kings 21:19–26*

A survey of the material in vv. 19–26 results in the following data regarding Ahab:

### a. *The Accusations concerning Ahab*

1. הֲרָצַחְתָּ וְגַם־יָרָשְׁתָּ ("Have you murdered and also taken possession?," v. 19a).
2. יַעַן הִתְמַכֶּרְךָ לַעֲשׂוֹת הָרַע בְּעֵינֵי יְהוָה ("because you have sold yourself to do evil in the eyes of the Lord," v. 20bβ and repeated in v. 25aβ).
3. אֶל־הַכַּעַס אֲשֶׁר הִכְעַסְתָּ ("for the anger with which you angered me," v. 22bα).
4. וַתַּחֲטִא אֶת־יִשְׂרָאֵל ("and [because] you caused Israel to sin, " v. 22bβ).
5. וַיַּתְעֵב מְאֹד לָלֶכֶת אַחֲרֵי הַגִּלֻּלִים כְּכֹל אֲשֶׁר עָשׂוּ הָאֱמֹרִי ("And he did very abominably in going after idols, like the Ammonites had done," v. 26a).

### b. *The Condemnations concerning Ahab*

1. בִּמְקוֹם אֲשֶׁר לָקְקוּ הַכְּלָבִים אֶת־דַּם נָבוֹת יָלֹקּוּ הַכְּלָבִים אֶת־דָּמְךָ גַּם־אָתָּה ("in the place where the dogs licked up Naboth's blood, the dogs will lick up your blood, your very own blood," v. 19b)

2. הִנְנִי (מֵבִי) [מֵבִיא] אֵלֶיךָ רָעָה וּבִעַרְתִּי אַחֲרֶיךָ וְהִכְרַתִּי לְאַחְאָב מַשְׁתִּין בְּקִיר וְעָצוּר וְעָזוּב בְּיִשְׂרָאֵל ("Behold, I will bring upon you evil and I will sweep away and cut off from Ahab the ones who urinate on the walls, both enslaved and freedmen, in Israel," v. 21).

3. וְנָתַתִּי אֶת־בֵּיתְךָ כְּבֵית יָרָבְעָם בֶּן־נְבָט וּכְבֵית בַּעְשָׁא בֶן־אֲחִיָּה ("And I will make your house like the house of Jeroboam, son of Nebat, and like Baasha, the son of Achiah," v. 22a)

4. הַמֵּת לְאַחְאָב בָּעִיר יֹאכְלוּ הַכְּלָבִים וְהַמֵּת בַּשָּׂדֶה יֹאכְלוּ עוֹף הַשָּׁמָיִם ("And the dead of Ahab in the city, the dogs shall eat, and the dead in the fields, the birds of the air shall eat," v. 24).

From the sheer proportions of the accusations and condemnations in this block of material it is obvious that the main focus of attention is Ahab. This is, however, the exact inverse of the situation found in vv. 1–16. Verses 1–16 focused everyones attention on the culpability of Jezebel. In vv. 19–26, however, Ahab is the recipient of nearly all the accusations and condemnations. In the compiler's mind, he is the one held primarily responsible for all that has transpired.

A closer analysis of these accusations and condemnations reveals interesting data concerning the chapter as a whole and the accusations and condemnations in particular. In the Naboth story (vv. 1–16) and in the accusation (v. 19a) there is an obvious absence of any Dtr influence (at least regarding common Dtr themes and terminology). This does not mean to imply that the Dtr could not have used a previously existing story and inserted it wholesale into his work, but it does mean that the first accusation against Ahab in v. 19a—הֲרָצַחְתָּ וְגַם־יָרָשְׁתָּ—is *not* specifically Dtr. This position is supported by M. Noth and M. Weinfeld.[41] In the accusation in v. 19a there is a perfect summation of, and correspondence with, the entire story of vv. 1–16. Following this "non-Dtr" accusation against Ahab in v. 19a, we perceive a very distinct difference in the remainder of the accusations. Accusations 2 through 5 (in the above list) can all be categorized as consisting of typical Dtr phraseology.[42]

When we look at the condemnations, we notice that the first condemnation in v. 19b, like the first accusation in v. 19a, does not appear to be from the hand of the Dtr: בִּמְקוֹם אֲשֶׁר לָקְקוּ הַכְּלָבִים אֶת־דַּם נָבוֹת יָלֹקּוּ הַכְּלָבִים אֶת־דָּמְךָ גַּם־אָתָּה. There is no recognizably Dtr terminology in this statement. All of the remaining condemnations are comprised of language that has been generally recognized and characterized as Dtr.[43] There is no preparation to be found for the condemnation

41. M. Noth, *The Deuteronomistic History* (2d ed.; JSOTSup 15; JSOT Press, 1991), 112; Weinfeld, *Deuteronomy and the Deuteronomic School*. None of vv. 1–19, nor their specific phrases, are directly mentioned in Weinfeld's list of Deuteronomic Phraseology—Appendix A, 320–65.

42. Noth, *The Deuteronomistic History*, 112, and Weinfeld, *Deuteronomy and the Deuteronomic School*, Appendix A, 320–65. Accusation 2 (v. 20bβ, repeated in v. 25aβ; see Weinfeld, 341, # 10 and 342, # 5); Accusation 3 (v. 22bα; see Weinfeld, 323, #5 and 340, # 5–6); Accusation 4 (v. 22bβ; see Weinfeld, 340, # 5–6); Accusation 5 (v. 26a–bα; see Weinfeld, 323, # 4).

43. Condemnation 2 (v. 21; see Weinfeld, 350, # 5 and 352, #12); Condemnation 3 (v. 22a; see Noth, *The Deuteronomistic History*, 112; Weinfeld does not discuss this passage); Condemnation 4 (v. 24; see Weinfeld, 349, # 22, and, 351, # 11). Condemnation of Jezebel: Condemnation 1 (v. 23: See Weinfeld, 349, #11a).

in v. 19b in the story of vv. 1–16, nor is there any further discussion or reference to it in the remainder of the story. We have never been told anything about the dogs licking up Naboth's blood. We have in this condemnation a theme that stands in total isolation from all that surrounds it.

## 2. *The Condemnation and Accusation against Jezebel in 1 Kings 21:23, 25b*

In vv. 23 and 25b we find the only condemnation and accusation made against Jezebel in the whole of 1 Kgs 21. This should cause us to question the apparent imbalance found in our text. In vv. 1–16, Ahab is a minor character and is presented as being ignorant of the crime committed against Naboth. On the other hand, Jezebel is presented as main actor and the one responsible for the crime. In vv. 17–29, however, we find a reverse emphasis. In these verses it is Ahab who receives the vast majority of the accusations and condemnations, whereas Jezebel merely receives one of each.

### a. *The Condemnation of Jezebel*

1.     וְגַם־לְאִיזֶבֶל דִּבֶּר יְהוָה לֵאמֹר הַכְּלָבִים יֹאכְלוּ אֶת־אִיזֶבֶל בְּחֵל יִזְרְעֶאל
   ("And also to Jezebel the Lord speaks, saying: 'The dogs will eat Jezebel in the ramparts[44] of Jezreel,'" v. 23)

### b. *The Accusation Concerning Jezebel*

1.     אֲשֶׁר־הֵסַתָּה אֹתוֹ אִיזֶבֶל אִשְׁתּוֹ ("whom his wife Jezebel incited/enticed," v. 25).

---

44. Regarding בְּחֵל יִזְרְעֶאל, as it occurs in the text, the term בְּחֵל is the preposition בְּ plus the construct singular form of the noun חֵל, which means "a rampart, fortress or fortification." According to BDB, 298, it can also refer to "the space between the outer and inner fortifications, including a moat." Both Burney (*Notes*, 250) and Snaith (*Notes on the Hebrew Text of I Kings*, 80) note that the LXX and Lucianus presume this term. They also note that, interestingly in this case, the Vulgate, Peshitta, and the Targums presume בְּחֶלְקָה—a common feminine singular noun plus preposition which means "in the portion, part, section," usually with regard to ground (BDB, 324)—which they both recommend be adopted. According to Burney (*Notes*, 250) the prediction is not fulfilled "by the rampart" (if the term בְּחֵל is kept) but rather is fulfilled "outside the palace *within* the city." He therefore argues for emending to בְּחֶלְקָה. In my opinion the use of the term בְּחֶלְקָה in these later texts and the recommended emendation by Burney and Snaith, is due to the influence of 2 Kgs 9 and represents an unnecessary harmonization. According to recent archaeological evidence from the site of Jezreel, there was in fact a large flat area between the walls of the city and the ramparts of the city. Also included in the fortifications was a huge moat. These findings would seem to support the position that the oracle technically could have been fulfilled "within the fortifications, or, ramparts" of Jezreel. This would in fact agree with the account of Jezebel's death in 2 Kgs 9:30–36, which took place in or near the gate to the city (despite the recollected oracle's use of בְּחֶלְקָה). See D. Ussishkin and J. Woodhead, "Excavations at Tel Jezreel 1992–1993: Second Preliminary Report." *The British School of Archaeology in Jerusalem* (reprint from *Levant* 26 [1994]: 1–71); H. G. M. Williamson, "Jezreel in Biblical Texts," *Tel Aviv* 18, no. 1 (1991): 72–92; D. Oredsson, "Jezreel—Its Contribution to Iron Age Chronology," *SJOT* 12 (1998): 86–101.

The accusation made against Jezebel demands special comment. The first thing we notice is that it is "couched" within a statement about Ahab: אֲשֶׁר־הֵסַתָּה אֹתוֹ אִיזֶבֶל אִשְׁתּוֹ ("whom his wife Jezebel incited/enticed," v. 25b). On the surface it appears to be a bit odd that according to the story of vv. 1–16 Jezebel was the main culprit, the arch-villain, yet when it comes to the accusations by the prophet, she receives only this indirect accusation. The explanation for this is two-fold. First, the whole of the story found in vv. 1–16 represents one large accusation against Jezebel, written in "bold print." The story itself needs no "interpretation" with regard to whom the guilty person really is. Secondly, if we search the concordance for the verb in this accusation, √סות, we find that its various forms only occur seventeen times in the Old Testament. Its semantic range includes: "to incite, entice, allure, instigate, seduce, and trick." Key to understanding its usage in 1 Kgs 21:25b is the fact that its "first" occurrence in the received order of the biblical text is found in Deut 13.

### 3. *1 Kings 21:23, 25b and Deuteronomy 13*

Deuteronomy 13 is comprised of three sections of material pertaining to warnings and prohibitions concerning those who would entice, allure or in any other way lead an Israelite into going after other gods. This chapter is part of the so-called, "Deuteronomic Law Code." According to S. R. Driver, it has no exact parallel in the other Law Codes.[45] Though the other codes do occasionally have strong prohibitions against the worship of other gods (see Exod 20:3; 22:19–20; 23:13) in this Deuteronomic code, an entire chapter is dedicated to condemnation of those who would tempt an Israelite to follow other gods.

Deuteronomy 13 can be seen as a continuation of the previous passage of Deut 12:29–31, which prohibits the Israelites from imitating the religious practices of the Canaanites whom they are going to dispossess of their land; land which YHWH has promised to give to them as an inheritance. These practices are presented as representing "traps" or "snares" for the Israelites; they are things that the Israelites may feel "tempted" to imitate (12:31a). These practices are also considered "hateful" to YHWH: לֹא־תַעֲשֶׂה כֵן לַיהוָה אֱלֹהֶיךָ כִּי כָל־תּוֹעֲבַת יְהוָה אֲשֶׁר שָׂנֵא עָשׂוּ לֵאלֹהֵיהֶם. The author goes on to emphasize the fact that they even practice infant sacrifice (12:31b). The fundamental article of faith that is at issue in these dangers and rules is the place of YHWH as Israel's sole and sovereign Lord and God. In order to protect the Israelites from these dangers, and especially because of the "insidious" nature of these dangers, this code of law proscribes even those whom, from among the Israelites themselves, might tempt a fellow-Israelite to follow after these gods and practices.

It is my contention that Deut 13 can be seen as an "interpretive key" for reading and understanding, especially, the role of Jezebel as it is portrayed in 1 Kgs 21:25b. Deuteronomy 13:7–12 contains within itself several features which are found also in 1 Kgs 21. These include, the use of the rare root √סות to indicate

---

45. S.R. Driver, *Deuteronomy* (ICC; Edinburgh: T. & T. Clark, 1896), 151.

the danger of apostasy, the mention of the "wife" as the one who seduces her husband into apostasy, and the punishment of death by stoning for such a crime. The author of 1 Kgs 21 was obviously very much aware of Deut 13. I maintain that he borrowed freely from Deut 13 the key terms and issues, and then, with literary freedom and acumen, rearranged the details to suit his own story. By so doing, he finds precedence for his vehement condemnation of Jezebel. Let us briefly look a little more closely at Deut 13 and how it might relate to 1 Kgs 21:25b.

In Deut 13:7–12 (following the Hebrew numbering) we read:

> Deut 13:7 "If your brother, the son of your mother, or your son, or your daughter, *or the wife* of your bosom, or your friend who is as your own soul, *entices you secretly* (כִּי יְסִיתְךָ בַסֵּתֶר), saying, *'Let us go and serve other gods,'* which neither you nor your fathers have known, 8 some of the gods of the peoples that are round about you, whether near you or far off from you, from the one end of the earth to the other, 9 you shall not yield to him or listen to him, nor shall your eye pity him, nor shall you spare him, nor shall you conceal him; 10 but *you shall kill him; your hand shall be first against him to put him to death, and afterwards the hand of all the people.* 11 *You shall stone him to death with stones* (וּסְקַלְתּוֹ בָאֲבָנִים וָמֵת), *because he sought to draw you away from the LORD your God, who brought you out of the land of Egypt, out of the house of bondage.* 12 *And all Israel shall hear, and fear, and never again do any such wickedness as this among you.*

In 1 Kgs 21:25–26 we read:

> There was none who sold himself to do what was evil in the sight of the LORD (אֲשֶׁר הִתְמַכֵּר לַעֲשׂוֹת הָרַע בְּעֵינֵי יְהוָה) like Ahab, whom Jezebel his wife incited (אֲשֶׁר־הֵסַתָּה אֹתוֹ אִיזֶבֶל אִשְׁתּוֹ). 26 He did very abominably in going after idols (וַיַּתְעֵב מְאֹד לָלֶכֶת אַחֲרֵי הַגִּלֻּלִים), as the Amorites had done, whom the LORD cast out before the people of Israel.

In the "first" occurrence of the root √סות in the received text of Deut 13:7, it is significant that it is found in the context of the "war" against idolatry and the "enticement" *to serve other gods*. Though this specific theme is never explicitly developed in 1 Kgs 21:1–16, it is one of the charges made against Ahab in v. 26, immediately following the use of the verb √סות in v. 25b. It is also one of the main themes or charges made against Ahab (and Jezebel) found throughout the whole of the Elijah Cycle. Alongside the active role that Jezebel is assigned in the murder and acquisition of the vineyard of Naboth in vv. 1–16, she is also charged with having enticed or seduced Ahab to sin (25b). This specific charge is connected directly with a charge against Ahab, אֲשֶׁר הִתְמַכֵּר לַעֲשׂוֹת הָרַע בְּעֵינֵי יְהוָה (v. 25aβ). This charge is a specifically Dtr accusation which is always connected with "going after other gods" (see v. 26).[46]

---

46. Regarding לַעֲשׂוֹת הָרַע בְּעֵינֵי יְהוָה, this charge occurs a total of forty-two times in Deuteronomy–2 Kings. In Deuteronomy and Judges it is found ten times, all of which are in reference to the people of Israel (Deut 4:25; 9:18; 17:2–3; 31:29; Judg 2:11; 3:7, 12; 4:1; 6:1; 13:1). There is also one reference to the kingdom of Israel in 2 Kgs 17:17. In 1 Sam 15:19 Saul is accused of this when he and the people broke the rules of *herem* against the Amalekites. Judah is accused of this sin three times in 1 Kgs 14:22 and 2 Kgs 21:15, 16. The remaining 26 occurrences of this accusation are all in reference

When we consider the specific verb סוּת√ in the accusation against Jezebel, we find that in nearly every occurrence it has to do with a *negative* enticement or instigation.[47] In Deut 13, the enticement is to idolatry; to pagan gods and religious practices which draw the people away from absolute faithfulness to YHWH. This is exactly what Jezebel is being accused of having done to Ahab in 1 Kgs 21:25b. However, once again, we are confronted with the stark reality that these charges have no direct or explicit connection with the story found in 1 Kgs 21:1–19a. The themes found in the accusations and condemnations of both Ahab and Jezebel are not connected in any *obvious* way with the injustices committed in the story of Naboth's vineyard. But the "obvious" may not always be the reality. For the moment, I return to a discussion of the accusations and condemnations in 1 Kgs 21:20bβ–26.

### 4. *The Accusations and Condemnations in 1 Kings 21:20bβ–26*

To appreciate the significance of the content of the accusations and condemnations in vv. 20bβ–26 it is helpful to compare them to the first occurrence of a similar list of accusations and condemnations as "formulaic statements" (see Table 3, on the next page). This occurrence is found in 1 Kgs 14:7–11 where they are spoken against Jeroboam, the first king of Israel and, for the Dtr author, the archetype for all evil kings, but especially for those in the Northern Kingdom.

The first thing we notice is that, though both accounts have strong similarities, they are by no means identical. On the level of the structure of the individual accounts we encounter the first difference. The Jeroboam account is perfectly symmetrically structured. There are four accusations (lines 2–5, which comprise one compound charge), followed by לָכֵן, followed by four announcements of punishment and condemnation (lines 7–11, comprising one compound condemnation), followed by a concluding statement of finality by the Lord: כִּי יְהוָה דִּבֵּר[48] (line 13). In the Ahab account we have an introductory accusation concerning Ahab's selling himself to do evil in the sight of the Lord (line 1). This is then followed by four condemnations or announcements of punishment against Ahab (lines 2–5), one condemnation of Jezebel (line 7), and a compound condemnation of Ahab (lines 8–9). The account is then concluded with a summary accusation of negative incomparability that contains three further charges against Ahab (lines 11–13).

---

to the kings of Israel and Judah. Solomon is accused of this in 1 Kgs 11:4–6; seventeen kings of the kingdom of Israel are accused of this sin (1 Kgs 15:26, 34; 16:19, 25, 30; 21:20, 25; 22:53; 2 Kgs 3:2; 13:2, 11; 14:24; 15:9, 18, 24, 28; 17:2); all are charged with it only one time with the exception of Ahab who is accused of it three times in 1 Kgs 16:30; 21:20; and 21:25. Also, nine kings of Judah are accused of this sin (2 Kgs 8:16, 27; 21:2, 6, 20; 23:32, 37; 24:9, 19).

47.  See Josh 15:18 (13–19) and its doublet in Judg 1:11–16; 1 Sam 26:19; 2 Sam 24:1; 2 Kgs 18:32, 35; 2 Chr 18:2; Job 2:3; 36:16, 18; Jer 38:22; 43:3.

48. Prior to 1 Kgs 14:11, this phrase is only found in Num 10:29. After our text, it only occurs seven times: Isa 1:2; 22:25; 24:3; 25:8; Jer 13:15; Joel 4:8; Obad 8.

Table 3. *Comparison of the Accusations and Condemnations against Jeroboam and Ahab*

| | | A. JEROBOAM: 1 KINGS 14:7–11 | |
|---|---|---|---|
| *Line* | | *Verse* | *Text* |
| 1 | Commission and Introduction | 7–8 | Go, tell Jeroboam, 'Thus says the LORD, the God of Israel: Because I exalted you from among the people, and made you leader over my people Israel, and tore the kingdom away from the house of David and gave it to you; and yet you have not been like my servant David, who kept my commandments, and followed me with all his heart, doing only that which was right in my eyes, |
| 2 | Accusation | 9 | —You have done more evil than all who were before you (*Negative Incomparability*) |
| 3 | Accusation | 9 | —You have gone and made for yourself other gods and וּמַסֵּכוֹת—libations or molten images |
| 4 | Accusation | 9 | —to provoke me to anger |
| 5 | Accusation | 9 | —and me, you cast behind your back. |
| 6 | | 10 | לָכֵן הִנְנִי—Therefore, Behold |
| 7 | Condemnation | 10 | —I will bring evil upon the house of Jeroboam |
| 8 | Condemnation | 10 | —I will cut off from Jeroboam every male, free or slave, in Israel |
| 9 | Condemnation | 10 | —I will consume/sweep away the house of Jeroboam; as one burns dung (הַגָּלָל) until it is gone |
| 10 | Condemnation | 10 | —The dead of Jeroboam who die in the city, the dogs will eat |
| 11 | | 11 | —and the dead of Jeroboam who die in the field, the birds of the sky shall eat |
| 12 | | 11 | כִּי יְהוָה דִּבֵּר—Thus says the Lord.' |

| | | B. AHAB: 1 KINGS 21:20–26 | |
|---|---|---|---|
| *Line* | | *Verse* | *Text* |
| 1 | Accusation | 20bβ | You have sold yourself to do evil in the sight of the Lord |
| 2 | Punishment | 21 | הִנְנִי (מֵבִי) [מֵבִיא]—Behold, I will bring upon you evil |
| 3 | Condemnation | 21 | —I will sweep away/consume your descendants |
| 4 | Condemnation | 21 | —I will cut off from Ahab every male, free or slave, in Israel |
| 5 | Condemnation | 22 | —and I will make (give) your house like the house of Jeroboam and the house of Baasha |
| 6 | Reasons | 22 | —for the anger to which you provoked me<br>—and because you caused Israel to sin |
| 7 | Condemnation | 23 | and also Jezebel, the dogs will eat her—בְּחֵל of Jezreel |
| 8 | Condemnation | 24 | —The dead belonging to Ahab who die in the city, the dog will eat, |
| 9 | | 24 | —and the dead belonging to Ahab who die in the field, the birds of the sky shall eat |
| 10 | Accusation | 25 | *There was none like Ahab: (Negative Incomparability)* |
| 11 | Accusation | 25 | —*who sold himself to do evil in the eyes of the Lord, and,* |
| 12 | Accusation | 26 | —*whom Jezebel, his wife, enticed/seduced/incited.* |
| 13 | Accusation | 26 | —*He did abominably, going after idols* (הַגִּלֻּלִים) *as did the Amorites whom the Lord cast out before the people Israel.* |

When we consider the individual elements of the two accounts we find many similarities and differences. In the Jeroboam account, the first charge against him is in fact a statement of negative incomparability[49] (line 2). This statement is reinforced by the previous verses of the chapter (vv. 7–8). In these verses, YHWH says that he "tore the kingdom (of Israel) away from the house of David and gave it to you; *yet, you have not been like my servant David, who kept my command-ments, and followed me with all his heart, doing only that which was right in my eyes*" (line 1). These verses give the basis for YHWH's judgment upon Jeroboam and the comparison of Jeroboam with David, the ideal king. Verses 7–9 together, then, represent a statement of negative incomparability: "you have *not* been like David," rather, "you have done more evil than all who were before you" (14:9). There is an ironic and mysterious element to be found in vv. 7–9. It is said that Jeroboam did more evil than *all* who were before him (line 2). Yet, he *was* the first king of Israel after the fall of the "United Kingdom" of David and Solomon. The only king between Jeroboam and the "ideal king," David, was Solomon.[50] Is this an indirect reference to Solomon and his sinfulness? The statement of negative incomparability found in 1 Kgs 14:9 (at the beginning of the pericope), however, can also be understood as a type of *proleptic summary*, which is then spelled out and clarified by the remaining charges that are made against Jeroboam.

In the Ahab account, we find that the statement of negative incomparability is found at the *end* of the account (1 Kgs 21:25–26, lines 11–13), instead of at the beginning as with the Jeroboam account. In this position, Ahab's negative incom-parability takes on the character of an emphatic restatement or summary of the previous charges concerning his wickedness:

1. he sold himself to do evil in the sight of the Lord (an exact repetition of the first charge from 21:20bβ [lines 11 and 1—forming a type of "book-end"]),
2. whom Jezebel his wife enticed/incited (line 12), and,
3. he did abominably; going after idols as did the Amorites whom the Lord dispossessed before Israel (line 13).

Unlike in the Jeroboam account, at the beginning of the account of the charges against Ahab, the first statement made against him is not an explicit statement of negative incomparability. Rather, the statement in v. 20bβ (line 1) is a proleptic summary introducing and summarizing all the charges that are to follow. In this sense it plays a similar role as does the statement of negative incomparability in 1 Kgs 14:9a. Both statements accuse the respective kings of doing evil. For the Dtr, the accusation of "doing evil" always carries the meaning of falling into idolatry or the worship of other gods. This is, in fact, highlighted in both accounts by direct references to these practices (1 Kgs 14:9b; 21:26). A survey of the occurrences of the phrase לַעֲשׂוֹת הָרַע בְּעֵינֵי יְהוָה, and other variant forms of the statement, shows that in nearly every occurrence in the books of Deuteronomy

---

49. See G. N. Knoppers, "'There was None Like Him': Incomparability in the Book of Kings," *CBQ* 54, no. 1 (1992): 411–31.
50. Solomon's son and successor was Rehoboam, a contemporay to Jeroboam.

through 2 Kings, it is related to the worship, making, or following of other gods and or idols.[51]

The statement of negative incomparability made against Jeroboam in 14:9a and the one made against Ahab in 21:20bβ are not worded in exactly the same way. In 14:9 we read: וַתֵּרַע לַעֲשׂוֹת מִכֹּל אֲשֶׁר־הָיוּ לְפָנֶיךָ. This statement uses a hiphil imperfect 2d masc. sing, converted form of the verb √רעע meaning, "to do injury," "to hurt," "to do evil or wickedly," "to break," or "shatter." Jeroboam is being accused of having caused/brought about or done evil more than anyone who was before him. In 21:20bβ, however, Ahab is accused of having "*sold himself* to do evil" (הִתְמַכֶּרְךָ לַעֲשׂוֹת הָרַע בְּעֵינֵי יְהוָה). In the Old Testament there are some six occurrences where this verb is used with reference to YHWH selling Israel into the power of an enemy because of their sinfulness and unfaithfulness—usually connected with idolatry or the worship of other gods.[52] Only in three cases is the verb used with regard to an individual or a nation "*selling themself* to do evil.*" Two of these are found in our text with reference to Ahab (1 Kgs 21:20bβ, 25). The other is found in 2 Kgs 17:17 where it is Israel who sells itself in this way. In those cases where YHWH is the subject of the verb, the act of selling Israel is *the punishment* for unfaithfulness and apostasy. In the case of Ahab, and through him all Israel, not only have they "done evil in the sight of the Lord" by going after other gods, but even more, they have *sold themselves* into this wickedness. They have, in other words, freely chosen to reject YHWH's sovereignty and to sell themselves into slavery to other gods. In the charge found in 1 Kgs 21:20bβ and 25, then, we see a continuation of the portrayal of Ahab as being *the most evil* of all the northern kings, a portrayal which is highlighted in the proleptic summary of his reign in 1 Kgs 16:30–34.

In the Jeroboam account, the second charge mentioned is that he had gone after, and made for himself, other gods and idols: וַתֵּלֶךְ וַתַּעֲשֶׂה־לְּךָ אֱלֹהִים אֲחֵרִים וּמַסֵּכוֹת. The term מַסֵּכוֹת with reference to "molten images" occurs some twenty-five times in the Old Testament, always referring to, or mentioned with, other gods.[53] The molten image of this charge finds its parallel at the very end of the Ahab account where it serves as the final element of the statement of negative incomparability. Significantly different in the Ahab version is the fact that the term used, instead of מַסֵּכוֹת, is הַגִּלֻּלִים ("the idols", 21:26). This term occurs only nine times outside the book of Ezekiel where it is found some thirty-nine times.[54] This fact may be significant in a discussion of the dating of these texts. In 1 Kings, the term is found only twice. The first reference in 15:12 is to Asa, king of Judah and is positive in the sense that he is accredited with destroying all these

---

51. See the discussion of this on p. 72 n. 46.
52. See Judg 2:3–4; 3:7–8; 4:2; 10:6–7; 1 Sam 12:9–10; Ps 44:13. In Joel 4:8 YHWH sells Tyre, Sidon, and Philistia to Judah for having mistreated her.
53. See Exod 32:4, 8; 34:17; Lev 19:4; Num 33:52; Deut 9:12, 16; 27:15; Judg 17:3, 4; 18:14, 17, 18; 1 Kgs 14:9; 2 Kgs 17:16; 2 Chr 28:2; 34, 3, 4; Neh 9:18; Isa 30:1(?), 22; 42:17; Hos 13:2; Nah 1:14; Hab 2:18.
54. See Lev 26:30; Deut 29:16; 1 Kgs 15:12; 21:26; 2 Kgs 17:12; 21:11, 21; 23:24; Jer 50:2; Ezek 6:4 + 38 other occurrences in Ezekiel.

גִּלְלִים. The second reference is our text concerning Ahab who is said to have followed these idols. Also significant in 1 Kgs 21:26 is the comparison that is made concerning Ahab's worship of these idols—"He did abominably, going after idols *as did the Amorites whom the Lord cast out before the people Israel.*" Reference to the Amorites is first found in the covenant of YHWH with Abraham in Gen 15:18–21. In this text YHWH promises to Abraham all of the territory between the Nile in Egypt and the Euphrates in Babylon,[55] all lands inhabited by other nations, including the Amorites. This promise is reiterated to the Israelites in Exod 3:8, 17; 13:5; 23:33; 33:2 and 34:11. YHWH then begins to fulfill the promise in Num 21:25–26, after which the Israelites dwelt in the Land of the Amorites (Num 21:31–32). This was all interpreted as the Lord's doing and credited to him. The context of this promise of the land of the Amorites (as well as of other nations) was that of a covenant in which YHWH was to become *the one and only God* for the Israelites. In this context, Deut 12:29–31 warns the Israelites:

> "When the LORD, your God cuts off before you the nations whom you go in to dispossess, and you dispossess them and dwell in their land, *take heed that you be not ensnared to follow them, after they have been destroyed before you, and that you not inquire about their gods, saying: 'How did these nations serve their gods?—that I may do likewise.'* You shall not do so to the Lord your God; for every abominable thing which the Lord hates they have done for their gods; for they even burn their sons and daughters in fire to their gods." (RSV translation)

Ahab is apparently being accused of multiple violations. He is charged with abandoning YHWH as his God, of breaking the covenant that YHWH had made with Israel, and of doing the exact things "which the Lord hates"—the very things for which YHWH dispossessed the Amorites in the first place. The implied question or threat in this narrative is therefore, "Should Ahab deserve anything less than the punishment that the Amorites received?"

Another element to be noticed in the structure of the account of 1 Kgs 21:20bβ–26 has to do with the juxtaposition of the "proleptic summary" of 20bβ—"You have sold yourself to do evil in the sight of the Lord"—with the first condemnation or announcement of punishment in v. 21a—"Behold, I will bring upon you evil." First, in the close proximity of these two phrases we see that the clear intention of the author was to emphasize the application of type of *Lex Talionis*, "an evil for an evil." This interpretation is supported by the apparent omission of לְכֵן in 1 Kgs 21:21a, which would normally introduce a statement of judgment or condemnation. This term is found in its normal usage in the account of Jeroboam at the beginning of v. 10. In both accounts the statement that YHWH will bring evil upon them is the first of the statements of judgment (14:10a; 21:21a). Significant as well is the fact that in the version found in the Jeroboam account, the pronouncement is that YHWH will bring evil *upon the house of Jeroboam.* In this case the punishment is, from the very beginning, to be upon the entire dynasty of Jeroboam. Jeroboam is not singled out as the sole

---

55. That is, the Davidic empire—Deut 11:24; 2 Sam 8:3; 1 Kgs 4:21 and 8:65.

object of any of the judgments made in this passage. This is not the case in the Ahab account. It is striking that when Ahab is informed that the Lord will bring evil, it is first specifically stated that this evil will be brought "upon you" (אֵלֶיךָ), that is, upon Ahab himself. Only in the following judgments is it extended to include his dynasty and all Israel. This is consistent with the statements of negative incomparability in which Ahab is worse than all others, including Jeroboam.[56]

The next difference between the two accounts also has to do with the first three judgments spoken against Jeroboam and the first four spoken against Ahab.

Table 4. *The Judgments against Jeroboam and against Ahab*

| Jeroboam—*1 Kings 14:10* | Ahab—*1 Kings 21:21–22* |
|---|---|
| I will bring evil *upon the house* of Jeroboam, | Behold, I will bring *upon you* evil, |
| | I will sweep away/consume *your* descendants, |
| I will cut off from Jeroboam *every* male, free or slave, in Israel, | I will cut off *every* male, free or slave, in Israel, |
| I will consume/sweep away *the house* of Jeroboam. | and I will make (give) *your house* like the house of Jeroboam and the house of Baasha. |

In the Jeroboam version, the primary emphasis and focus of the entire judgment is against the *whole* dynasty of Jeroboam. All three of these judgments deal with the annihilation of his dynasty, which necessarily includes Jeroboam himself. The emphasis of this punishment is upon its total inclusivity. The objects of the three judgments are Jeroboam's "house," his "males," and his "house." "House" can be understood to represent the entire dynasty, both males and females, as well as his whole royal line, in a more general way. The reference to "every male" is probably a specific reference to the kingship within the dynasty, though it can also be a reference to the ongoing generation of the dynasty.

When we consider the judgments against Ahab, however, we see that the first judgment is spoken *directly against Ahab*; the evil that YHWH will bring is to fall directly upon him. This judgment is then followed by three other judgments that define how this evil will take place. It is as if Ahab must himself witness all that is going to happen, one step at a time. In the judgments against Ahab, the objects of the judgments are "yourself," "your descendants," "your males," and "your house." Whereas with Jeroboam the punishment of having his house consumed/ swept away by YHWH is the third action, with Ahab it appears in the second position and its object is even more specifically designated as "your descendants" (וּבִעַרְתִּי אַחֲרֶיךָ). This would include both males and females. Then, as if to emphasize the point even further, it specifies that all his males (free and slave)— all from his line who might dare to make a claim for the throne—are to be "cut off." Finally, as if to reiterate, the fourth judgment is again all-inclusive, his entire house (dynasty) will be "given away" as was that of Jeroboam and Baasha

---

56. See 1 Kgs 16:30–34, the proleptic summary for his entire reign, and 1 Kgs 21:25–26.

(1 Kgs 21:22). Because of the extreme gravity of Ahab's sin,[57] his punishment is likewise "to be to the extreme."

Added to the fourth judgment against Ahab (v. 22), as if to supply justification, are two further charges: (1) "for the anger which you provoked me," and (2) "because you caused/made Israel to sin." The first of these has a parallel in the third charge against Jeroboam (14:9). In Deuteronomy through 2 Kings, the provocation of the Lord to anger is usually connected with the causing of Israel to sin—which is usually understood as practicing idolatry and worshipping other gods. In 1 and 2 Kings, it is a charge made against nearly every one of the northern kings and against several southern kings as well. The two main ways in which these texts express the Lord's anger is with the phrase, אֶל־הַכַּעַס אֲשֶׁר הִכְעַסְתָּ (as in 1 Kgs 21.22),[58] or a form of the phrase וַיִּחַר אַף יְהוָה (see Num 12:9).[59] Interestingly, when we look for a parallel in the account of the accusations and condemnations of Jeroboam in the pericope of 1 Kgs 14:9–11, the charge of "causing Israel to sin" does not appear. Jeroboam is, however, accused of this sin in 1 Kgs 14:16, which reads: וְיִתֵּן אֶת־יִשְׂרָאֵל בִּגְלַל חַטֹּאות יָרָבְעָם אֲשֶׁר חָטָא וַאֲשֶׁר הֶחֱטִיא אֶת־יִשְׂרָאֵל. In this verse Israel will be "given away" because of the "sin which Jeroboam sinned, and which he made Israel to sin." In 1 Kgs 21:22 the comment on angering the Lord and the one on causing Israel to sin can be seen as the reasons or explications of the original proleptic statement in v. 20bβ.

Added to the third charge against Jeroboam is a further explication of how the Lord will sweep away his house, כַּאֲשֶׁר יְבַעֵר הַגָּלָל עַד־תֻּמּוֹ ("as one sweeps away dung until it is done away with"). This statement is probably intended to be an implied word-play in that the house of Jeroboam is to be swept away like dung (הַגָּלָל) for its having gone after other gods and molten images (מַסֵּכוֹת, 14:9). A word frequently used for "idols" is הַגִּלֻּלִים, the precise thing which Ahab is accused of following in 21:26. The similarity of the two words הַגָּלָל and הַגִּלֻּלִים, suggests the possibility of a word-play. The use of the image of sweeping away dung in the Jeroboam account could be seen as a subtle reference to the specific crime for which his house is being swept away—idolatry. It might just as well be a commentary on the part of the author with regard to his view of the practice of idol worship. In Ahab's case the word-play could be a reversed version of the above commentary. The גִּלֻּלִים which Ahab is accused of following could also represent an equivalence in the mind of the author with the image of הַגָּלָל in the Jeroboam account.

The remaining common elements between the two accounts are found in the condemnations regarding the deceased members of the royal families: in 14:11 for Jeroboam, and in 21:24 for Ahab. These condemnations are equivalent to a

57. See 1 Kgs 16:30, 33—Ahab "did more evil than all before them."

58. Jeroboam: Deut 4:25; 9:18; 31:29; 32:16, 19, 21; Judg 2:12, 14; 1 Kgs 14:9, 15; Nadab: 1 Kgs 15:30; Baasha 1Kgs 16:2, 7, 13; Ahab: 1 Kgs 16:13, 26; 21:22; Ahaziah: 1 Kgs 22:54; Israel: 2 Kgs 17:11, 17; Manasseh of Judah: 2 Kgs 21:6; Judah: 2 Kgs 21:15, 17; the kings of Israel: 2 Kgs 23:19; and Manasseh: 2 Kgs 23:26.

59. See Judg 2:14; Num 25:3–4; Deut 6:14–15; 7:3–4; 11:17; 29:17–19, 24–26; Josh 7:1; 23:16; Judg 2:11–14; 2:19–20; 3:7–8; 10:6–7; 2 Sam 7:7; 24:1; 2 Kgs 13:2–3; 24:19–20.

condemnation of non-burial,[60] in which the corpses will be consumed by dogs and birds. None of the members of these dynasties are to receive proper ritual burials in their family tombs. This condemnation is also a prediction of violent deaths after which the dead will not "sleep with their fathers," the traditional statement for those who died peacefully.

This brings us to the final elements of these two accounts, those elements that are unique to each. In the Jeroboam account, one statement which finds no explicit equivalent in the Ahab account, is the charge: "and me, you have cast behind your back" (14:9). In this particular form, this phrase is only found three times in the Old Testament. In 1 Kgs 14:9 it is a charge made against Jeroboam. In a similar negative sense it is found in Ezek 23:35 where the whole of ch. 23 is an allegory of two sisters who have sold themselves into adultery/idolatry. The sisters represent Jerusalem/Judah and Samaria/Israel. They are both charged with the same crime: יַעַן שָׁכַחַתְּ אוֹתִי וַתַּשְׁלִיכִי אוֹתִי אַחֲרֵי גַוֵּךְ. The only other similar occurrence of the phrase is in a positive statement found in Isa 38:17. In this case, Hezekiah is ill and prays to YHWH. Within his prayer he states that YHWH has cast all his (Hezekiah's) sins behind his back: כִּי הִשְׁלַכְתָּ אַחֲרֵי גֵוְךָ כָּל־חֲטָאָי. In both of these cases, in which the subject of the action is not YHWH (1 Kgs 14:9; Ezek 23:35), the act described is one of abandoning YHWH to chase after other gods.

The final unique element in the Jeroboam account is the solemn concluding statement of finality by the Lord: כִּי יְהוָה דִּבֵּר. There is no equivalent to this formula found at the end of the Ahab account. However, we do find in the account of the commissioning of Elijah to announce the accusations and condemnations against Ahab in v. 19 the twice repeated formula: כֹּה אָמַר יְהוָה. These two statements function in similar ways in that they both express the source of the accusations and condemnations and they express the guarantor of the authority of the prophet who announces them.

When we turn our attention to the Ahab account we find two elements that have no parallel in the Jeroboam account. Both of these elements have to do with Jezebel. The first is her condemnation/judgment found in 21:23: וְגַם־לְאִיזֶבֶל דִּבֶּר יְהוָה לֵאמֹר הַכְּלָבִים יֹאכְלוּ אֶת־אִיזֶבֶל בְּחֵל יִזְרְעֶאל. This condemnation is said by some to interrupt the condemnations of Ahab and therefore represents a late gloss. It is true that it does have the feel of an "after-thought"; of something which causes a certain roughness in the account of the accusations and condemnations of Ahab. However, as Table 3 (above) shows, this condemnation follows upon the condemnations of Ahab himself, of his descendants, his male offspring in particular, and his whole house. It can be said that, given the dominant role that Jezebel played in vv. 1–16, this condemnation does fit and that it represents another example of the application of a *Lex Talionis* style of justice. Not only this, but by including her condemnation in the list of Ahab's condemnations, the author makes the condemnation of the dynasty of Ahab 100 per cent complete; nobody, patrilineally or matrilineally, will escape the condemnation.

---

60. See the above discussion of the command to Bidkar to cast Jehoram's body upon the field of Naboth, pp. 27–29.

The final unique element in the Ahab account is found in 21:25b, the charge that Jezebel, Ahab's wife, enticed/seduced/incited him: אֲשֶׁר־הֵסַתָּה אֹתוֹ אִיזֶבֶל אִשְׁתּוֹ. The key to understanding this subtle but strong charge is found in Deut 12:29–13:19 where the regulations are defined for dealing with all those who would entice, incite, or seduce an Israelite from his/her absolute and exclusive commitment to YHWH, the God of Israel. The fact that Jezebel is accused in 1 Kgs 21:25b of enticing Ahab, with no further explanation, is sufficient for the informed and attentive reader of the books of Deuteronomy through 2 Kings to know exactly what it was that Jezebel is being accused of in this statement. She is the source of the temptation to worship other gods that Ahab was incapable of resisting. This charge finds no basis in the story of vv. 1–16 where, though her actions are cruel, deceitful, and morally repulsive, there is no clue of her having tempted or enticed anyone to follow other gods. This charge represents more precisely the Jezebel found in the other stories of the Elijah Cycle; the Jezebel who was the strong promoter and patroness of the Baal cult and the vehement opponent of Elijah the prophet of YHWH. In the remainder of the Elijah Cycle, Jezebel represents for the author(s) of those texts the very symbol of the danger of mixing with foreigners (especially of foreign wives and politically motivated marriages). Throughout the Old Testament this danger is spelled out as idolatry and the worship of gods other than YHWH. It is *this* Jezebel who is condemned and accused in 1 Kgs 21:23 and 25b.

Having considered the accusations and condemnations of both Ahab and Jezebel found in 1 Kgs 21:20–26, we now turn to a consideration of the final three verses of the chapter. First Kings 21:27–29 present the reaction of Ahab to Elijah's charges and the transferal of the oracle spoken against Ahab to "his son's generation."

# Chapter 6

## AHAB'S RESPONSE TO HIS CONDEMNATION
## AND THE "ORACLE OF TRANSFERAL": 1 KINGS 21:27–29

The Elijah–Naboth Fragment in 1 Kgs 21:17–19a, 20aα–bα is related to the Jehu-Apologetic Redaction found in 2 Kgs 9:21bγ, 25–26 by means of the Dtr "oracle of transferal" found in 1 Kgs 21:27–29. These verses require detailed analyses.

### 1. *Verse 27: Ahab's Response to YHWH's Accusation and Condemnation*

First Kings 21:27 begins in the exact same way as did v. 15 (re. Jezebel) and v. 16 (re. Ahab), with the use of the temporal phrase: וַיְהִי כִשְׁמֹעַ. In v. 27 the reference is once again to Ahab. In both v. 16 and v. 27 the messages "which he heard" led Ahab from a state of passivity to a state of action. In v. 16, after hearing the message concerning Naboth's death, he gets up to go down to take the vineyard into his possession. This is the first "action" or "active role" that Ahab has played since he recounted to Jezebel Naboth's refusal to sell or trade his vineyard back in v. 6. In v. 27, after hearing the accusation and condemnation of God through the prophet Elijah, he is once again provoked to action, this time to an act of repentance. The connection between vv. 15–16 and v. 27 could possibly be seen as a sign of the originality of vv. 27–29, forming a unity in the overall story.

There are two reasons for arguing for this unity. First, there is no change of characters or location that would indicate a new scene. Secondly, it is only "natural" in a logical reading of the text that after Elijah announces the accusations and condemnations in vv. 17–19 there would be some indication of Ahab's response to this announcement. This response is supplied to us in v. 27: וַיְהִי כִשְׁמֹעַ אַחְאָב אֶת־הַדְּבָרִים הָאֵלֶּה וַיִּקְרַע בְּגָדָיו וַיָּשֶׂם־שַׂק עַל־בְּשָׂרוֹ וַיָּצוֹם וַיִּשְׁכַּב בַּשָּׂק וַיְהַלֵּךְ אַט ("And when Ahab heard those words, he rent his clothes, and put sackcloth upon his flesh, and fasted and lay in sackcloth, and went about dejectedly"). This verse describes Ahab's reaction to the proclamation of Elijah as the traditional ritual acts of penance and mourning. It can be said that Ahab performs six actions. The first is, וַיְהִי כִשְׁמֹעַ אַחְאָב אֶת־הַדְּבָרִים הָאֵלֶּה. I include this as one of the actions because of the fact that Ahab might have been able to choose *not* to listen. Also, the fact that we are informed of the subsequent actions that he takes means that he *truly* and *actively* listened; that he took seriously what he was told. But there is an important question to ask regarding the referent for the verb: To what does the phrase הַדְּבָרִים הָאֵלֶּה refer?

The answer to this question is not as simple as it may appear. Perhaps the "obvious" answer according to the logic of the narrative would be that the referent is the whole speech of Elijah in vv. 20bβ–26. If we consider the text of vv. 25–26 closely, we notice that there is a change of voice from vv. 20bβ–24 to vv. 25–26. This change of voice has led many scholars to consider vv. 25–26 to be a "narrative aside" representing the opinion of the narrator himself and therefore they are not to be considered an original part of the speech of Elijah. The insertion of this narrative aside causes a break between vv. 27–29 and the remainder of the chapter. This break has subsequently created a debate among scholars. This debate concerns the precise place/verse to which vv. 27–29 connect in the text, prior to the insertion of the narrative aside. Opinion varies widely as to the answer to this question.

The first opinion is that v. 27 follows directly upon v. 16a. This is the conjecture of A. Klostermann. He reconstructs the original v. 16 to read as follows:

וַיְהִי כִּשְׁמֹעַ אַחְאָב כִּי מֵת נָבוֹת וַיָּקָם וַיִּקְרַע בְּגָדָיו וַיָּשֶׂם־שַׂק עַל־בְּשָׂרוֹ וַיָּצוֹם וַיִּשְׁכַּב בַּשָּׂק
וַיְהַלֵּךְ אַט וַיְהִי אַחֲרֵי כֵן וַיָּקָם אַחְאָב לָרֶדֶת אֶל־כֶּרֶם נָבוֹת הַיִּזְרְעֵאלִי לְרִשְׁתּוֹ

He explains the current state of the MT as the result of haplography in which the scribe's eye jumped from the first occurrence of וַיָּקָם to the second וַיָּקָם, thus resulting in the present form of v. 16. The same scribe, however, after discovering his error and realizing that the missing text could not be left out, added it to the end of the chapter at the present v. 27.[1]

A second opinion is that v. 27 refers back to vv. 17–19b. A. Šanda maintains that if v. 27 belongs to the oldest layer of the tradition, then so too must vv. 28–29. In this case, he argues, the repentance of Ahab only makes sense when it is understood as modifying or clarifying, in Ahab's favor, the effects of the mentioned threats in vv. 17–26 (especially of v. 19b). Šanda holds that this clarification is supplied by vv. 27–29 in two ways. First, in vv. 27–29 the threat of v. 19b is transferred to the son—interpreting the blood of Ahab in v. 19b as the blood of Ahab that flows in his son's veins. Secondly, in vv. 27–29 for the first time in the oldest layer of the tradition (which does not include vv. 21–22, 24), the destruction of the whole dynasty is clearly indicated: בִּימֵי בְנוֹ אָבִיא הָרָעָה עַל־בֵּיתוֹ.[2] Montgomery and Gehman, in agreement with I. Benzinger[3] and contrary to Šanda, maintain that vv. 27–29 are secondary additions. They see them as "an attempt to ameliorate the judgment upon Ahab in v. 19, which was fulfilled only in his son."[4] M. Weinfeld, E. Würthwein, and Y. Zakovitch all see vv. 27–29 as sequential to the original prophetic narrative of vv. 17–19.[5]

1. Klostermann, *Die Bücher Samuelis und der Könige*, 384–85.
2. Šanda, *Das erste Buch der Könige*, 468.
3. Benzinger, *Die Bücher der Könige*, 116.
4. Montgomery and Gehman, *A Critical and Exegetical Commentary*, 333.
5. Weinfeld, *Deuteronomy and the Deuteronomic School*, 18; Würthwein, "Naboth-Novelle und Elia-Wort," 395; also in *Die Bücher der Könige: 1. Kön. 17– 2 Kön. 25*, 252–53; Zakovitch, "The Tale of Naboth's Vineyard," 399–401.

A third opinion is that the antecedent to vv. 27–29 is found in vv. 17–20a.
Following upon Stade and Schwally,[6] R. Kittel, in his complex evaluation of the
origins of these verses, states that "it is probably better to assign vv. 27–29 to the
hand of the Rd (his exilic editor), in which case v. 29 probably refers back to
v. 21. However, it is also very possible that v. 27 is still part of the older story, as
a continuation of v. 20a."[7] O. H. Steck maintains that v. 27 "can only link back to
vv. 17–20bα."[8] S. Timm maintains that "most, if not all, of v. 27 is *not* original
and he specifically highlights the phrases אֶת־הַדְּבָרִים הָאֵלֶּה and וַיֵּלֶךְ אַט as
"hardly original." In his opinion, "vv. 28–29 go directly back to the event of the
encounter between Elijah and Ahab in vv. 17–20bα."[9] S. DeVries maintains that
vv. 27–29 represent a "surprise ending of a royal self-judgment narrative" which
continues from v. 20. He considers vv. 21–26 to be late additions.[10]

A fourth opinion is proposed by M. White who maintains that vv. 27–29 are
original to the vineyard story.[11] She rejects the final phrase, עַל־בֵּיתוֹ, based upon
the Greek traditions. After this, she then attempts to find the antecedent to the last
words of v. 29, אָבִיא הָרָעָה. She finds this antecedent in v. 21aα. For a variety of
reasons she questions the Dtr assignation of v. 21 and then concludes that, at
least in some form, v. 21 was original to the vineyard story. In her opinion, then,
the antecedent for vv. 27–29 is v. 21.[12]

J. T. Walsh presents a fifth opinion. He maintains that it is not possible for
הַדְּבָרִים הָאֵלֶּה to be a reference to the narrator's aside in vv. 25–26, nor to the
"ambiguously voiced words in 23–24" which don't pertain to the individual
punishment of Ahab. He considers all these verses to be "a lengthy digression"
and that הַדְּבָרִים הָאֵלֶּה refers to Elijah's oracle of doom against Ahab and his
dynasty which is found in vv. 20–22.[13]

A sixth opinion is held by a group which maintains that the antecedent to
vv. 27–29 is found in vv. 21–24 (though most do not include v. 23). N. Schlögl,
when speaking about v. 16 notes that Lucianus and the Syriac both contain the
acts of repentance. These, according to Schlögl, "are only a remnant of the original reading which was transferred to v. 27." He therefore agrees with Klostermann's enlarging of the text of v. 16. When commenting on v. 27, Schlögl notes
"that the discrepancies between Lucianus and the Syriac, both between themselves and with the MT, show that v. 29 (like v. 22) speak of a condemnation of
Ahab for the sin of 'idol worship' and not for the murder of Naboth. The Syriac
blends both of these condemnations together (vv. 16. 19. 21–22. 24)." Schlögl
then goes on to state that "from the simplicity of the Hebrew text, which bears

6.   Stade and Schwally, *The Book of Kings*, 38.
7.   Kittel, *Die Bücher der Könige*, 158.
8.   Steck, *Überlieferung und Zeitgeschichte*, 46 n. 1.
9.   Timm, *Die Dynastie Omri*, 130 n. 27.
10.  DeVries, *Prophet against Prophet*, 115–16 and n. 17, 131, and *I Kings*, 255, 258.
11   White, "Naboth's Vineyard and Jehu's Coup," 23.
12.  White, "Naboth's Vineyard and Jehu's Coup," 33–34.
13.  J. T. Walsh, *I Kings* (ed. D. W. Cotter; Berit Olam: Studies in Hebrew Narrative and Poetry;
Collegeville: Liturgical Press, 1996), 335.

the stamp of genuineness, it is to be understood that Ahab repented after the second condemnation (v. 27) just as he had after the first condemnation in v. 16." He concludes that "vv. 27–29 follow very well upon v. 24 and refer back to the content of vv. 21, 22 and 24."[14] R. de Vaux maintains that "since vv. 27–29 must follow directly upon the words of Elijah, the intervening vv. 25–26 are secondary."[15] A. Jepsen argues that "vv. 27–29 strongly resemble the Chronicler's language. As far as the literary ordering of the text is concerned, vv. 27–29 are connected to, or dependent upon, vv. 21–22, 24 and all of them are of Dtr or post-Dtr provenance."[16] W. Dietrich maintains that "vv. 27–29 and 20bβ–24 are from the same hand and the phrase הַדְּבָרִים הָאֵלֶּה refers to the sayings in vv. 20bβ–24."[17] A similar position is held by G. H. Jones, H. Schmoldt, S. L. McKenzie, W. M. Schniedewind, and J. M. Hamilton.[18]

The second action of which v. 27 informs us is that Ahab וַיִּקְרַע בְּגָדָיו. This action is significant for several reasons. It is found in texts which indicate that it is a gesture of remorse, as when Reuben discovers that Joseph is no longer in the cistern (Gen 37:29), or when Benjamin's brothers hear that Benjamin is accused of stealing the cup from Joseph (Gen 44:13).[19] In other cases it implies a reaction of mourning as when Jacob is informed of Joseph's supposed death (Gen 37:34), or Elisha's reaction when he sees Elijah taken up to heaven (2 Kgs 2:12). In the above-mentioned instances, the action is usually mentioned in isolation from other ritual actions. In other texts it appears to be a part of the ritual for penance or mourning where it is one of several actions taken. This is the case in our verse where it is mentioned with the acts of hearing, putting on sackcloth, fasting, lying down in sackcloth, and going about gently/dejectedly. Similar lists are found often in the Old Testament with slight variations in the individual elements.[20] In the case of Ahab this action is meant to show his sincere repentance, and as with all the examples of this type of behavior, the purpose of this behavior is to attempt to dissuade YHWH from expressing his wrath.

The final action that Ahab performs deserves special comment. We are told at the end of v. 27 that Ahab וַיְהַלֵּךְ אַט. As a phrase, this is a *hapax*. The term אַט occurs only five times in the Old Testament. In Gen 33:14 it describes the manner in which Esau and his men will "go slowly before" Jacob and his people. In 2 Sam 18:5 it is found in David's plea that Absalom be treated "gently" for his (David's) sake. In Job 15:11, Eliphaz asks Job (in a critical manner of speech)

---

14. Schlögl, *Die Bücher der Könige, Die Bücher der Chronik*, 175, 178.

15. De Vaux, *Les livres des Rois*, 71 n. e.

16. Jepsen, *Die Quellen des Königsbuches*, 147–48.

17. Dietrich, *Prophetie und Geschichte*, 36–37.

18. Jones, *1–2 Kings* 2:360; H. Schmoldt, "Elijas Botschaft an Ahab," 52; McKenzie, *The Trouble with Kings*, 69; W. M. Schniedewind, "History and Interpretation: The Religion of Ahab and Manasseh in the Book of Kings," *CBQ* 55, no. 4 (1993): 649–61 (654); J. M. Hamilton, "Caught in the Nets of Prophecy? The Death of King Ahab and the Character of God," *CBQ* 56, no. 1 (1994): 649–53 (651).

19. Other texts which imply the sense of remorse are Num 14:6; Judg 11:35.

20. See 2 Sam 1:11–12; 3:31; 13:31; 2 Kgs 19:1; Ezra 9:3, 5; Esth 4:1; Isa 22:12; 37:1; 58:5; Jer 6:26; 36:24; 48:37; 49:3; Ezek 7:8; 27:31; Neh 9:1; Ps 35:13; Lam 2:10; Joel 1:8, 13; Dan 9:1.

"Are the consolations of YHWH too small for you, or, his word too *gentle* with you?" In Isa 8:6 the term is used to describe the way in which the waters of Shiloah flow, "gently." In none of these cases is this term used within a context of penitence as we find in 1 Kgs 21:27. There are other accounts of repentance in which an action is mentioned which might be synonymous with Ahab's "walking about gently." In Ezra 9:3, 5 we are informed of the actions of Ezra which are clearly acts of penitence. We find in the final position of both lists the statements: "and he sat in desolation/appalled" (מְשׁוֹמֵם וָאֵשְׁבָה, v. 3), and ". . . I fell on my knees and spread out my palms (my hands) to the Lord, my God" (וָאֶכְרְעָה עַל־בִּרְכַּי וָאֶפְרְשָׂה כַפַּי אֶל־יְהוָה אֱלֹהָי, v. 5). In Neh 9:1 we also find as the final action the placing of dirt upon their heads; in Ps 35:13 the final action is to pray "with my head bowed down," and in Isa 58:5, though in a critique of practices, it mentions the act of "bowing down one's head" in the repentance ritual. All of these actions connote humility. Based upon these examples of similar types of actions, we can interpret the statement אַט וַיְהַלֵּךְ to mean that Ahab's attitude was one of humility, penitence and sorrow and this was expressed in his manner of bearing.[21]

Concerning their interpretations of the phrase אַט וַיְהַלֵּךְ, it is again instructive to consult the scholars. Keil and Delitzsch translate the phrase as "er ging leise (still) einher" ("he went about quietly"), as if he were "ein Tiefbetrübter" ("deeply grieved").[22] A. Klostermann, followed by I. Benzinger,[23] held that the Hebrew phrase made no sense and replaced it with the conjectured phrase וַיָּלֶן אַרְצָה, which they translated, "und übernachtete auf der Erde."[24] R. Kittel retains the Hebrew text and translates it as "und ging gedrückt einher." He maintained that "the Hebrew, אַט, appears to have the idea of 'slowness' (Leisen), 'gentleness' (Sachten) and 'softness' (Sanften), as in 2 Sam 18:5." He interprets the Hebrew as equivalent to the German "gedrückt" ("depressed").[25] C. F. Burney simply states that it is a "substantive used adverbially" and translates it as "and went about quietly."[26] According to Stade and Schwally, the Hebrew phrase was unintelligible even to the ancient versions as evidenced by the fact that the LXX replaces it with κλαίων, and the Targum and the Syriac interpret it as יָחֵף, meaning "barefoot." According to Stade and Schwally these interpretations are "nothing but guesses." They go on to argue that "the Hebrew adverb אַט is so strongly supported by other biblical texts such as Gen 33:14 and Isa 8:6 that no emendation of the text can be acceptable." They critique Klostermann's

---

21. Regarding אַט וַיְהַלֵּךְ, the term אַט is a substantive used as an adverb. The probable root is אטט√ meaning "to emit a moaning or creaking sound" (BDB, 31); it usually appears with the ל prefix as in Isa 8:6 where we read: מִי הַשִּׁלֹחַ הַהֹלְכִים לְאַט. In our verse, the context is that of penitential behavior, thus most often it is translated as "humbly, gently, quietly." Theoretically speaking, we could also say that he went about "mumbling softly" or "groaning" in the sense of mumbling his sorrow or groaning in sorrow for his sins.

22. Keil and Delitzsch, *Das Alte Testament*, 226.

23. Benzinger, *Die Bücher der Könige*, 116.

24. Klostermann, *Die Bücher Samuelis und der Könige*, 385–86.

25. Kittel, *Die Bücher der Könige*, 159.

26. Burney, *Notes*, 250.

conjecture of וַיֵּלֶךְ אַרְצָה as being "without any foundation." The only change which they might find acceptable would be to read אַט as לְאַט.[27] N. Schlögl translates the phrase as "er ging gesenkten Hauptes einher" ("he went about bowed over") and suggests that the Hebrew should be read as אָבֵל, "sad" or "bowed," or, with Lucianus, בְּכֶה, as in Ps 37:7 ("he went about weeping").[28]

A. Šanda reasons that "when a person is repenting and fasting (in the Bible) they often go about barefoot (see Ezek 24:17; Isa 20:3; Mic 1:8; 2 Sam 15:30)." He conjectures that "perhaps אַט is a euphemism for 'barefoot' as it is in the Targum and the Syriac." He maintains that "one can take it as an outward expression of an inner depression or heartfelt remorse which manifests itself by going about 'leise' or 'sachte' as in Isa 8:6; 2 Sam 18:5 and Gen 33:14."[29] The remainder of the scholars consulted simply translate the phrase without much comment: O. Eissfeldt reads "und ging still umher";[30] R. de Vaux has "et marcha à pas lents," which he notes is a sign of moral depression and humiliation;[31] Montgomery and Gehman offer "he went softly," or "he went about depressed";[32] É. Dhorme translates it as "et il marchait doucement";[33] J. Gray has "he went about quietly";[34] W. Dietrich translates אַט as "sanft" and notes that only twice is it found in conjunction with the verb הלך√ (Isa 8:6; 1 Kgs 21:27).[35] He maintains that Isa 8:6 is based upon 1 Kgs 21:27. R. Bohlen translates the phrase as "und ging gedrückt umher";[36] Y. Zakovitch as "he walked about subdued";[37] S. DeVries as "contrite" or "dejected";[38] P.-M. Bogaert as "et il allait pleurant" ("and he went about weeping");[39] and finally J. T. Walsh as "he went about meekly." Walsh comments that the word is debated, but that "it probably refers to the sort of withdrawal from everyday activities that often characterizes a period of mourning or repentance."[40]

In conclusion, despite the many interpretations and opinions on the part of the scholars, we are left with the fact that וַיְהַלֵּךְ אַט represents a *hapax legomenon*. Its importance is found in its uniqueness, and therefore, its uniqueness is no reason for eliminating it from the text. The fact that it is not a cliché found

27. Stade and Schwally, *The Book of Kings*, 167.
28. Schlögl, *Die Bücher der Könige, Die Bücher der Chronik*, 178.
29. Šanda, *Das erste Buch der Könige*, 468.
30. Eissfeldt, *Das erste Buch der Könige*, 540.
31. De Vaux, "Le Cycle d'Élie," 72 and n. b.
32. Montgomery and Gehman, *A Critical and Exegetical Commentary*, 333, 335.
33. Dhorme, *La Bible*, 1128.
34. Gray, *I & II Kings*, 444.
35. Dietrich, *Prophetie und Geschichte*, 81.
36. Bohlen, *Der Fall Nabot*, 449.
37. Zakovitch, "The Tale of Naboth's Vineyard," 402.
38. DeVries, *I Kings*, 253, 258.
39. P.-M. Bogaert, "Le Repentir d'Achab d'après la Bible Hébraïque (I R 21) et d'après la Septante (3 Règnes 20)," in *Élie le Prophète: Bible, Tradition, Iconographie colloque des 10 et 11 novembre 1985, Bruxelles* (ed. G. E. Willems; Publications de l'Instituttum Iudaicum 6: Leuven: Peeters, 1986), 39–57 (51).
40. Walsh, *I Kings*, 336.

elsewhere, or belonging to a recognized "school" of thought, could argue for its originality and authenticity in the text.

### 2. *Verses 28–29: The Reprieve—YHWH Recognizes and Accepts Ahab's Repentance and Transfers the Punishment*

#### a. *Verse 28*

Verse 28 is an exact duplication of the introduction to the first encounter between YHWH and Elijah the Tishbite found in v. 17. In that scene, YHWH commissions Elijah (v. 18) to go down and confront Ahab in Naboth's vineyard with the question: הֲרָצַחְתָּ וְגַם־יָרָשְׁתָּ (v. 19aβ). In the present scene, YHWH's question is addressed directly to Elijah (v. 29): הֲרָאִיתָ כִּי־נִכְנַע אַחְאָב מִלְּפָנָי.

The first observation concerning this question has to do with the "perspective" which it implies. The setting appears to be an encounter between YHWH and Elijah in which they are alone. Yet, at the end of the previous scene there is no indication that Elijah had departed from his encounter with Ahab. It is as if this meeting between YHWH and Elijah is taking place outside of time and space; that all action on the narrative stage has frozen while this "mystical" encounter between YHWH and Elijah takes place.

Linked to the "mystical" aspect of this encounter between YHWH and Elijah is the fact that both the scene and the story/chapter comes to an abrupt end after the account of this encounter. We are never told that Elijah communicated to Ahab the postponement of the punishment that YHWH spoke about in their encounter. In this respect, this scene is similar to that of the commissioning scene in vv. 17–19, which was followed by a "time warp" in which the account of the actual initial encounter between Elijah and Ahab appears to be missing. Instead of an account of the actual "meeting" of Elijah and Ahab, the text places us in the midst of a conversation between Ahab and Elijah that is already "in process." The big difference between these two scenes is that in this final scene YHWH tells Elijah that he will postpone the punishment, but, God does not commission Elijah to communicate this postponement to Ahab. Instead, the scene suddenly ends, as if in the midst of this meeting, leaving everyone "up in the air" with several unanswered questions: Did Elijah communicate this message to Ahab? What was Ahab's response? How was it that Elijah and Ahab parted? Was it as bitter enemies or as friends? The fact is that the story of 1 Kgs 21 gives us no clues as to how the encounter between Elijah and Ahab began or ended. Again we have to ask whether this is a deliberate narrative ploy on the part of the author. The story comes to a conclusion in a certain sense, in that the threatened punishment of Ahab is delayed. But this very decision on the part of YHWH to delay the punishment until Ahab's son's day has the effect of leaving the reader hanging; of tickling his interest even more to see what will really happen. So, in the end, the author has brought this particular story to a "sort of ending." At the same time, he has maintained both the narrative tension and the interest of the reader, and projected both of these into the future by means of ending this chapter with a promise/prediction. The stage is set for the sequel.

b. *Verse 29*

Verse 29 begins with a question directed to Elijah by YHWH: הֲרָאִיתָ כִּי־נִכְנַע
אַחְאָב מִלְּפָנָי. The verb √כנע occurs only in the niphal and hiphil conjugations in
the MT. In the hiphil it means "to humble or subdue." In the niphal it is found
both as a reflexive, meaning "to humble oneself," and as a passive, meaning "to
be humbled." In our verse, the niphal reflexive form is found twice, both in the
perfect, 3d masc. sing. In the eyes of YHWH (at least as presented by the author
of this verse), Ahab's penitential actions in v. 27 are construed as an act of
sincere repentance and self-humbling. When we search the concordance for the
root of this verb we find that it occurs some thirty-six times in the Old Testament.
The various niphal forms occur twenty-five times: sixteen times in the books of
Chronicles[41] and nine times in the other books of the Old Testament.[42]

The use of this particular verb has caused a debate among some recent scholars in terms of the dating of this verse. In 1968, O. H. Steck[43] discerned three
main contexts in which the verb √כנע occurs in the niphal. In each of these contexts, the verb is used with a specific type of theological application. In the first
context, this verb serves to qualify the usual or proper relationship of a victim or
loser to the victor, namely, humiliation. In these cases, YHWH brings about this
"humiliation" for the victor (usually Israel).[44]

According to Steck, a second context where the verb √כנע occurs in the niphal
is in the Holiness Code in Lev 26:41. Here we find a grouping of Deuteronomis-
tic-type sayings in which the Exile/Dispersion of 587 B.C.E. is understood and
presented as "your (Israel's) humiliation," a type of national self-humiliation.
Chronicles takes this interpretation and applies it in the DtrH to specific instances
of individual distress.[45] To be highlighted in this particular application of the verb
√כנע within Chronicles is the fact that the humiliation always follows upon an
evil or disaster *which has already occurred.* It differs greatly from Lev 26, in
which we find it used in a "generalized" way in which an action of YHWH transforms a situation of communal suffering into a moment of grace. The Chronicler's
emphasis is specifically upon individual or singular moments of need. According
to Steck, this is definitely not the case in 1 Kgs 21:27–29. Steck criticizes
A. Jepsen for disregarding this fact when he assigned 1 Kgs 21:27–29 to a post-
exilic addition.[46] Steck may be over-reacting in this case.

Steck maintains that there is a third context for the usage of the verb √כנע in
the niphal. This context has nothing to do with the Dtr view of history, but rather,
"it is connected with 2 Chr 36:12, a tradition that was formulated well before

---

41. See 1 Chr 20:4; 2 Chr 7:14; 12:6, 7 (×2); 13:18; 30:11; 32:26; 33:12, 19, 23 (×2); 34:27 (×2);
36:12.

42. See Lev 26:41; Judg 3:30; 8:28; 11:33; 1 Sam 7:13; 1 Kgs 21:29 (×2); 2 Kgs 22:19;
Ps 106:42.

43. Steck, *Überlieferung und Zeitgeschichte*, 46–47 n. 3.

44. See Judg 3:30; 8:28; 11:33; 1 Sam 7:13; Ps. 106:42; 1 Chr 20:4; 2 Chr 13:8.

45. See 2 Chr 7:13, 14; 30:11; 32:26; 33:12, 19, 23

46. Steck, *Überlieferung und Zeitgeschichte*, 46–47 n. 3. *Contra* Jepsen, *Die Quellen des
Königsbuches*, 8, 120.

587 B.C.E. Connected with this tradition are our verses 1 Kgs 21:27–29, the pre-Dtr formulation in 2 Kgs 22:19, and the pre-Chronicles formulation found in 2 Chr 12:6f." In Steck's opinion,

> the particular use of the verb √כנע in these verses is to be distinguished from the much younger use found elsewhere in Chronicles. In these particular verses, the humiliation results not from a conscious and freely chosen conversion or a 'turning back' on the part of the individual, but rather, it occurs because of prophetic announcements of judgment or doom. In these cases, the act/s of humiliation have the effect of causing YHWH to delay the immediate fulfillment of the judgment.

For Steck,

> the appearance of this type of postponement due to the prophetic announcement in 1 Kgs 21:27–29 is a piece of *pre-exilic tradition*. This fact does not preclude that the Dtr was capable of using this pre-exilic formulation for his own purpose. This in fact appears to be what he did . . . he used it to justify the postponement of the punishment until Ahab's son's time.[47]

Steck is followed in his position that 1 Kgs 21:27–29 are pre-Dtr by H. Seebass, W. Thiel, and W. M. Schniedewind.[48]

In 1970, A. Jepsen argued that "the use of this form of the verb is reflective of a late, post-Dtr theological perspective which is found mainly in the Books of Chronicles and in the Priestly tradition (see Lev 26:41; 2 Chr 7:14, etc.)."[49] R. Bohlen, A. Rofé, and S. L. McKenzie follow him in this position.[50] There is also a small group of scholars who argue that 1 Kgs 21:27–29 are from the hand of the Dtr. This group includes M. Weinfeld, G. H. Jones, and H. J. Stipp.[51] Thus, some scholars date this verb's usage in our verse to the pre-Dtr period, others to the Dtr, and still others to the post-Dtr period.

---

47. Steck, *Überlieferung und Zeitgeschichte*, 46–47 n. 3 (author's translation, emphasis added).

48. Seebass, "Der Fall Naboth in 1 Reg. XXI," 484; W. Thiel, "Deuteronomische Redaktionsarb it in den Elia-Erzählungen," in *Congress Volume: Leuven, 1989* (VTSup 43; Leiden: Brill, 1991), 14–171 (164) (Thiel holds that v. 29's use of the verb √כנע is Dtr, but that vv. 27–28 are pre-Dtr); Schniedewind, "History and Interpretation, 654 n. 14.

49. Jepsen, "Ahabs Buße," esp. 150–54.

50. Bohlen, *Der Fall Nabot*, 318–19; McKenzie, *The Trouble with Kings*, 69; Rofé, "The Vineyard of Naboth," 95.

51. Weinfeld, *Deuteronomy and the Deuteronomic School*, 24 n. 2; Jones, *1–2 Kings* 2:360; H.-J. Stipp, "Ahabs Buße und die Komposition des deuteronomistischen Geschichtswerks," *Bib* 76 (1995): 471–97 (480).

# Chapter 7

## THE SOURCES, ORIGINS, AND COMPOSITION
## OF 1 KINGS 21:17–29 AND 2 KINGS 9:21, 25–26

Two important questions to be considered at this point of our investigation are whether or not 1 Kgs 21:17–29 and 2 Kgs 9:25–26 come from the same or different sources or authors, and whether it is possible to decide which is the older of the two traditions. A review of some of the scholarship regarding these questions reveals a variety of opinions. It is a fact that in the work of most of the scholars, a discussion of the sources, origins, and dating of these texts is not very clearly delineated.

### 1. *A Review of Scholarly Opinion*

Writing at the end of the nineteenth century, I. Benzinger recognized that it was highly unlikely that 1 Kgs 21 and 2 Kgs 9:25–26 came from the same narrator:

> it is from the very beginning highly unlikely that one and the same narrator, who narrated the Ahab story with such warmth and love for his heroes, now here with a conscious joy should describe the extermination of Ahab's house as the just punishment of God concerning Ahab's outrages. From the way in which 2 Kgs 9:25f. refers to 1 Kgs 21:19, it is not possible to conclude that both variations come from the same narrator.[1]

For Benzinger, "the form of the prophecy and judgment found in 2 Kgs 9:25–26 is the simplest form of the tradition and is even more primitive than that which is found in 1 Kgs 21:19. It is from this primitive form that all the later renditions have developed."[2] For Benzinger, therefore, it is clear that 2 Kgs 9:25–26 are to be considered the oldest layer of the tradition and that 1 Kgs 21:17–29 are from a later hand.

A. Šanda, in his attempt to correlate the data in the two accounts, conjectured that Jehu must have been present when Ahab and Elijah met, as recounted in 1 Kgs 21:20–24. It is because of this that he knows the prophecies that were spoken at that meeting. Because Jehu was there, he also knew that the punishment for Ahab's sins had been postponed to his son (1 Kgs 21:21; see 2 Kgs 10:10). According to Šanda, in 2 Kgs 9:25–26 the word of YHWH is found in a slightly different form, especially concerning אֱמֶשׁ and דְּמֵי בָנָיו. Neither of these elements were known to the author of 1 Kgs 21, otherwise he would have

---

1 Benzinger, *Die Bücher der Könige*, 148–49 (author's translation).
2. Benzinger, *Die Bücher der Könige*, 151.

certainly used them. "Chapters 9 and 10 [of 2 Kgs] are, therefore, literarily different from 1 Kgs 21."[3] Though Šanda does not go on specifically to state it, I believe that his observations support the position that these two accounts came from different authors. This is further supported by his dating of the Naboth story in 1 Kgs 21 to a time between 740–721 based upon the use of the term מֶלֶךְ שֹׁמְרוֹן.[4] Šanda argues that the caution which the author of 2 Kgs 9–10 uses in his judgment of Jehu indicates that

> He was Jehu's contemporary and this fixes chapters 9 and 10 in a period where Jehu and his dynasty had not yet been compromised by their failure against the Arameans and were still surrounded by the unspoiled aura of their election by God.[5]

J. A. Montgomery and H. S. Gehman conclude that the Jehu accession narrative in 2 Kgs 9–10 is contemporary to the events that it describes.[6] They see the source of this story being "the school of the prophets" who express "full *sub-voce* approval of the revolt and Jehu's bloody deeds."[7] Specifically with regard to 2 Kgs 9:25–26 and their relationship to 1 Kgs 21, Montgomery and Gehman maintain that 2 Kgs 9:25–26 are indeed original to the story and that

> We may not claim more than that the two histories (1 Kgs 21 and 2 Kgs 9–10) come from a common literary tradition, and, if indeed from different composers, light is cast upon a remarkable culture inspired in and by the early prophets.[8]

According to A. Jepsen, we have in 2 Kgs 9–10 "one of the best examples of Hebrew storytelling." For him, this story is either "the official or semi-official account" of the Jehu accession. Jepsen maintains that

> the actions of Jehu were not self-motivated, but rather, they were the direct result of God's will and plan, and therefore we cannot accuse or blame Jehu of wrongdoing. The story in 2 Kgs 9–10 is about YHWH's calling of Jehu for the purpose of the extermination of the Baal cult and the Omride dynasty. We are not dealing here, therefore, with a prophetic legend . . . concerning Elisha.[9]

Jepsen goes on to say that "the oldest historical story (concerning the accessions of kings) is that found in 2 Kgs 9."[10]

J. M. Miller holds that the narratives found in 1 Kgs 21 and 2 Kgs 9:25–26 reflect different scenes for Naboth's murder and that "the brief reference in the account of Jehu's rebellion, regardless of its textual difficulties, is probably *the most accurate* of the two".[11] Being most accurate, however, does not necessarily imply that it is older or younger. It merely makes a statement concerning the dependability of its detail, historical or otherwise. Miller goes on to say:

---

3. Šanda, *Das zweite Buch der Könige*, 98–99.
4. Šanda, *Das erste Buch der Könige*, 470.
5. Šanda, *Das zweite Buch der Könige*, 123.
6. Montgomery and Gehman, *A Critical and Exegetical Commentary*, 399.
7. Montgomery and Gehman, *A Critical and Exegetical Commentary*, 399.
8. Montgomery and Gehman, *A Critical and Exegetical Commentary*, 399.
9. Jepsen, *Nabi*, 73.
10. Jepsen, *Nabi*, 124.
11. Miller, "The Fall of the House of Ahab," 308–9 (emphasis added).

> Moreover, whether one regards the latter [1 Kgs 21] as a late novelette, or whether one treats it as an early Ephraimitish legend, priority in historical reconstruction must be given to the details of the Naboth affair which the author of the account of Jehu's rebellion—who lived soon after the events which he described—took for granted were commonly known. In short, Naboth was not murdered during Ahab's reign, but soon before the death of Ahab's son, Jehoram. Indeed, one may even speculate that . . . the Naboth affair may have been one of the elements which touched off Jehu's rebellion.[12]

In Miller's opinion, then, the Naboth material found in 2 Kgs 9:25–26 is more original than that found in 1 Kgs 21, and the king involved in the affair was not Ahab, but Joram.

O. H. Steck holds that both 1 Kgs 21 and 2 Kgs 9:25–26 were written about the same event, but it is here that the similarities end. For Steck, there is clearly no literary relation between the two stories, rather they relate only by the fact that they partake of "parallel oral traditions." The differences are so many between the two stories that the authors must have been unaware of each other. The similarities between the two stories can be explained as being due to the fact that the authors are writing during the same time-period and they are writing about the same topic. Steck maintains that the author of 1 Kgs 21 is from a prophetic school, whereas the author of the Jehu story in 2 Kgs 9 is a court historian.[13]

H.-C. Schmitt holds that the many differences found between the "Deuteronomistic Naboth story" in 1 Kgs 21 and the prophetic reference found in 2 Kgs 9:25–26 argue against an attempt to assign 2 Kgs 9:25–26 to Dtr. At the same time, the data that are found in 2 Kgs 9:25–26 appear to be historically reliable in juxtaposition to those found in 1 Kgs 21. Second Kings 9:26 also corresponds to family/clan legal codes and obligations known from the ninth century BCE. In this, Schmitt's view is similar to that found in Steck. However, Schmitt disagrees with Steck's position that 1 Kgs 21 and 2 Kgs 9:25–26 were written in the same time-period. Schmitt argues:

> 1 Kgs 21 sets forth an obviously later legal tradition than 2 Kgs 9:25f. This can be seen especially by the fact that 1 Kgs 21 no longer sees the family code as the standard and thus is arranged according to Deuteronomy's manifestly developed legal thought (see Deut 24:16). Fundamentally, that which argues against placing 1 Kgs 21:1ff in the period of Jehu is that the historically false picture of Ahab presented therein[14] according to which Ahab stands completely under the influence of Jezebel, is not imaginable in a specific time when a large portion of the population personally knew Ahab.[15]

According to Schmitt,

> since the statements from 9:25f. are older than those from the Dtr Naboth story from 1 Kgs 21, this work is therefore, to be placed before the Dtr. Their apologetic tendency in favor of Jehu is best understood if we date them to the last period of the Jehu dynasty. Perhaps the reproaches such as are found in Hosea 1:4 can be understood as the background for such an apologetic tendency.[16]

---

12. Miller, "The Fall of the House of Ahab," 316–17.
13. Steck, *Überlieferung und Zeitgeschichte*, 40–53.
14. Steck, *Überlieferung und Zeitgeschichte*, 65–71, 75
15. Schmitt, *Elisa*, 26 n. 54 (author's translation).
16. Schmitt, *Elisa*, 27.

This position with regard to the dating of 2 Kgs 9:25–26 also has ramifications for the dating of 1 Kgs 21. "If 9:25f. belongs in the first half of the eighth century, then one can hardly be led to hold that the considerably younger form of the Naboth Story from 1 Kgs 21 also comes from the Kingdom of Israel."[17]

S. DeVries, in agreement with Montgomery and Gehman and in opposition to Jepsen, holds that 2 Kgs 9:25–26 in fact comes from a prophetic legend. He says concerning 2 Kgs 8:29–10:28, that "though relatively early in origin, this political document was added at a fairly late stage to the existing Elijah–Elisha collection."[18] Within this "political document" the narrator used several different historical reports, but perhaps his most important source was what DeVries refers to as

> the prophetic legend of 8:29b–9:36a. This story, an instrumental fulfillment narrative, with a high level of historical factuality, itself reflects an attitude of stern censure toward Jezebel, but the accession historian has intensified this element of censure at 9:8a. 25b–26. 36b–37 with his own political polemic.[19]

G. Hentschel agrees with O. H. Steck that 1 Kgs 21:1–20bα belongs to a younger stratum of the tradition.[20] He recognizes and attempts to clarify why in 2 Kgs 9:25–26 "a very different tradition concerning similar events is presented."[21] He notes that "there are even similar forms to the curses in both traditions but within these similar forms there are also differences in details." He concludes by saying:

> We must recognize, for better or for worse, that the tradition in 1 Kgs 21:1–20bα and 2 Kgs 9:25–26 go back to the same event, and the differences are due to the fact that the traditions preserved for us have been considerably altered in the oral stage of transmission.[22]

## 2. A Summary and Conclusions based upon the Scholarly Review

What can we conclude from the above survey of scholarly opinion? The first point of general, though not universal, agreement among these scholars is that the account that is found in 2 Kgs 9:25–26 appears to be rather "historically reliable,"[23] and that it should be dated to some time during the Jehu dynasty.[24] Some hold that 2 Kgs 9:25–26 is the more "primitive" or older of the two stories or traditions.[25] This is, however, not the position held by everyone. Others prefer to

---

17. Schmitt, *Elisa*, 27 n. 56.
18. DeVries, *Prophet against Prophet*, 122.
19. DeVries, *Prophet against Prophet*, 122.
20. Hentschel, *Die Elijaerzählungen*, 150.
21. Hentschel, *Die Elijaerzählungen*, 155.
22. Hentschel, *Die Elijaerzählungen*, 155.
23. Jepsen, *Nabi*; Miller, "The Fall of the House of Ahab"; Steck, *Überlieferung und Zeitgeschichte*; Schmitt, *Elisa*; DeVries, *Prophet against Prophet*.
24. Šanda, *Das zweite Buch der Könige*; Jepsen, *Nabi*; Montgomery and Gehman, *A Critical and Exegetical Commentary*; Schmitt, *Elisa*; Miller, "The Fall of the House of Ahab."
25. Benzinger, *Die Bücher der Könige*; Jepsen, *Nabi*; DeVries, *Prophet against Prophet*; Schmitt, *Elisa*; Hentschel, *Die Elijaerzählungen*.

see both stories as coming from the same period of time but from different literary traditions and authors.[26] The problem with the positions taken by the above-mentioned scholars is that they appear to have fallen victim to an overly strong influence of "historicity." It is probably true, as many have also argued, that there is an "historical account" at the basis of the text of 2 Kgs 9–10. However, as I and some others have argued, this "historical account" does not comprise the entirety of the two chapters. These texts have been heavily redacted and reworked and one must exercise a great deal of caution when interpreting them. I take the position that the "historical account," to the extent that it can be discerned, is comprised of the following verses: 2 Kgs 9:14–15aα, 15b–21bα, 23–24; 10:1–9, 11–17a, 32–33. The text found in 2 Kgs 9:21bγ, 25–26, the Jehu-Apologetic Redaction, does *not* belong to this account, but is a secondary insertion from the hand of an apologist writing some time during the Jehu dynasty. The oracle in v. 26a is most likely a fragment of an old oracle (a "Naboth Fragment") which, though not exactly the same as the Elijah–Naboth Fragment in detail, does give substantiation to that fragment.[27] The oracle in v. 26a was secondarily inserted into the Jehu coup account as part of the Jehu-Apologetic Redaction and was connected to 1 Kgs 21:17–19aβ, 20a–bα by means of the insertion of the oracle of transfer found in 1 Kgs 21:27–29. I conclude, therefore, that 2 Kgs 9:21bγ, 25–26 are neither original to the account of Jehu's coup d'etat in 2 Kgs 9–10, nor are they "historical" in the sense of the so-called "historical account" of that coup.

### 3. *The Deuteronomistic Composition of 1 Kings 21:17–29 and its Relationship with the Jehu-Apologetic Redaction in 2 Kings 9:21bγ, 25–26*

In the received text of 1–2 Kings, there is definitely some relationship between the Dtr texts of 1 Kgs 21:17–29,[28] and the Jehu-Apologetic Redaction in 2 Kgs 9:21bγ, 25–26. This relationship is secondary in nature. It was constructed by the Dtr Historian using the "prophecy–fulfillment" pattern, and as a part of the thorough editing of the received texts and traditions in the preparation of his comprehensive history. Second Kings 9:21bγ, 25–26 were used by the historian despite the fact that the author was well aware that the details of the oracle in 2 Kgs 9:26 did not match perfectly those of the Elijah–Naboth Fragment. The fact that the two traditions were related with regard to the righteous Israelite, Naboth, and also with regard to the evil and unrighteous king, Ahab, allowed the historian to use them both and to "create" an artificial relationship between them by means of the insertion of 1 Kgs 21:27–29.

---

26. See Benzinger, *Die Bücher der Könige*; Steck, *Überlieferung und Zeitgeschichte*; Hentschel, *Die Elijaerzählungen*, and contrary to Montgomery and Gehman, *A Critical and Exegetical Commentary*, who see them as being from a common literary tradition.

27. See the discussion in Chapter 2.

28. These texts include: the old Elijah–Naboth Fragment in 1 Kgs 21:17–19aβ, 20aα–bα; the Dtr accusations and curses of Ahab and his dynasty in vv. 20b–22, 24–26; and, the verses transferring the personal punishment of Ahab to his son's time in vv. 27–29.

The historian's particular dislike and disapproval of Ahab was the motivation for the creation of his account. Building upon his antipathy toward the Northern Kingdom and his negative opinion of all the northern kings, he saw in Ahab the one whom he could epitomize as the "worst of the worst." Ahab did evil in the eyes of the Lord more than all those kings who came before him. He not only "followed in all the sins of Jeroboam" and lead Israel into sin, but above all of this, he married a pagan wife and priestess of Baal, Jezebel, the daughter Ethbaal, king of the Sidonians. He then went over to the worship of Baal. Ahab did more to anger the Lord than did any of the kings of Israel before him (1 Kgs 16:29–33).

The question arose for the historian as to how to conjoin the old Naboth fragments that were clearly critical of Ahab for the unjust murder of Naboth, with his own list of accusations and condemnations of Ahab which arose out of his other sources, namely, the stories from the Elijah Cycle found in 1 Kgs 17–19. The solution he arrived at was to borrow a narrative framework from another of his stories which was also critical of a king for the unjust theft of "property" that belonged to another man and which also involved the unjust murder of the owner of that "property." This story was none other that that of David and Bathsheba (2 Sam 11:2–12:15). Borrowing the narrative framework from this story, the Dtr Historian was able to begin to create his text of 1 Kgs 21:17–29.

With the creation of the secondary relationship between the Elijah–Naboth Fragment and the Jehu-Apologetic Redaction's Naboth Fragment (9:26), the Dtr Historian needed to create or borrow a narrative framework for his account that would weave them together into a seemingly unified account. He borrowed this framework from the story of David and Bathsheba (2 Sam 11:2–12:15). In this narrative framework, I believe he found the perfect structure within which to insert his accusations and condemnations of Ahab and his dynasty. On initial consideration, one might react and say that these two stories have nothing to do with each other, and in terms of the events recounted and the personalities involved, this would be correct. However, I suggest that the Dtr Historian was looking for *a narrative framework only*, and that he borrowed this alone from the story of David and Bathsheba. This becomes visible only when we do a side-by-side comparison of the texts of the two accounts.

As indicated in the following chart (next page), several elements of this framework are already *implicitly* present in the Elijah–Naboth Fragment. These include the facts that the king wanted the property of Naboth, that he killed Naboth (or had him killed) in order to obtain this property, and that he finally did take possession of the deceased man's property. The fragment is not in and of itself a complete narrative; rather, it appears to be merely the ending of a story that is no longer extant. This fragment was then expanded by the Dtr "commentary" or "explication" found in the accusations and condemnations in vv. 20b–22, 24–26. Finally, the Dtr connected this event concerning Naboth's death with the other independent account in 2 Kgs 9:25–26 by adding 1 Kgs 21:27–29 to transfer the punishment for the crime to Ahab's son's day. We can see, therefore, that nearly the entire narrative frame of the David and Bathsheba story is found either implicitly or explicitly in the text of 1 Kgs 21:17–29.

Table 5. *The Narrative Framework of 2 Samuel 11:2–12:15 and 1 Kings 21:17–29*

| Line | The Narrative Frame | 2 Samuel 11:2–12:5 | 1 Kings 21:17–29 |
|---|---|---|---|
| | | DAVID | AHAB |
| 1 | The Object of Desire is Stated | 11:2–4a: Bathsheba | |
| 2 | A First Complication Occurs | 11:5: Bathsheba is pregnant to David but married to Uriah | |
| 3 | A Second Complication Occurs | 11:6–13: Uriah refuses to go home and sleep with his wife | |
| 4 | The Communication of a Plan for Resolving the Complications | 11:14–15: David writes to Joab and communicates his plan for having Uriah killed | These elements are *implicit* in the Elijah–Naboth Fragment (vv. 17–19a, 20a–bα) |
| 5 | The Resolution of the Complications | 11:16–17: the plan is enacted and Uriah is killed | |
| 6 | The Communication of Fulfillment of the Action | 11:18–25: Joab sends a messenger to David with the news of Uriah's death | |
| 7 | The Taking Possession of the Desired Object | 11:26–27: When Bathsheba hears of Uriah's death she mourns and David takes her as his wife | |
| 8 | The Lord's Displeasure and Notification of the Lord's Sending of a Prophet | 11:24e–12:1: YHWH is displeased and sends Nathan to David | 21:17–18: YHWH calls and sends Elijah to Ahab |
| 9 | A First Accusation | 12:1b–6: The parable of the stolen ewe—David's self-accusation | 21:19aβ: the accusation of a civil crime |
| 10 | A Second Accusation | 12:7–10: Nathan accuses David in YHWH's name | 21:20b: the accusation of a cultic crime |
| 11 | The Condemnation | 12:10–12: The sword will never depart . . . I will bring evil upon you. . . | 21:20b–24: I will bring evil upon you; I will utterly sweep you away, and will cut off from Ahab every male, bond or free, in Israel . . . |
| 12 | An Evaluative Judgment | * * * * * * * * * * * | 21:25–26: There was none who sold himself to do what was evil in the sight of the LORD like Ahab, whom Jezebel his wife incited.[26] He did very abominably in going after idols, as the Amorites had done, whom the LORD cast out before the people of Israel.) |
| 13 | The Repentance of the Guilty Person | 12:13a: David admits his sin | 21:27: Ahab repents and puts on sackcloth, etc. |
| 14 | The Transference of the Punishment to Offspring | 12:13b–23: And Nathan said to David, "The LORD also has put away your sin; you shall not die.[14] Nevertheless, because by this deed you have utterly scorned the LORD, the child that is born to you shall die." | 21:28–29: Because he has humbled himself before me, I will not bring the evil in his days; but in his son's days I will bring the evil upon his house. |

As the above chart shows, the elements of the framework found in 1 Kgs 21:17–29 and in 2 Sam 11–12 match perfectly. In both accounts it is *the king* who is confronted by a prophet, it is *the king* who is accused and condemned for murder and taking possession of property, and it is *the king* who repents and as a result the punishment is transferred to another. From this perspective, the frame has no need for 1 Kgs 21:1–16, and it has no need for Jezebel. In fact, Jezebel's presence actually "breaks" or "complicates" the frame when the frame is secondarily expanded to include vv. 1–16.[29] This highlights the fact that there is a major "break" between the story of the vineyard in 1 Kgs 21:1–16 and the Dtr story of the accusations and condemnations of Ahab in vv. 17–29. It is to a detailed discussion of 1 Kgs 21:1–16 that we must now turn our attention.

---

29. See the further development of this discussion in Chapter 16, pp. 190–93.

Part III

THE STORY OF THE ACQUISITION OF NABOTH'S VINEYARD:
1 KINGS 21:1-16

# Chapter 8

## GENERAL INTRODUCTION, APPROACH, AND NARRATIVE OUTLINE

When we turn our attention to "the Story of the Acquisition of Naboth's Vineyard" we find that there are several difficulties with assigning its verses to a specific source. First, we find in these verses no typical Dtr terminology, so it is questionable whether they would have come from the hand of a Dtr. Second, this story is presented as a parable. It begins with the phrase, . . . כֶּרֶם הָיָה לְ, which in every case where it is used (see Isa 5:1; Cant. 8:11) introduces a parable-type story which is meant to be interpreted neither literally nor historically. Third, there are other elements in these verses which highlight the "unbelievable" or the "incredible" aspects of the events and which should warn everyone against a literal or historical interpretation. These elements include:

1. a king being presented as so feeble and impotent in the face of the rejection of a request to a commoner
2. that he would go to his bed and refuse to eat, acting like a spoiled child over his inability to get a vineyard;
3. that his wife would be presented as the one who truly rules, who takes things into her own hands and has the power and authority to use the kings seals, to design the plan, and to command the elders and nobles of a free Israelite city to comply with what is obviously a crime of murder;
4. that the plan would be written in letters and sent to the elders and nobles;
5. that upon the completion of the crime, the wife would command the king to go and take possession of the dead man's vineyard;
6. finally, that after all of this, the wife would never be "charged" or "convicted" for this gross and criminal misuse of royal power and authority.

All of these things should caution, even the uninformed reader, that there is something more profound and subtle going on in this story.

Nearly all commentators recognize the presence of a break or a roughness in the text between v. 16 and v. 17. The Elijah–Naboth Fragment in vv. 17–19a, 20a–20bα, though showing no sign of Dtr authorship, is apparently old and may be presumed to have been either already in place prior to the Dtr, or to have been part of an old oral tradition which was inserted by the Dtr Historian when he compiled this part of his history concerning Ahab. Most scholars also maintain that vv. 20b–22, 24–26 show evident Dtr traits and are therefore easily assumed to have come from that "school" of redaction. Most also recognize the clear absence of any trace of these same Dtr traits in vv. 1–16. The conclusion drawn, therefore, is that the two halves of 1 Kgs 21 do not originate from the same author(s). So, from where do vv. 1–16 come?

I will begin our discussion of 1 Kgs 21:1–16 with what I call "a linear 'expository reading'" of the text.[1] By this I mean, first, that I will read the text in "chronological" sense from v. 1 to v. 16. I will attempt *not* to presume a fore-knowledge of the story or its outcome; I will read it as if doing so for the first time. Second, I will analyze each scene by first defining which are the "active voices"[2] and where the action is situated. I will also discuss the interrelationship that exists between the scene being studied and those which preceded it. Third, I will attempt to address any significant questions that might arise from the text of the scene. Thus, I will discuss such issues as textual difficulties, logical diffi-culties, prophecy/fulfillment, and differences between various elements in the text itself or between its various scenes. Throughout all of this, I will weave in a *status questionis* by engaging with and presenting the opinions of a wide range of scholars concerning the various questions and difficulties of the text.

Such a reading presents a limitation to this approach, namely, that I will be performing a synchronic reading of the text. This approach is based upon the following premises. First, that the text of 1 Kgs 21, as *a whole and complete unit*, makes sense as it is found in the MT. Second, that there is an internal logic to the text. (These first two premises are not meant to imply that the text is without difficulties.) Third, that in its present form, the text evinces an author who knows how to keep the reader/listener involved in the story by means of manipulating the narrative tension of the story.

The reasons for this type of reading and analysis of each scene of the narrative are threefold. First, it is to gain a familiarity with the text. Second, it is to dis-cover the narrative and textual difficulties of the story and the proposed solutions to these on the part of scholars and commentators. Third, it is to gather informa-tion that will help us to make decisions concerning the history of the compilation of the received text of 1 Kgs 21.

A survey of a selection of scholars concerning their opinions and delimitations of the narrative outline of the Naboth story is already revealing. These scholars generally fall into two main categories. The first are those who see a narrative outline *for the whole of the chapter*.[3] (See Table 6, opposite.) The second cate-gory is comprised of those who consider *only the first part of the chapter* (vv. 1–16 or 1–20a) to be the oldest layer of the tradition and therefore use it as the limit for their narrative outlines.[4] (See Table 7, opposite.)

1. I borrow this term "expository reading" from Barré, *The Rhetoric of Political Persuasion*, 56.
2. By "active" I mean the ones responsible for saying that which is being *spoken or thought*, that is, the communicators. In some cases this will include the narrator.
3. Schlögl, *Die Bücher der Könige, Die Bücher der Chronik*, 172; Snaith, "The First and Second Book of Kings," 172–78; de Vaux, "Le Cycle d'Élie"; B. O. Long, *I Kings, with an Introduction to Historical Literature* (FOTL 9; Grand Rapids: Eerdmans, 1984), 223; J. T. Walsh, "Methods and Meanings: Multiple Studies of I Kings 21," *JBL* 111, no. 2 (1992): 193–211, and *I Kings*, 316–41.
4. Gressmann, *Die älteste Geschichtsschreibung*, 271–73; Welten, "Naboth's Weinberg," 18–32; Würthwein, "Naboth-Novelle und Elia-Wort," 375–97 (see also his more recent work where he maintains the same outline: *Die Bücher der Könige 1. Kön. 17–2 Kön. 25*, 248–51); Zakovitch, "The Tale of Naboth's Vineyard"; Rofé, "The Vineyard of Naboth," 89–104; T. Schaack, *Die Ungeduld des Papiers: Studien zum alttestamentlichen Verständnis des Schreibens anhand des Verbums katab im Kontext administrativer Vorgänge* (BZAW 262; Berlin: de Gruyter, 1998), 51–52.

Table 6. *A Survey of Scholarly Opinion on the Narrative Outline of 1 Kings 21:*
*A. Includes the Whole of the Chapter*

| N. Schlögl (1911) | N. H. Snaith (1954) |
|---|---|
| Part 1: Naboth's Vineyard, vv. 1–4 | Part 1: Naboth's Refusal, vv. 1–4 |
| Part 2: Jezebel's lets Naboth be stoned, vv. 5–12 | Part 2: Jezebel's Plot, vv. 5–12 |
| Part 3: Oracles against Ahab and Jezebel, vv. 15–26 | Part 3: Naboth's Death, vv. 13–16 |
| Part 4 : Ahab's repentance, vv. 27–29 | Part 4 : Elijah's Intervention, vv. 17–29 |
| **R. de Vaux (1956)** | **B. O. Long (1984)** |
| Part 1: Naboth refuses to part with his Vineyard, vv. 1–3 | Part 1: The Narrative Situation, v. 1 |
| Part 2: Ahab and Jezebel, vv. 4–7 | Part 2: The Complication, vv. 2–7 |
| Part 3: The Murder of Naboth, vv. 8–16 | Part 3: The Resolution /New Complication, vv. 8–16 |
| Part 4: The Rage of Elijah, vv. 17–26 | Part 4: The Climax, vv. 17–26 |
| Part 5: The Repentance of Ahab, vv. 27–29 | Part 5: The Aftermath, vv. 27–29 |
| *J. T. Walsh (1992 and 1996)* | |
| Part I: | Part II: |
| Scene 1: Ahab and Naboth, vv. 1–4a | Scene 1: YHWH and Elijah, vv. 17–19 |
| Scene 2: Ahab and Jezebel, vv. 4b–7 | Scene 2: Ahab and Elijah, vv. 20–22 |
| Scene 3: Jezebel's letter, vv. 8–10 | Scene 3: Narrative Aside 1, vv. 23–24 |
| Scene 4: The Trial and Execution, vv. 11–14 | Scene 4: Narrative Aside 2, vv. 25–26 |
| Scene 5: Jezebel and Ahab, v. 15 | Scene 5: Ahab, v. 27 |
| Scene 6: Ahab in the Vineyard, v. 16 | Scene 6: YHWH and Elijah, vv. 28–29 |

Table 7. *A Survey of Scholarly Opinion on the Narrative Outline of 1 Kings 21:*
*B. Includes only a Part of the Chapter*

| H. Gressmann (1921) | P. Welten (1973) |
|---|---|
| Introduction, Ahab and Naboth, vv. 1–4 | Scene 1: Ahab and Naboth, vv. 1–4 |
| Scene I: Ahab and Jezebel, vv. 5–7 | Scene 2: Ahab and Jezebel, vv. 5–9 |
| Scene II: in Jezreel, vv. 8–14 | Scene 3: Naboth and Jezebel, vv. 11–16 |
| Scene III: in the vineyard, vv. 15–20 | Scene 4: Elijah and Ahab, vv. 17–20a |
| **E. Würthwein (1978/1984)** | **Y. Zakovitch (1984)** |
| | Exposition, v. 1 |
| Scene 1: Ahab and Naboth, vv. 1aβ–4 | Scene 1: Ahab and Naboth, vv. 2–3 |
| Scene 2: Ahab and Jezebel, vv. 5–7 | Scene 2: Ahab and Jezebel, vv. 4–10 |
| Scene 3: Jezebel's letter, vv. 8–13 | Scene 3: Naboth's trial & Execution, vv. 11–13 |
| Scene 4: Conclusion, vv. 14–16 | Scene 4: Ahab and Jezebel, vv. 14–16 |
| | Scene 5: Ahab and Elijah, vv. 17–19, 27–29 |
| **A. Rofé (1988)** | |
| Introduction, v. 1 | |
| Scene 1: Ahab and Naboth, vv. 2–4 | |
| Scene 2: Ahab and Jezebel, vv. 5–7 | |
| Scene 3: the Letter, vv. 8–10 | |
| Scene 4: Naboth's trial and execution, vv. 11–14 | |
| Scene 5: Ahab and Jezebel, vv. 15–16 | |
| Scene 6: Ahab and Elijah, vv. 17–20bα | |

Using the received text of 1 Kgs 21, it is indeed possible to perform a narrative analysis of the whole of the chapter. However, as I have already argued, this is tenuous at best because of the clear and obvious break between vv. 16 and 17 and because of the long and complex history to the compilation of this chapter. My analysis of the narrative of 1 Kgs 21:1–16 results in the following structural outline. I have divided the narrative into "Acts" based upon "themes" and have subdivided these (where appropriate) based upon changes in the active characters on the "stage" of action.

Table 8. *The Narrative Outline of the Story of the Acquisition of Naboth's Vineyard, 1 Kings 21:1–16*

|  | General narrative introduction for the whole of the chapter | v. 1a |
|---|---|---|
| *Act I:* | *Ahab's Offer to Buy or Trade for Naboth's Vineyard and its Rejection* | *vv. 1b–4* |
| Scene 1: | Ahab and Naboth discuss the offer | vv. 1b–4 |
| *Act II:* | *The Acquisition of the Vineyard of Naboth* | *vv. 5–16* |
| Scene 1: | Jezebel and Ahab discuss the offer made to Naboth | vv. 5–7 |
| Scene 2: | Jezebel writes to the Elders and Nobles of Jezreel | vv. 8–10 |
| Scene 3: | The Elders and Nobles of Jezreel fulfill Jezebel's orders | vv. 11–14 |
| Scene 4: | Jezebel commands Ahab to take possession of the vineyard | vv. 15–16 |

# Chapter 9

## AN EXPOSITORY READING OF ACT I: SCENE 1—1 KINGS 21:1B–4: AHAB'S OFFER TO BUY OR TRADE FOR NABOTH'S VINEYARD AND ITS REJECTION

In this scene the "actors" include Naboth the Jezreelite (v. 3b), Ahab the king of Samaria (v. 2aβ–b), and the Narrator (vv. 1–2aα, 3a, 4). The "what" or the "focus" of the scene is Ahab's offer to Naboth the Jezreelite to trade or to buy his vineyard. Naboth, invoking an oath, refuses to sell or trade his ancestral inheritance. It is here that the first "difference in point of view" occurs. As far as Ahab is concerned, the property he is interested in obtaining is merely a "vineyard." For Naboth, however, it is much more significant; it is his ancestral inheritance, which he has a duty to maintain and then pass on to his own children.[1] This difference in point of view concerning the vineyard serves as the catalyst for the entire story.

Another difficulty arises when we consider the temporal indicators found in our scene. The first of these is found at the beginning of v. 1: וַיְהִי אַחַר הַדְּבָרִים הָאֵלֶּה. This is a type of "generic" temporal indicator that is used simply to link what follows with that which precedes it. I refer to it as "generic" because its purpose is not to express a specific time, per se, but rather to denote a sequentiality of events. In the Old Testament this particular introduction is rarely used.[2] In the context of our text the only thing that we can conclude concerning this phrase is that it indicates that the following story concerning Naboth was preceded by certain other events. Whether or not those events are the events narrated in ch. 20 is questionable.

A second temporal indicator can be found in the phrase . . . כֶּרֶם הָיָה לְ. Though not usually considered a temporal indicator, the phrase acts in this case as an indicator of an indefinite period of time in the past. It fulfills the same function as do the phrases "Once upon a time . . ." or "There once was . . ." in English

---

1. See the regulations and customs concerning ancestral inheritance in Num 25 (esp. vv. 7–8); 27:1–11; 36:1–12.

2. The phrase וַיְהִי אַחַר הַדְּבָרִים הָאֵלֶּה occurs a total of thirteen times in three variations: (a) in Gen 22:1; 39:7; 1 Kgs 17:17; 21:1, we have the exact form found in 1 Kgs 21.1—וַיְהִי אַחַר הַדְּבָרִים הָאֵלֶּה; (b) in Gen 15:1; Esth 2:1; 3:1; Ezra 7:1, we have the form אַחַר הַדְּבָרִים הָאֵלֶּה—the same phrase as in 1 Kgs 21.1 but minus the temporal indicator וַיְהִי; (c) in Gen 22:20; 48:1; Josh 24:29 we have the form used in 1 Kgs 21.1 but with a change of preposition—וַיְהִי אַחֲרֵי הַדְּבָרִים הָאֵלֶּה. In 1 Kgs 21.1 the phrase appears to be used for the sole purpose of making a connection between the end of the previous chapter and the subsequent story.

fables. These phrases are used to introduce stories that, though they might be based upon some element of historical truth, have become "parabolic" in the sense that they have free license to cross the boundaries between fact and fiction for the purpose of enhancing the story and communicating their message.

The temporal aspect of . . . כֶּרֶם הָיָה לְ is based upon the particular form of the noun כֶּרֶם. This term (and in fact the phrase as a whole) only functions in a temporal sense when the noun is precisely "indefinite" and when it is used to introduce a narrative about an incident which is deliberately being placed in the realm of the indefinite past. As such it is found only three times in the MT: 1 Kgs 21:1; Isa 5:1;[3] and Cant 8:11.[4] All three of these occurrences introduce stories about vineyards that occurred "once upon a time." In stories introduced in this manner, all other temporal indicators, no matter how precise they may otherwise appear to be,[5] must be understood within the "indefiniteness" of the entire story. In this sense all the events and personalities mentioned in the story take on the aspect of indefiniteness; they become, in a sense, "universalized" or "symbolic."

The final phrase which gives an indication as to when these events *might* have taken place is the specific reference to אַחְאָב מֶלֶךְ שֹׁמְרוֹן. This term gives us an historical referent to a period of time when Ahab was ruling in Samaria. However, this referent is not exactly precise, nor is it without difficulty. First of all, the indefiniteness or the "timeless" character of the overall story should caution us against "believing" or accepting as "literal" any specific temporal reference which is found in the context of the story. However, like any good story, this one is probably based upon some historical incident involving an unjust murder and taking of property, which was at a later time reformulated into a universally applicable didactic parable. A more probable possibility would be that the story was written long after Ahab's time and was then "retrojected" to the period when Ahab reigned in Israel. If this story does refer to the historical period when Ahab ruled, with Samaria as his capital, then it would be possible to date it to approximately 870–851 B.C.E. However, at that time his kingdom was apparently known only as the "Kingdom of Israel." The terms "king of Samaria" or "kingdom of Samaria" only came into use with reference to a geographic/political entity after 722 B.C.E. and the annexation of the conquered kingdom of Israel by Assyria.[6] The most probable explanation for this reference to Ahab as מֶלֶךְ שֹׁמְרוֹן is that it is an anachronism on the part of the author of the story. The intention of the author of the text as it now stands in the MT appears to be to make the reader understand that the story took place when Ahab was king, regardless of whether his kingdom was known as Israel or Samaria.

The location of this scene also presents a problem. Where does the action of the scene take place? We find several indications of location in this scene. The first of these indicators is in v. 1: אֲשֶׁר בְּיִזְרְעֶאל. This relative clause situates

---

3.   Like our verse, Isa 5:1 is preceded by an introductory phrase.
4.   A similar temporal usage, but using different terms, is found in Job 1:1, which is introduced by the phrase אִישׁ הָיָה בְאֶרֶץ־עוּץ.
5.   For example, the specific mention of "Ahab the king of Samaria."
6.   See Rofé, "The Vineyard of Naboth," 97.

something "in Jezreel." The Hebrew wording is not precise and could be a reference to either the Valley of Jezreel[7] or to the town of Jezreel itself. This location was the place of origin of a certain נָבוֹת הַיִּזְרְעֵאלִי.[8]

Yet another problem exists with this relative clause, namely, what is its specific referent? In its present location in the sentence it would appear to refer to its immediately preceding phrase נָבוֹת הַיִּזְרְעֵאלִי. In this case, its purpose would be to modify Naboth the Jezreelite. If this is so, however, it would appear to cause a redundancy. We have already been informed that Naboth is from Jezreel by the use of the gentilic adjective הַיִּזְרְעֵאלִי. To maintain that the relative clause אֲשֶׁר בְּיִזְרְעֶאל refers to Naboth would cause either the gentilic adjective or the relative clause to be redundant. The most common solution to this problem is to see the relative clause as modifying, not Naboth, but the vineyard. In this case the relative clause would situate the vineyard owned by Naboth in Jezreel. This interpretation would seem to be further supported by the following locale indicator which also appears to refer to the vineyard: קָרוֹב אֵצֶל הֵיכַל אַחְאָב מֶלֶךְ שֹׁמְרוֹן.[9]

Though technically it is possible to say that the phrase קָרוֹב אֵצֶל הֵיכַל אַחְאָב מֶלֶךְ שֹׁמְרוֹן is a reference to Naboth, according to the inner logic of the text it would make more sense as a reference to the vineyard. If this is the case, then the first verse would be constructed in the following manner:

1. a declarative statement—"There once was a vineyard";
2. three descriptive statements modifying the declarative statement:
   a. "belonging to Naboth the Jezreelite" (ownership),
   b. "which was in Jezreel" (general location of the vineyard),
   c. "near the palace of Ahab the king of Samaria" (the specific location of the vineyard).

If the above interpretation of the verse is correct, then it would appear that the author was very concerned with emphasizing the location of the vineyard in Jezreel. However, the last phrase of the sentence raises a difficulty that throws the above interpretation into question. This final "specific locator," קָרוֹב אֵצֶל הֵיכַל אַחְאָב מֶלֶךְ שֹׁמְרוֹן, highlights a further difficulty in our text. The reference to "Ahab the king of Samaria" is a very rare term[10] which in the present context raises two questions and difficulties: (1) What is the "king of Samaria" doing with "a palace" in Jezreel? And, (2) is the location of the "palace of Ahab the king of Samaria" (and therefore the events of this story) in Jezreel or in Samaria? At this stage in the story we do not have the information with which to answer these questions.

---

7. This forms the southeastern part of the large plain that separated the region of Samaria from Galilee.

8. In the phrase לְנָבוֹת הַיִּזְרְעֵאלִי, Naboth is "defined" by his place of origin.

9. Regarding אֵצֶל הֵיכַל, this is the first time in the present order of the MT that הֵיכַל is *not* used with reference to a temple, but rather with the meaning of "palace." Throughout the rest of ch. 21, הֵיכַל is never again used; rather, the kings residence is referred to as his "house" (בֵּיתוֹ).

10. The title מֶלֶךְ שֹׁמְרוֹן occurs only in 1 Kgs 21:1 and 2 Kgs 1:3. Note that in 1 Kgs 21:18 Ahab is referred to as מֶלֶךְ־יִשְׂרָאֵל, a much more common title.

The fact is that a couple of features in the text of v. 1 raise the possibility that the events may not have occurred in Jezreel, but rather in Samaria. Key among these is the reference in v. 1 (already mentioned) to Ahab as מֶלֶךְ שֹׁמְרוֹן. A second is the gentilic designator for Naboth: הַיִּזְרְעֵאלִי. The difficulty here is the fact that the use of gentilic modifiers would be senseless if the person to whom they are applied was, in fact, living in their town of origin where the same gentilic would apply to everyone native to that town. The use of this type of modifier makes logical sense only when the person to whom it is applied is *not* living in their town of origin.[11] If this is the case in our verse then we would have to conclude that the vineyard was located in Jezreel, Naboth's town of origin, but that Naboth himself was living or visiting elsewhere whereby the gentilic modifier would be applicable. The text, on the one hand, appears insistent that the affair took place in Jezreel, while, on the other hand, certain forms and references appear to contradict this insistence and to raise the possibility that the location was in Samaria. The type of confusion evident in our text could result from a confusion of the facts by the author, from the combination of various and different traditions, or from different editorial redactions. The simple fact remains that the text of v. 1 in the MT is unclear. This is not, however, the case in the text of the LXX, which situates everything in Samaria.

The next locale indicator is found in v. 2, in the phrase כִּי הוּא קָרוֹב אֵצֶל בֵּיתִי. This is again a reference to the location of the vineyard of Naboth. This time it is Ahab himself who is speaking. The הֵיכַל[12] of v. 1 (which was from the

11. With Šanda, *Das erste Buch der Könige*, 465.
12. It is possible that the use of the term הֵיכַל, in this case, could be construed as a late usage. This is, in fact, the first time in the canonical arrangement of the Bible that the term is used in the common sense of "palace" instead of it's usual meaning of "temple." According to BDB, 228, it is used "rather seldom as 'palace.'" With the exception of 1 Kgs 21:1, it is found with the meaning of "palace" only in late texts (exilic and post-exilic). These late texts include 2 Kgs 20:18, which Montgomery and Gehman (*A Critical and Exegetical Commentary*, 510) say cannot be dated much later than 597 and which Gray (*I & II Kings*, 702) sees as possibly a trace of Isaiah of Jerusalem in the Exile after 597. (Note that 2 Kgs 20:18 is also found in Isa 39:7, a text which is considered to be part of a late insertion into Isa 1–39 by O. Kaiser, *Isaiah 13–39* [trans. R. A. Wilson; OTL; Philadelphia: Westminster, 1974], 408–10; R. E. Clements, *Isaiah 1–39* [The New Century Bible Commentary; Grand Rapids: Eerdmans, 1980], 293 [who places it post-598]; J. D. W. Watts, *Isaiah 34–66* [WBC 25; Waco, Tex.: Word Books, 1987], 66–67 [who places it post-605 B.C.E.]; S. H. Widyapranawa, *The Lord is Savior: Faith in National Crisis: Isaiah 1–39* [ITC; Grand Rapids: Eerdmans, 1990], 260 [who says, "chapter 39 gives the impression of being a prophecy from an exilic or post-exilic date"].) Other late texts containing reference to הֵיכַל are 2 Chr 36:7; Dan 1:4. In the plural the term is found in Isa 13:22, a text considered late by J. Skinner (*The Book of the Prophet Isaiah I–XXXIX* [Cambridge: Cambridge University Press, 1930], 112–13 [who places it "in the closing years of the Babylonian Exile"]), Clements (*Isaiah 1–39*, 137 [who places it in the period "immediately preceding the fall of Babylon to the Persians and the Medes in 538]), Widyapranawa (*The Lord is Savior*, 82 [who places it between the death of Nebuchadnezzar in 561 and the defeat of Babylon in 539]), J. Barton (*Isaiah 1–39* [Old Testament Guides; Sheffield: Sheffield Academic Press, 1995], 85). Plural forms of הֵיכַל are also found in Nah 2:7; Ps 45:9, 16—the latter text being considered late by R. J. Tournay ("Les Affinités du Ps. XLV avec le Cantique des Cantiques et leur Interprétation Messianique," in *Congress Volume: Bonn, 1962* [VTSup 9: Leiden: Brill, 1963], 168–212 [212]), who places it in Jerusalem in the last decade of the Persian occupation, and E. L. Hossfeld

mouth of the narrator) is here referred to in Ahab's own words as בֵּיתִי ("my house"). As a matter of fact, never again in our chapter is the palace referred to explicitly as הֵיכָל but only as בֵּיתִי. That בֵּיתִי is a reference to the הֵיכָל is clear from the context. The fact that the term used for Ahab's residence by the narrator differs from that used by Ahab might be an indication that the two usages come from different sources. But at this stage in our analysis it is too early to make a definitive decision on this issue. Naboth's vineyard is located somewhere קְרוֹב אֵצֶל ("close by")[13] Ahab's בֵּיתִי/הֵיכָל. Ahab desires this vineyard for a גַּן יָרָק ("green/vegetable garden").[14]

Another locale indicator is found in the phrase וַיָּבֹא אַחְאָב אֶל־בֵּיתוֹ ("and Ahab went to his house") (v. 4a). Here again the problem is one of indefiniteness. Based upon the information given thus far in the narrative, this reference would have to be to the same place as the בֵּיתִי in v. 2 and the הֵיכָל of v. 1. A final indication of place or location is found near the end of v. 4: וַיִּשְׁכַּב עַל־מִטָּתוֹ ("and he lay upon his bed"). With this phrase we are informed of the physical location of Ahab at the end of this scene; he is lying upon his bed. The question of precisely where the encounter between Ahab and Naboth took place is an element of the scene that is not clear. The text, as we have it, gives us no indication at all as to the precise location of this conversation. It tells us where the vineyard was located, where Naboth was originally from, where Ahab had a palace, and that the vineyard of Naboth was near Ahab's house, but it gives no clue whatsoever as to where the conversation between the two men took place. We cannot say, based upon the text itself, that the conversation took place in the vineyard, in the palace of Ahab, in Naboth's house nor in any other location in the town or valley of Jezreel. All we are told is that the two men had a "conversation." There is no further precision as to the location of this conversation. This "silence" on the part of the narrator is significant in light of the fact that throughout the first two verses his purpose and goal is to "set the stage" for the reader/hearer. He gives all the pertinent information for the general location (Jezreel), the actors (Naboth and Ahab), and the central object of focus (the vineyard). If it were significant for the narrator to place this conversation in a specific location, and given his propensity

and E. Zenger (*Die Psalmen, I: Psalm 1–50* [Die Neue Echter Bibel 29; Würzburg: Echter Verlag, 1993], 279) who maintain that there was a pre-exilic basis to the psalm which in the exilic period was expanded and in the post-exilic period was inserted between Pss 44 and 46 as an interpretive key for those psalms. Psalm 144:12 is considered late by some scholars, including A. A. Anderson (*The Book of Psalms*, vol. 2, *Psalms 73–150* [London: Oliphants, 1972 (2d ed. 1977)], 931), who maintains that the psalm probably came from "the Judean community of the Persian period," and L. C. Allen (*Psalms 101–150* [WBC 21; Waco, Tex.: Word Books, 1993], 290), who, based upon the language of the psalm, places it in the post-exilic period. See also Hos 8:14; Amos 8:3; Job 4:5; Prov 30:28.

13. The phrase קְרוֹב אֵצֶל is a *hapax legomenon* in the MT. According to Rofé, "The Vineyard of Naboth," 98, this particular usage is of late origin.

14. A combination of otherwise attested terms, לְגַן־יָרָק represents a *hapax legomenon* in the MT. The term גַּן appears a total of forty-two times and יָרָק occurs a total of fourteen times, but in no other place are the two found together. Nelson (*First and Second Kings*, 141) maintains that this term appears to be "an ironic reference to Deut 11:10 which contrasts the land of promise to the "vegetable garden of Egypt" (כְּגַן הַיָּרָק). Nelson (p. 141) also considers רֵשׁ in v. 15 to be a Dtr code-word for the conquest (see Deut 12:12; 14:27).

for detail, then surely he would have mentioned exactly where the conversation took place.

A consultation of scholarship spanning nearly a century and a half reveals that the location of the conversation was, until recently, a non-issue. Of the scholars consulted, only three (recent) writers have made an issue of situating this conversation specifically *within* Naboth's vineyard. Y. Zakovitch says, when discussing his "Scene I, Ahab's Proposal" (vv. 2–3), that, "The exchange takes place outside Ahab's palace (to which the king returns in v. 4), *apparently in Naboth's vineyard.*"[15] This detail, which here appears to be somewhat tentative, later becomes one of the key elements in Zakovitch's presentation of the "symmetrical structure of the story's five scenes" (which he presented as a chiasm).[16] Another scholar who considers the location of the discussion between Ahab and Naboth to have been in the vineyard itself is A. Rofé. In discussing his first scene, Rofé makes reference to "the dialogue between Ahab and Naboth, [which took place] *presumably in the vineyard* (see v. 4 where Ahab comes back home)."[17] He makes no further comment on the issue. The third scholar who places the conversation in the vineyard proper is J. T. Walsh. He maintains that the chapter can be broken down into two perfectly balanced chiastic units with scenes that are distinguished mainly by means of changes in place and/or characters. In the first scene (vv. 1–4a) the setting is *"in Naboth's vineyard."*[18] Despite these interpretations, the fact remains that the text gives absolutely no indication of the location of this conversation.

The above examples highlight a potential difficulty. Especially with regard to Zakovitch and Walsh's positions, which involve the construction of "chiastic" analyses of the whole chapter, the problem is that if this conversation between Ahab and Naboth *cannot* be located in the actual vineyard, then their chiastic analysis falls apart. These two studies highlight the problem of the imposition of narrative structures which in all probability are not to be found in the text itself. This is often particularly true of chiasms.[19] It is specifically this problem which I find in the studies of Zakovitch and Walsh. In order for their chiastic structures to be perfectly balanced, they must place the conversation between Ahab and Naboth specifically *in the vineyard.* But there is no evidence in the text that this was the case. The best we can say is that the text does not say where this conversation took place.

---

15. Zakovitch, "The Tale of Naboth's Vineyard," 384 (emphasis added).
16. Zakovitch, "The Tale of Naboth's Vineyard," 397.
17. Rofé, "The Vineyard of Naboth," 90 (emphasis added).
18. Walsh, "Methods and Meanings," 194–95 (emphasis added).
19. This problem has been presented by, among others, J. Murphy-O'Connor, *Paul the Letter-Writer: His World, His Options, His Skills* (GNS 41; Collegeville: Liturgical Press, 1995). Though Murphy-O'Connor's study is directly concerned with the writings of St Paul, it has implications for the analysis of any text. According to Murphy-O'Connor, the concentric (chiastic) approach to the text offers "unlimited scope . . . for subjective eisegesis." After consulting both ancient and modern studies on Rhetoric, he continues: "The search for concentric structures covering a complete letter has little to recommend it. Such an arrangement has no basis in the rhetorical tradition. The approach necessarily involves generalizations which become progressively more subjective as they approach higher degrees of abstraction" (pp. 89–90).

# Chapter 10

## AN EXPOSITORY READING OF ACT II: SCENE 1—1 KINGS 21:5-7: JEZEBEL AND AHAB DISCUSS THE OFFER MADE TO NABOTH

### 1. *Analysis*

The "actors" in this scene are the narrator (vv. 5a, 6aα, 7a), Jezebel the wife[1] of Ahab (vv. 5b, 7b), and Ahab (v. 6aβ–b). Following upon the previous scene in which Ahab returns to his house in a sour mood and goes to his bed, refusing to eat, Jezebel appears on the stage and confronts Ahab. Ahab explains that he spoke to Naboth the Jezreelite concerning the vineyard but that his offer was rebuffed. Jezebel responds with what might be interpreted as a "sarcastic" question: אַתָּה עַתָּה תַּעֲשֶׂה מְלוּכָה עַל־יִשְׂרָאֵל ("You, are you now ruling over Israel?").[2] This question could be construed as a critique of Ahab's method of exercising his royal authority. It could also be interpreted simply as the concern of a wife for

1. Jezebel is referred to as אִשְׁתּוֹ ("his wife"). Nowhere in this chapter is Jezebel referred to as "queen."

2. Appearing in the initial position in the clause, אַתָּה can be interpreted as an emphatic (see *GK* §135a). With regard to the function of the clause, scholarly opinion is divided. The fact is that our statement can be interpreted both as a question (rhetorical or direct) and as a statement. Those who argue that it is a question usually base their position upon the opinions of H. G. Mitchell ("The Omission of the Interrogative Particle," in *Old Testament and Semitic Studies in Memory of W. R. Harper* [ed. Robert Francis Harper, Francis Brown and George Foot Moore; Chicago: University of Chicago Press, 1908], 113–29), and *GK* §150, 1. These scholars note that a question is not always introduced by an interrogative pronoun or adverb. Klostermann, *Die Bücher Samuelis und der Könige*, 382, rewrites the text to אִשׁ תָּם and then reads the text as follows: "You are a simple man! Do you want to make him (Naboth) king over Israel?" I see no grounds whatsoever for this rewriting. Some of the scholars who maintain that our phrase is a question include: Benzinger, *Die Bücher der Könige*, 114; Kittel, *Die Bücher der Könige*, 156; Burney, *Notes*, 7, 244; Gressmann, *Die älteste Geschichtsschreibung*, 270; Šanda, *Das erste Buch der Könige*, 459, 462; Snaith, "The First and Second Book of Kings," 72; Dhorme, *La Bible*, 1125; Gray, *I & II Kings*, 437; K. Baltzer, "Naboths Weinberg," *Wort und Dienst*, n.s., 8 (1965): 73–88 (77); Jones, *1–2 Kings* 2.354. Some of those who see our phrase as a statement include: Stade and Schwally, *The Book of Kings*, 270 (a translator's note on the issue); Schlögl, *Die Bücher der Könige, Die Bücher der Chronik*, 174; Eissfeldt, *Das erste Buch der Könige*, 539; Montgomery and Gehman, *A Critical and Exegetical Commentary*, 331; Fohrer, *Elia*, 23; F. I. Anderson, "The Socio-Juridical Background," 46–46; Seebass, "Der Fall Naboth in 1 Reg. XXI," 479; Würthwein, "Naboth-Novelle und Elia-Wort," 386; Bohlen, *Der Fall Nabot*, 444 (on p. 129 he does mention that it could be interpreted as either a question or statement); DeVries, *I Kings*, 252; Walsh "I Kings," 321. Recently, Schaack (*Die Ungeduld des Papiers*, 55–57), though he does not directly address whether this phrase is a question or statement, does argue that Jezebel's response represents a desire to demonstrate her own power, a power which could serve the king well. I agree with Bohlen and others who maintain that it can be seen as either a question or a statement. I chose to translate it as a question in order to convey a tone of sarcasm or irony into the conversation and scene.

her despondent husband. Regardless, Jezebel promises to give Naboth's vineyard to Ahab.

There are no explicit temporal indicators mentioned in these verses. The only sense of time is supplied by means of the verb tenses and sequences used in this scene. These follow the standard forms for past-tense narration and for discourse within the context of past-tense narration. From these sequences, we can conclude that the conversation between Ahab and Naboth concerning the vineyard (in Scene 1) took place prior to the conversation between Jezebel and Ahab that is being recounted in this scene. In v. 7 we hear Jezebel command Ahab to get up, eat, and let his heart rejoice, for she "*will* give" him Naboth's vineyard. This unconverted qal imperfect with a future sense moves the action forward toward the next scene.

As with the temporal indicators, the locale indicators for this scene are dependent upon the previous scene. No explicit indicators are mentioned in this scene. We can presume that the scene takes place in the "house" of Ahab, the place to which Ahab had returned at the end of the last scene. We can also presume that the present scene takes place in the royal bedchamber, where, we were told at the end of the last scene, Ahab had taken to his bed. This is verified in the present scene by the series of commands which Jezebel issues to Ahab in v. 7, included among which is the command קוּם ("arise, get up"). This command presumes that Ahab was still lying in his bed and confirms the situating of this scene in his bedchamber.

A key bit of information that is supplied to the reader in this scene is found in v. 6. Here Ahab recounts to Jezebel, by way of explanation for his sour mood, his rendition of what transpired in his conversation with Naboth. The attentive reader should be struck by the shift in the details in this report from those of the original conversation.

### 2. *Ahab's Offer to Buy Naboth's Vineyard and Subsequent References to this Offer*

In 21:2 we find Ahab's offer to Naboth to trade or to buy his vineyard. In v. 3 we hear Naboth's response to Ahab's offer. In v. 4 we are informed of Ahab's "thoughts" as he returns to his house "angry and sullen."[3] In these thoughts we are again informed about the offer. Then, in v. 6, Ahab recounts to Jezebel both his offer to Naboth and Naboth's response to his offer. Finally, in v. 7, Jezebel refers to the object of desire, the vineyard. There are striking similarities and differences in these various references to the original offer as can be seen in the following table.

---

3.    Regarding סַר וְזָעֵף, this pair of adjectives found in parallel construction only occurs here and shortly before in 1 Kgs 20:43. Both occurrences refer to Ahab. The adjective סַר occurs in the masculine form only in 1 Kgs 20:43 and 21:4, and once in the feminine in 1 Kgs 21:5. BDB (711) defines it as "stubborn, resentful, sullen, implacable." The adjective וְזָעֵף occurs only in 1 Kgs 20:43 and 21:4. It is defined in BDB (277) as "out of humor, vexed." The verbal root also carries the sense of "enraged, fuming, storming." In the participial form זֹעֲפִים it occurs in Gen 40:6 where it is used to describe the outward appearance or expression of the imprisoned butler and cup-bearer of Pharaoh.

Table 9. Ahab's Offer to Naboth in its Various Expressions

| Row | Column 1<br>v. 2<br>Ahab's Offer to Naboth | Column 2<br>v. 3<br>Naboth's Response to Ahab | Column 3<br>v. 4<br>Ahab's Thoughts | Column 4<br>v. 6<br>Ahab's Offer Reported to Jezebel | Column 5<br>v. 6<br>Naboth's Reported Response | Column 6<br>v. 7<br>Jezebel's Promise to Ahab |
|---|---|---|---|---|---|---|
| A |  | חָלִילָה לִּי מֵיהוָה |  |  |  |  |
| B | תְּנָה־לִּי | מִתִּתִּי | לֹא־אֶתֵּן לְךָ | תְּנָה־לִּי | לֹא־אֶתֵּן לְךָ | אֲנִי אֶתֵּן לְךָ |
| C | אֶת־כַּרְמְךָ | אֶת־נַחֲלַת אֲבֹתַי לָךְ | אֶת־נַחֲלַת אֲבוֹתָי | אֶת־כַּרְמְךָ | אֶת־כַּרְמִי | אֶת־כֶּרֶם נָבוֹת הַיִּזְרְעֵאלִי |
| D | וִיהִי־לִי לְגַן־יָרָק כִּי הוּא קָרוֹב אֵצֶל בֵּיתִי | (—) | (—) | (—) | (—) | (—) |
| E | וְאֶתְּנָה לְךָ תַּחְתָּיו כֶּרֶם טוֹב מִמֶּנּוּ |  |  | בְּכָסֶף |  |  |
| F | אִם טוֹב בְּעֵינֶיךָ אֶתְּנָה־לְךָ כֶסֶף מְחִיר זֶה |  |  | אוֹ אִם־חָפֵץ אַתָּה אֶתְּנָה־לְךָ כֶרֶם תַּחְתָּיו |  |  |

The first observation regarding this chart has to do with row B. All six references to the desired vineyard are connected together by the use of the verb נתן√ ("to give"). In Ahab's offer (v. 2—col. 1) and in his report of the offer to Jezebel (v. 6—col. 4), the exact same imperative form is used, תְּנָה־לִּי. In Naboth's response to Ahab's offer (v. 3—col. 2), he uses an oath formula which conveys a negative response: חָלִילָה לִּי מֵיהוָה מִתִּתִּי.[4] In this phrase the verb used is the qal infinitive construct + 1st com. sing. suffix. The verb is prefixed by the partitive, מִן. In Ahab's recollection of Naboth's answer (v. 4—col. 3), and in his report of Naboth's answer to Jezebel (v. 6—col. 5), we have the exact same negative form of the verb, לֹא־אֶתֵּן לְךָ. Finally, in the promise of Jezebel to Ahab (v. 7—col. 6) we find the emphatic positive use of the verb: אֲנִי אֶתֵּן לְךָ. The verb נתן√ also occurs three other times within these six references. In Ahab's offer to Naboth in v. 2 we have Ahab using twice the cohortative form אֶתְּנָה and the same form is used once in Ahab's report to Jezebel (v. 6—col. 4).

When we consider row C, the *objects* of this central verb נתן√, we see another interesting element. I will list the objects in order to see this element more clearly.

Table 10. *The "Objects" of the Verb* נתן√

| | | | |
|---|---|---|---|
| 1. | Col. 1 | Ahab's Offer | אֶת־כַּרְמְךָ |
| 2. | Col. 2 | Naboth's Response | אֶת־נַחֲלַת אֲבֹתַי |
| 3. | Col. 3 | Ahab's Thoughts | אֶת־נַחֲלַת אֲבֹתַי |
| 4. | Col. 4 | Ahab's Reported offer | אֶת־כַּרְמְךָ |
| 5. | Col. 5 | Naboth's Reported Response | אֶת־כַּרְמִי |
| 6. | Col. 6 | Jezebel's Promise | אֶת־כֶּרֶם נָבוֹת הַזִּרְעֵאלִי |

A question that has always haunted interpreters of our story is: Did Jezebel know and understand that the vineyard was Naboth's ancestral inheritance? In my view, the way in which these verses are structured, and the way in which the verb and its objects occur (whether intentionally on the part of the author, or accidentally), gives us the answer to this question. According to these verses, Ahab and Naboth are the *only* ones in the story who know this crucial information. In Ahab's offer, the king refers to the object of desire as "your vineyard" (col. 1, row C). Naboth responds and refers to the same object as "the inheritance of my fathers" (col. 2, row C). When Ahab recalls Naboth's answer, he does so literally, "the inheritance of my fathers" (col. 3, row C). It should be noted that this particular recollection is actually from the voice of the narrator telling the reader of the *thoughts* of Ahab and may therefore reflect more the narrator's perspective. As far as Ahab is personally concerned, whenever he speaks about the object of his desire he refers to it only as "vineyard" and never as anything

---

4.   See also 1 Sam 24:7 and 26:11 for the same negative oath. See 2 Sam 23:17 for a slight variant. For a discussion of oath formulae in the Old Testament, see H. S. Gehman, "The Oath in the Old Testament," in *Grace upon Grace: Essays in Honor of Lester J. Kuyper* (ed. J. I. Cook; Grand Rapids; Eerdmans, 1975), 51–63.

else (see col. 1, row C; col. 4, row C; and col. 5, row C). For understanding exactly what Jezebel knew with regard to the object of Ahab's desire, his report to Jezebel of his offer is the key (col. 4, row C). Ahab tells her that he asked Naboth for "your vineyard" using the exact words of his original request regarding the vineyard. This is then reinforced by his further report of Naboth's answer, in which he changes Naboth's words from "the inheritance of my fathers" to "my vineyard." Why this sudden change? Might this possibly be evidence that Ahab was in fact not as "naïve" as is generally thought with regard to this affair? Might Ahab have deliberately been controlling what Jezebel knew about the situation and thereby manipulating her reaction? Possibly! Though the text does not address these questions, we should not be at all surprised when we hear Jezebel merely refer to the object of desire as "vineyard" (col. C, row C). After all, that is *the only way* that she has heard it referred to in Ahab's report.

Another important question should be raised with regard to Naboth's response to Ahab's offer as reported in v. 3. Naboth invokes an oath formula: חָלִילָה לִּי מֵיהוָה מִתִּתִּי אֶת־נַחֲלַת אֲבֹתַי לָךְ ("God forbid that I should give my ancestral inheritance to you"). This is the only time in the entire narrative in which Naboth speaks directly. This response of Naboth can be interpreted in at least two different ways: Naboth *could* not sell his ancestral inheritance, or Naboth *would* not sell it. The way it is apparently interpreted by Ahab, and thus by Jezebel (whether or not due to the manipulation of Ahab), is that Naboth deliberately snubs the king's more than fair offer for the trade or purchase of the vineyard— Naboth *would* not sell. In this interpretation, Naboth could be seen as acting arrogantly and spitefully. This is the way in which Naboth's refusal appears to have been communicated to Jezebel. But there are two counter-arguments that suggest that this perceived snub was not what it appeared. The first argument is that *Ahab's* response to Naboth's refusal to sell or trade his vineyard suggests that the king had no other options, that he knew that if the vineyard was part of Naboth's ancestral inheritance there was nothing he could legally do to obtain the property. This could be the reason why, after Naboth's refusal, Ahab is said to have simply returned to his home and gone to bed in a sour mood. There is no appeal made to "royal prerogative," no reaction of imposing royal authority in the sense of an application of some form of the right of "eminent domain."

The second argument is implied by Naboth's response to Ahab's offer for the vineyard: חָלִילָה לִּי מֵיהוָה מִתִּתִּי אֶת־נַחֲלַת אֲבֹתַי לָךְ. This is an apparent appeal to YHWH for protection from the perceived "sin" of selling or parting with his ancestral inheritance ("God forbid that I should sell" can be understood as, "Lord protect me from selling"). This can be interpreted as an expression of Naboth's sincere piety and fidelity to the traditions of his people—a tradition in which evidently he believed that he *could* not sell his inheritance. This tradition was apparently based upon those beliefs which maintain that YHWH himself is the owner of the land which, in his generosity, he has entrusted to the various tribes of Israel for use and safekeeping. As such, since they were not the true owners of the land, it was not their prerogative to sell or part with their inheritance.[5] There

5.  See Gen 12:7; Lev 25:8–55 (esp. v. 23–24); Josh 21:43–45; 24:12–13.

was only one exception to this custom, namely, in the case of dire circumstances, the land can be temporarily "sold." In these cases the sale was for a determined period of time and always with the right of the seller to have the land returned to him (redeemed) at a later period of time (see Lev 25:25–28).[6] Since there is no indication in 1 Kgs 21 that Naboth is in a situation where he *has* to sell his inheritance, then we must conclude that his refusal to sell was based upon his fidelity to these traditions. In Naboth's mind, and according to these traditions, *he could not sell*.

The impression left by the text regarding this question, however, is ambiguous. It appears that for Naboth, his refusal to sell or trade his vineyard was a matter of fidelity to tradition and it appears from Ahab's initial response that indeed even Ahab recognized that he could not forcibly compel Naboth to part with his inheritance. On the other hand, the report that Ahab gives to Jezebel concerning his offer to Naboth (and in particular the changes he makes in the details) leaves open the question as to whether or not he deliberately misled Jezebel into obtaining the vineyard for him by the use of "less ethical" means. This apparent ambiguity in the text could also be a deliberate attempt on the part of the author simply to heighten the narrative tension and the listener's interest and emotional involvement in the story.

Column 1, row D of the above chart gives us Ahab's rationale for his offer to trade or buy Naboth's vineyard. It is significant that after its initial mention in the conversation between Ahab and Naboth, this rationale is never again mentioned. It is conveniently left out of Ahab's reports to Jezebel. We can only guess as to the reason for this absence. It may be simply that the author of the narrative thought it insignificant. It may be that the author felt that its absence would raise the narrative tension. It may also be that the reader is meant to think that Ahab deliberately left it out of his report so as not to make himself appear weak in Jezebel's eyes for having made such a "generous" offer to a commoner. All of these are possible interpretations—none is absolutely certain.

Rows E and F have to do with the terms of the offer that Ahab made to Naboth (col. 1) and as he reported them to Jezebel (col. 4). Once again, we notice significant changes between these two references. The original offer was in two parts: (1) "I shall give you in its place a vineyard which is better than it" (col. 1, row E), and, (2) "If it is better in your eyes, I shall give you money (silver) according to its value" (col. 1, row F). This is indeed a generous offer. However, this "generosity" suddenly disappears in the report that Ahab gives to Jezebel (col. 4). In this report, the basic elements are mentioned but with significant differences. First of all, the order of the things offered is reversed from that of the original offer. Now it is the money that is said to have been offered first. But even here there is an important difference. In the first element of Ahab's report to Jezebel he tells her that he said to Naboth: "Give me your vineyard for money (silver)" (col. 4, row E). The descriptive and explicative element of the original offer of money is conveniently left out of the report. In place of "*If it is better in*

6.   See the discussion in Baltzer, "Naboths Weinberg," 78–81.

*your eyes*, I shall give you money (silver) *according to its value*" (col. 1, row F), we now have simply and directly: "Give me your vineyard for money (silver)" (col. 4, row E).[7]

A similar change takes place in the other element of the original offer. In col. 1, row E the offer was that Ahab would give Naboth in place of his vineyard, "a vineyard that is better than it." In the report to Jezebel, the important description, "a vineyard that is better than it" disappears. Ahab simply mentions the offer as a trade of *equal* value. Once again, we must ask the question: Why? Why does Ahab eliminate all the qualifiers that he used in his original offer to Naboth when he subsequently reports it to Jezebel? Are we meant to infer from these changes that Ahab was afraid of Jezebel and therefore gave her only the barest of details to minimize the negative response that he might have otherwise received from her? Or are we meant to see in these changes a deliberate and conniving Ahab who is manipulating Jezebel into doing his "dirty work" for him by arranging to have Naboth eliminated? The answer to both of these questions is "probably." We are dealing in this text with a dramatic narrative in which suspense and intrigue play important roles. The purpose of such changes in information may well be the deliberate work of the narrator/author to heighten the narrative tension and to involve the reader more emotionally in this tragic story. If this is the case, and if the narrator has been successful in this technique, then we should be asking at this point: By what devious or criminal means is Jezebel going to get the vineyard? And: Will Ahab and/or Jezebel get away with it?

---

7.    The term כֶּסֶף most commonly refers to silver. When silver was used for barter or exchange for commodities it bore the sense of "money." See BDB, 494.

# Chapter 11

## AN EXPOSITORY READING OF ACT II: SCENE 2—1 KINGS 21:8–10: JEZEBEL WRITES LETTERS TO THE ELDERS AND NOBLES OF JEZREEL

In this scene the two main characters are the narrator (who recounts/ speaks) and Jezebel (who writes the letters). There is also mention of several "passive" parties with reference to the letters: Ahab (v. 8), the "elders and nobles" (v. 8), Naboth (vv. 8, 9), the people (v. 9), the "two worthless men" (v. 10). The narrator recounts the actions and plan of Jezebel subsequent to her promise to Ahab that she would get the vineyard for him (Scene 1, v. 7). Jezebel is the only "active" actor upon the stage. She writes letters in Ahab's name and under his authority (using his seal) to the elders and nobles of Naboth's town. In these letters, she orders them to call a fast and to set Naboth at the front of the people. They are then to call forth two "sons of worthlessness," two untrustworthy or unscrupulous men, who are to accuse Naboth of cursing God and the king— crimes for which the punishment was apparently death (see Exod 22:27). They are then to take Naboth out of the town and stone him to death.

This scene is dependent upon the previous scenes for its temporal aspect and its location. In terms of the location of Jezebel as she writes her letters, we can presume that she is situated somewhere in the royal residence where she has shortly before spoken with Ahab in his bedchamber. Jezebel takes it upon herself to write the letters and send them to the elders and nobles living in Naboth's city. With the exception of אֲשֶׁר בְּעִירוֹ הַיֹּשְׁבִים אֶת־נָבוֹת ("who are in his city, who are citizens/dwelling with Naboth"), there are no specific locale indicators mentioned in this scene. This phrase has to do with the location of the recipients of the letters which Jezebel is writing—they are "those who are in his city, those dwelling[1] with Naboth."

This scene raises several important questions. First of all, we are informed in very clear terms, almost emphatically, how Jezebel went about writing her letters: וַתִּכְתֹּב סְפָרִים בְּשֵׁם אַחְאָב וַתַּחְתֹּם[2] בְּחֹתָמוֹ ("and she wrote letters in Ahab's

---

1. See below (pp. 1344–35) for a discussion of this term.
2. This verb is found in only two texts prior to ours, Lev 15:3 and Deut 32:3, where it has the meaning of "to seal something up in something." The root occurs a total of twenty-seven times. Besides these two texts and the one occurrence in 1 Kgs 21:8, where it means to "seal a letter," the verb √חתם is only found in later texts—Neh 10:1–2; Esth 3:12; 8:8 (×2), 10; Job 9:7; 14:17; 24:16; 33:16; Cant 4:2; Isa 8:16; 29:11; 32:10, 11, 14, 44; Ezek 12; Dan 9:24; 12:4, 9. Both BDB, 367, and *NK–B* 1:364 indicate the term could be Late Biblical Hebrew and it is also found in Phoenician and Aramaic.

name and sealed them with his seal"). This explicit statement raises two questions: (1) Is the plan about which Jezebel writes truly her own plan, or is it Ahab's, or even both Jezebel's and Ahab's? (2) Who is ultimately responsible for the results of this plan—Jezebel or Ahab?

Regarding the first of these questions, the text allows for the impression to be given that the plan was Jezebel's. After all, Ahab, we are told, is in his bed pouting and refusing to eat. He is seemingly unable to function. This gives the impression that the originator and initiator of the plan is Jezebel alone. As is apparently the intention of the text, most scholars and commentators place the responsibility for both the plan and its outcome directly with Jezebel.[3]

The explicit mention that she wrote "in Ahab's name" and then "sealed the letters with Ahab's seal" throws a shadow of doubt over the impression that Jezebel held sole responsibility for the plan. Did she consult with Ahab and obtain his permission to use his name and seal, thus giving her plan royal approval and authority? If so, then this would indicate that Ahab was indeed involved from the very beginning. Who, then, would be ultimately responsible for the results of this plan—Jezebel or Ahab? A relatively small group of scholars and commentators attempt to answer the question of ultimate responsibility for the plan and its results at this point in the text. E. Würthwein held that Jezebel was exercising royal power in a manner that Ahab, himself, would never have dared to do.[4] S. Timm holds that Jezebel manipulated Ahab throughout.[5] G. H. Jones holds that Jezebel "takes the initiative; the decision to confiscate the vineyard for Ahab (v. 7) and the plan to stage a trial against Naboth (vv. 8–10) are attributed to the queen."[6] Others, including G. Fohrer, K. Baltzer, B. Uffenheimer, P. Welten, and H. Seebass, hold that since Ahab's name and seal were used he was ultimately responsible.[7]

The next question which this scene raises has to do with the addressees of the letters—the זְקֵנִים and the חֹרִים.[8] Who are they? The זְקֵנִים comprised a traditional

---

3. See Klostermann, *Die Bücher Samuelis und der Könige*, 382–83, who, in Jezebel's remark to Ahab in v. 7, emends the text to read "you are a simpleton . . ." For him, the plan is completely Jezebel's. See also Gressmann, *Die älteste Geschichtsschreibung*, 272; Montgomery and Gehman, *A Critical and Exegetical Commentary*, 330–31; Fohrer, *Elia*, 23; Gray, *I & II Kings*, 440–41; B. Uffenheimer, "The Deeds of Naboth the Jezreelite," in *Sefer Yosef Braslavi* (Jerusalem: Kiryat-Sepher, 1970 [Hebrew]), 47–78 (73); Rofé, "The Vineyard of Naboth," 91–92; Zakovitch, "The Tale of Naboth's Vineyard," 389–90; Jones, *1–2 Kings* 2:354; DeVries, *I Kings*, 257; Walsh, *I Kings*, 321–22.

4. Würthwein, "Naboth-Novelle und Elia-Wort," 377.

5. Timm, *Die Dynastie Omri*, 115.

6. Jones, *1–2 Kings* 2:354.

7. Fohrer (*Elia*, 62–63) holds that in the original layer Ahab alone was responsible; there was no role for Jezebel in this layer. Baltzer ("Naboths Weinberg," 85) holds that by the use of the seals Ahab is responsible; Uffenheimer ("The Deeds of Naboth the Jezreelite," 73) sees Jezebel as the main culprit in the crime but that Ahab, himself, was very interested in the death of Naboth. Welten ("Naboth's Weinberg," 25) maintains that Ahab is fully responsible in every scene. Seebass ("Der Fall Naboth in 1 Reg. XXI," 479) holds that Ahab was involved from the very start.

8. In this scene, these two groups occur together in both v. 8 and v. 11. These are the only occurrences in the Old Testament where they are found together.

group within most ancient Near Eastern societies, probably originating within early nomadic cultures.[9] Within Israelite society there appears to have been a development of the meaning and role of this group. Apparently, by the time of the dissolution of the United Monarchy in Israel, the elders had become part of the upper class with a role in the governance of the individual kingdoms.[10] They are frequently mentioned alongside other groups of nobles, as is the case in our text. Their role developed and changed from period to period. By the time of our story,[11] and based upon the description of their role in Deut 21:1–9, 18–21, and 22:13–21, the elders of the various cities apparently were responsible for legal decision-making, including cases involving capital offenses.[12] As a recognizable entity, they are found throughout nearly the whole of the Old Testament.

The חֹרִים are much more difficult to identify precisely. The noun חֹרִים is found in Deut 2:12 as the name for the former residents of Seir, who had been defeated and dispossessed by the sons of Esau. It occurs again in 1 Sam 14:11 where it refers to the "holes" (caves), in which, according to the Philistines, the Hebrews had hidden for protection. In our verse, 1 Kgs 21:8 (also v. 11), it occurs for the first time with the sense of a particular group in Israelite society. The exact role, position, and identity of this group is still open to conjecture. After 1 Kgs 21, the term always connotes this specific group of people in Israelite society.

The discussion among the scholars concerning the precise meaning of the term has resulted in some refinement of the positions. In 1899, Benzinger translated the term as "die Vornehmen" ("the nobles") and said that they appear to be fellow members with the Elders in the municipal court, part of the municipal administration. He also noted that later in the texts of Nehemiah they appear to be known as authorities or some sort of government officials.[13] The following year, 1900, Kittel also translated the term as "Vornehmen" but forcefully stated that the term is a much later gloss (based upon Neh 2:16 etc.) which meant the same thing as הַזְּקֵנִים and which translates or explains this term for the post-exilic readers.[14] F. I. Anderson and Würthwein follow Kittel in this position.[15]

A. Šanda[16] translates the term as "die Freien" ("the freedmen"), and says that they appear to be a type of noble. He notes that they appear in Jer 27:20 and 39:6, texts that come from the beginning of the Babylonian Exile and which seem to indicate that the זְקֵנִים was an already established institution. Šanda then remarks

9. See J. Conrad, "זָקֵן," *TDOT* 4:122–31. According to Conrad, the one exception to this phenomenon was Egypt.
10. Conrad, "זָקֵן," 127.
11. This could be either the "implied time"—the time of Ahab, or the "actual time" of the writing or telling of the story.
12. Conrad, "זָקֵן," 128.
13. Benzinger, *Die Bücher der Könige*, 114.
14. Kittel, *Die Bücher der Könige*, 156.
15. F. I. Anderson, "The Socio-Juridical Background," 55, sees the two terms as a hendiadys for "elders." See also Würthwein, "Naboth-Novelle und Elia-Wort," 387 n. 35.
16. Šanda, *Das erste Buch der Könige*, 462–63.

(with Kittel) that in the latter books זִקְנֵי יִשְׂרָאֵל is no longer used, and that הַחֹרִים could well be a gloss used to replace it. After these remarks, however, he goes on to theorize even further. He says that it is also possible that under the influence of the kingship they might have developed into a specific class of aristocracy which may have existed for a long time side by side with the older group known as "the elders." He suggests that these aristocrats were not necessarily comprised of, or considered to be elders, but rather that their position was one of royal privilege.[17] Šanda is followed in this position by G. Fohrer. According to him, it is a loan-word from Aramaic which in other Semitic languages means "freedman," and this is how it was used in Israel. In Judean literature of post-exilic times, the term was modified to mean "noble" or "aristocrat." Fohrer notes, however, that this sense is not found in the Elijah traditions where the term הַחֹרִים had a meaning equivalent to the Judean term עַם הָאָרֶץ ("free, or, full citizens").[18] Following Šanda and Fohrer is R. de Vaux who sees the הַחֹרִים as paralleled with the שָׂרִים in Isa 34:12 and Eccl 10:17, and who says that in Jer 27:20 it replaces שָׂרִים. He also held that הַחֹרִים is paralleled in 2 Kgs 24:14 with שָׂרִים. Based upon these observations, de Vaux concluded that these words are almost synonymous and that they denote a ruling class of the Monarchic period. They were administrators and heads of families—men of position.

This term, referring to some sort of "noble," is found for the first time in 1 Kgs 21:8, 11. All other occurrences of the term with this meaning are found in late exilic or post-exilic texts.[19] A. Rofé claims that the term "is a loan-word from Aramaic, Imperial Aramaic to be sure."[20] After citing several late sources in which the term occurs, he concludes:

---

17. Šanda's position may have been built upon that of Gressmann, *Die älteste Geschichts-schreibung*, 271, who translates the term as "Adlingen," which has the sense of having been "knighted" or elevated in rank by the royalty. Šanda's theory that the הַחֹרִים may have obtained their position as a royal privilege has gained a following among some later scholars, including: Gray, *I & II Kings*, 440, who feels that they may have been politically aligned with the Omrides; Seebass, "Der Fall Naboth in 1 Reg. XXI," 479, who says that they had a special affiliation to the royal house, perhaps as landed or privileged freedmen; Jones, *1–2 Kings* 2:355, who holds that they were probably a rank of gentry that developed around the kingship; Oeming, "Naboth, der Jesreeliter," 373, who accepts Seebass' definition and adds that they may have been a type of vassal to the king.

18. Fohrer, *Elia*, 23–24 n. 41.

19. See Isa. 34:12 which is found within the context of what has been called the "little Apocalypse" found in Isa 34–35. These chapters are believed by many to be a secondary insertion into First Isaiah based and dependant upon the prophecy of salvation found in Second Isaiah. See, among others: J. Jensen and W. H. Irwin, "Isaiah 1–39," in *The New Jerome Biblical Commentary* (ed. R. E. Brown, J. A. Fitzmyer, and R. E. Murphy; Englewoods Cliffs, N.J.: Prentice–Hall, 1990), 229–48 (230); O. H. Steck, *Bereitete Heimkehr: Jesaja 35 als redactionelle Brücke zwischen dem Ersten und Zweiten Jesaja* (SBS 121; Stuttgart: Verlag Katholisches Bibelwerk, 1985), 94–96; S. L. Harris and R. L. Platzner, *The Old Testament: An Introduction to the Hebrew Bible* (Boston: McGraw-Hill, 2003), 232. It appears that the term is comes primarily from the late exilic or the post-exilic period. The term is found particularly frequently in Nehemiah; Neh 2:16; 4:8, 13; 5:7; 6:17; 7:5; 13:17; and see also; Eccl 10:17; Jer 27:20; 39:6.

20. Rofé, "The Vineyard of Naboth," 98.

Presumably the title was derived from their being free from compulsory labour to the Persian king, in exchange for services rendered to the crown. The appearance of the title *hōrîm* as the leaders of the town of Naboth fully conforms with the socio-political reality of 5th century Judah.[21]

Certainty concerning the identity of the הַחֹרִים, however, still evades us. Perhaps they were a recognizable group within Israelite society which at the time of the writing of our text might or might not have been distinct from "the elders." In other traditions and texts, mostly of the late exilic and Persian periods, the distinction is perhaps more clear and they are perhaps directly connected in some way with the kingship. But this is not absolutely clear in our text. The majority opinion is to translate the term as "nobles"[22] and, recognizing the difficulties, this is the translation that I accept in this work.

Connected with the elders and nobles is a relative clause comprised of two appositive statements: אֲשֶׁר בְּעִירוֹ and הַיֹּשְׁבִים אֶת־נָבוֹת. Besides the fact that these two clauses cause an awkwardness in the text, the second statement, הַיֹּשְׁבִים אֶת־נָבוֹת, has also caused some differences in interpretation. The specific issue has to do with the meaning of the participle הַיֹּשְׁבִים. In 1887, Klostermann translated this phrase as "those who govern with him in his city."[23] This interpretation was picked up by Burney who translated it as "those who preside with Naboth."[24] Burney argues that both here and in v. 11 this reference means that Naboth was one of the elders and nobles *who governed the city*. Burney bases his translation upon Isa 28:6; Pss 9:8; 29:10, and Joel 4:12, in which cases a form of the same verb is used to refer to the exercise of judgment or of ruling.[25]

I maintain, however, that Burney was mistaken in his application of the particular usage found in Isa 28:6; Ps 29:10, and Joel 4:12 to our verse in 1 Kgs 21. In every verse to which Burney refers for support, the subject of the verb is YHWH and not human beings. Second, in Isa 28:6; Ps 9:8, and Joel 4:12, the verb √ישׁב is always found with, and takes its meaning from being coupled to, the term מִשְׁפָּט. In Ps 29:10 the term מִשְׁפָּט does not appear, though the verb √ישׁב is used in reference to YHWH "sitting upon his throne." I conclude from these texts that the verb √ישׁב does not appear with the explicit meaning of "judgment" without its being directly connected with the word מִשְׁפָּט, or at least being in a context

---

21. Rofé, "The Vineyard of Naboth," 99. Others who either specifically date the term to the Persian period, or who suggest that it is from this period, include: Kittel, *Die Bücher der Könige*, 156; Šanda, *Das erste Buch der Könige*, 462–63; F. I. Anderson, "The Socio-Juridical Background," 55; Würthwein, "Naboth-Novelle und Elia-Wort," 387.

22. Among those not already mentioned and who translate our term in this way, are: Klostermann, *Die Bücher Samuelis und der Könige*, 382; Burney, *Notes*, 244; Schlögl, *Die Bücher der Könige, Die Bücher der Chronik*, 174; Eissfeldt, *Das erste Buch der Könige*, 539; Montgomery and Gehman, *A Critical and Exegetical Commentary*, 331; Snaith, "The First and Second Book of Kings," 174; Uffenheimer, "The Deeds of Naboth the Jezreelite," 72–73; Bohlen, *Der Fall Nabot*, 61; Rofé, "The Vineyard of Naboth," 91.

23. Klostermann, *Die Bücher Samuelis und der Könige*, 383.

24. Burney, *Notes*, 244.

25. Note also Exod 18:13; Judg 4:4–5; Isa 16:5; Jer 26:10; Prov 20:8; and Dan 7:9–10.

which clearly defines the legal nature of the situation, such as we find in Prov 20:8 where the phrase used is יוֹשֵׁב עַל־כִּסֵּא־דִין. Neither of these connections is found in our chapter. The specific context of our phrase is a letter written by Jezebel to the elders and nobles of Jezreel and the *explicit* purpose is the calling of a fast, *not* a public trial. If Jezebel would have wanted a public trial, she could have ordered one to be called. There was no need to use the ruse of a public fast. Klostermann and Burney, however, did gather a group of followers for their position.[26]

A larger number of scholars either disagree with Klostermann and Burney's position or follow others who disagree with them. For example, two years after Klostermann published his commentary, I. Benzinger wrote that הַיֹּשְׁבִים אֶת־נָבוֹת, and the preceding phrase, אֲשֶׁר בְּעִירוֹ, had the same meaning = "die Mitbürger Naboths." He goes on to say: "That Naboth, himself, belonged to the city leaders is in no way indicated (Klostermann), so we have no right to translate, הַיֹּשְׁבִים, as a 'member' (i.e., of the city council)".[27] I concur with Benzinger's position.

A further question that this scene raises for us is that of power or authority. What power or authority do/does Jezebel/Ahab have over the townsfolk of Jezreel (or Samaria), and specifically, over the "elders and nobles" of the town? Naturally, one would answer that they hold their legitimate authority as royalty. But how far does this authority reach? Does it have limits beyond which even it cannot go? Though a thorough investigation of these matters is beyond the scope of the present work, at this point we can surmise that evidently there were limits to royal power and authority as evinced by the first scene. Ahab went to Naboth, a free citizen of Israel, and attempted to trade or buy the vineyard from him. There is no sign of the use of royal authority in this scene. When Naboth refused to part with his family inheritance, even then Ahab did not appeal to any royal authority to forcibly take the vineyard. Why? The obvious, or at least the logical, reason for this appears to be that it was beyond the power of the crown to take the property. In a certain sense, the entire story revolves around this detail.

In our present scene, because there was apparently no legal means for Ahab to obtain the vineyard, Jezebel takes it upon herself to obtain it through "other" means. She writes letters to the elders and nobles of the town in which she tells them what to do. This raises the question of authority again: Was it within her power to do this? Evidently, since she wrote under Ahab's name and used his

---

26. Stade and Schwally, *The Book of Kings*, 165; Schlögl, *Die Bücher der Könige, Die Bücher der Chronik*, 174; Snaith, "The First and Second Book of Kings," 74; Brichto, *The Problem of "Curse"* (JBLMS 13; Philadelphia: Society of Biblical Literature, 1963), 160–61; Zakovitch, "The Tale of Naboth's Vineyard," 390–91.

27. Author's translation (with added emphasis) of: "Dass Naboth selbst zu den Ratherren gehört (Klostermann), wird mit keiner Silbe angedeutet, also haben wir kein Recht, הַיֹּשְׁבִים mit 'Beisitzer' zu übersetzen" (Benzinger, *Die Bücher der Könige*, 114). Following Benzinger are: Kittel, *Die Bücher der Könige*, 156; Gressmann, *Die älteste Geschichtsschreibung*, 271; Šanda, *Das erste Buch der Könige*, 459; Eissfeldt, *Das erste Buch der Könige*, 539; de Vaux, *Les livres des Rois*, 70; Montgomery and Gehman, *A Critical and Exegetical Commentary*, 331; Fohrer, *Elia*, 23 n. 40; Gray, *I & II Kings*, 437; Seebass, "Der Fall Naboth in 1 Reg. XXI," 479; Bohlen, *Der Fall Nabot*, 61, 444; Jones, *1–2 Kings* 2:355; DeVries, *I Kings*, 252; Schaack, *Die Ungeduld des Papiers*, 53

seal, she realized that in order to obtain complete compliance with her plan she needed the full backing of the king's authority. We may assume therefore that her own authority as Ahab's wife was "insufficient" to gain the compliance of the elders and nobles. Though there is considerable reason to question the actual legal authority of such letters, for the purpose of our narrative, the author evidently feels free to "stretch" or exaggerate the actual authority of Jezebel. The narrator/author also does not bother to explain why the elders and nobles comply with the orders in the letters. He simply presents them as complying. This lacuna in the information supplied, and perhaps the lack of contact with actual realities, allows for the reader to raise in his/her own mind this question of authority. It is a result of this apparent discontinuity with "reality" that some scholars have ventured to speculate that there may have been close and powerful links between the חֹרִים and the royal family. This relationship may have been the source of the authority or power that Jezebel exercised in her letters and plan. However, this type of reasoning is, in my opinion, based upon an overly "historical" interpretation of this didactic parable about Naboth's vineyard.[28] At any rate, the end of this scene leaves us asking the questions: Will they do it? Will the elders and nobles obey Jezebel?

Another important issue that arises concerning our present scene has to do with v. 10. In this verse we are told that Jezebel orders the elders and nobles to place before Naboth שְׁנַיִם אֲנָשִׁים בְּנֵי־בְלִיַּעַל[29] ("two worthless men") to witness against him. The very fact that Jezebel would order "worthless men" to be used immediately causes the reader to flinch with distaste. It also has the effect of raising the narrative tension to an even higher pitch.

A final issue with regard to this scene concerns the use of a letter as a means of transmitting such a plan. Many have questioned the "historicity" or the "factuality" of the account on the basis of this detail. Would the king's wife, even if she were writing in his name and under his authority, write such detailed plans which were so explicitly illegal (i.e. the use of false witnesses) in a letter? Would this

---

28. An example of this type of speculation is found in Gray, *I & II Kings*, 440, where he conjectures: "The fiction of communal justice is noteworthy. Jezebel's reliance on the local elders and freeborn men of Jezreel suggests that Ahab was personally influential. This indicates perhaps that the persons in question had long been accustomed to follow the lead of the family of Ahab. This situation is readily intelligible if Ahab's family was from Jezreel, the modern Arab analogy suggesting that the influence of a powerful local family to whom all in the locality are in some degree attached is permanently dominant." This type of speculation regarding Ahab's influence, or his place of origin, finds no direct support in the biblical record.

29. בְּנֵי־בְלִיַּעַל is a term whose origins are very obscure and difficult. Its contexts appear to be negative in sense. As Burney (*Notes*, 245–47) points out, there are various explanations for the derivation of the term which fall into one of two main groups: (1) it is a combination of the term בְּלִי (= "not") and יַעַל (= "worth" or "use") which comes to mean "worthlessness" or "uselessness"; (2) it is a combination of בְּלִי (= "not") and יַעַל which stands for יַעֲלֶה and which means "that which comes up" or, "that which arises." In this case the meaning would be "that which does not arise or come up" (= "unsuccessful"). Burney then goes on to suggest that the term might in fact be a diminutive form of *bulai 'âl*, from the root בלע√, meaning "to engulf in ruin" or "perdition." With this, the difficulty of the term remains and the scholars generally interpret it with one of the above meanings.

not have been dangerous in the sense that the letter could later serve as evidence of the criminal involvement of the senders? Attempts to deal with questions of this sort have led a number of scholars to attempt to "correct" the text. These scholars suggest the elimination of the reference to the two false witnesses in v. 10 as a late intrusion on the part of a redactor who was under the influence of v. 13.[30] If this reference is eliminated, then the elders and nobles would not be implicated as co-conspirators in the crime and the difficulty of the culpability of the royal couple would not be explicit in the text. I am against such a solution for two reasons. The first is that what we have in this story is biblical narrative in the form of a didactic parable, *not an historical record*. The author of this narrative supplies many details and bits of information (e.g. the conversation between Jezebel and Ahab in the bedchamber) through the mouth of the narrator. This is information that may or may not have been known to the actors on the "stage" of the narrative, if indeed these events ever transpired in the first place. This is part and parcel of good narrative and of artistic license. The second reason is that on at least one other occasion we find the same type of explicit detail being delivered in a letter instigating the same type of illegal activity on the part of royalty. This parallel is found in 2 Sam 11:14–15 where King David wrote to Joab detailing the plan for having Uriah the Hittite killed. This similarity of 1 Kgs 21:1–16 to the David and Bathsheba story is only one of many such parallels between these two stories.[31] The fact that Jezebel details her plans in the letters and that she refers to the two false witnesses in terms which express what they truly were, is a deliberate attempt on the part of the author of our text continually to heighten the narrative tension of the story.

30. This issue will be discussed in detail in the next scene.
31. See the above discussion on pp. 106–9. ·

Chapter 12

AN EXPOSITORY READING OF ACT II: SCENE 3—1 KINGS 21:11–14:
THE ELDERS AND NOBLES OF JEZREEL FULFILL JEZEBEL'S ORDERS

The narrator is the active voice in this entire scene. Those who play active roles in the account are "the people of his (Naboth's) city, the elders, and the nobles who were inhabitants of his city," and the "two worthless men." Naboth is presented as being totally passive and Jezebel is merely mentioned as the one to whom the message is sent at the end of the scene.

This scene recounts the fulfillment of the orders and plan sent to the elders and nobles by Jezebel. They call a fast, place Naboth at the front of the people, and two "sons of unrighteousness" accuse him of cursing God and king. They take Naboth outside the town and stone him to death. The elders and nobles then send[1] word to Jezebel that Naboth was stoned and is dead.

The first question to ask with regard to Jezebel's plan of the last scene and its execution in this scene is: Why proclaim a fast? This apparently innocent question is in the end rather important since its answer will, in large part, affect one's interpretation of the role of the elders and nobles. H. A. Brongers maintains that fasting was used for several reasons and on different occasions, both individually and communally. According to him there were seven types (or reasons/occasions for) fasting: (a) fasting after a death (2 Sam 1:12; 7:16–23); (b) war-fasting (1 Sam 14:24); (c) preparatory or introductory fasting (Exod 34:28; Judg 20:26; 1 Sam 28:20; and 1 Kgs 21:9); (d) fasting as a potent auxiliary to prayer (1 Sam 7:5–6; 2 Sam 12; Neh 1:4–11); (e) expiatory fasting (1 Sam 7:6; Jer 36:9; Joel 2:12; Jonah 3); (f) concomitant fasting (Esth 4:16); and (g) the so-called "Zechariah-fastings" (Zech 8:19). As is seen, he interprets the fast proclaimed in our chapter as a preparatory or introductory fast (c). He maintains that the sole reason for the proclamation of this type of fast was that "the people as a whole are ordered to prepare themselves for this trial not only mentally but physically as well. To this very intent a fast was proclaimed and to nothing else."[2]

The difficulty with Brongers' position is not his classification of the fast in 1 Kgs 21 as a preparatory or introductory fast, but rather with his supporting

<hr />

1. The subject of this verb will be discussed in the analysis of vv. 8–14 as a unit in Chapter 13, pp. 146–50.

2. H. A. Brongers, "Fasting in Israel in Biblical and Post-Biblical Times," in *Instruction and Interpretation: Studies in Hebrew Language, Palestinian Archaeology, and Biblical Exegesis* (ed. A. S. Van Der Woude; OTS 20 (Leiden: Brill, 1977), 1–21 (9).

argumentation. He maintains that the calling of the fast and the command to "set Naboth at the head of the people" made it abundantly clear that what Jezebel was calling for was a public trial in which Naboth stood accused and that everyone in Jezreel would know this. For him, Naboth is accused of blasphemy and *lèse majesté* that threaten the life of the community. He continues: "In consequence of this, other explanations put forward in the course of time are in our opinion to be rejected." Obviously Brongers' position is based upon his interpretation of the implied meaning of sitting someone "at the head of the people." But if the meaning of this phrase and action were truly so self-evident then why has it been such a debated issue throughout the history of the critical analysis of the passage? Brongers' categorical elimination of any other possible interpretation, and thus, of constructive discussion or debate, is a difficult position to maintain.

The simple fact is that the text (the author) does not reveal the reason for the calling of the fast. We have here perhaps another example of the author's deliberate raising of questions of logic in the mind of the reader for which there are no explicit answers given. The effect of this technique is that the narrative tension continues to mount. As a result of the lack of any overt explanation for the fast, scholars (and everyone else) have been left with the task of asking why, and then of seeking explanations.

It appears to me that the focus of attention in the majority of these explanations has been overly influenced by the subsequent commands in Jezebel's letters: "set Naboth in front/at the head of the people. Then, sit two worthless men opposite him and let them bear witness saying: 'You have cursed/blasphemed God and the king.' And then take him out and stone him and let him die (stone him to death)." Because the author tells us about these further commands, many are led to believe that the whole purpose of the fast was to commence, and perhaps even to disguise, the process of a trial. But here too we must be careful not to prejudge the text based upon our familiarity with or preknowledge of the story. What did the elders and nobles really know? How deeply, if at all, were they actively and willingly involved in the whole affair? These are questions to which we still must turn our attention. For the present, however, we must proceed with caution.

A review of the scholarship with regard to the reason for the calling of the public fast shows the ongoing struggle to understand both the act of calling the fast and the meaning of the fast itself. It is a complex issue. We must keep in mind that the text and its author do not inform us of the reason for the fast, nor does Jezebel mention the specific reason in her letters. All we can infer from the text is that the calling of the fast was to serve as the backdrop or pretext for the remaining parts of her plan—to have Naboth charged and put to death. From this we might suspect the purpose for the calling of this fast was purely utilitarian; that is, it was not meant to be used for the purpose for which a fast was normally called, but rather for some ulterior motive. We may speculate that this ulterior motive was ultimately the gathering together of all the townsfolk to witness and partake in the demise of Naboth. But, in the text itself, we are never explicitly told this.

The majority of scholars believe that the main purpose for calling a *public fast* was to assemble the people together to pray and do penance in order to atone for some known or unknown sin. This sin presented a real or immanent danger to the community. The assembled community was to attempt through this fast, prayer, and penance to discover both the sin and the sinner responsible for the danger to the community. They were then to eliminate these from the community in an attempt to assuage the evident anger and immanent judgment of God against them.[3] It is still an open discussion as to who had the legal authority to call these fasts. S. Timm notes that it is remarkable that for the author of our text and his followers, the imposition of a fast day upon a free Israelite community by their king appears to be a common occurrence. He notes, however, that there is no further evidence for such a practice in which an Israelite king apparently exercises this type of religious function. It is unclear, according to Timm, whether in fact the crown had the authority to call a localized fast, especially during the implied time of this narrative—the reign of Ahab.[4] I would also point out that according to our narrative, though the command to call the fast was allegedly written to the elders and nobles of Jezreel by Jezebel and sent by her in Ahab's name and under his seal, it is in fact the elders and nobles themselves who call the fast—not Ahab or Jezebel. This would appear to be more consistent with the tradition concerning the calling of public fasts according to the biblical texts. In those verses I have found concerning the calling of "general" or "public" fasts, five instances have the fast being proclaimed either by "the people" in general or by a specific group of people.[5] In five other texts the fast is called by an individual other than the king (usually a prophet or priest). In Joel 1:14 and 2:15, fasts are declared by the Lord through the prophet Joel. In Esth 4:3 and 4:15, the fast is declared by Queen Esther, but without the knowledge, approval, or seal of the king. In Ezra 8:21, the fast is proclaimed by Ezra the priest. Only in one verse was I able find a king specifically proclaiming a public fast—King Jehoshaphat in 2 Chr 20:3.[6]

According to the text of 1 Kgs 21, it is possible to conclude that Jezebel called the fast with no sense of religious purpose. Instead, she called it with the sole purpose of gathering the people together as a legal body capable of condemning

3. This is the generally accepted rationale for the calling of a general fast. See Keil and Delitzsch, *Das Alte Testament*, 224–25; Benzinger, *Die Bücher der Könige*, 115; Kittel, *Die Bücher der Könige*, 157–58; Gressmann, *Die älteste Geschichtsschreibung*, 272; Schlögl, *Die Bücher der Könige, Die Bücher der Chronik*, 174; Šanda, *Das erste Buch der Könige*, 463; Eissfeldt, *Das erste Buch der Könige*, 539 n. a; de Vaux, *Les livres des Rois*, 70 n. b; J. A. Montgomery, "Ascetic Strains in Early Judaism," *JBL* 51 (1932): 183–213 (187); Montgomery and Gehman, *A Critical and Exegetical Commentary*, 331; Snaith, "The First and Second Book of Kings," 174; Dhorme, *La Bible*, 1125; Fohrer, *Elia*, 24; Brichto, *The Problem of "Curse,"* 161–62; Gray, *I & II Kings*, 440; Welten, "Naboth's Weinberg," 23; Zakovitch, "The Tale of Naboth's Vineyard," 391.

4. Timm, *Die Dynastie Omri*, 122. See also Baltzer, "Naboths Weinberg," 85, and Welten, "Naboth's Weinberg," 23 n. 26.

5. See Judg 20:26; 1 Sam 7:6; 2 Sam 1:12; Jer 36:9; and Jonah 3:5, 7–9.

6. There is also in 1 Sam 14:24 the account of Saul imposing a type of "fast" upon his men and enforcing it with a curse on anyone who eats. In this instance, however, the term צום is not used.

Naboth.[7] If the people, with the exception of the elders and nobles who received her letters, believed that the reason for the fast was that there was some immanent threat to their peace and security, then it was all the better for Jezebel's plan. In this case, they would apparently have been predisposed to act decisively to rid themselves of the "cause" of the immanent danger and thus perhaps ward off the danger itself. This predisposition would serve Jezebel's purposes very well. This fact was recognized by some of the earlier scholars, including Keil and Delitzsch, Benzinger, and Kittel.[8] In more recent scholarship, however, there appears to be a trend toward a much more blunt and straightforward analysis.

In 1964, K. Baltzer, recognizing that the reason for the fast was not given in the text itself, held that it was obvious from the text that it was a misuse of a very earnest and important type of religious holiday; a type of "day of repentance."[9] F. I. Anderson took a firm position when he said that "Presumably to 'proclaim a fast' means to announce a court session with a suspension of other business so that the citizens could assemble." He does note, however, that this particular "connection of jurisprudence with fasting is without parallel" and therefore remains obscure.[10] B. Uffenheimer found the substance of Jezebel's letter to be more shocking than the story of David's letter arranging to have Uriah killed. For him, the submission of the nobles and elders in our story is much more shameful. He comments: "As judges there was to be nothing in their hands except the word of God as it was formulated in the traditional constitution/law."[11] He maintains that their duty was to oppose or resist Jezebel's arbitrary command, which was harmful to the very foundations of Hebrew law. He goes on to say that the calling of the public fast before the trial of Naboth makes no sense at all except to emphasize the severity and the extraordinary character of the charges—that there was both a curse of God and of the king.[12] H. Seebass maintained that the use of the fast was both for its "shock value" and in order to obtain a rapid conclusion.[13] R. Bohlen held that the author had no other purpose in having Jezebel call the fast than to gather together a legal body that was capable of delivering the death penalty.[14] A. Rofé applied the calling of the fast to "Jezebel's exigency." She was in need of a sudden and quick trial in which Naboth would have no chance of preparing his defense. It was, in his words, a "lynch law" of ancient times.[15]

---

7. Klostermann, *Die Bücher Samuelis und der Könige*, 383, interpreted the proclamation of the fast as "an invitation to an important act of the state."

8. See the discussions in Keil and Delitzsch, *Das Alte Testament*, 202; Benzinger, *Die Bücher der Könige*, 539 n. a; Kittel, *Die Bücher der Könige*, 157–58.

9. Baltzer, "Naboths Weinberg," 85.

10. F. I. Anderson, "The Socio-Juridical Background," 56. This is the same position held by Jones, *1–2 Kings* 2:355–56.

11. Uffenheimer, "The Deeds of Naboth the Jezreelite," 65, בחוקה המסורתית כשופטים אין בידם כשופטים אין בידם אלא דבר ה' כפי שהוא נתנסח ("As judges, there was to be nothing in their hand except the word of God as it was formulated in the traditional constitution") (author's translation).

12. Uffenheimer, "The Deeds of Naboth the Jezreelite," 65–66, 72.

13. Seebass, "Der Fall Naboth in 1 Reg. XXI," 480–81.

14. Bohlen, *Der Fall Nabot*, 378.

15. Rofé, "The Vineyard of Naboth," 92.

In the preceding discussion of the proclamation of the fast I have touched upon the complexity of the issue. We have looked at the occasions on which fasts were proclaimed and have discussed the situations in which they were normally called. We have also seen that the text and situation in 1 Kgs 21 does not fit neatly into these categories. In the end we must admit that it is an anomaly. The author obviously felt free enough to take a known practice in Israel and to use it, or perhaps even to misuse it, in order to heighten the tension in this story. In the final analysis, we are left with the stark reality that the author has chosen not to reveal his reasons for having Jezebel call the fast. As Šanda has pointed out, a public fast of this sort had to have an obvious reason that would have been known by everyone. This would not have been the case with the so-called "curses" of Naboth, which apparently were secret offenses for which there were supposedly only the two disreputable witnesses.[16] On the basis of this type of logic, some authors have attempted to conjecture what the specific "cause" might have been.[17] But this type of conjecturing is not necessary, nor is it helpful, since it presumes an historical event in this story, and since the author does not give even a clue as to the cause. A plain reading of the text shows that it is not the fast or its supposed cause that is of primary interest; rather, attention focuses on the fact that the calling of the fast was a façade, a ruse in order to make possible the public condemnation of Naboth.

The next issue for consideration is the sense of the phrase וְהוֹשִׁיבוּ אֶת־נָבוֹת בְּרֹאשׁ הָעָם (v. 12b). What does it mean "to set Naboth at the head (front, foremost part) of the people"? The phrase בְּרֹאשׁ הָעָם occurs only three times in the Old Testament. The first occurrence is in Deut 20:9, in the context of the "rules for warfare." Our phrase is found in the specific rule to commanders that they are to muster (or be appointed) at the "head of the people." They are, in other words, to lead the Hebrew forces into battle. The only other two occurrences of the phrase are found in our story with reference to Naboth (vv. 9, 12).

Scholars are divided into two main groups over the interpretation of the phrase. The first group understands it to mean that Naboth is to be given a place of honor from which he will be toppled through Jezebel's plan.[18] The second group is comprised of those who do not interpret the phrase as the giving of a place of honor to Naboth. There are two basic subdivisions in this group. The first is comprised of those scholars who believe that the phrase means that

---

16. Šanda, *Das erste Buch der Könige*, 463. See also Uffenheimer, "The Deeds of Naboth the Jezreelite," 65–66 for the same type of interpretation.

17. See Šanda, *Das erste Buch der Könige*, 463, who conjectured that it might be the arrival of the Autumn and the danger of a possible draught. Eissfeldt, *Das erste Buch der Könige*, 539 n. a, sees the cause as possibly the draught of chs. 17–18, and he is followed by Jones, *1–2 Kings* 2:355–56. R. de Vaux, "Le Cycle d'Élie," 70 n. b, also conjectured draught or famine.

18. See Benzinger, *Die Bücher der Könige*, 11; Burney, *Notes*, 245; Gressmann, *Die älteste Geschichtsschreibung*, 272; Schlögl, *Die Bücher der Könige, Die Bücher der Chronik*, 174; Šanda, *Das erste Buch der Könige*, 463; Eissfeldt, *Das erste Buch der Könige*, 539 n. a; de Vaux, "Le Cycle d'Élie," 70 n. b; Gray, *I & II Kings*, 440–41; Uffenheimer, "The Deeds of Naboth the Jezreelite," 65; Würthwein, "Naboth-Novelle und Elia-Wort," 387; Zakovitch, "The Tale of Naboth's Vineyard," 391.

Naboth is being made to sit in the seat/place of the defendant in a public trial.[19] The second subgroup is comprised of those who interpret the phrase to mean that Naboth is being made into some sort of leader. A. Klostermann held that the fast was an invitation to an important function of the state during which Naboth was to be elected or appointed as the new town leader.[20] Montgomery and Gehman interpret it to mean that Naboth was presiding "in the capacity of head of the people."[21] H. C. Brichto,[22] following E. A. Speiser,[23] interprets the phrase to mean that Naboth was made a נָשִׂיא, a prince or leader of the people.

There are, therefore, various interpretations of the meaning of the phrase וְהוֹשִׁיבוּ אֶת־נָבוֹת בְּרֹאשׁ הָעָם. The text itself offers no explicit explanation as to the rationale behind the command. The reader is once again placed in the position of having to ask the question: Why? The author has stepped up the tension level another notch and now has the complete attention of the reader.

---

19. Keil and Delitzsch, *Das Alte Testament*, 225, conjecture a placement at the front of the gathering where the elders sit together for the judicial hearing of cases. This position is somewhat ambiguous since it could be read as either a place where the judges sit (a place of honor), or as an indication that it was Naboth's "case" that was being heard and that he was to be seated in the defendant's seat. See also Kittel, *Die Bücher der Könige*, 157; Dhorme, *La Bible*, 1125; Brongers, "Fasting in Israel," 10; Jones, *1–2 Kings* 2:356.

20. Klostermann, *Die Bücher Samuelis und der Könige*, 383.

21. Montgomery and Gehman, *A Critical and Exegetical Commentary*, 331.

22. H.C. Brichto, "Background and Function of the Biblical *nāśī*," *CBQ* 25 (1963): 111–17.

23. E. A. Speiser, "An Angelic 'Curse': Exodus 14:20," *JAOS* 80 (1960): 198–200 (199 n. 8).

# Chapter 13

## THE LITERARY RELATIONSHIP BETWEEN
## ACT II: SCENE 2 (1 KINGS 8–10) AND ACT II: SCENE 3 (1 KINGS 11–14)

### 1. The Similarities and Difference in the Texts of the Two Scenes

Both scenes are introduced by a narrative comment. Scene 2 is introduced by v. 8, which describes the circumstances of Jezebel's writing of the letters, the individuals to whom the letters were sent, and the location where these individuals were located. Scene 3 is introduced by v. 11, which states that the leaders of Naboth's town did exactly as Jezebel had written to them. Each of these introductions is then followed by an explication of the specifics. A close comparison of these two texts shows a variety of differences between the commands and their fulfillments.[1]

Table 11. *The Texts of Act II: Scenes 2 and 3*
(Asterisk indicates unique or otherwise special elements in the text)

| Scene 2: <br> The Letter (vv. 9–10) | Scene 3: <br> The Fulfillment (vv. 12–13) |
|---|---|
| (v. 9) וַתִּכְתֹּב בַּסְּפָרִים לֵאמֹר <br> קִרְאוּ־צֹום <br> וְהֹושִׁיבוּ אֶת־נָבֹות <br> בְּרֹאשׁ הָעָם: | (v. 12) קָרְאוּ צֹום <br> וְהֹשִׁיבוּ אֶת־נָבֹות <br> בְּרֹאשׁ הָעָם: |
| (v. 10) וְהֹושִׁיבוּ <br> שְׁנַיִם אֲנָשִׁים בְּנֵי־בְלִיַּעַל <br><br> נֶגְדֹּו <br> וִיעִדֻהוּ <br><br> לֵאמֹר <br> * בֵּרַכְתָּ <br><br> אֱלֹהִים וָמֶלֶךְ <br> וְהֹוצִיאֻהוּ <br><br> וְסִקְלֻהוּ <br><br> וַיָּמֹת: | * (v. 13) וַיָּבֹאוּ <br> שְׁנֵי הָאֲנָשִׁים בְּנֵי־בְלִיַּעַל <br> * וַיֵּשְׁבוּ <br> נֶגְדֹּו <br> וַיְעִדֻהוּ <br> * אַנְשֵׁי הַבְּלִיַּעַל אֶת־נָבֹות נֶגֶד הָעָם <br> לֵאמֹר <br> בֵּרַךְ <br> נָבֹות <br> אֱלֹהִים וָמֶלֶךְ <br> וַיֹּצִאֻהוּ <br> * מִחוּץ לָעִיר <br> וַיִּסְקְלֻהוּ <br> * בָּאֲבָנִים <br> וַיָּמֹת: |

---

1. Verses 10b–13a are missing from Codex Vaticanus. This omission is most likely due to homoioteleuton from υἱοὺς παρανόμων in v. 10b to the similar phrase found in v. 13a. This will be discussed further when I explore the issue with v. 10—pp. 156–59.

In Scene 2 we have the account of Jezebel writing and sending the letters containing her orders for the elders and nobles. In Scene 3 we have the account of the fulfillment of those orders. In v. 9 the verb קְרָאוּ is a qal imperative, masc. pl. of √קרא. The fulfillment of this command in v. 12 is the expected form, קָרְאוּ, which is a qal perfect, 3d com. pl. Also in v. 9 is the verb וְהֹשִׁיבוּ, which is a hiphil imperative, masc. pl. + *waw*-conjunctive of √ישׁב. In v. 12 the form used for the notification of its fulfillment is probably a mistake. The expected form would be וַיֹּשִׁיבוּ, a 3d pl. hiphil converted imperfect. Instead, we have וְהֹשִׁיבוּ, the exact form as is found in the command of v. 9. According to N. H. Snaith, this error is due to the influence of the previous hiphil imperative (v. 9) and is not intended to be a hiphil perfect, 3d pl. + *waw*-conjunctive.[2]

In v. 10 we find the command: וְהֹשִׁיבוּ שְׁנַיִם אֲנָשִׁים בְּנֵי־בְלִיַּעַל נֶגְדּוֹ. The verb in this case is the same as the previous imperative, וְהֹשִׁיבוּ (v. 9b), and serves as a parallel to the command to sit Naboth at the head of the people. However, the expected statement of fulfillment in v. 13 is not found. Here we have the first significant change between the two texts. In v. 13 we find: וַיָּבֹאוּ שְׁנֵי הָאֲנָשִׁים בְּנֵי־בְלִיַּעַל וַיֵּשְׁבוּ נֶגְדּוֹ. Instead of a single verb to parallel the single occurrance found in the command, we find two verbs, neither of which carries the exact meaning or sense of the command in v. 10. In v. 13 we find a pair of qal converted imperfects, 3d masc. pl., וַיָּבֹאוּ and וַיֵּשְׁבוּ. These verbs, in juxtaposition to וְהֹשִׁיבוּ in v. 10, are both active in meaning—the two worthless men came and sat by their own volition. This is not the sense of the command of Jezebel that mandated that the elders and nobles were to sit/place (causative) the two worthless men across from Naboth.

One other slight difference between the first parts of v. 10 and v. 13 is to be found in the references to the two men. Verse 10 reads שְׁנַיִם אֲנָשִׁים, which is a masculine dual adjective followed by a common masculine plural *indefinite* noun. In v. 13 we have שְׁנֵי הָאֲנָשִׁים, which is composed of a masculine dual adjective in construct state followed by a common masculine noun with the *definite article*.

With the next verb, we have another change between the command and the fulfillment. The verb in v. 10b, וִיעִדֻהוּ, is a hiphil imperfect, 3d masc. pl. of √עוד with a 3d masc. sing. suffix and a *waw*-conjunctive. It is situated in a volitive + imperfect/cohortative sequence which has the translation value of purpose or result.[3] As such, it expresses the reason why the two worthless men are to be set across from Naboth, "so that they might witness against him." In v. 13 and the fulfillment of this command we have the form וַיְעִדֻהוּ, which is a hiphil converted imperfect 3d pl. + a 3d masc. sing. suffix. This verb cannot be said to fulfill a

2. Snaith, *Notes on the Hebrew Text of I Kings*, 75. The same position is held by, among others, Benzinger, *Die Bücher der Könige*, 115; Burney, *Notes*, 247–48; Stade and Schwally, *The Book of Kings*, 165; Eissfeldt, *Das erste Buch der Könige*, 539.

3. T. O. Lambdin, *Introduction to Biblical Hebrew* (9th ed.; London: Darton, Longman & Todd, 1990), 119. For the syntax of verbal structures and sequences, see also A. Niccacci, *The Syntax of the Verb in Classical Hebrew Prose* (trans. W. G. E. Watson; JSOTSup 86; Sheffield: JSOT Press, 1990), 168–97 (esp. the chart on 168–69).

command of v. 10 in the same sense as the other instances of the command–fulfillment pattern, since the form found in v. 10 is not in the imperative. It does, however, fulfill the "wish" of the volitive form found in v. 10. In its own context in v. 13, this verb "appears" to follow in sequence with the previous two active verbal forms, וַיָּבֹאוּ and וַיֵּשְׁבוּ—"they came, they sat, and they witnessed . . . ." There is, however, a significant difficulty with regard to the interpretation of the verbal sequence of this and the remaining verbs in v. 13. This difficulty will be addressed in more detail later when I discuss the overall analysis of vv. 8–14.

The use of the verb עוד√ in the hiphil with the active meaning of "to witness" is rare. It is found with this sense in 1 Kgs 21:10, 13; 2 Chr 24:19; Mal 2:14, and Job 29:11. It is also found with a causative meaning in Deut 4:26; 30:19; 31:28; Jer 32:10, 25, 44; Lam 2:13, and possibly in Isa 48:6.[4] With the exception of our particular verses of 1 Kgs 21:10, 13, this verb is found only in texts considered to be from the exilic to the post-exilic period. This might be an indication that its presence in 1 Kgs 21 could also be of late provenance.[5] According to Rofé, the Classical Biblical Hebrew term for "giving witness" was composed of the verb ענה√ usually followed by ב.[6] In our verses we do not find this classical verbal construction.

The next part of the phrase in v. 13, אַנְשֵׁי הַבְּלִיַּעַל אֶת־נָבוֹת נֶגֶד הָעָם, has no parallel in the original letters of Jezebel. This phrase seems somewhat strange and redundant since we have just seen in the first part of the same verse the phrase וַיָּבֹאוּ שְׁנֵי הָאֲנָשִׁים בְּנֵי־בְלִיַּעַל וַיֵּשְׁבוּ נֶגְדּוֹ. I would suggest that it is because of the differences between these two phrases, and not because of the similarities, that we may have here not a redundancy, but rather a deliberate attempt on the part of the author/narrator to delineate the specific sequence of actions that he is recounting. In the first part of the sentence, the phrase refers to two specific (the definite state of the construct form) worthless men who came and sat across from him (Naboth). In this statement, "the two worthless men" are the subjects of both verbs. In the phrase which follows, וַיְעִדֻהוּ אַנְשֵׁי הַבְּלִיַּעַל אֶת־נָבוֹת נֶגֶד הָעָם, again these same אַנְשֵׁי הַבְּלִיַּעַל ("worthless men") are the subjects of the verb. In this case the repetition of the subject places stronger emphasis upon this verb—in a sense, setting it somewhat apart from the previous two verbs. The repetition of the subject is not exact. In v. 13a the author uses the form of the definite noun with the specific numerical adjective שְׁנֵי. In v. 13b he reverts to a general or less specific, though still definite, אַנְשֵׁי הַבְּלִיַּעַל. This "generality" or lack of specification in terms of number is most likely due to the close proximity of the other specific reference, בְּנֵי־בְלִיַּעַל שְׁנֵי הָאֲנָשִׁים, and the desire to avoid an exact duplication.

---

4. *NK–B* 2:795 has a comment that the verb חֲנִידוּ in Isa 48:6 should be read as תָּעִידוּ. See also BDB, 730 for עדל√ II.

5. With Rofé, "The Vineyard of Naboth," 99–100.

6. Rofé, "The Vineyard of Naboth," 100 and n. 44. Two of the references given by Rofé are dubious (Deut 31:21 and Num 35:20). The remainder are clear examples—see Gen 30:33; Exod 20:16 = Deut 5:20; Deut 19:16 and 18 (both of which are coupled with the verb עוד√); 1 Sam 12:3; 2 Sam 1:16; Isa 3:9; 59:12; Jer 14:7; Hos 5:5 = 7:10; Mic 6:3; Prov 25:18; Job 15:6; 16.8.

Perhaps the most significant change between the commands in v. 10, the first mention of the worthless men in v. 13a, and the phrase which appears in v. 13b, is the addition to the end of the phrase in v. 13b of אֶת־נָבוֹת נֶגֶד הָעָם. This phrase informs us of two essential facts: (1) that the worthless men witness specifically *against* (or about) Naboth, and (2) that they addressed their testimony not *to* Naboth, but rather directly *to the people*. This change, congruent with the change from passive to active verbs in v. 13a, is important because it will necessitate further changes in the "person" of the specific elements of the alleged curses.

In v. 10 the command of Jezebel was to have the worthless men witness against (specifically "to" or "toward") Naboth, and she even supplied the specific quote they were to use in their testimony—בֵּרַכְתָּ אֱלֹהִים וָמֶלֶךְ, meaning "*You* cursed God and the king."[7] The verb is the piel perfect *2d* masc. sing. But in v. 13, where these worthless men have taken an active rather than passive role, and where the author or narrator has supplied the above-mentioned additions, these worthless men address their testimony directly to the whole of the people. Therefore, of necessity, they must recount Naboth's alleged curse in the 3d masc. sing., בֵּרַךְ ("he cursed"), and they must specify who it was that did the cursing, נָבוֹת ("Naboth").

The next difference between Jezebel's letter and the account of its fulfillment is to be found in the verb יצא√ ("to go out"). In v. 10 we find the hiphil imperative, masc. pl. + 3d masc. sing. suffix, וְהוֹצִיאֻהוּ ("take him out"). In v. 13 we find the expected hiphil converted imperfect 3d, masc. pl., + 3d masc. sing. suffix, וַיֹּצִאֻהוּ ("they took him out"). Following this verb in v. 13 we have the added מִחוּץ לָעִיר ("outside of the city") which supplies detail and precision which, though not needed in the command itself, clarifies the action of the verb in the narrative fulfillment account.

A similar situation is found with the following verb. In v. 10 the command is simply to "stone him," וְסִקְלֻהוּ, a qal imperative, masc. pl. + 3d masc. sing. suffix. In the fulfillment account we find an expected form, וַיִּסְקְלֻהוּ, a qal converted imperfect 3d masc. pl. + 3d masc. sing. suffix. This verb is also followed by an explicative addition vis-à-vis the command, בָּאֲבָנִים ("with stones").

The final difference between the two accounts has to do with the last verb. In v. 10 we have the form וְיָמֹת ("and he died"), which is a qal imperfect 3d masc. sing. apocopated form with a *waw*-conjunctive. This form follows in sequence upon the previous imperative and, as we have seen above, is to be understood as expressing purpose or result, "so that he might die." In the fulfillment narrative, we find the form וַיָּמֹת, which is a qal converted imperfect 3d masc. sing. apocopated form, "and he died." This form is expected and it follows logically in sequence with the previous verb.

---

7.   The phrase בֵּרַךְ נָבוֹת אֱלֹהִים וָמֶלֶךְ ("Naboth cursed God and the king") is here used as a euphemism for cursing or blaspheming. See Job 1:5, 11; 2:5, 9; Ps 10:3 (with BDB, 139; Burney, *Notes*, 247). The prohibition against cursing God and the king derives from the Covenant Code in Exod 22:27: אֱלֹהִים לֹא תְקַלֵּל וְנָשִׂיא בְעַמְּךָ לֹא תָאֹר.

## 2. Verses 8–14 as a Unit

When we consider vv. 8–14 as a unit we see that it is constructed of integrated narrative units: the text of the letters and the account of its fulfillment. Having noted the differences between these two units, we now need to look at their internal structures. An overview of both scenes, taken as an integrated unit, presents the following schematic outline:

Table 12. *A Schematic Outline of the Narrative of Act II: Scenes 2 and 3*

|  |  |  |  |
|---|---|---|---|
| I | | A Narrative Introduction for the Unit as a whole and for Scene 2: | v. 8 |
| *Scene 2* | II | The Writing of the Letters: | |
| | a) | Narrative introduction: | v. 9a |
| | b) | The Letter's Content (Instructive/Hortatory discourse): | vv. 9b–10 |
| *Narrative Bridge* | III | Narrative Bridge/Introduction to Scene 3: | v. 11 |
| *Scene 3* | IV | The Fulfillment: | |
| | a) | The Enactment of the Commands: | vv. 12–13 |
| | b) | The Report: | v. 14 |

The first way in which this block of materials is integrated is in terms of recounting the specific commands of Jezebel and their fulfillment. Internally all three units are linked together by the verb שלח√ ("to send"). This verb actually forms an *inclusio* around the entire unit (v. 8 and v. 14). It is also found twice in v. 11, in the middle of the two scenes, a verse which serves as a narrative bridge. In v. 8, Jezebel "sends" her orders via letters to the elders and nobles. In v. 11 we are emphatically told that these same elders and nobles did exactly as Jezebel had commanded in the letters which "she sent." In v. 11 we find a general description of "the people of his town" followed by two modifying clauses describing in greater detail and precision exactly who these people were who did what Jezebel commanded. This is then followed by two parallel relative clauses which modify the verb וַיַּעֲשׂוּ by telling us that *they did* "as Jezebel *sent* to them" and "as was written in the letters." This second relative clause is then even further modified by yet another relative clause that modifies the word "letters" and which reads, "which she sent to them." This hyper-emphatic verse is also hyper-redundant in the same style as 1 Kgs 21.1. Its syntactical breakdown is as follows:

Table 13. *The Syntactical Diagram of 1 Kings 21:11*

Finally, in v. 14, the elders and nobles "send" to Jezebel to inform her that her orders had been carried out and that Naboth was dead.

A second view of the internal unity and integration of these scenes can be obtained by means of an analysis of the verbal sequences and syntax of these scenes. The following is a schematic outline of Scene 2 (vv. 8–10) highlighting the verbal structure and sequence of the scene:

Table 14. *A Schematic Outline of Act II: Scene 2*

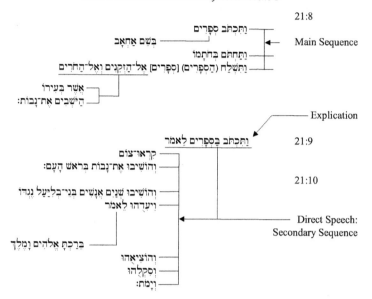

This scene opens with what I will call a "Narrative Introduction", an introduction which functions for both the unit as a whole and for Scene 2, in particular. This introduction is found in v. 8. This verse initiates the main verbal sequence of the scene which is comprised of three *wayyiqtol* forms having Jezebel as their subject: (1) וַתִּכְתֹּב, (2) וַתַּחְתֹּם, and (3) וַתִּשְׁלַח. The verb which follows these, the fourth verb in the sequence (v. 9), is the same verb as the initial verb in the verse, וַתִּכְתֹּב. I will call this verb "explicative" since it is a deliberate repetition of the initial verb of the verse and it serves as the introduction for a major secondary sequence of verbs. This secondary sequence serves to explain exactly what it was that Jezebel wrote in the letters. Its introductory nature is highlighted by the two words which immediately follow the verb, בַּסְּפָרִים לֵאמֹר, and in particular by the use of the infinitive construct, לֵאמֹר. This infinitive construct, and in fact the entire clause, introduces the section of the scene which, comprised of direct speech (*qatals*, direct volitive forms), recounts the content of the letter which Jezebel wrote in Ahab's name, sealed with his seal, and sent to the elders and nobles of Naboth's town. This section of the scene (the content of the letter) is comprised of a chain of seven imperatives addressed to the elders and nobles. In the center of this chain, we are supplied with the specific content of the testimony that the two false witnesses are to give. This explication of the content of the testimony contains a piel perfect verb (a *qatal* in direct discourse), בֵּרַכְתָּ אֱלֹהִים וָמֶלֶךְ.

We can summarize the scene by saying that the main action is performed by Jezebel, who wrote the letters, sealed them, and then sent them to the elders and nobles. This information is supplemented by the explication of the content of the letters. The verbal sequences and forms in this scene are normal and expected. Scene 3 can be outlined schematically as follows:

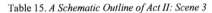

Table 15. *A Schematic Outline of Act II: Scene 3*

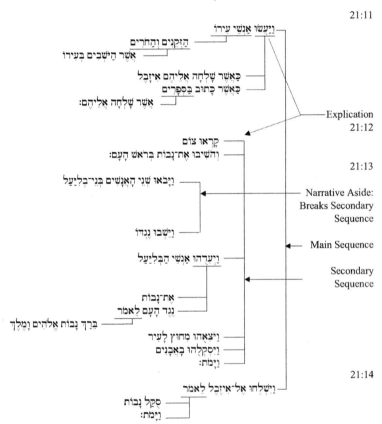

As with Scene 2, Scene 3 contains a main sequence of verbs (*wayyiqtol*) and an explication which contains a secondary sequence of verbs. In this scene, the subject of the main sequence is the elders and the nobles of Naboth's town. At the beginning of v. 11 we are told that they did as Jezebel had written to them: וַיַּעֲשׂוּ אַנְשֵׁי עִירוֹ הַזְּקֵנִים וְהַחֹרִים כַּאֲשֶׁר שָׁלְחָה אֲלֵיהֶם אִיזָבֶל. These same people are the subject of the next verb in the main sequence, which is found at the beginning of v. 14, וַיִּשְׁלְחוּ אֶל־אִיזֶבֶל לֵאמֹר. Both of these verbs in the main sequence, וַיַּעֲשׂוּ and וַיִּשְׁלְחוּ, are then followed by further explicative information.

In the case of the first verb of the scene, וַיַּעֲשׂוּ, we have the same situation as in Scene 2 where the explication is in the form of a major secondary sequence of verbs. In Scene 3 the secondary sequence serves as the "fulfillment" of the secondary sequence of verbs in Scene 2 (which is comprised mostly of *qatal* imperatives). In this case, the sequence is in the form of a narrative report which explicates exactly how the nobles and elders fulfilled that which Jezebel had commanded them in her letters (Scene 2). Verses 12–13, therefore, function as the explication of the opening verb of v. 11, וַיַּעֲשׂוּ. As was seen above when I discussed the difference between these two scenes' verbs, there is a near-perfect parallel between the verbs of the secondary sequence in Scene 2 and those found in the secondary sequence in Scene 3. The one exception is what I consider to be a break caused by the replacement of the second וְהוֹשִׁיבוּ שְׁנַיִם אֲנָשִׁים בְּנֵי־בְלִיַּעַל (v. 10a) in Scene 2 with וַיָּבֹאוּ שְׁנֵי הָאֲנָשִׁים בְּנֵי־בְלִיַּעַל וַיֵּשְׁבוּ נֶגְדּוֹ in Scene 3 (v. 13a). The change from the hiphil (causative) of the command in v. 10 to the qal (active) in this verse not only causes a break in the hiphil chain which surrounds it, but also necessitates the addition of the second verb וַיֵּשְׁבוּ (a qal perfect) in order to re-establish a link with the verb of the original command.[8] This interruption also necessitates the additional repetition of the subject for the following verb, וַיְעִדֻהוּ אַנְשֵׁי הַבְּלִיַּעַל, in order to clarify that this verb belongs to the secondary sequence and not to the main sequence of the scene. This repetition of the subject also serves to re-establish the link with the original command in v. 10 making sure that there is no confusion as to the verb's subjects—it is the "worthless men" who witnessed against Naboth and not the elders and nobles. The repetition of the subject of this verb, however, causes yet another problem in the interpretation of these verses, namely, the question concerning who is the subject of the verbs which follow, וַיֹּצִאֻהוּ and וַיִּסְקְלֻהוּ in v. 13, and וַיִּשְׁלְחוּ in v. 14. Since I interpret the verbs וַיָּבֹאוּ and וַיֵּשְׁבוּ to be an interruption or break in the sequence of the overall secondary verbal sequence of vv. 11–13, I conclude that the subjects of these three verbs in vv. 13–14 can only be the elders and nobles and the people of Naboth's town. This group also most probably included the two false witnesses following the prescription of the law of Deut 17:7. However, in my opinion, the verbal system of this scene clearly does not intend to imply or restrict the subjects of these verbs *only* to the two false witnesses.[9]

---

8. We have the following sequence chains:

| vv. 9b–10: | vv. 12–13: |
|---|---|
| qal imperative | qal imperfect |
| hiphil imperative | hiphil imperfect |
| *hiphil imperative* | *qal imperfect* |
| | *qal imperfect* |
| hiphil imperative | hiphil imperfect |
| hiphil imperative | hiphil imperfect |
| qal imperative | qal imperfect |
| qal imperative | qal imperfect |

9. With Jones, *1–2 Kings* 2:357, who notes regarding the subject of "and they sent" in v. 14 that, "The last subject given to a verb lies as far back as the 'two base fellows' in v. 13a but it is not to be assumed that they were responsible for the actions mentioned in 13b–14a. The council or court was responsible for the stoning in v. 13b, and probably official messengers were sent to Jezebel by the elders and nobles. The task of the scoundrels had been completed when they acted as witnesses." Also with Schaack, *Die Ungeduld des Papiers*, 53–55, and *contra* Bohlen, *Der Fall Nabot*, 67, who

The final verb in the main sequence, וַיִּשְׁלְחוּ, is followed by a brief explication which contains two verbal forms: סֻקַּל נָבוֹת וַיָּמֹת. This explication presents the content of the message sent from the elders and nobles to Jezebel concerning the successful completion of her commands. It is brief and to the point.

In both Scenes 2 and 3, then, we have strikingly similar verbal sequences which form the skeleton of the unit. We have a main sequence which narrates the primary action of the scenes: in Scene 2 Jezebel wrote letters, sealed them, and sent them to the elders and nobles; in Scene 3 the elders and nobles did as Jezebel commanded in the letters she had sent, before sending back to her their own message of completion. Each of these main sequences is supplemented by a large secondary sequence which supplies the details for the main sequences: in Scene 2 it gives the contents of the letter; in Scene 3 it gives the details of the fulfillment of the commands. From this, we can see the internal unity and integrity of these two scenes. They are surrounded and woven together by the *inclusio* of √שׁלח which is also used in the central v. 11 (twice). We have a near perfect symmetry between the two secondary sequences in terms of command–fulfillment. In conclusion, we can say that these two scenes form a well-integrated and balanced unit of narrative.

### 3. *Further Questions Regarding Scenes 2 and 3*

I now return to the questions that were put off in the discussion of Scene 2—namely, the question of the role of the elders and nobles, and the question of

says that, in contrast to the orders received in which the imperative has as its subject the addressees of the letter, here in v. 13 the plural subject of the verb is the שְׁנֵי הָאֲנָשִׁים. He continues by noting that since no change of subject is indicated, this means that the following verbs in 13e–f have also the witnesses as the subjects. In n. 70 on the same page, however, Schnaack states that from this one should not deduce that they alone did the stoning. If this is indeed the case, then how can he argue that the subjects of the verbs are only the false witnesses? Also *contra* Walsh, *I Kings*, 324–25, who argues that the false witnesses, Jezebel's agents, are the subjects of these verbs. He argues that this is in conformity with Israelite law, which says that the accusers in a capital crime are to be the first to cast the stones at the convict (Deut 17:7). This interpretation, however, is only partially correct since this law, states: "The hand of the witnesses shall be *first* against him to put him to death, *and after-ward the hand of all the people*" (RSV [emphasis added]). The witnesses are to be first among *all the people* to cast stones at the convict, not *just* the witnesses alone. I also fail to see how this reference to the legal practice in Deut 17:7 serves as an argument for the false witnesses being the subject of the other two verbs—וַיֹּצִאֻהוּ and וַיִּשְׁלְחוּ. Walsh argues that "the grammar is clear, the scoundrels are the subjects of the verbs." But as I have shown in the above verbal analysis, this clarity is not self-evident. Walsh also footnotes his previous categorical statement with the admission that, in fact, it is *not so clear* who the subjects are—"It is possible to read 'the people' (v. 13) as the subject of the verbs 'took him out' and 'stoned him.' But the verb in verse 14, 'sent to Jezebel,' is coordinate to those in v. 13b, and it is difficult to imagine the whole people sending the report back to Jezebel" (n. 9). In this note, Walsh contradicts, or at least modifies to the point of nullification, his categorical statement in the preceding text. Secondly, there is no reason to see the subject of the verb in v. 14a as "all the people" since the subject of the verb would have been the original addressees of the letters from Jezebel—the elders and the nobles. Interestingly, Kittel, *Die Bücher der Könige*, 157, appar-ently attempts to avoid the problem by translating the subject of these verbs as the German "man"—that is, with the generic, "one" or "someone."

the role of the two false witnesses. As we shall see, these two questions are intimately related.

What was the role of the elders and nobles in the plan of Jezebel? Were they active and willing participants, or were they passive and unwitting tools in Jeze-bel's intrigue? A superficial reading of the text of 1 Kgs 21 gives the appearance that these people were willing and knowing participants in Jezebel's plan. The data from the text that support this interpretation include the following bits of information. First, we are told that the letters from Jezebel were addressed and sent to them (v. 8). As we have already seen, it was also apparently rare that a king would call a general fast (Jehoshaphat being the one example). It was more often the case that the town leaders were the ones who called such fasts. Second, it is questionable whether the Israelite king had the legal authority unilaterally to impose a death sentence upon a free citizen of Israel. According to K. Baltzer, the "queen" (Baltzer's designation) had no legal means to use against Naboth since, "The king in Israel had no legal jurisdiction" (my translation).[10] He goes on to say, "the bearer of the legal authority is first of all the town/city commu-nity."[11] Third, in v. 11 it is emphatically stated that they (the elders and nobles) did "as Jezebel had sent to them; as was written in the letters that she sent to them." Finally, in v. 14 the elders and nobles report back to Jezebel the com-pletion of their orders. From all of this, one gets the clear impression that the elders and nobles were indeed active participants in the completion of Jezebel's plan.

There remains, however, the difficulty that arises in v. 13a with the shift from the hiphil to the qal verbs concerning the appearance on the scene of the two worthless men. This shift from the causative to the active verbal forms has raised another possible interpretation. In the letter to the elders and nobles, *they* were commanded to set (or cause to sit) two worthless men over against Naboth. Here in the fulfillment of those commands we are told that these two worthless men came forward *on their own volition* (the active form of the verb). This shift raises not only the question of the active or passive involvement of the false witnesses, it also raises the possibility that these witnesses came forward on their own. If this were the case, then perhaps the elders and nobles were not privy to this part of the plan and were, therefore, "used" by Jezebel solely to set the stage—they were simply to call a fast and sit Naboth at the head of the people. This could then support the interpretation that as far as the elders and nobles knew, the fast was for some real or threatening danger, or that the positioning of Naboth was for the purpose of bestowing some honor upon him. But this particular interpretation would raise an even further problem, namely, what to do with the statement in the letter (v. 10) in which Jezebel commands the elders and nobles to seat before Naboth the two worthless men. Would the town leaders knowingly and willingly employ two corrupt witnesses? We are in a dilemma which has intrigued interpreters and which has given rise to two opposing positions with regard to the role of the elders and nobles.

---

10. Baltzer, "Naboths Weinberg," 85, "Die Könige in Israel hatten keine Rechtshoheit."
11. Baltzer, "Naboths Weinberg," 85.

The first position interprets the role of the elders and nobles as an active one. Following the sense of the text itself, the proponents of this position consider the leaders of Naboth's town to have been totally informed and willingly involved in Jezebel's plan. Keil and Delitzsch maintain that the elders of Jezreel carried out the orders of Jezebel without hesitation. These scholars see this as an indication of the depth of the elders' and nobles' moral corruption, that they would do this out of "a slavish fear before the tyranny of the wicked queen."[12] I. Benzinger notes that "one can wonder about the brazenness with which Jezebel involved the elders of the town, and even more about the willingness with which they gave themselves over to being her pliable instruments . . . ."[13] J. Mauchline states that "it is evidence of Jezebel's power that the elders and the nobles, who were privy to the plot, conspired with her."[14] K. Baltzer holds that this scene indicates "the failure of a further ancient institution in Israel—the legal institution/community ('der Rechtsgemeinde')." The actions of the elders and nobles represent for him, and in his view for the author of the text, "a serious danger or threat to the distinctive legal system of Israel."[15] J. Gray holds that the elders and nobles were perhaps supporters of the Ahab family in Jezreel and as such were open to and accustomed to following the dictates of the royal family.[16] Scholars holding the same general position include Brichto, Miller, Uffenheimer, Seebass, Würthwein, and Zakovitch, who characterizes them as "her lackeys."[17] DeVries says that "It is certainly a sad spectacle that Israel's most powerful and revered classes could thus be instructed by royal edict to arrange for corrupt witnesses to destroy a righteous man in their midst, but so it was."[18] M. Oeming sees the whole city leadership as corrupt and under the "long arm of Jezebel."[19] Rofé refers to them as "Jezebel's accomplices,"[20] and Walsh holds that their obedience shows their complicity.[21]

The other position maintains that the elders and nobles were passive instruments in the hands of Jezebel. Generally, this group holds that the elders and nobles had no knowledge of what Jezebel had planned and that they were as surprised by the events as was perhaps Naboth himself. A. Klostermann maintains that the letter to the elders and nobles intentionally left them in the dark as to Jezebel's plans.[22] H. Gressmann holds that "Jezebel made use of some sort of

---

12. Keil and Delitzsch, *Das Alte Testament*, 225.

13. Benzinger, *Die Bücher der Könige*, 115.

14. J. Mauchline, *I–II Kings* (Peakes Commentary on the Bible; ed. M. Black and H. H. Rowley; London: Thomas Nelson, 1962), 347.

15. Baltzer, "Naboths Weinberg," 84–85.

16. Gray, *I & II Kings*, 440.

17. Brichto, *The Problem of "Curse,"* 162; Miller, "The Fall of the House of Ahab," 308; Uffenheimer, "The Deeds of Naboth the Jezreelite," 65, 72; Seebass, "Der Fall Naboth in 1 Reg. XXI," 480–81; Würthwein, "Naboth-Novelle und Elia-Wort," 387, 391; Zakovitch, "The Tale of Naboth's Vineyard," 390–92.

18. DeVries, *I Kings*, 257.

19. Oeming, "Naboth, der Jesreeliter," 373.

20. Rofé, "The Vineyard of Naboth," 91.

21. Walsh, "Methods and Meanings," 201.

22. Klostermann, *Die Bücher Samuelis und der Könige*, 383.

pretense to call the fast and set Naboth at the front. These commands applied also to the elders and town leaders. Secretly, according to the original story (v. 10 as gloss[23]), Jezebel hired two unworthy men as libelous witnesses. It was an insidious plan which worked."[24] N. Schlögl categorizes v. 10 as a gloss, saying that "Jezebel certainly would not write this in a letter to the magistrates, rather, would send it secretly by means of one of her faithful servants. With this verse eliminated, the elders and nobles would not have been privy to the plan."[25] He further notes that "if v. 10 were original then the town elders would have known and would have been as guilty as Jezebel. However, if the original text (without v. 10) is correct then they can only be said to have believed the two witnesses."[26] A. Šanda also maintains that v. 10 is secondary and "that therefore the elders and nobles would not have known the reason for the calling of the fast and the placing of Naboth at the head of the people."[27] G. Fohrer holds that as far as the people of the town were concerned, including the elders and nobles, they were to hold a fast and place Naboth at the head of the people as a sign of honor and also as a sign that Ahab and Jezebel held no grudge against him for not selling them his vineyard. The false witnesses, whom Jezebel had secretly prepared, were a surprise to everyone.[28]

F. I. Anderson theorizes that the letters sent to the elders and nobles included not only orders to hold a hearing concerning Naboth's claim of ownership of the vineyard, but also the documentation to use in the trial. He goes on to conjecture that additional documents were also sent which procured the services of false witnesses. For him, "the court officials may not have known all these facts, and so may be exonerated, if not from negligence, at least from collusion."[29] R. Bohlen holds that the letters to the elders and nobles contained only the commands to hold a fast and to sit Naboth at the head of the people.[30] This is the same position held by J. T. Walsh when he says, "They [the two worthless men] are not merely tools of the elders and nobles; they are, in fact, direct agents of the Baalist queen."[31]

In the above presentation we have seen how the question of the role of the elders and nobles in large part hinges upon the interpretation of v. 10. The presence or absence of v. 10 in the text impacts in a similar way upon the interpretation of the role of the "worthless men." If v. 10 is original, then it would mean that not only were the elders and nobles directly involved with Jezebel's plan, but also that as part of their role in the plot, they themselves were to find two false

---

23. The argumentation for the originality or the secondary nature of v. 10 will be discussed in more detail below—pp. 156–59.

24. Gressmann, *Die älteste Geschichtsschreibung*, 272. This is the same position held by de Vaux, *Les livres des Rois*, 70 n. * (my translation).

25. Schlögl, *Die Bücher der Könige, Die Bücher der Chronik*, 174 (my translation).

26. Schlögl, *Die Bücher der Könige, Die Bücher der Chronik*, 175 (my translation).

27. Šanda, *Das erste Buch der Könige*, 463 (my translation).

28. Fohrer, *Elia*, 24–25.

29. F. I. Anderson, "The Socio-Juridical Background," 55.

30. Bohlen, *Der Fall Nabot*, 68.

31. Walsh, *I Kings*, 324; see also "Methods and Meanings," 198.

witnesses to give testimony against Naboth. On the other hand, if v. 10 is secondary, then the elders and nobles had no idea what was going on and the appearance of the two worthless men is the sole doing of Jezebel. In this regard, the same group of scholars who argue for the passive role of the elders and nobles also argue that the two false witnesses were "agents" of Jezebel.

A. Klostermann and F. I. Anderson hold that the false witnesses were agents of Jezebel to whom she sent a private letter alongside the official letters she sent to the town leaders.[32] P. N. Schlögl sees it as a situation in which Jezebel worked together in secret with her "pliable servants."[33] Gressmann, Šanda, de Vaux, and Walsh hold that they were Jezebel's "agents."[34] H. Seebass holds that the false witnesses "were Jezebel's backup plan in case the elders and nobles were unfaithful to her orders."[35]

The apparent emphasis of the text is upon the active involvement of the elders and nobles and the "passive" involvement of the worthless men (they were "to be set" across from Naboth and "made" to witness against him). The elders and nobles are the addressees of the letters in v. 8, and in vv. 9–10 the content of the letters sent to them includes knowledge of the whole plan including the use of false witnesses. Verse 11 emphasizes that *they* (the elders and nobles) *did exactly as Jezebel had commanded them*. Verses 12–13 explain in detail how they complied with the commands from Jezebel. Finally, v. 14 recounts how they (the elders and nobles) sent word back to Jezebel to inform her of the completion of her orders. However, we have also seen how the shift in verbal aspect (from hiphil-causative to qal-active) in v. 13b disturbs and throws into doubt this apparent emphasis of the text. It raises the possibility that the role of the false witnesses was more active than passive and that the role of the elders and nobles was more passive than active. The whole issue revolves around v. 10.

### 4. *The Issue of Verse 10*

The overall emphasis of the entire section (Scenes 2 and 3) is that the elders and nobles were both privy to Jezebel's plan and were accomplices in it. This emphasis is interrupted by the shift in verbal aspect in v. 13b, which casts a shadow of doubt over this apparent involvement. There are two significant issues which arise in v. 10, one text-critical and the other interpretive. The solution to the question of the role of the elders and nobles depends upon the resolution of these two issues.

The text-critical issue focuses upon the fact that the entire section of text in v. 10a, from immediately following the phrase וְהוֹשִׁיבוּ שְׁנַיִם אֲנָשִׁים בְּנֵי־בְלִיַּעַל and continuing through to (and including) the term בְּנֵי־בְלִיַּעַל in v. 13a, is

---

32. Klostermann, *Die Bücher Samuelis und der Könige*, 383; F. I. Anderson, "The Socio-Juridical Background," 55.

33. Schlögl, *Die Bücher der Könige, Die Bücher der Chronik*, 174.

34. Gressmann, *Die älteste Geschichtsschreibung*, 272; Šanda, *Das erste Buch der Könige*, 463–64; de Vaux, "Le Cycle d'Élie," 70 n. *; Walsh, "Methods and Meanings," 198–99.

35. Seebass, "Der Fall Naboth in 1 Reg. XXI," 481.

missing in Codex Vaticanus (LXX^B). This lacuna is generally attributed to either haplography or to homoioteleuton.[36] The attribution of the lacuna to this sort of scribal error implies that the missing text, in fact, was there originally. R. Kittel, though recognizing that the LXX^B keeps little of the text, says that it appears to have dropped out accidentally. He observes that the gap in the LXX^B and that in the Syro-Hexaplar are not exactly the same and that in neither of these documents do the remaining pieces fit together without the addition of the texts found in the MT and Theodotion.[37]

Despite this possible explanation for the presence of the lacuna in the LXX^B, some have used its absence in this Codex as partial support for their arguments that these verses were not original to the text, and therefore that the elders and nobles were definitely not privy to Jezebel's plan and thus did not play an active role in it. A. Klostermann argues that v. 10 must be deleted since it causes awkwardness in the text with regard to the explicit statements in vv. 11–12. For him, "Jezebel had secretly arranged the whole thing and the letter to the elders and nobles deliberately left them in the dark."[38] H. Gressmann and G. Fohrer similarly argue that it is not part of the original story and that with its interwoven plan it causes a roughness in the text.[39] N. Schlögl sees v. 10 as a gloss since "Jezebel would certainly not have written this in a letter to the town leaders, but rather, she would have sent it secretly by means of a servant."[40] J. Gray holds that v. 10 "is part of Jezebel's plan rather than her overt instructions to the people of Jezreel, and may be secondary to the narration."[41] R. Bohlen also argues that "v. 10 is a secondary enlargement to the letter which originally comprised only the command to call a fast and place Naboth at the front of the people."[42] Lastly, J. T. Walsh goes back and forth on the retention or deletion of v. 10. In the end, he seems to accept v. 10 as an addition since, without it, the elders and nobles would not have been part of the plan of Jezebel. Verse 10 implicates them and, for Walsh, "transforms the story from a poignant tale of individual tragedy to an ethical exemplum that invites the reader to make moral judgments about widespread responsibility for an act of judicial murder."[43]

Linked to the above text-critical issue is an interpretive one which centers, not on the whole of v. 10, but rather on the presence of the term בְּנֵי־בְלִיַּעַל within it. A substantial number of scholars argue for the deletion of this term. The predominant argument is that Jezebel would not have used this term in reference to her own agents, especially in a letter spelling out her plan to the elders and

36. Codex Vaticanus is missing all the text between v. 10, from immediately after υἱοὺς παρανόμων, through υἱοὶ παρανόμων in v. 13. The missing text is found in other significant textual traditions, such as Alexandrinus, Cod. N, Lucianics, Armenian, Ethiopic, and Syriac. Origen includes the text under the asterisk and notes that it is in Theodotion.

37. Kittel, *Die Bücher der Könige*, 157.

38. Klostermann, *Die Bücher Samuelis und der Könige*, 383 (my translation).

39. Gressmann, *Die älteste Geschichtsschreibung*, 272; Fohrer, *Elia*, 24–25 n. 42.

40. Schlögl, *Die Bücher der Könige, Die Bücher der Chronik*, 174 (my translation).

41. Gray, *I & II Kings*, 441.

42. Bohlen, *Der Fall Nabot*, 62–68, 69 n. 71 (my translation).

43. Walsh, *I Kings*, 324–25.

nobles. Those who argue this position generally hold that the term entered v. 10 through v. 13 and that it is an expression of the narrator's opinion of the two false witnesses. Besides those already mentioned above who argue that the whole of v. 10 should be eliminated or seen as a gloss, there are some who argue only for the elimination of בְנֵי־בְלִיַּעַל. In 1904, Stade and Schwally noted that even though the term is found in the Greek, it is probably taken from v. 13: "In Jezebel's letter the expression was neither proper nor necessary; and there would have been no reason to repeat it in v. 13 if the two witnesses were already described by this epithet in v. 10."[44] A. Šanda and J. T. Walsh also maintain that the term is not original to the letter but entered under the influence of v. 13.[45] B. Uffenheimer says that it is not to be assumed that Jezebel used this term in her letter to the elders.[46] Y. Zakovitch sees the term as the narrator's words put into Jezebel's speech.[47]

The weakness in the above position, however, is that it presupposes the "historicity" of the account; that the account, as we have it, is reporting actual events as they occurred. One needs to ask whether the very reasons for which the above-mentioned scholars argue for the elimination of בְנֵי־בְלִיַּעַל from v. 10, may have been themselves "influenced" by their own perception of Jezebel and her plan. If v. 13b were to be called into question in terms of its originality in the text, a possibility given the syntactical problem caused by the shift in aspect of the verbs used, then there would be no reason at all to question the active involvement of the elders and nobles in Jezebel's plan or the use of two worthless men as witnesses in this plan (v. 10). In fact, there is also a group of scholars who maintain that the term should be retained in v. 10.

This group argues that what we have in this text (v. 10) is not an "historical" or actual account of the events as they occurred. Rather, we have here a narrative about certain events; a novel or story that recounts in artistic form an event which supposedly transpired in the past and which supposedly involved the unjust death of Naboth. The author's interest was not in the actual historical details, but rather in expressing a message about the moral and ethical injustices which may have occurred if the story were historical, or which are presently occurring at the time in which he is writing—it functions as a didactic parable. To do this, the author was free to adapt in his own "version" of what happened any of the details he may have received. Montgomery and Gehman maintain that in these verses "we are not dealing with the original indictment, and in any case the queen's arrogance knew no bounds."[48] H. Seebass, though he does not directly comment on our specific term, does maintain that the only phrases in vv. 8–13 which could be eliminated are אֲשֶׁר בְעִירוֹ in v. 8 and the second half of v. 11.[49] E. Würthwein, after presenting the arguments for the elimination of the term בְנֵי־בְלִיַּעַל,

44. Stade and Schwally, *The Book of Kings*, 165.
45. Šanda, *Das erste Buch der Könige*, 463; Walsh, "Methods and Meanings," 197–98.
46. Uffenheimer, "The Deeds of Naboth the Jezreelite," 67 n. 3.
47. Zakovitch, "The Tale of Naboth's Vineyard," 392.
48. Montgomery and Gehman, *A Critical and Exegetical Commentary*, 331.
49. Seebass, "Der Fall Naboth in 1 Reg. XXI," 479 n. 5.

counters these arguments by saying that in vv. 1–16 we are not dealing with an historical report, but rather with "a novel (eine Novelle), in which the author allows his presentation to develop and by means of this he characterizes the people and his use of time." He goes on to say that "v. 10 is actually indispensable to the unity of the 'Novelle'." He ends by arguing that "in fact v. 14 is dependent upon v. 10 and from this we can know that v. 10 is original to the story."[50] G. H. Jones maintains that the verse can be retained. He explains that it was possible "that the official correspondences only contained a legal document, the other instructions being carried by word of mouth."[51] Finally, A. Rofé maintains that v. 10 does not need to be deleted as being "too overt a game." He maintains that "what we have here is not a police report about Jezebel's crime, but a piece of fiction which does not necessarily relate 'plausible facts.'"[52]

One final question with regard to Scene 3 which is also related to the above discussions, is the question as to why the message concerning the completion of the trial, the condemnation, and the execution of Naboth is sent back to Jezebel and not to Ahab. After all, the initial letters were signed and sealed with Ahab's name and seal. Several factors touch upon this question, which I have already discussed above. Who is the subject of the verb? If it is the elders and nobles, then this again would imply that they were active participants in the plan. If it is the false witnesses, then it would indicate the innocence of the elders and nobles and the fact that these false witnesses were the secret agents of Jezebel. As with the previous issues and difficulties, the answers to this question are open to interpretation since the hard fact is that the text itself gives no indication as to the reason the message was sent to Jezebel. The only possible conclusion is that the author here, as elsewhere, is not concerned with recording the details as if he were writing a factual "police report" of the events, as if they might have actually happened. Rather, he is writing a story in which, from a narrative perspective, the reader is in a position of having "privileged" information—information for which the details do not need to be supplied. In v. 14, as with the overall emphasis of the entire two-scene section, the intention of the author is to convey that the elders and nobles of Naboth's town *were* involved with the plan from the start. They knew precisely who had sent the letters, regardless of the signature and seal attached to them, and they knew precisely to whom they had to report.

---

50. Würthwein, "Naboth-Novelle und Elia-Wort," 387–88 (my translation). More recently, similar argumentation is put forward by Schaack, "Die Ungeduld des Papiers," 53–55.

51. Jones, *1–2 Kings* 2:356.

52. Rofé, "The Vineyard of Naboth," 91.

# Chapter 14

## AN EXPOSITORY READING OF ACT II: SCENE 4—
## 1 KINGS 21:15–16

In Act II: Scene 4 the active voices and characters are the narrator (vv. 15–16), Jezebel (v. 15b), and Ahab (v. 16). Upon receiving the news that her orders concerning Naboth had been successfully carried out, Jezebel approaches Ahab and again commands him to get up. This time, instead of ordering him to eat and be happy, she tells him to go and lay claim to Naboth's vineyard for he is dead. Upon hearing this, Ahab silently obeys and goes down to take possession of the vineyard.

The location of this scene begins once again in the royal residence, perhaps even in the royal bedchamber, inferred by the command to "get up" similar to that in v. 7, though here it is not specifically connected with Ahab's being in his bed. This scene parallels Act II: Scene 1 in terms of the actors and the location. Regarding the narrative structure of the story, we have in this scene what can be called a "false climax" which is then followed by a "new complication." [1] The reason for this designation is that, in terms of a basic narrative, we have in this scene the resolution to the initial complication in the story—the vineyard which Ahab desired back in v. 2, is now his for the taking. Technically, the story could end here. [2] However, it does not. This "would-be ending" turns out to be only a "dramatic pause" leading to, and setting up, the introduction of YHWH and Elijah. Despite the fact that the story as we have it continues after v. 16, vv. 1–16 do form an identifiable narrative unit based upon the plot of an "object desired and object obtained." [3]

In the discussion of Scenes 2 and 3 we saw that there was a unity based upon command and fulfillment between the scenes. This unity was further strengthened by means of the verbal syntax and by the repetition of key terminology. We have the same situation in the present scene. Verse 15 portrays Jezebel once

---

1. J. L. Ska, *"Our Fathers Have Told Us": Introduction to the Analysis of Hebrew Narratives* (SubBib 13; Rome: Editrice Pontificio Istituto Biblico, 1990), 27. The climax of the narrative is normally the moment of highest tension. It can be triggered by the appearance of a decisive bit of new information, a new character, or a new element in the narrative. It is normally the moment when the narrative tension is relieved and the solution to the initial problem is reached. However, as in our story, there can be further complications, even after an apparent climax is reached. In these cases, the initial climax is characterized as "false."

2. See Appendix 1, below, for a discussion of the difficulty of the "end" of the original layer of the story of the vineyard.

3. Some, like Schaack, *Die Ungeduld des Papiers*, 51–52, 55–57, argue that vv. 1–16 form a complete and independent story. For further discussion see Chapter 8 and Appendix 1.

again as the one giving the commands. Verse 16 portrays Ahab as obeying and fulfilling (or at least beginning to fulfill) the commands issued by Jezebel. We note, therefore, that there is also in these two verses a unity based upon command and fulfillment.

If we step back from the text of this scene and look at the whole of Act II, we see that there is a similar type of unity between the first scene of Act II (vv. 5–7) and this, the final scene (vv. 15–16). This unity is also based upon the theme of "promise" and "fulfillment" and it becomes visible when we compare the texts in parallel.

Table 16. *The Internal Unity between Act II: Scene 1 and Act II: Scene 4*

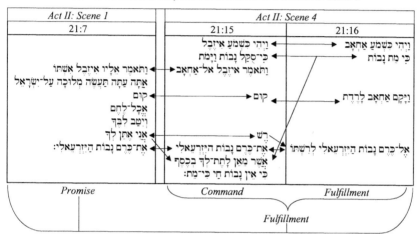

| Act II: Scene 1 | Act II: Scene 4 | |
|---|---|---|
| 21:7 | 21:15 | 21:16 |

*Promise*          *Command*          *Fulfillment*

*Fulfillment*

In Act II: Scene 4, both verses open with the same temporal phrase, וַיְהִי כִשְׁמֹעַ. In v. 15a, Jezebel is the subject and the referent is the message which the elders and nobles sent to her at the end of the last scene (v. 14). In v. 16a, the same phrase has Ahab as the subject and the referent is Jezebel's message to him concerning Naboth's demise.

The second area of similarity between vv. 15 and 16 is found in the content of the reported messages that were communicated to Jezebel and Ahab. In v. 15 the content is reported as כִּי־סֻקַּל נָבוֹת וַיָּמֹת. This report replicates exactly the message that was sent to Jezebel in v. 14. This message is then communicated by Jezebel to Ahab at the end of v. 15 by means of the following form: כִּי אֵין נָבוֹת חַי כִּי־מֵת . . .. The first thing to notice regarding this report to Ahab from Jezebel is that it does not repeat the entire report that she received from the elders and nobles. Missing is the reference to the method of Naboth's death. In the report to Ahab, Jezebel merely gives "the bottom line," the fact that Naboth is dead. In this report she actually states that Naboth is dead in two different ways: כִּי אֵין נָבוֹת חַי and כִּי־מֵת. The construction of these two clauses with their use of כִּי אֵין followed by the simple כִּי is not very common.[4] It is probably best

---

4.   Another instance of this rare combination occurs in Josh 18:7.

explained as a causal construction in which the כִּי-forms represent כִּי יַעַן, meaning "for," "because," or "on account of the fact that."[5] The second כִּי is probably best explained as a pleonastic with a causal or adversative sense which introduces a statement that repeats (albeit in a different form) the same message as the first part of the phrase and which serves the purpose of emphasizing the message.[6]

In v. 16, the message which Ahab hears from Jezebel is reported (in the voice of the narrator) as simply: כִּי מֵת נָבוֹת. In this statement, there is no longer any detail as to the cause of Naboth's death, nor any explication of the fact of his death; rather, there is just the plain fact of his death. This news of Naboth's death serves as the impetus for Ahab to take action for the first time since Act II: Scene 1, where we were informed that he had gone to his bed in a "sour mood."

The changes in the reporting of the events follows a similar pattern to that which we saw when we examined Ahab's report to Jezebel concerning his offer to buy Naboth's vineyard and Naboth's consequent rejection of the offer (vv. 2–7).[7] There we saw that the negative response of Naboth to Ahab's offer—חָלִילָה לִּי מֵיהוָה מִתִּתִי אֶת־נַחֲלַת אֲבֹתַי לָךְ (v. 3)—which was repeated exactly in Ahab's recollection of the event (v. 4), and which became in Ahab's report to Jezebel in v. 6, לֹא־אֶתֵּן לְךָ אֶת־כַּרְמִי. In both reports, a key bit of information has been left out, perhaps deliberately. In both cases, the final form of the delivered message prompts the recipients into action—Jezebel in v. 7 promises to obtain the vineyard and then does so (vv. 8–14), and Ahab in v. 16 obediently gets up from his bed to go down and take possession of the same vineyard.

This brings us to the first overt link between Act II: Scene 1 and Scene 4. Both scenes use the same verb form with Jezebel as the subject, namely, וַתֹּאמֶר. In Scene 1 the phrase serves the double purpose of introducing Jezebel as Ahab's

---

5.  See *GK* §158b.

6.  Muraoka, *Emphatic Words and Structures in Biblical Hebrew*, 106, lists the first phrase as one of only a few verses which follow the pattern of אֵין + definite noun + adjective (see also Lev 13:31), which he interprets as an emphatic usage. Joüon and Muraoka, *A Grammar of Biblical Hebrew* 2:605 §160h see this verse as a striking example of an unsuffixed form of אֵין with a determinate subject. The second occurrence of כִּי has caused some difficulties in terms of interpretation. Snaith, *Notes on the Hebrew Text of I Kings*, 77, says that the form of the verb in the phrase כִּי־מֵת can be either a qal perfect 3d masc. sing., or, a qal active participle. He then says that "since it is preceded by כִּי, it is probably the perfect meaning, 'for he had died.' He notes that about ten manuscripts have כִּי אָם in place of כִּי, which is good Hebrew for 'but/except' after a negative. He therefore translates our phrase as, 'for Naboth is not alive, but dead.'" The key difficulty in our phrase is the translation value of כִּי. According to BDB, 473, among other things, כִּי can serve to enunciate the conditions under which a future action is conceived as possible and it can also be understood as explicative in the sense of justifying a statement by unfolding the particulars which establish or exemplify it (474). BDB includes the second כִּי in our clause (though the reference which they give is 1 Kgs 21:17 instead of 21:15) in a subgroup of those occurrences where כִּי follows a negative (in our case, the first clause, אֵין כִּי). In these cases they translate it as "but" (474). Joüon and Muraoka, *A Grammar of Biblical Hebrew* 2:642 §172c n. 1, comment: "The adversative sense probably derives from the causal one, and must have developed in cases where there is virtual equivalence between *for* and *but*: Gen 17:15 . . . In 1 Kgs 21:15, after the initial כִּי in the sense of *for*, this explanation seems quite natural."

7.  See above, Chapter 10, pp. 124–29.

wife, and, as the introduction to the promise that she is going to make regarding the obtaining of the vineyard. In v. 15, the phrase introduces the fact that the vineyard is now available for Ahab to take into his possession. In both instances, the introductory statement, "Jezebel then said . . . ," is immediately followed by a chain of imperatives. In v. 7 we find קוּם אֱכָל־לֶחֶם וְיִטַב לִבֶּךָ, and in v. 15 we find קוּם רֵשׁ אֶת־כֶּרֶם נָבוֹת הַיִּזְרְעֵאלִי. In both cases, this imperative chain is followed by emphatic explicative statements that give the reason why the commands should be obeyed: v. 7, (כִּי—אֶתֵּן לְךָ אֶת־כֶּרֶם נָבוֹת הַיִּזְרְעֵאלִי אֲנִי—implicit), and v. 15, כִּי אֵין נָבוֹת חַי כִּי־מֵת.

The next element that links Scene 1 and Scene 4 is found in the verb קוּם√. This verb occurs as the first of the commands that Jezebel gives to Ahab in both scenes (v. 7 and v. 15). It also occurs in the notification of the fulfillment of the command in v. 16, וַיָּקָם (a qal converted imperfect).

Another link is found with the verb נתן√. This verb occurs in the emphatic promise of Jezebel in v. 7: אֲנִי אֶתֵּן לְךָ אֶת־כֶּרֶם נָבוֹת הַיִּזְרְעֵאלִי. In v. 15 it occurs in the context of Jezebel's explication of the reason for her new commands to Ahab to "get up and take into possession." In this context she refers to the fact that the vineyard which she now commands Ahab to take into possession is the same one which Naboth refused "to give to you for money" (אֲשֶׁר מֵאֵן לָתֶת־לְךָ בְכֶסֶף). What Naboth refused to give to Ahab in v. 3, and that which Jezebel promised to give to him in v. 7, Jezebel now gives to Ahab in v. 15. This is the first occurrence of this verb since the promise made by Jezebel to Ahab back in v. 7 (a hiatus of eight verses). Every usage of the verb נתן√ to this point in the chapter has had the vineyard of Naboth as its object.[8]

Scene 1 and Scene 4 are also linked together by references to the "object of desire." In v. 7, Jezebel promised to give to Ahab, אֶת־כֶּרֶם נָבוֹת הַיִּזְרְעֵאלִי. In v. 15, she commands Ahab to take possession of the same: אֶת־כֶּרֶם נָבוֹת הַיִּזְרְעֵאלִי. Finally, in v. 16, we are informed that Ahab arose in order to go down: אֶל־כֶּרֶם נָבוֹת הַיִּזְרְעֵאלִי.

A final internal link is found within Scene 4 itself and has to do with the verb ירשׁ√. In v. 15 we find the qal imperative form רֵשׁ. In v. 16 we have the infinitive construct form plus the 3d masc. sing. suffix, לְרִשְׁתּוֹ. This is another instance of the command–fulfillment pattern. Though there is no direct linkage between this root and Scene 1, there is a thematic linkage with Jezebel's promise to give to Ahab the vineyard of Naboth. The object of this promise and that of the verb ירשׁ√ is the same vineyard. As a pair of commands, קוּם רֵשׁ only occurs in this verse in the Old Testament.

---

8. There remains in 1 Kgs 21 only one further use of this verb in v. 22. Once again, there is a substantial hiatus of seven verses between the usage of נתן√ in v. 15 and its occurrence in v. 22. In v. 22, however, the subject of the verb is YHWH and its object is not related to the vineyard of Naboth; rather it is the condemnation of Ahab's house/descendants because of his crime against Naboth. In this occurrence of the verb, we can conclude that other than being the same basic verb, it is not connected to the use of this verb in the previous instances—neither in terms of theme (the vineyard) nor in terms of subjects (YHWH plays no active role in the story of the acquisition of the vineyard, vv. 1–16).

A final element of Act II: Scene 4 is the presence of Naboth. In this scene we find the densest usage of Naboth's name in the entire chapter—five times in two verses.[9] Interestingly, though Naboth only speaks once (in v. 3), his constant presence is strongly felt throughout the rest of the story by means of the use of his name. This presence is almost haunting and it is particularly strongly felt in these two verses.

As a result of the above discussion concerning the many connections between Act II: Scene 1 and Scene 4, as well as between the two verses within Scene 4, we can conclude that these scenes are very closely related in theme, forms, and terminology. The overriding theme that links these two scenes together is that of promise/command and fulfillment. Together these two scenes form "bookends" for the whole of Act II.

9.    Act I: Scene 1 (×4); Act II: Scene 1 (×2); Scene 2 (×2); Scene 3 (×4); Scene 4 (×5).

## Part IV

### THE SOURCES AND ORIGINS OF THE STORY OF NABOTH'S VINEYARD IN 1 KINGS 21:1–16: AN HYPOTHESIS

## Chapter 15

### WHEN WAS THIS STORY OF NABOTH'S VINEYARD CREATED?

The question of dating is perhaps one of the most difficult questions concerning any ancient text. It is, however, the fundamental question for the formulation of any hypothesis for the origins of a text. Once a text has been situated on the chronological continuum, then it becomes possible to conjecture answers to the other necessary historical questions.

In the course of the history of the interpretation of 1 Kgs 21, there has been general, though by no means unanimous, agreement that the origin of 1 Kgs 21:20b–22, 24–29 is Deuteronomistic. The greatest difficulties have had to do with identifying the sources and origins of vv. 1–16, the story of Naboth's vineyard. These difficulties, coupled with the apparent lack of any recognizable Dtr linguistic characteristics, have led the majority of commentators to take the position that the story must be "an old tradition" which was subsequently used by the author/compiler in the creation of 1 Kgs 21. This position has then led many of these same scholars to interpret the events recounted in this story as having actually happened in the historical period of Ahab, king of Israel. This conclusion is mistaken. It is based upon a circular argument which maintains that there is no evidence that vv. 1–16 are from Dtr, therefore it must be an old tradition; and because it is an old tradition, there is no evidence of Dtr found within it.

This type of argumentation has had the effect of causing a somewhat "near-sighted" approach to the question of the origins of vv. 1–16 among those scholars who have actually attempted to discern the historicity of the text of vv. 1–16.[1] This approach develops its position in the following manner. First, vv. 1–16 "must" antedate the Dtr material in vv. 17–29 since they contain no obvious Dtr language. Second, if vv. 1–16 are indeed older than the Dtr material, then it is only logical that they come from the historical period of Ahab and Elijah, since they recount events concerning their time. Third, if vv. 1–16 come from the time of Ahab and Elijah, then they must be historical. This type of "logic" has had the effect of preventing the vast majority of scholars from ever even considering the possibility that vv. 1–16 could be anachronistic and that they could indeed post-date the Dtr texts in vv. 17–29.

We need to step back from the incidents and persons of the text of 1 Kgs 21:1–16, and away from the obvious Dtr material found in the chapter, in order to be able to re-ask the question concerning the sources and origins of the story.

---

1.  There are many scholars who, without doing independent research, "presume" or accept the historicity of these verses simply because previous scholars held them to be historical.

If we do this, then the "problem" of the lack of any Dtr language in vv. 1–16, and that of the magnetic attraction of the Dtr materials in vv. 20–29, fade in both importance and influence.

The foregoing analysis of 1 Kgs 21 has shown that there are indeed elements of ch. 21 and its related texts that are from the Dtr traditions. But it has also shown that there are other elements which cannot be assigned in any direct way to the Dtr traditions, namely, what we have called the "Elijah–Naboth Fragment," the "Jehu-Apologetic Redaction," and the entire "Anti-Jezebel Redaction." I have argued that the Elijah–Naboth Fragment and the Jehu-Apologetic Redaction are in fact of pre-Dtr provenance and were "reused" or "kept" by the Dtr in his construction of his history. The Anti-Jezebel Redaction, however, I have argued is of late, post-Dtr provenance.[2] But what of vv. 1b–16, 23, 25bα? What are their origins and why were they written?

The author of 1 Kgs 21:1b–16, 23, 25bα must have had certain themes, concerns, or issues that he wished to present, and these would undoubtedly be linked with concerns and issues of his own day. It is my contention that these are detectable in our verses by means of the author's symbolic characterization of the individuals in his story of the vineyard. It is therefore important first to focus attention upon these characterizations in order to situate the text of 1 Kgs 21:1–16 chronologically. I will limit my focus to the three main characters: Ahab, Naboth, and Jezebel.

### 1. *Ahab the Wicked King*

The name "Ahab" occurs fifteen times in 1 Kgs 21. In v. 1 he is introduced as אַחְאָב מֶלֶךְ שֹׁמְרוֹן ("Ahab, king of Samaria") and in v. 18 he is referred to as אַחְאָב מֶלֶךְ־יִשְׂרָאֵל ("Ahab, king of Israel"). All the other occurrences of the name are in the simple form of אַחְאָב.

The presentation of Ahab in this chapter is very complex. Verse 1 introduces him as the "king of Samaria" who owned a palace in the town of Jezreel beside which Naboth the Jezreelite owned a vineyard. Ahab desired to have possession of this vineyard and so he entered into discussion and negotiation with Naboth concerning this possibility (v. 2). In this verse, Ahab is presented as a king who was both just and respectful of his citizens' rights. This is demonstrated by the fairness and, in fact, the generosity of the offer that he made to Naboth. Even in the following verses (vv. 3–4), when Naboth refuses to part with his family inheritance (the vineyard), Ahab's response is not one of tyrannical megalomania. He does not (according to the text) resort to the exercise of regal authority or to the right of "eminent domain" in order to take possession of the vineyard by force. Instead, at Naboth's refusal, Ahab simply returned to his house סַר וְזָעֵף עַל־הַדָּבָר אֲשֶׁר־דִּבֶּר אֵלָיו נָבוֹת הַיִּזְרְעֵאלִי . . . וַיִּשְׁכַּב עַל־מִטָּתוֹ וַיַּסֵּב אֶת־פָּנָיו וְלֹא־אָכַל לָחֶם ("sullen and displeased about that which Naboth the Jezreelite had spoken to him . . . and he laid down upon his bed and he turned away his face and would

---

2. See above, p. 47 n. 43.

not eat food") (v. 4). The presentation of Ahab in vv. 1–3 as fair and just and as one who consults others perhaps best reflects the Ahab we met in 1 Kgs 20. There Ahab was willing to consult and listen to both the elders and the various prophets who were sent to him by YHWH.

Between vv. 3 and 4, the presentation of Ahab shifts suddenly from one of a just and fair king to a king who is dejected, upset, and totally immobilized by Naboth's rejection of his offer. Now the king is presented as reacting like a small child who has not had his own way. This shift serves to set the stage for the remainder of the story of the acquisition of the vineyard (vv. 5–16), with its presentation of Jezebel as the one who exercises true royal "authority." Throughout all of vv. 5–14, Ahab is totally absent from the narrative—presumably he is still lying in his bed totally immobilized.

When next we hear of Ahab in vv. 15–16, Jezebel announces to him the fact that Naboth is dead and that his vineyard is now available for Ahab to take it into his possession. When Ahab hears this, the text says that he "arose to go down to the vineyard of Naboth the Jezreelite to take possession of it" (v. 16). Verses 15–16 present Ahab as one who mutely and unquestionably obeys his wife Jezebel, who has both the will and power to command her husband. In reality, vv. 1–16 are more a story about Jezebel than about Ahab. Ahab is merely a secondary character, a "stage prop" whose presence simply serves to contextualize the actions and the presentation of Jezebel.

In vv. 17–20a we have a scene in which YHWH calls upon Elijah to go down and meet Ahab (v. 18), to confront him with the accusation of murder and of taking possession (v. 19), and to condemn him to death (v. 19). The account of the actual encounter between Ahab and Elijah opens *in medio res* in v. 20a. Ahab is speaking in a style very similar to that which is found in 1 Kgs 18:17. In both scenes Ahab is presented as being "aggressive" toward Elijah. He accuses Elijah of being a "troubler of Israel" (18:17) and refers to Elijah as, "O my enemy" (21:20a). In both cases, Elijah reverses the "charge" of being a "troubler" back upon Ahab, after which Ahab then becomes humbly obedient to the prophet. In 1 Kgs 18:19–20 he obeys Elijah's command to call together all Israel and all the prophets of Baal and Asherah, and in 1 Kgs 21:27 Ahab rent his clothing, put on sackcloth, fasted, and "went about quietly."

In the remainder of the verses of the chapter, 21:20bβ–26, we find a collection of accusations and condemnations spoken against Ahab (with the exception of v. 23, which is against Jezebel). As has already been discussed, these verses are characteristic of the Dtr editor in both language and style. These verses have nothing to do with the events of 1 Kgs 21:1–20a. Rather, they are accusations and condemnations for supposed "sins" of Ahab which were presented primarily in the proleptic summary in 1 Kgs 16:29–34, but also throughout all of chs. 17–20 and 22. In 1 Kgs 21:20bβ, Ahab is portrayed as having "sold himself to do what was evil in the sight of the Lord." For this all his descendants are to die (v. 21); his entire house/dynasty is to be wiped out because of the anger to which he provoked YHWH and because he caused Israel to sin (vv. 22, 24). Verses 25–26, in the form of a narrative aside, reiterate the incomparability of Ahab's wickedness (see 1 Kgs 16:30–34) and link it directly to the sin of "going after other gods" (v. 26). The presentation of Ahab in 1 Kgs 21, therefore, is drawn from a variety of different sources. It is a constructed or compiled characterization that combines features from his characterizations in 1 Kgs 16:30–34; 1 Kgs 17–19; 20; and 22.

Ahab is presented in 1 Kgs 21 as the incomparably wicked king (vv. 17–26). This characterization as a wicked and even abominable character is not necessarily a late or post-exilic invention. In 1 Kgs 21, Ahab is symbolic of both Israelite and Judean kingship, at least in the eyes of the Dtr Historian. Kingship became the focal point and the target of prophetic opposition when, in the prophets' eyes, it began to over-reach its intended function and to become like the kingship of the countries that surrounded Israel. The prophets opposed the centralization of power, authority, and wealth in the hands of the crown. This centralization was nearly always at the expense of the poor and the powerless classes of society. This theme is found in both the story of the vineyard in 1 Kgs 21:1–16, and in the confrontation of Elijah and Ahab regarding the murder of Naboth and the confiscation of his property by the crown in vv. 17–19a, 20aα–bα. The motif of the abusive king/crown/ruler in Israel recalls the debate concerning kingship found throughout the Old Testament.[3]

Ahab is accused of being worse than all the other kings who were before him (v. 25a). This accusation of "negative incomparability" is then further defined in vv. 25b–26. He is charged with having been "seduced" by his (foreign) wife, וַיַּתְעֵב מְאֹד לָלֶכֶת אַחֲרֵי הַגִּלֻּלִים כְּכֹל אֲשֶׁר עָשׂוּ הָאֱמֹרִי אֲשֶׁר הוֹרִישׁ יְהוָה מִפְּנֵי בְּנֵי יִשְׂרָאֵל ("and he did very abominably in following after idols, like all that the Amorites had done, whom the LORD dispossessed before the people of Israel", v. 26). Ahab is accused and condemned, not only for having abused and ignored the rights of Naboth the Jezreelite, but also for having abused and ignored the rights of YHWH. In all these things, in the Dtr Historian's view, Ahab becomes symbolic of the wicked and corrupt kings of both Israel and Judah. It is no small wonder, then, that he also becomes the one who ultimately is blamed for the eventual destruction of Israel and who becomes known as the worst of all Israelite kings. His wickedness and sinfulness are so great that they even "infect" the

---

3. The discussion of the role of kingship in Israel and the ancient Near East is a complex and heated one. As this is not our direct topic of interest, I will here only present a brief bibliography: H. J. Boecker, *Die Beurteilung der Anfänge des Königtums in den deuteronomistischen Abschnitten. Ein Beitrag zum Problem des "deuteronomistischen Geschichtswerks"* (WMANT 31; Neukirchen–Vluyn: Neukirchener Verlag, 1969); W. H. Schmidt, "Kritik am Königtum," in *Probleme biblischer Theologie: Gerhard von Rad zum 70. Geburtstag* (ed. H. W. Wolff; Munich: Chr. Kaiser, 1971), 440–61; R. E. Clements, "The Deuteronomistic Interpretations of the Founding of the Monarchy in I Sam. VIII," *VT* 24 (1974): 398–410; Veijola, *Das Königtum*; B. Halpern, *The Constitution of the Monarchy in Israel* (HMS 25; Chico, CA: Scholars Press, 1981); G. E. Gerbrandt, *Kingship According to the Deuteronomistic History* (SBLDS 87; Atlanta: Scholars Press, 1986); J. J. M. Roberts, "In Defense of the Monarchy: The Contribution of Israelite Kingship to Biblical Theology," in *Ancient Israelite Religion: Essays in Honor of Franck Moore Cross* (ed. P. D. Miller, Jr., P. D. Hanson and S. D. McBride; Philadelphia: Fortress, 1987), 377–96; W. Riley, *King and Cultus in Chronicles: Worship and the Reinterpretation of History* (JSOTSup 160: Sheffield: JSOT Press, 1993).

kingdom of Judah through the marriage/treaties made by himself and his sons. Ahab and his dynasty become the "measure" by which King Manasseh, and all Judah itself, will be condemned to destruction and exile (2 Kgs 21:13; Mic. 6:16). One needs only to consult such Dtr texts as those found in 2 Kgs 8:18, 26–27; 21:3, 13, to see that Ahab had already become, in the eyes of the Dtr, this "measure":

> And I will stretch over Jerusalem the measuring line of Samaria, and the plummet of the house of Ahab; and I will wipe Jerusalem as one wipes a dish, wiping it and turning it upside down. (2 Kgs 21:13 RSV)

I conclude, therefore, that there is evidence in the presentation of Ahab in 1 Kgs 21:17–26 that betrays the perspectives of the Dtr. When we look at vv. 1–16, however, we must say that this particularly Dtr symbolic presentation of Ahab is not found. In these verses, Ahab is not the epitome of the wicked king, but rather he is the epitome of an incompetent, whimpering, spoiled, and childish weakling. When he does not get his way with the vineyard, he does not act as a king normally would; rather, he merely returns home, goes to bed, and refuses to eat. He is incapacitated by Naboth's refusal, and certainly does not reflect the type of wicked king portrayed in the Dtr passages. We must ask, therefore: If this is the case, then from where does this picture of Ahab come? Before we can answer this question fully, we must first look at the presentations of Naboth and Jezebel.

## 2. *Naboth the Jezreelite*

References to Naboth occur only in 1 Kgs 21 and in 2 Kgs 9:21bγ, 25–26. Within these texts, Naboth is referred to by the simple form of his name, נָבוֹת, a total of fourteen times and with the compound of the name + gentilic, הַיִּזְרְעֵאלִי, a total of eight times.

When we look at the presentation of Naboth in 1 Kgs 21, the first thing we notice is that, despite his very frequent mention by name within the first eighteen verses (×19), he is really only a secondary character. He actively speaks only once, in v. 3. In all the other references which use his name, he is a passive character—he is either being quoted or spoken about. The fact that Naboth only actively speaks once is very important in his presentation in this story. This fact focuses the attention of the reader or listener upon that which Naboth says. The remainder of the story results from, and hinges upon, what Naboth says. From this perspective, his single statement becomes the key for understanding the whole of the story and, as such, it becomes the perfect channel for the expression of the central issue for the author.

Naboth is introduced in v. 1. This introduction supplies us with the setting and background for his statement. We learn from this verse that Naboth is a Jezreelite and that he owns a vineyard that is located next to the palace of Ahab, the king in Samaria.[4] In v. 2 we are informed that Ahab, the king, desired to have Naboth's

---

4. This verse contains many interesting textual, redactional, and logical difficulties. A detailed discussion of these is beyond the scope of the present work. What is important here is that the vineyard is located closeby the palace of Ahab.

vineyard for a "green garden" and proposed to trade a better vineyard for Naboth's vineyard, or to buy the vineyard from him. To this point, there is nothing untoward or extraordinary about the situation—a king offers to trade or buy a piece of property (a vineyard) from one of his citizens with what appears to be a very fair and even generous offer. However, Naboth refuses the offer.

In v. 3 we find Naboth's only spoken words in response to the king's offer: חָלִילָה לִּי מֵיהוָה אֶת־נַחֲלַת אֲבֹתַי לָךְ מִתְּתִי ("God forbid that I should give my ancestral inheritance to you"). This response has the effect of shocking both the reader/listener, and the king. One's reaction is to ask why Naboth would refuse such a generous offer by the king. Naboth's response supplies this reason. The vineyard is not just an ordinary vineyard, it is the "inheritance of my fathers." Naboth's answer has been interpreted in two opposite ways: either he *would not sell* his vineyard, or, he *could not sell* his vineyard.[5] The way one interprets Naboth's statement will greatly impact the way in which one interprets the presentation of Naboth in this story. Based upon the information supplied by the text of 1 Kgs 21:1–16, it is my position that Naboth was not in a situation where, according to Israelite traditions and customs, he might have *had* to sell his property (Lev 25:25–28). Therefore, based upon these same Israelite traditions and customs,[6] I conclude that *he could not sell his vineyard*. The reasons why he could not sell his vineyard are based upon the traditions and practices of his ancestors, which (at least according to 1 Kgs 21) were apparently still in effect at the time of its author. Whether or not these traditions carried with them the full weight of civil or religious law is open to question. What is not so much open to question is the moral or ethical weight of the traditions that prevented Naboth from even considering trading or selling his family inheritance. By creating this situation in the text, the author symbolically portrays Naboth as the epitome of the faithful Israelite. Naboth maintains and protects the land-inheritance of his tribe and all the other traditions of his forefathers that are being threatened by the "modern advances" of the political realities of the time of the compiler of this text.

In the only other references to Naboth in the Old Testament, 2 Kgs 9:21bγ, 25–26, Naboth is presented as a person from Jezreel who had owned properties (fields) near that city. He and his sons had been murdered and as a result of this the Lord is said to have uttered an oracle of doom against Ahab. Jehu, after murdering Ahab's son Joram, the reigning monarch, commands his adjutant to cast Joram's body upon "the field of Naboth." The only thing we can gain from these passages is that Naboth and his sons were murdered. The reason for these murders and the name of the murderer(s), are never given. We also learn that Naboth owned properties other than the vineyard which was near the palace of Ahab (1 Kgs 21). These fields are still being referred to as "the fields of Naboth" several years after Naboth's death.[7]

---

5.   See Appendix 2 for a presentation of scholarly opinion regarding this question.
6.   See Gen 12:7; Lev 25:8–55, especially vv. 23–24; Josh 21:43–45; 24:12–13; etc.
7.   See the discussion of these texts in Chapter 2.

The information in these verses is presented in a very general way and with a noticeable lack of precision or detail. Effectively, rather than detracting from the symbolic nature of Naboth's presentation in 1 Kgs 21, this material's generic nature, in fact, reinforces this symbolic presentation.

### 3. *Jezebel the Wife of Ahab and the "Counterpart" to Ahab in Wickedness*

In 1 Kgs 21:1–16, Ahab is portrayed as being "manipulated" and "controlled" by his wife, Jezebel. In a certain sense, Jezebel acts as the "counterpart" to Ahab in these verses. She fulfills the role of the strong, ruthless, sinful ruler (Ahab's Dtr role) and the role of the dangerous foreign wife. She is in control of everything. She is decisive, industrious (the plan and the letters), powerful (she commands the elders and nobles). She is unethical (using false witnesses and having an innocent Israelite "juridically murdered"), and she is successful (she attains that which she sets out to obtain). In vv. 1–16, by means of the way Jezebel is presented, all the "blame" is placed squarely upon her. This serves to balance all the blame that is placed upon Ahab in vv. 17–26. By the end of the chapter, they have been accused, condemned, and "sentenced" to death for their wicked behavior. Through the characterizations of Ahab and Jezebel, 1 Kgs 21 comes to represent a very strong indictment and judgment upon abusive and uncontrolled rulers in Israel and Judah—kings, their wives, nobles, and elders. This indictment might still be considered to be of Deuteronomistic origin were it not for its being affiliated and combined with the role and character of Jezebel. Jezebel, as Ahab's wicked foreign wife, does not "fit" into the typical Dtr schema and material.

### a. *Jezebel the Wicked Foreign Woman/Wife*

In the presentation of Jezebel in 1 Kgs 21, and in fact in her entire biblical presentation, the major emphasis is place squarely upon the fact that she is *a foreign wife/woman* married to King Ahab whom she "seduced" into apostasy. The only explicit accusation made against Jezebel (v. 25b) is situated within the context of an accusation against Ahab. It is possible to read this charge on at least two different levels. On the surface, it is a charge that she "seduced" her husband Ahab to follow after the idols (see v. 26). On a deeper or more subtle level, this charge comes to characterize the entire biblical presentation of Jezebel found throughout the whole of the Elijah Cycle. She is presented as a "harlot and sorceress" who seduces, not only Ahab, but also all of Israel away from fidelity to YHWH and his laws (2 Kgs 9:22). She is presented as the protectress and promoter of worship of the "foreign" gods, Baal and Asherah (1 Kgs 18:19). She is introduced in 1 Kgs 16:31–33 as the sure sign of Ahab's negative incomparability—of his being even worse than Jeroboam. Through his marriage to this foreign woman Jezebel, it is implied that Ahab became an apostate (vv. 31b–34). Jezebel, for the author of these texts, becomes symbolic of the dangerous and seductive nature of apostasy. This danger is specifically personified in the figure of the "foreign wife," who, once given entrance into the special realm of the covenant community, eventually corrupts and takes control of the minds and hearts of all, king and citizen alike, and leads them away from sole reliance upon, and true faith in, YHWH.

b. *Jezebel in 1 Kings 21—The Story of Naboth's Vineyard*

When we focus our attention upon the presentation of Jezebel in the overall story of 1 Kgs 21, the first thing that strikes us is the emphasis that is placed upon the fact that Jezebel is Ahab's "wife". She is referred to as אִיזֶבֶל אִשְׁתּוֹ (in reference to Ahab), a total of three times in the whole of the Elijah/Elisha Cycles. All three of these references are found in the story of Naboth's vineyard (1 Kgs 21:5, 7, 25). This theme of Jezebel as Ahab's wife is tightly linked to the introduction of Jezebel in the proleptic summary of Ahab's reign found in 1 Kgs 16:29–34. Within this summary, which in its final form strongly highlights the negative effects of Jezebel becoming Ahab's wife, is found the only other reference to Jezebel as Ahab's wife outside the anti-Jezebel redactional material: וַיִּקַּח אִשָּׁה אֶת־אִיזֶבֶל בַּת־אֶתְבַּעַל מֶלֶךְ צִידֹנִים ("and he took as his wife Jezebel, the daughter of Ethbaal, King of Sidon") (v. 31). This statement, in my opinion, is the only original Dtr reference to Jezebel.

(1) *Jezebel in the story of the acquisition of Naboth's Vineyard—vv. 1b–16.* In this story, Jezebel is *the* main actress. It is she who takes things into her own hands in order to obtain the desired vineyard for her incapacitated husband. According to the logic of the text, Jezebel is presented as the one who comes up with the plan for obtaining the vineyard and she is the one who puts it into action. Ahab is presented as not having been involved at all.

Jezebel first appears in v. 5 where she is introduced as Ahab's wife who comes to the dejected Ahab and asks why he was so upset and refusing to eat. Ahab tells her about Naboth's rejection of his offer (v. 6). In v. 7, "Jezebel, his wife," responds to him. The repetition of the relationship of Jezebel to Ahab in this verse, so close upon the same introduction in v. 5, can only be understood as being meant to add emphasis. Together with the tight link of these references to 1 Kgs 16:31, this emphasis implies that Jezebel is not only Ahab's wife, but more specifically, that Jezebel is Ahab's "Sidonian (= foreign) wife." Though no direct reference is found in 1 Kgs 21:1b–16 to the fact of Jezebel's foreign origins, the linkage with 16:31 makes this very clear. The dialogue between Ahab and Jezebel in vv. 5–7 further supports this. In this dialogue, Jezebel is the one in control of the situation. She first comments on Ahab's method of exercising kingship in Israel, and then she promises to get the vineyard herself. In this we see a deliberate attempt on the part of the author to highlight the differences, not only between Ahab and Jezebel as individuals, but also on the implied level, between understandings or methods of rule in Israel and Sidon.

In 21:8–14 we have the account of Jezebel's ruthless plan for obtaining the vineyard and of its fulfillment. Naboth is accused of blasphemy and "treason"[8]

---

8. N. M. Sarna notes that there is no biblical law or legal text that mentions a punishment for cursing the king. He then proceeds to draw the same conclusion as most have done in the past. He says that since both God and king are paired together implicitly in Exod 22:27 and explicitly in our text (1 Kgs 21:10, 13) and in Isa 8:21 (though in reverse order) it is reasonable to assume that the offense of cursing the king was considered to be on the same level of high crime as cursing God. Both were taken to be a great threat to the established social and religious order, as a crime against

and is stoned to death. Then at the beginning of v. 14 we are informed that the elders and nobles sent word back *to Jezebel* that the orders had been fulfilled and Naboth was dead. This should strike us as somewhat odd. Why was word sent back to Jezebel, *and not to the king* whose name and seal were used on the letters? How did the elders and nobles know to send the message to Jezebel? The text itself does not address the answers to these questions. It would appear, however, that the text does want to imply that the elders and nobles were in collusion with Jezebel, or in some way were under her control. Jezebel is presented in these verses as a ruthless feminine and foreign potentate.

In vv. 15–16 we once again see Jezebel in action. Upon receiving word of Naboth's death, she goes to Ahab, who is presumably still in his bed, and she *commands* him to "arise and go down and take possession of Naboth's vineyard, for Naboth was dead." Ahab is portrayed as obediently doing all that Jezebel commands. Who, then, is acting the part of king? It is Jezebel!

In summary, we can say that in 1 Kgs 21:1b–16 Jezebel is first of all presented as Ahab's (foreign) wife. As such, she is shown capable of both confronting her husband and of taking charge. In vv. 8–13 she is presented as a "ruthless potentate." Finally, in vv. 15–16, she is presented as the one in charge; the one in command. A plain reading of the text of vv. 1–16 presents a Jezebel who is a prime example of a powerful and ruthless foreign woman/wife. Though it is true that in the text of 1 Kgs 21 there is no explicit mention of the fact that Jezebel was a "foreigner," we "know" this information as attentive "listeners" from the connection of this story with 1 Kgs 16:31. Her character and actions are always presented in such a way as to highlight the fact that both she and her actions are "foreign" in comparison to those of a "faithful Israelite." In 1 Kgs 21:1b–16,

the state meriting capital punishment (N. M. Sarna, "Naboth's Vineyard Revisited [1 Kings 21]," in *Tehillah le-Moshe: Biblical and Judaic Studies in Honor of Moshe Greenberg* [ed. M. Cogan, B. L. Eichler and J. H. Tigay; Winona Lake, Ind.: Eisenbrauns, 1997], 119–26 [121–22]). The main difficulty with this position is that there is no textual evidence to support the position that cursing the king was held to be on the same level as cursing God in the Old Testament in general, and in our specific text in particular. Keil and Delitzsch arrived at a conclusion similar to Sarna, but based it more on a "religious" or "theological" foundation. They maintained that "the cursing of the king is not to be taken as a second crime added to that of cursing God, but rather, the cursing of the king as the visible representative of God was *eo ipso* also cursing God" (Keil and Delitzsch, *Das Alte Testament*, 225). Klostermann maintained that "Naboth's refusal was an unmotivated insult against the king" (Klostermann, *Die Bücher Samuelis und der Könige*, 382). Gressmann maintained that "the one who cursed the king, just as the one who cursed God, was, according to accepted law, to be stoned to death." How much more so in the case where Naboth, "a stiff-necked farmer . . . so viciously abused the special trust of his king" (Gressmann, *Die älteste Geschichtsschreibung*, 271–72). Šanda argues that "the accusation of cursing God does not appear to be very strong in the text. The account presents the offense or insult against the king as the most significant of the charges . . . "Naboth was made to appear as a *rebel* against the crown and, as such, deserved to be put to death as in the account found in 2 Sam 16:5–15" (Šanda, *Das erste Buch der Könige*, 464). Z. Ben-Barak maintained that the Naboth story contains all the elements which allowed for the conclusion that Naboth was tried and convicted as a rebel against the king and the state (Z. Ben-Barak, "The Confiscation of Land in Israel and the Ancient Near East," *Shnaton, An Annual for Biblical and Ancient Near Eastern Studies* [Tel Aviv: The Israel Bible Society, 1982 (Hebrew)], 101–17 [110–11]).

then, she is characterized as being cunning (it is her plan), ruthless (she had Naboth put to death), unethical (she used false witnesses), and domineering (she was the one who commands Ahab, the king). Just as in 1 Kgs 18–19, so also in 1 Kgs 21:1b–16, Jezebel is presented as a powerful force that inspires fear and who is capable of achieving what she wants, despite or regardless of the king.

(2) *The presentation of Jezebel in vv. 20bβ–26—the Dtr additions.* It is a fact that Jezebel is portrayed as the "prime mover" or the "prime actor" in vv. 1–16. When we look at the Dtr additions that "supposedly" spell out the punishments for the murder of Naboth, however, we find that the person punished the most is not Jezebel but Ahab, who spent most of vv. 1–16 in his bed. In vv. 20bβ–26 it is Ahab who gleans the major portion of the accusations and condemnations. Technically, as I have already noted, these Dtr verses have more to do with Ahab's having succumbed to the powers and seductions of his (foreign) wife Jezebel portrayed in chs. 17–19, than with the events of 1 Kgs 21:1–16. Within the context of 1 Kgs 21, however, they are meant to be understood in relation to vv. 1–16. In this regard and in this context, there is an inverse proportion of punishment to responsibility for the crime in these verses as compared to vv. 1–16. According to the author/editor of 1 Kgs 21:20bβ–26, Ahab is the one who is held mainly responsible for Naboth's death and for taking possession of his vineyard (v. 20a).

For this reason we find one condemnation after another for Ahab in vv. 20bβ–26. Stuck into the middle of these, literally interrupting and breaking the flow of Ahab's condemnations, we find in v. 23 the only condemnation mentioned for Jezebel: וְגַם־לְאִיזֶבֶל דִּבֶּר יְהוָה לֵאמֹר הַכְּלָבִים יֹאכְלוּ אֶת־אִיזֶבֶל בְּחֵל יִזְרְעֶאל ("and also concerning Jezebel, says the LORD, the dogs will eat Jezebel in the territory [ramparts] of Jezreel"). We are compelled to question the "justice" of the imbalance of punishments vis-à-vis the responsibility for the crime. Yes, Jezebel will die just as Ahab (v. 23), but Ahab according to 21:1b–16 supposedly had nothing to do with the crime. In the long list of condemnations of Ahab, Jezebel's single condemnation seems to be somehow "insufficient" and "out of place." Jezebel's condemnation, however, does make a definite and clear connection with the other stories of the Elijah/Elisha Cycles. Her condemnation is then repeated with slight variation in 2 Kgs 9:10a, where it is connected with a notice of non-burial— וְאֶת־אִיזֶבֶל יֹאכְלוּ הַכְּלָבִים בְּחֵלֶק יִזְרְעֶאל וְאֵין קֹבֵר ("and the dogs will eat Jezebel in the portion of Jezreel, and there will be no burial")—and again in the account of Jezebel's death in 2 Kgs 9:36, where it is Jehu who repeats the oracle.

*1 Kings 21:23, 25b.* These two verses are related together through the pattern of accusation (21:25b) and condemnation (21:23). Verse 23 clearly breaks the flow of the Dtr oracles in vv. 20bβ–22 and 24. It is clearly not from the same hand as the verses that surround it. Most scholars recognize the secondary nature of v. 23 within 1 Kgs 21.[9] I have taken the position that 21:23, 25b come from

---

9.   Benzinger, *Die Bücher der Könige*, 116; Kittel, *Die Bücher der Könige*, 255; Gressmann, *Die älteste Geschichtsschreibung*, 271 n. *; Schlögl, *Die Bücher der Könige, Die Bücher der Chronik*, 177; Eissfeldt, *Das erste Buch der Könige*, 538; Jepsen, *Nabi*, 93; de Vaux, *Les livres des Rois*, 116

the hand of the "anti-Jezebel" redactor.[10] Together with the other verses that I have attributed to this redactional layer, and as a part of the prophecy–fulfillment pattern imposed upon these texts by this redactor, these verses are well integrated and are related closely together. Since they derive from the same author/redactor and from the same redactional pattern, it cannot be maintained that they derive one from the other.[11] As part of the prophecy–fulfillment pattern imposed by the anti-Jezebel redactor, and as the text of the passage now reads, 2 Kgs 9:36 is presented as the fulfillment of both 1 Kgs 21:23[12] and 2 Kgs 9:10.[13]

The pattern of prophecy–fulfillment is frequently considered one of the "hallmarks" of the Dtr texts.[14] However, as I have already indicated with regard to

n. c; Montgomery and Gehman, *A Critical and Exegetical Commentary*, 399, 403–4; Fohrer, *Elia*, 26; Gray, *I & II Kings*, 436; Miller, "The Fall of the House of Ahab," 310; Fricke, *Das zweite Buch von den Königen*, 127–28; Weinfeld, *Deuteronomy and the Deuteronomic School*, 20–21; J. Fichtner, *Das erste Buch von den Königen* (BAT 12/1; Stuttgart: Calwer, 1972), 321; DeVries, *Prophet against Prophet*, 131 n. 17; Hentschel, *Die Elijaerzählungen*, 42; Bohlen, *Der Fall Nabot*, 301, 319; Rehm, *Das erste Buch der Könige*, 208; Würthwein *Die Bücher der Könige, 1. Kön. 17–2 Kön. 25*, 251, 334; Jones, *1–2 Kings* 2:351, 463; R. Smend, "The Deuteronomistic Elijah: A Contribution to the Old Testament Portrayal of the Prophets" (trans. D. A. Knight) *OTE* 4 (1986): 28–45 (42–43); Campbell, *Of Prophets and Kings*, 98 n. 80; McKenzie, *The Trouble with Kings*, 75. A few of the earlier scholars were uncertain or hesitant: Skinner (*Kings*, 260) maintained that it was either original or an interpolation based on 9:36; Burney (*Notes*, 311) maintained that the relationship between 21:23 and 9:36 cannot be insisted upon since 21:19–26 have been largely amplified by the Dtr Redactor; and Šanda (*Das zweite Buch der Könige*, 101) held that 9:36 sounds more original than 21:23.

10. With Minokami, *Die Revolution des Jehu*, 59–60.

11. *Contra* those who maintain that 21:23 is derived from 9:36: Benzinger, *Die Bücher der Könige*, 116; Kittel, *Die Bücher der Könige*, 255; Gressmann, *Die älteste Geschichtsschreibung*, 271 n*; Schlögl, *Die Bücher der Könige, Die Bücher der Chronik*, 177; Eissfeldt, *Das erste Buch der Könige*, 538; Jepsen, *Nabi*, 93; Montgomery and Gehman, *A Critical and Exegetical Commentary*, 403–4; Fohrer, *Elia*, 26; Miller, "The Fall of the House of Ahab," 310; Fricke, *Das zweite Buch von den Königen*, 127–28; Hentschel, *Die Elijaerzählungen*, 40–42, 150; Rehm, *Das erste Buch der Könige*, 208; Jones, *1–2 Kings* 2:463; Würthwein *Die Bücher der Könige, 1. Kön. 17–2 Kön. 25*, 208. *Contra* also those who maintain that 9:36 is derived from 21:23: Gunkel, *Geschichten von Elisa*, 73; 99 nn. 15–16; Snaith, "The First and Second Book of Kings," 177–78; Seebass, "Der Fall Naboth in 1 Reg. XXI," 488; Bohlen, *Der Fall Nabot*, 301; Zakovitch, "The Tale of Naboth's Vineyard," 401.

12. This relationship is recognized by: Klostermann, *Die Bücher Samuelis und der Könige*, 384; Skinner, *Kings*, 326–27; Kittel, *Die Bücher der Könige*, 255; Fricke, *Das zweite Buch von den Königen*, 126–27; Dietrich, *Prophetie und Geschichte*, 26; Weinfeld, *Deuteronomy and the Deuteronomic School*, 20–21; Hentschel, *Die Elijaerzählungen*, 40–42; Bohlen, *Der Fall Nabot*, 301; Rehm, *Das erste Buch der Könige*, 208; Würthwein *Die Bücher der Könige, 1. Kön. 17–2 Kön. 25*, 251, 334; Hobbs, *2 Kings*, 113; Nelson, *First and Second Kings*, 144; Barré, *The Rhetoric of Political Persuasion*, 125; O'Brien, *The Deuteronomistic History Hypothesis*, 199–200; McKenzie, *The Trouble with Kings*, 75.

13. Weinfeld (*Deuteronomy and the Deuteronomic School*, 20–21) and Barré (*The Rhetoric of Political Persuasion*, 125) maintain that both 9:7–10 and 9:36 are the fulfillment notices of 21:23. Long (*I Kings*, 127, 129) maintains that only 9:7–10 fulfill 21:23.

14. The particular Dtr usage of the prophecy–fulfillment pattern is held by many scholars. See for example: Benzinger, *Die Bücher der Könige*, 152; von Rad, "Die deuteronomistische Geschichtstheologie in den Königsbüchern," 54–57; Bernhardt, "Prophetie und Geschichte," 22; Weinfeld, *Deuteronomy and the Deuteronomic School*, 15; Hoffmann, *Reform und Reformen*, 99; Peckham, *The Composition of the Deuteronomistic History*, 66; Van Seters, *In Search of History*, 315–16.

2 Kgs 9:10a and 9:36, these texts are more likely "imitations" of the Dtr pattern coming from the hand of the anti-Jezebel redactor.[15] In the case of 9:10a, it actually interrupts the Dtr redaction, indicating that it is, in fact, a later insertion to the already secondary Dtr redaction. This appears to be the case also in 1 Kgs 21:23. This oracle against Jezebel, though "imitating" the Dtr oracle against Ahab that follows in v. 24, is not worded exactly like the Dtr oracle. Also, it breaks the linkage between, and interrupts the long chain of oracles against, Ahab. I maintain, therefore, that 1 Kgs 21:23 is a secondary insertion from the hand of the late anti-Jezebel redactor.

A second feature that refers to Jezebel in the Dtr section of 1 Kgs 21 is found in v. 25b. This is the only explicit accusation made *against Jezebel* in vv. 20bβ–26. Again, this accusation, like the condemnation of Jezebel in v. 23, is couched within an accusation against Ahab. Verse 25, together with v. 26, forms a type of "editorial comment" or "parenthetical remark":

> There was none who sold himself to do what was evil in the sight of the LORD like Ahab, *whom Jezebel his wife incited.* He did very abominably in going after idols, as the Amorites had done, whom the LORD cast out before the people of Israel. (1 Kgs 21:25–26 RSV)

In this accusation, Jezebel, again referred to as Ahab's "wife," is said to have "enticed, or seduced, or lured" Ahab; אֲשֶׁר־הֵסַתָּה אֹתוֹ אִיזֶבֶל אִשְׁתּוֹ. But what does this mean? What does it refer to in the story of vv. 1–16? Can it be said that Jezebel "seduced" Ahab into agreement with her plan, since she is said to have used his seals? This is unlikely. If this were the case we would expect that the anti-Jezebel redactor would have pounced upon this and used it against Ahab, but he did not do so. According to the text, Jezebel never discussed her plan with Ahab, nor are we told that Ahab told her to use his seals. Also, when the elders and nobles report back, it is to Jezebel that they report, and not to Ahab whose seal had been used. All this would seem to indicate that Ahab did not know that Jezebel used his seals. The fact of the matter is that there is no mention, direct or indirect, in vv. 1–16 that Jezebel ever seduced or enticed Ahab in any way.

The accusation of seduction made against Jezebel found in v. 26, therefore, has nothing at all to do with the story of Naboth's vineyard. However, it is very much the theme found in the presentation of Jezebel that we find in the other stories of the Elijah Cycle which come from the hand of the anti-Jezebel redactor. The connection between the accusation of seduction in 1 Kgs 21:25 and the remainder of the Elijah Cycle is made and explicated in v. 26 which indicates precisely what it was that Ahab was "seduced" into by Jezebel. According to the author of this verse, "He did very abominably in going after idols, as the Amorites had done, whom the LORD cast out before the people of Israel."[16] This same accusation of "seduction into apostasy" resulting from marriage to foreign women is also strongly implied in the proleptic summary of Ahab's reign in 1 Kgs 16:31–32. In this text we find these same two elements intimately linked

---

15. See Chapter 4 for a discussion of the Anti-Jezebel Redaction and the prophecy–fulfillment pattern.

16. See the discussion of 1 Kgs 21:23. 25b and Deut 13, on pp. 82–84.

together in the anti-Jezebel insertion that is found immediately before the typical Dtr accusation of going and serving and worshipping Baal.

Jezebel is first introduced in 1 Kgs 16:31bα, which is situated within the Dtr expansion to the proleptic summary of Ahab's reign found in 1 Kgs 16:28–34:

> And as if it had been a light thing for him to walk in the sins of Jeroboam the son of Nebat, *he took for his wife Jezebel the daughter of Ethbaal king of the Sidonians*, and went and served Baal, and worshiped him. (1 Kgs 16:31 RSV)

The presentation of Jezebel found in this proleptic summary is both explicit and implicit, and it represents the judgment of its author and redactors concerning Jezebel. This judgment forms the basis for her entire presentation in the Bible. As it reads in its present context, Ahab's marriage to Jezebel was tantamount to an act of apostasy. It was not bad enough for Ahab to carry on the tradition of the "sinfulness of Jeroboam," the sin of failing to worship YHWH alone. Ahab, like Jeroboam, worshipped other gods and idols and he encouraged the people to do so as well. He even built shrines (בָּמוֹת) on high places. After this, "he went and served Baal, and worshipped him" (v. 31bβ). These are all typical Dtr accusations. But the Dtr text concerning Ahab has been redacted and augmented by a secondary expansion found in v. 31bα. According to this insertion into the summary, Ahab did even worse than Jeroboam when he entered into a marriage with the (foreign) princess, Jezebel, the daughter of Ethbaal the Phoenician ruler of Sidon.

This insertion is from the hand of the anti-Jezebel redactor. Its insertion has the effect of shifting the focus of attention of the entire summary from the negative influences and activities of Ahab as king, to the negative *influences and effects of Jezebel upon Ahab*. In the eye's of the anti-Jezebel redactor, the marriage of Ahab to Jezebel was the root cause for the fall of the Ahabite (Omride) dynasty and it was seen by this redactor as a type of "prostitution" of Israel to Baal through Ahab the king. It is no surprise that eventually we will hear of Jezebel being accused of "seducing" Ahab in 1 Kgs 21:25, and of her being referred to as a harlot in 2 Kgs 9:22.

One final indicator that the emphasis on Jezebel in the text of 1 Kgs 16:31 might be secondary is found in the fact that in none of the summaries of the northern kings, *prior to Ahab*, is there found any mention of the king's wife or the effect of the king's marriage upon his judgment. This feature only begins with Ahab's marriage to Jezebel. That this marriage had a profoundly negative effect, in the eyes of this editor, is seen by the fact that Jezebel even plays a role in the summaries of each of Ahab's sons. These are found in 2 Kgs 22:52–53 regarding Ahaziah—"and he walked in the way of his father *and in the way of his mother*"—and in 2 Kgs 3:2 regarding Joram—"He did what was evil in the sight of YHWH, though not like his father *and mother*." It is possible that this anti-Jezebel editor saw the negative effects of Jezebel's marriage to Ahab as passing on also through the women's line. In 2 Kgs 8:18 we find regarding Jehoram: "And he walked in the way of the kings of Israel, as the house of Ahab had done." This would normally have been sufficient condemnation for the Dtr!

However, the verse continues by giving a further explanation: "for the daughter of Ahab (and perhaps of Jezebel?) was his wife." We find a similar situation with regard to Ahaziah of Judah. In 2 Kgs 8:26 we read: "His mother's name was Athalia; she was a granddaughter of Omri, king of Israel (i.e. the daughter of Ahab and Jezebel?)." In 8:27 we find: "He also walked in the way of the house of Ahab, and did evil in the sight of the LORD, as the house of Ahab had done, for he was son-in-law to the house of Ahab." With these last two kings from Judah, it appears that the author wishes to imply that the sinfulness for which they are condemned had as its origins Ahab's marriage to Jezebel and the children that that marriage produced. It also emphasizes that this wickedness was passed on from generation to generation, not only patrilineally, but also matrilineally.

We now return to the redaction of 1 Kgs 21:25. By means of the insertion of v. 25b the anti-Jezebel redactor has effectively shifted the responsibility for Ahab's apostasy from himself to Jezebel, his wife. This exact same phenomenon is seen in the other elements of the Anti-Jezebel Redaction. Verse 25b is the final occurrence of reference to Jezebel as "Ahab's wife." This reference links its use here with the other uses of this *title*. Each of the references to Jezebel as Ahab's wife is effectively a shorthand statement which always implies and emphasizes the fact that she is Ahab's *foreign* wife, a fact which is explicitly stated in her introduction in 1 Kgs 16:31. In 1 Kgs 21:25b, therefore, the accusation of seduction made against Jezebel is once again an attempt on the part of the anti-Jezebel editor to shift the responsibility for Ahab's apostasy from himself to his wicked foreign wife Jezebel.

Like all the other Dtr accusations made against Ahab in vv. 20bβ–26, v. 25b also has no *direct* connection whatsoever with the story of the acquisition of Naboth's Vineyard. Nowhere in vv. 1–16 is there any indication that Ahab or Jezebel worshipped or went after other gods. Verse 25b, however, *is* linked to vv. 1–16 by the reference to Jezebel as Ahab's *wife*. This connection is not a Dtr connection, but was a deliberate thematic link made by the anti-Jezebel redactor when he created and prefaced the story of the vineyard to the pre-existent Dtr text of the accusations and condemnations of Ahab.

*c. Conclusions Regarding the Biblical Presentation of Jezebel*

The treatment that Jezebel receives at the hands of the anti-Jezebel author/ redactor is anything but gentle. She is presented as a wicked, power-hungry, abusive, conniving, deceptive, malicious, and vengeful "foreign" woman/wife. She is accused of having "seduced" Ahab into apostasy and idolatry (1 Kgs 16:31; 21:25b), she directed a deliberate persecution of the prophets of YHWH in an apparent attempt to establish her own religion of Baal and Asherah in her new home and kingdom.[17] In 1 Kgs 19:1–3a she vows to kill Elijah the prophet and in 1 Kgs 21:5–16 she arranges the death of Naboth and the confiscation of his property for the palace, all based upon false charges and false witnesses. She is

---

17. At least this is how it now appears in the texts—see 1 Kgs 18:4, 13, 19; 2 Kgs 3:2, 13; 9:7, 22.

eventually killed, at Jehu's order, during the revolt led by him, and for which revolt Jezebel is presented as part of the cause (2 Kgs 9:7, 10a). This revolt brought about the end of the Omride dynasty. Jezebel represents in these texts an example of the dangerous foreign woman/wife who has the power and the means to seduce her Israelite husband (and king), and through him all of Israel as well, away from faithfulness to YHWH.[18] Jezebel comes to represent the seductive character of apostasy itself. Once it is given entrance into the special realm of the covenant community, it will eventually corrupt the minds and hearts of king, elders, nobles, and citizens, and lead them away from sole faith in, and worship of, YHWH.

Jezebel, therefore, becomes the symbol for the seductive and destructive influences of the "wicked foreign woman/wife." This fact, coupled with the distinct possibility that nearly her entire biblical presentation has been secondarily inserted by the anti-Jezebel redactor,[19] should cause us to be cautious about reading and interpreting the texts about her as an historical account. Both her symbolic presentation and the secondary nature of her presentation can assist in helping to date this material. When was the issue of marriage to *foreign* women highlighted as a major problem for the Israelites? It was one of *the* major problems which Ezra and Nehemiah faced in Persian-period Jehud (Ezra 9:2). But is there any evidence that could link the story we find in 1 Kgs 21:1–16 to this late period? The evidence for a positive answer to this question will continue to grow.

## 4. Synthesis

The characterization of Ahab, Naboth, and Jezebel in the texts we have analyzed is the result of the work of the authors and redactors of these texts. This characterization as presented in the above analysis can be briefly synthesized in the following manner:

1.  Ahab: Ahab is by far the most wicked of all the kings of Israel. *He is the epitome of the evil and incompetent kingship of the kingdom of Israel (and perhaps of kingship in general).* His greatest sin, and that which epitomizes the greatest danger to the Israelite people, was his marriage to the Phoenician princess, Jezebel. In relation to Jezebel, Ahab is presented as being powerless, incapacitated, timid, and childish. Jezebel, his foreign wife, to whom he has effectively given over control of the kingdom, also controls him. He has, in effect, "sold his soul" to the seductions of his wife to follow the Baalim and he has led Israel into the same sin.

---

18. See Rofé, "The Vineyard of Naboth," 101–2; J. A. Soggin, "Jezabel, oder die fremde Frau," in *Mélanges bibliques et orientaux en l'honneur de M. Henri Cazelles* (ed. A. Caquot and M. Delcor; AOAT 212; Kevelaer: Butzon & Bercker, 1981), 453–59.

19. Perhaps the only truly Dtr text concerning Jezebel is the mention of her name and marriage to Ahab in 1 Kgs 16:31: ". . . He even married Jezebel, daughter of Ethbaal, king of the Sidonians . . ." (see below, p. 196-98).

2.  Naboth: *Naboth is characterized in 1 Kgs 21 as the epitome of the faithful Israelite.* His refusal to trade or sell his vineyard to Ahab the king is presented as a refusal to abandon the ancient traditions, customs and laws regarding the inalienability of the "inheritance of the fathers." For this refusal, he is murdered and Ahab took his property. He becomes a type of "martyr" which motivates the ongoing battle of the faithful prophet Elijah (fighting for YHWH) against the evil king Ahab and his wicked wife Jezebel. It is his death that precipitates the beginning of the end of the Ahabite dynasty.

3.  Jezebel: *Jezebel is the epitome of the dangerous and wicked foreign wife.* Whenever a king of Israel marries a foreign wife, such as Jezebel, this wife will seduce her husband, and through him all Israel, away from fidelity to YHWH. Therefore, she is characterized as the great "whore and sorceress" (1 Kgs 9:22). As such she seduces one and all to follow Baal and Asherah. She persecutes and kills the legitimate prophets of YHWH and replaces them with her own prophets of Baal and Asherah, "who dine at her table" (1 Kgs 19:19). She will go to any length to obtain what she wants, she will murder, use false witnesses, threats, and seduction. It is because of Jezebel and her great wickedness that the dynasty of Omri, and perhaps even the entire kingdom of Israel, was destroyed.

## 5. When was the Story of 1 Kings 21:1–16 Created?

*a. Linguistic and Textual Evidence for a Late Provenance of 1 Kings 21:1–16*
Linguistic evidence is rarely 100 per cent reliable. Language is malleable and can be manipulated by an author in a variety of ways and for a variety of reasons. The use of archaic words adds richness and charm to a text. The use or creation of new terms, idioms, or styles may be an attempt to show sophistication. Yet, despite the malleability of language, it is nonetheless a human endeavor to communicate. The human element is always present and reveals itself in a variety of ways in the written text. Even in texts that are intended by their authors to appear to be more ancient than the date of creation, there are indications in the language and style of the text which inevitably betray the period and time in which they were created. This type of evidence is present within 1 Kgs 21:1–16.

(1) *"Late" terminology found in 21:1–16.* Since most of the following terminology and linguistic features have already been discussed, I will simply list them and refer the reader to the appropriate locations for the discussion. There is evidence in our text that indicates a late date for its creation.
     Terms that *strongly* suggest late origins:
     1.  v. 1          הֵיכָל          (p. 120 n. 12)
     2.  v. 8          חתם√          (p. 130 n. 2)
     3.  vv. 8, 10     הַחֹרִים        (pp. 132–34)
     4.  vv. 10, 13    עוד√           (pp. 145–46)

Terms which *possibly* suggest late origins:

1. v. 1     מֶלֶךְ שֹׁמְרוֹ    (p. 118)
2. v. 2     קָרוֹב אֵצֶל    (pp. 119–20 and n. 13)
3. v. 2     לְנַי־יָרָק    (p. 121 n. 14)
4. vv. 5, 6     דבר√    not followed by לֵאמֹר, or any other form of
√אמר,[20] but having the same meaning as
√אמר.[21]

The presence of four terms which strongly suggest origins or usage in Late Biblical Hebrew, plus four other features which I categorize as "possible" evidence, argues that the author at the time of the writing of this pericope was probably "late." But what does "late" mean? The four terms I list as "strong" evidence are categorized by either, or both, BDB and Koehler and Baumgartner as "NH" (New [Late] Hebrew) or as "MHb" (Middle Hebrew). Both of these designations represent what other scholars refer to as "LBH" (Late Biblical Hebrew), which is the Hebrew found mainly in the late exilic and post-exilic books of the Old Testament. The presence of this type of language in the text of 1 Kgs 21:1–16 would, therefore, appear to indicate that the author of these verses was writing at a late exilic, perhaps even post-exilic, date.

(2) *Other possible indicators.* On a more superficial, but still indicative level, we find other terms and issues that might chronologically and geographically point to a similar setting for the texts of Ezra–Nehemiah, Chronicles, and that of 1 Kgs 21. In 1 Kgs 21:8, 11 we find a pair of terms representing the town leaders in Jezreel, הַזְּקֵנִים וְהַחֹרִים. A similar pair of terms is found in Ezra 10:8, which shares one term with the pair found in 1 Kgs 21, הַשָּׂרִים וְהַזְּקֵנִים. Also similar to 1 Kgs 21:8, 11 and its use of the term הַחֹרִים is the frequent presence of this same group in Nehemiah (×7).[22] In most of the cases in Nehemiah, הַחֹרִים is found within lists of various Jewish groups (2:16; 4:8, 19; 7:5). In Neh 5:7 we find them paired with the "officials" (הַסְּגָנִים) as the object of charges brought against them by Nehemiah. These charges included those of oppressing and abusing their own people. This is very similar to the situation found in 1 Kgs 21. The term also occurs in the construct form, חֹרֵי יְהוּדָה, in Neh 6:17 and 13:17 (where, similar to our text, they are also being accused), Jer 27:20 and 39:6. This particular usage could indicate a southern, post-exilic dialectical usage with the same sense as the older term, הַזְּקֵנִים.

First Kings 21:26 states that Ahab, וַיַּתְעֵב מְאֹד לָלֶכֶת אַחֲרֵי הַגִּלֻּלִים. Though the verbal root √תעב and its nominal forms are quite frequent in the Old Testament, in our particular verse it is significant to note that Ahab is said to have been

---

20. Rofé, "The Vineyard of Naboth," 97–98. Rofé argues for this position, saying that "this stylistic feature occurs in other stories which show additional signs of late composition (1 Kgs 8; 2 Kgs 1)." See also Rofé's *The Prophetical Stories*, 37 and n. 23, where he also discusses this feature.

21. See also Exod 32:7–14; Josh 22; 1 Kgs 13; 2 Kgs 1:6, 7, 9 (×2), 10, 11, 12, 13, 15, 16, etc., which are considered late for other reasons.

22. See also Neh 2:16; 4:8, 13; 5:7; 6:17; 7:5; 13:17. There are a total of 13 occurrences in the Old Testament, all of which are generally considered to be post-exilic.

first seduced by Jezebel, his (foreign) wife (v. 25b), and then he is said to have "done very *abominably* in going after the idols." In Ezra 9:1, 11, and 14 the same root, תעב√, in its nominal forms, is linked closely with the problem of marriage to foreign women—women who either practice these abominable things themselves or who convince their husbands to do so (see Neh 13:26–27).

A third connection between 1 Kgs 21 and both Ezra and Nehemiah is found in the terms based upon the root ירש√. In 1 Kgs 21 derivatives of the root ירש√ are found in vv. 15, 16, 18, and 19 where it is always in reference to Ahab's improper taking of Naboth's נַחֲלַת אֲבֹתָי ("ancestral inheritance"). Naboth's ancestral inheritance is his share of his tribe's allotment dating back to the "original" occupation of the Promised Land under Joshua. In Ezra 9:11–12, Ezra speaks of the return from the Exile as a type of "New Conquest." It is the new "taking possession of the land." For Ezra and Nehemiah, however, this is being endangered by the peoples' intermarriage with foreign women. In Neh 9:15, 22, 23, 24, and 25, Ezra is recounting the story of the conquest within the context of what has come to be called "the Great Confession." Ezra sees the "taking possession" of the land as God's doing, and its coming to fruition is dependent upon Israel's strict obedience to the Law.

Nehemiah 9:25–26 is especially interesting when seen in relationship to 1 Kgs 21. In Neh 9:25, the Israelites entered Canaan and "took their fortified cities and a rich land." It then lists all the good things they took into their possession, among which we find specific mention of *vineyards*. In v. 26, however, the Israelites' infidelity to YHWH is highlighted in that "they rebelled against thee and cast the law behind their back and *killed the prophets*." The charge of murdering the prophets of YHWH is also made against Jezebel, implicitly in 1 Kgs 16:13, and explicitly in 1 Kgs 18:4, 13 and 19:2.

The final usage of the term ירש√ in 1 Kgs 21 is in v. 26 and is found in the accusation that Ahab followed in the abominations of the Amorites whom YHWH had dispossessed for Israel. This theme is always found in connection with the sin of apostasy and with going after the "abominations" of foreigners. We see it used in the condemnations of Rehoboam (1 Kgs 14:24), Ahab (1 Kgs 21:26), Ahaz (2 Kgs 16:3), Israel (2 Kgs 21:8; see vv. 6–18), and Manasseh (2 Kgs 21:2; 2 Chr 33:2). In Ezra 9:1 it is found specifically connected with marriage to foreign women.

Finally, in 1 Kgs 21:25b Jezebel is accused of "seducing" (סות√) Ahab, who then goes after the idols. In Ezra 9:1, 11, 14, the condemnation of marriages with foreign women from among the "peoples of the land" is also connected with the "abominations" and the idols of these women. In Neh 13:26 this sentiment is made very clear in the writer's judgment upon Solomon:

> Did not Solomon king of Israel sin on account of such women? Among the many nations there was no king like him, and he was beloved by his God, and God made him king over all Israel; nevertheless foreign women made even him to sin. (RSV)

This same root and theme is found in 2 Chr 18:2, in the story of Ahab trying to convince Jehoshaphat to go to battle with him at Ramoth-Gilead against the Assyrians. In this post-exilic version of the story, *Ahab* is said to have "seduced or enticed" Jehoshaphat. The use of this particular verbal root is not found in the parallel account of the same story found in 1 Kgs 22 (see v. 4). Finally, at the end of the account of the battle, Jehoshaphat is saved from the Assyrian soldiers by YHWH, who is said to have "seduced or lured" the Assyrians away from Jehoshaphat (2 Chr 18:31). This verse is also missing in the account in 1 Kgs 22 (see vv. 32–33). The use of the root √סות in the Chronicle texts, when it is not found in the older parallel texts of the books of Kings, would appear to indicate a late usage for this root.

b. *Conclusions and Proposed Dating for the Story of Naboth's Vineyard*
We have seen in the symbolic presentation of the characters involved in the story of Naboth's vineyard that there are strong thematic connections with the post-exilic texts of Ezra, Nehemiah, and Chronicles. These themes include: (1) Ahab, the wicked king; (2) Jezebel as the "counterbalance" to Ahab, the wicked king; and (3) Jezebel, the wicked foreign woman/wife. There are also "thematic" elements in the texts based upon the usage of certain terms which, though not necessarily unique to late texts, do make strong connections between the text of 1 Kgs 21 and the post-exilic texts texts of Ezra, Nehemiah, and Chronicles. We have also found within the text of vv. 1–16 linguistic indications of a post-exilic setting, namely, four terms which appear to be of Late Biblical Hebrew provenance, and four other terms or usages which are possibly late. When these data are all put together, it would appear to give rather strong indications that the account in 1 Kgs 21:1–16 was added to the Dtr evaluation of Ahab found in 1 Kgs 21:17–22, 24–25a, 26 some time during the Persian period from the late sixth to fourth century B.C.E.[23]

---

23. With Rofé, "The Vineyard of Naboth," 101–2, who dates the story to the Persian period, fifth–fourth century. However, I disagree with Rofé when he maintains that it is a "re-telling of the old story of Naboth shifting the guilt from Ahab to Jezebel." Rofé presumes that it is an old story that is being retold—I do not.

# Chapter 16

## WHERE, HOW, WHY, AND BY WHOM
## WAS THE STORY OF 1 KINGS 21:1–16 CREATED?

### 1. *Where was the Story of 1 Kings 21:1–16 Created?*

If it is true, as I have suggested, that the story in 1 Kgs 21:1–16 comes from the Persian period and that it bears strong thematic and linguistic similarities with the texts of Ezra, Nehemiah, and Chronicles, then it becomes somewhat easier to attempt an answer to the question: Where was the story in 1 Kgs 21:1–16 created? The only logical place where the writing of the story of 1 Kgs 21:1–16 would have made sense, and where it would have been pertinent to the context and issues which it addresses, would be in the Persian province of Jehud, and most likely, in Jerusalem.

### 2. *How, Why, and by Whom was the Story of 1 Kings 21:1–16 Created?*

Because the last three of our questions are dependent upon each other for answers, it is necessary to deal with them together. Now that we have situated the story in time and place of origin, the next questions have to do with *how*, *why*, and *by whom* this story was created. It is these questions which will highlight not only the sources used in the creation of the story of 1 Kgs 21:1–16, but also its origins.

In its present context, the story of Naboth's vineyard consists not only of vv. 1–16, but includes the *entirety* of the chapter. The chapter in the present text of the books of Kings is presented as comprising an integral whole. Nevertheless, this is a *compiled* whole. In my opinion, it is the end result of a deliberate and creative intervention of a Persian-period author. It did not come about by means of a long process of development and redaction or retellings, as many scholars maintain; rather, it is an artistically created "original" work which incorporates, builds upon, and reorients the Dtr accusations and condemnations of Ahab and his dynasty. I maintain that it is possible to discern the process by which it came into being by a consideration of the various sources and elements used in its creation.

### a. *The "Elijah–Naboth Fragment" and the Dtr Accusations and Condemnations of Ahab*

The original DtrH had been expanded and updated during the Exile by an editor of the same Dtr tradition (sometimes referred to as "Dtr2"). In this comprehensive history the author of 1 Kgs 21:1–16 found tremendous support and useful evidence for his desire to create a very negative and categorical characterization of Israelite rulers and officials. This was especially the case with regard to all of the northern kings and for many of the later kings of Judah, particularly the post-Josianic kings. Among Dtr's many presentations of wicked kings, however, the most wicked of all, the veritable model of wickedness, was non-other than Ahab.

I have taken the position that the author of 1 Kgs 21:1–16 had as one of his main sources the "Dtr History," in an already relatively fixed form. From this source, he had at his disposal the old Elijah–Naboth Fragment in vv. 17–19aβ, 20a–20bα, and the Dtr vv. 20bβ–22, 24–25a, 26. The Elijah–Naboth Fragment has led scholars to conjecture that it represents merely the conclusion of an otherwise lost account of a confrontation between the prophet Elijah and King Ahab regarding the murder of a certain Naboth and the attempt on Ahab's part to take possession of the dead man's property. The focus in this fragment is solely upon Ahab and his guilt and punishment. In strong juxtaposition to the clearly Dtr verses found in vv. 20b–22, 24–25a, 26, the Elijah–Naboth Fragment contains no Dtr language and has nothing to do with dynastic ramifications or punishments. It is also a fact that vv. 1–16 contain no typically Dtr language.

The Elijah–Naboth Fragment, however, does cause a tension with the other clearly Dtr oracles which follow it. Whereas in the Elijah–Naboth Fragment Elijah's oracle is spoken only against Ahab and is presented as his personal punishment, in the Dtr oracles the punishment is comprehensive of the entire dynasty. Whereas the fragment's oracle is for the civil crimes of murder and taking possession, the Dtr oracles which follow it are for the religious crime of apostasy and leading the Israelites astray (i.e. into apostasy). Whereas the fragment places the crimes specifically within the time of Elijah the prophet, in the Dtr oracles that follow there is no mention of Elijah or any other prophet. It appears justifiable, therefore, to maintain that the fragment and the Dtr oracles where both intentionally, and secondarily, placed together. I have conjectured that this was done by the Dtr despite the fact that the insertion caused tensions between the fragment and his collection of oracles of accusation and judgment. His purpose for the insertion of the fragment was twofold. First, it was to create a context for his collection of oracles against Ahab. Second, it was to give these oracles the weight of prophetic authority by placing them into the mouth of the powerful prophet, Elijah the Tishbite.

I also contend that the author of 1 Kgs 21:1–16, situated in Jehud, had access to a variety of sources and traditions from both pre-exilic Judah and from the period of the Exile. Among these was the DtrH within which was already found the account of Ahab's confrontational encounter with Elijah and the resultant condemnations of himself and his entire dynasty (1 Kgs 21:17–19aβ, 20a, 22, 24–26). In the Elijah–Naboth Fragment concerning Ahab's crime against one of his own citizens, and in the judgments and oracles (Dtr) which followed upon it, the post-exilic author of 1 Kgs 21:1–16 found the perfect parallel to one of his own major concerns/themes, namely, the corruption and wickedness of rulers both in pre-exilic Judah and in Persian-period Jehud. He therefore decided to use this fragment as the basis upon which to create a "didactic parable" which would both express most forcefully his particular concerns and themes, and which would make explicit that which was already implicit in the Elijah–Naboth Fragment. This fragment supplied our post-exilic author with basic "evidence" which included: (1) the names of the main characters (Ahab, Elijah, and Naboth), (2) a crime representing the wickedness of a king (murder and taking inherited property from an apparently faithful Israelite citizen), and (3) prophetic and divine punishment for this crime, both in vv. 19b and in 20b–29. With this evidence, the author had all he needed to create his didactic parable.

b. *The Pre-Dtr "Jehu-Apologetic Redaction"*

A second source that was used in the compilation of 1 Kgs 21 was found in what I refer to as the pre-Dtr "Jehu-Apologetic Redaction." Related to the Elijah–Naboth Fragment, is a variant and independent prophetic oracle of YHWH spoken against an anonymous person and promising vengeance for the murder of Naboth and his sons. This oracle is presently found in 2 Kgs 9:26:

אִם־לֹא אֶת־דְּמֵי נָבוֹת וְאֶת־דְּמֵי בָנָיו רָאִיתִי אֶמֶשׁ נְאֻם־יְהוָה וְשִׁלַּמְתִּי לְךָ
בַּחֶלְקָה הַזֹּאת נְאֻם־יְהוָה וְעַתָּה שָׂא הַשְׁלִכֵהוּ בַּחֶלְקָה כִּדְבַר יְהוָה׃

Among the layers of early sources and redactions in the texts of the "Historical Books" is a layer of pre-Dtr Jehu-Apologetic Redaction.[1] I would include in this layer of redaction those references having to do with Naboth and his death in 2 Kgs 9:21bγ[2] (as well as reference to the meeting at the property of Naboth the Jezreelite[3]) and vv. 25–26.[4] Second Kings 9:26 contains a fragmentary relic from

---

1. Those who maintain this type of redaction include: Schmitt, *Elisa*, 24–29; Sekine, "Literatursoziologische Beobachtungen zu den Elisaerzählungen," 56; Bohlen, *Der Fall Nabot*, 288; Olyan, "*Ḥāšālôm*," 654; White, *The Elijah Legends and Jehu's Coup*, 17.

2. The secondary nature of this part of v. 21 is also noted by: Schmitt, *Elisa*, 27; Sekine, "Literatursoziologische Beobachtungen zu den Elisaerzählungen," 56; Van Seters, *In Search of History*, 305; Rehm, *Das zweite Buch der Könige*, 96; Würthwein *Die Bücher der Könige, 1. Kön. 17–2 Kön. 25*, 332; Hentschel, *2 Könige*, 43; Barré, *The Rhetoric of Political Persuasion*, 14; Minokami, *Die Revolution des Jehu*, 37–39.

3. The use of the gentilic adjective with Naboth's name in these references is one signal that they are later insertions into the text. The references are to the specific field which was owned by Naboth who had been murdered. The deliberate intent of this usage is to imply that the field *was well known to all*. The difficulty that indicates its secondary nature is the fact that the entire scene of the story is taking place *within view of Jezreel*. If we take these two facts into consideration (Naboth's field being well known and its being within view of Jezreel) then the use of the gentilic becomes both redundant and unnecessary.

4. See Chapter 2 for a detailed discussion of this redaction. Again, many of the older scholars hold these verses to be original to the story: Klostermann, *Die Bücher Samuelis und der Könige*, 422; Benzinger, *Die Bücher der Könige*, 148–49, 151; Kittel, *Die Bücher der Könige*, 232; Stade and Schwally, *The Book of Kings*, 39; Gressmann, *Die älteste Geschichtsschreibung*, 305; Schlögl, *Die Bücher der Könige, Die Bücher der Chronik*, 245; Montgomery and Gehman, *A Critical and Exegetical Commentary*, 399; and recently Olyan, "*Ḥāšālôm*," 658–59. More recent scholarship has generally tended to see these two verses as secondary to the text: Whitley, "The Deuteronomic Presentation of the House of Omri," 149; Schmitt, *Elisa*, 25–27; Sekine, "Literatursoziologische Beobachtungen zu den Elisaerzählungen," 56; DeVries, *Prophet against Prophet*, 90; Bohlen, *Der*

a pre-Dtr, but non-extant, account of an incident concerning the murder of a certain Naboth and his sons. I will therefore refer to it simply as a "Naboth Fragment." In its present setting, it forms a part of the Jehu-Apologetic Redaction. The oracle found in v. 26 is, in my opinion, an old oracle, indeed only a Naboth Fragment, which is from a different and independent tradition from that found in 1 Kgs 21:17–19a, 20aα–bα (the Elijah–Naboth Fragment). In order to insert the oracle of v. 26 into the account of Jehu's coup, the redactor created a context for it with v. 21bγ and v. 25. The purpose of the insertion was to give prophetic justification to Jehu's murder of Joram and to the desecration (non-burial) of his body. In my estimation, the "context" of the "remembered" occasion when the original oracle was pronounced was "unknown" or already "lost" by the time of its insertion into this new context. That it was deliberately assigned to the time of "Ahab his father" was merely a matter of convenience in order to apply it to the case at hand, the murder of Joram. I suggest that this insertion was made into the account of the Jehu coup some time between the writing of the coup account itself and the end of the Jehu's dynasty.

I refer to the two groups of verses—1 Kgs 21:17–19a, 20aα–bα, and 2 Kgs 9:21bγ, 25–26—as "fragments" because neither of them comprises an entire account of the events surrounding the death of Naboth. They are "independent traditions" in the sense that the details they provide do not match well, and at times even contradict each other. On the other hand, they are related together by the fact of the murder of Naboth. These two old fragments belong to separate tradition histories concerning a crime that was committed against Naboth. In my opinion, both fragments were already a part of the pre-Dtr books of Kings, or at least part of early oral traditions.

Both traditions were eventually linked together when the prophecy found in 1 Kgs 21:19b was transferred to one of Ahab's son by means of 1 Kgs 21:27–29. The prophecy in 21:19b is spoken against Ahab alone and focuses upon the fulfillment of the oracle taking place in the specific location where a crime against Naboth took place. This personal condemnation of Ahab was secondarily "transferred" to the time of his son Joram by means of 1 Kgs 21:27–29. These verses were most likely inserted by the Dtr redactor of the books of Kings when he compiled his accusations and condemnations against Ahab and his dynasty in 1 Kgs 21:20b–22, 24–26. This Dtr redaction of the books of Kings as a part of the creation of the "Dtr History" allowed this editor to "transfer" the individual punishment of Ahab which, though probably not the original ending to the fragment, may already have been in place when the Dtr Historian was creating his work. Having also the separate and independent tradition in the Jehu-Apologetic Redaction of 2 Kgs 9, the Dtr Historian was able to link these two independent traditions by means of inserting the "transfer" in 1 Kgs 21:27–29. I therefore

*Fall Nabot,* 282–84; Timm, *Die Dynastie Omri,* 140–41; Rehm, *Das zweite Buch der Könige,* 96; Würthwein *Die Bücher der Könige, 1. Kön. 17–2 Kön. 25,* 332; Trebolle Barrera, *Jehú y Joás,* 132; Schmoldt, "Elijas Botschaft an Ahab", 42; Barré, *The Rhetoric of Political Persuasion,* 13–14; Minokami, *Die Revolution des Jehu,* 373–39; Long, *II Kings,* 115; McKenzie, *The Trouble with Kings,* 73–74.

maintain that the "prophecy–fulfillment" relationship that exists between 1 Kgs 21:27–29 and 2 Kgs 9:25–26 is from the hand of the Dtr Historian. The strong emphasis on prophecy–fulfillment is often argued to be one of the characteristic features of the Dtr redactions.[5]

### c. *The Narrative Framework*
Thus far, I conclude that 1 Kgs 21:17–29 is a Dtr compilation which includes the distinct elements of the Elijah–Naboth Fragment, the Dtr accusations and condemnations of Ahab and his dynasty found in vv. 20b–22, 24–26, and the verses transferring the personal punishment of Ahab to his son's time in vv. 27–29. There is also a definite relationship between 1 Kgs 21:17–19 and the Jehu-Apologetic Redaction in 2 Kgs 9:21bγ, 25–26. This relationship is "secondary" in nature. It was constructed by the Dtr Historian using the "prophecy–fulfillment" pattern as a part of the thorough editing of the received texts and traditions in the preparation of his comprehensive history. Second Kings 9:21bγ, 25–26 were kept by the historian despite the fact that the author was already well aware that the details of the oracle in 2 Kgs 9:26 did not match perfectly those of the Elijah–Naboth Fragment. The fact that there were some similarities between the two fragments allowed for the use of both and for the "creation" of a secondary relationship between them by means of the insertion of 1 Kgs 21:27–29.

We have already argued that the Dtr Historian had borrowed the narrative framework of the David and Bathsheba story and used it to compile his text of 1 Kgs 21:17–29.[6] First Kings 21:1–16 is a secondary parabolic expansion to the Dtr account found in vv. 17–29. The addition of vv. 1–16 serves to fill out and develop the frame and the story that was already implicitly present in the Elijah–Naboth Fragment. In this expansion and development, Jezebel is introduced into the story. But her presence departs from a strict following of the David–Bathsheba narrative frame. Her presence serves the purpose of shifting the responsibility and the blame for the crime from Ahab the king to Jezebel. In the first sixteen verses of 1 Kgs 21 it is now *Jezebel* who parallels David, not Ahab. I maintain that this shift in roles was deliberate and was, in fact, the specific intent of the anti-Jezebel redactor who wrote these sixteen verses.

The story of the vineyard in 1 Kgs 21:1–16 also fills out with explicit detail that which was only implicit in the original Dtr account in vv. 17–29. For these reasons, vv. 1–16 should be considered a fictional expansion to the Dtr text. It was only after the addition of vv. 1–16 that 1 Kgs 21 came to be the "didactic parable" of a Persian-period, Jehudite author. Included with the addition of vv. 1–16 was also the insertion of the anti-Jezebel passages in v. 23 and in v. 25bα. The end result is that with the addition of the vineyard story in vv. 1–16, the David and Bathsheba framework presented above in Chapter 7 has been artistically expanded and filled out until it now looks as follows:

---

5.   The fact that the specific prophecies are not "exactly" fulfilled, but only "generally" fulfilled, is a problem and represents an indication of the secondary nature of the relationship.

6.   See the discussion on pp. 107–9, and especially the chart on p. 108.

Table 17. *The Narrative Framework of 2 Samuel 11:2–12:5 and 1 Kings 21:17–29*

| Line | The Narrative Frame | 2 Samuel 11:2–12:5 | 1 Kings 21:17–29 |
|---|---|---|---|
| | | DAVID | AHAB |
| 1 | The Object of Desire is Stated | 11:2–4a: Bathsheba | vv. 1b–2: Naboth's Vineyard |
| 2 | A First Complication Occurs | 11:5: Bathsheba is pregnant to David but married to Uriah | v. 3: Naboth's refusal |
| 3 | A Second Complication Occurs | 11:6–13: Uriah refuses to go home and sleep with his wife | v. 4: Ahab is withdrawn, dejected and unable to function |
| 4 | The Communication of a Plan for Resolving the Complications | 11:14–15: David writes to Joab and communicates his plan for having Uriah killed | vv. 8–10: *Jezebel writes* letters in Ahab's name communicating her plan to have Naboth killed |
| 5 | The Resolution of the Complications | 11:16–17: The plan is enacted and Uriah is killed | vv. 11–13: The plan is enacted and Naboth is killed |
| 6 | The Communication of Fulfillment of the Action | 11:18–25: Joab sends a messenger to David with the news of Uriah's death | v. 14: The elders and nobles *sent to Jezebel* saying the deed was accomplished |
| 7 | The Taking Possession of the Desired Object | 11:26–27: When Bathsheba hears of Uriah's death she mourns and David takes her as his wife | vv. 15–16: Upon hearing of Naboth's death Ahab takes possession of the vineyard |
| 8 | The Lord's Displeasure and Notification of the Lord's Sending of a Prophet | 11:24e–12:1: YHWH is displeased and sends Nathan to David | 21:17–18: YHWH calls and sends Elijah to Ahab |
| 9 | A First Accusation | 12:1b–6: The parable of the stolen ewe—David's self-accusation | 21:19aβ: The accusation of a civil crime |
| 10 | A Second Accusation | 12:7–10: Nathan accuses David in YHWH's name | 21:20b: The accusation of a cultic crime |
| 11 | The Condemnation | 12:10–12: The sword will never depart . . . I will bring evil upon you . . . | 21:20b–24: I will bring evil upon you; I will utterly sweep you away, and will cut off from Ahab every male, bond or free, in Israel . . . |
| 12 | An Evaluative Judgment | * * * * * * * * * * * | 21:25–26: There was none who sold himself to do what was evil in the sight of the LORD like Ahab, whom Jezebel his wife incited.[26] He did very abominably in going after idols, as the Amorites had done, whom the LORD cast out before the people of Israel.) |
| 13 | The Repentance of the Guilty Person | 12:13a: David admits his sin | 21:27: Ahab repents and puts on sackcloth, etc. |
| 14 | The Transference of the Punishment to Off-Spring | 12:13b–23: "And Nathan said to David, 'The LORD also has put away your sin; you shall not die.[14] Nevertheless, because by this deed you have utterly scorned the LORD, the child that is born to you shall die.'" | 21:28–29: Because he has humbled himself before me, I will not bring the evil in his days; but in his son's days I will bring the evil upon his house. |

Very few scholars have noted the relationship between 1 Kgs 21 and the David and Bathsheba story in 2 Sam 11–12. J. A. Soggin suggests that the story as found in 1 Kgs 21 contains "considerable expansions" of "novelistic" style. He proposes that the story might deal with a "conflict between the Israelite land law and that of Canaan," and he maintains that

> the story could be one of a number in circulation seeking to discredit Ahab and his wife. This possibility is strongly suggested by its resemblance to another analogous episode, that of the prophet Nathan and David after his adultery with Bathsheba and the killing of her husband (II Sam. 11:2–12:15).[7]

The only other scholar I found who deals at any length with the possible relationship between 1 Kgs 21 and 2 Sam 11:2–12:15 is Marsha White. Though both White and I have arrived at very similar analyses of the parallels between these two stories, we did so independently of each other's work and we approach the texts very differently. The fact is that though we agree on the *fact* of a relationship between these two stories (based upon narrative features), we disagree on the motive and purpose of the relationship.

In White's *The Elijah Legends and Jehu's Coup*, her goal is to "dispute the notion that there was a mid-ninth century prophetic 'revolution' linked with the Jehu-led 'revolt' against the 'oppressive' house of Omri, implying a broad popular base for the 'revolt.'"[8] White maintains the basic historicity of the account found in 2 Kgs 9–10 admitting only to the possibility of only one redactional "seam" located between 2 Kgs 10:17–18. "Otherwise, 2 Kgs 9:1–10:25 is a seamless whole that proceeds smoothly and logically from Jehu's anointing to his divinely-ordained commission to his execution of the commission."[9] Accepting the "historicity" of 9:25b–26a, White unquestionably reads the anonymous oracle found there as having been spoken against Ahab. She is also forced by her argumentation to accept the "historicity" of 1 Kgs 21:27–29 since these verses postpone the punishment of Ahab to the time of Jehu's revolution. She states:

> The integrity of the dynastic extermination prophecy and its deferral to Ahab's son's time mean that the prophecy together with its fulfillment in the narration of Jehu's coup d'état did not enter at a later time, but belonged with the vineyard story from the start. Stated differently, the vineyard story as a whole is an *ex eventu* prophecy that is fulfilled only in the narrative of Jehu's exterminations. This story [1 Kgs 21—P.T.C.] . . . was almost certainly authored by a supporter of King Jehu, most likely a member of his scribal corps. It was composed to legitimate Jehu's overthrow of the Omrides and massacre of everyone associated with them, probably shortly after the event.[10]

White, therefore, sees the Naboth Vineyard story in 1 Kgs 21:1–29 as a "retelling" of the crime of Ahab against Naboth which is originally found in 2 Kgs 9:25b–26a. In order to accomplish his aim, the author "casts" Elijah

---

7.   J. A. Soggin, *A History of Israel: From the Beginnings to the Bar Kochba Revolt, AD 135* (London: SCM Press, 1984), 207.
8.   White, *The Elijah Legends and Jehu's Coup*, 1.
9.   White, *The Elijah Legends and Jehu's Coup*, 36.
10.   White, *The Elijah Legends and Jehu's Coup*, 36.

as a second Nathan, who confronts the guilty king and pronounces the divine decree against him, later transferring the sentence to his son as a result of the king's repentance (II. Sam 12:1–14). That is, the structure of the David and Bathsheba story was borrowed as a vehicle for the condemnation of Ahab's dynasty, additionally providing an opportunity for an *ex eventu* prediction of when the exterminations would occur.[11]

The weakness with White's approach to these texts lies primarily in her initial presupposition that 2 Kgs 9–10 form an accurate and unified historical account of the events. Her position that 2 Kgs 9:25–26 are historical, in particular, causes her to have to conjecture that the anonymous oracle therein was spoken specifically and historically against Ahab. There is no basis for this conjecture in the biblical text. Her position regarding 2 Kgs 9:25–26 also forces her to develop a theory as to the relationship of 2 Kgs 9:25–26 with 1 Kgs 21 and 2 Sam 11–12. She rightly sees the dependence of 1 Kgs 21 on the narrative framework of 2 Sam 11–12; seeing no such relationship between 2 Sam 11–12 and 2 Kgs 9:25–26, however, she conjectures that the story of 1 Kgs 21 is a "re-telling" of the crime and conviction of Ahab in 2 Kgs 9:25–26 modeled upon 2 Sam 11–12. All of this was done, in her estimation, shortly after the coup of Jehu and as a type of apologetic for it.

White's position is built upon her opinion that 2 Kgs 9:25–26 are original and historical to the Jehu account. I disagree with her position. I maintain that 2 Kgs 9:21bγ, 25–26 are, in fact, secondary to the "historical account" of Jehu's coup. Both White and I maintain that the David and Bathsheba framework was used by the Dtr Historian to shape and link his accusations and condemnations of Ahab and his dynasty to the Elijah–Naboth Fragment. We both also maintain that 1 Kgs 21:27–29 were created by him to make a link with a separate and independent tradition found in the secondary Jehu-Apologetic Redaction in 2 Kgs 9. However, it is my position that at the time of Dtr's work, 1 Kgs 21:1–16, the story of the Vineyard of Naboth, *did not yet exist* and therefore did *not* yet play any role in this framework. Therefore, though I agree with White's opinion regarding the fact that 1 Kgs 21 and 2 Sam 11–12 share a narrative pattern or framework, I do not agree with her explanation of the relationship between 1 Kgs 21 and 2 Kgs 9:25–26.

### d. *The Actual Situation in Jehud*

If, as I have argued, the final form of 1 Kgs 21 was compiled in Persian-period Jehud, then we must now ask whether there is any evidence of Persian-period Jehudite concerns or themes found in our text which would help to substantiate this date and location.

In the books of Ezra and Nehemiah there is abundant information concerning the situations which Ezra, the priest/governor, and Nehemiah, the governor of Jehud, found when they arrived in Jehud from Babylon. These situations would have also served as "source material" for our author, since they were in fact the very objects of his didactic parable/critique. Two of the main themes which are at

---

11. White, *The Elijah Legends and Jehu's Coup*, 17.

times addressed together, and at times separately, are those of the "wicked rulers" and the very negative and dangerous threat caused by the "wicked foreign wife/woman" (or even of "wicked foreigners," in general). Another theme found in the texts of Ezra and Nehemiah is that of "vineyards." These appear to have been the main issues our author had in mind, and in fact "borrowed" when he created the parable of Naboth's vineyard in 1 Kgs 21:1–16.

(1) *The "anti-wicked ruler" theme.* Nehemiah 5 stands as an exemplary description of the situation that Nehemiah faced when he arrived in Jerusalem to oversee the reconstruction of the city walls. A "great outcry" arose from the people "against their Jewish brethren" (v. 1). The problems listed appear to have been the result of the total concentration of resources upon the reconstruction projects to the detriment of the people themselves. There was not enough food for their families, people were forced to mortgage their property to the wealthy and to the rulers, including their fields, *their vineyards*, and their homes, in order to buy food (v. 3). Not only this, but the people were being forced by the conditions to borrow money in order to pay "the king's tax upon our fields and vineyards" (v. 4). Even worse, the people were, in effect, being forced into slavery to the wealthy and rulers. The people felt helpless and frustrated because "other men have our fields and vineyards" (v. 5).

Nehemiah was furious at this. After taking time to consider the charges, he called a general assembly and we are told:

> I took counsel with myself, and I brought charges against the nobles and the officials (אֶת־הַחֹרִים וְאֶת־הַסְּגָנִים). I said to them, 'You are exacting interest, each from his brother.' And I held a great assembly against them . . . . (Neh 5:7 RSV)

As a result of this assembly, Nehemiah orders these nobles and officials to restore everything they had taken from the people:

> Return to them this very day their fields, their vineyards, their olive orchards, and their houses, and the hundredth of money, grain, wine, and oil which you have been exacting of them. (Neh 5:11 RSV)

After this crisis concerning the abuse of the returnees by their own people, Nehemiah continues his reflections and recounts how, since his arrival as governor in Jehud, *he* had not been like his predecessors:

> The former governors who were before me laid heavy burdens upon the people, and took from them food and wine, besides forty shekels of silver. Even their servants lorded it over the people. But I did not do so, because of the fear of God. (Neh 5:15 RSV)

This situation described in Neh 5 undoubtedly was based upon real facts in everyday life in Jehud. The suffering of the people under the burden of reconstruction was exacerbated by crooked, cruel, and wicked leaders and rulers, both Jewish and non-Jewish. It would only be logical to expect that the theme of the wickedness and injustice of the rulers would also be one of the main themes of our author's "didactic parable" in 1 Kgs 21:1–16 if it were written at the same period of time, as I maintain.

(2) *The "anti-foreign wife/woman" theme.* The first thing to mention here is that the anti-foreign wife/woman theme is not unique to post-exilic Jehud. It is a theme found throughout the Old Testament, to lesser or greater degrees. In Deut 7 we find a case in point. In this account, Moses is exhorting the people of Israel in the context of their anticipated entrance into the Promised Land of Canaan. We find many of the same elements in this text which are also found in Ezra and Nehemiah and 1 Kgs 21. We find, for example, the technical term "to possess/dispossess" connected with the settlement in the land. In vv. 3–5, we also find the prohibition of mixed marriages:

> You shall not make marriages with them (the peoples of the nations), giving your daughters to their sons or taking their daughters for your sons. *For they would turn away your sons from following me, to serve other gods*; then the anger of the LORD would be kindled against you, and he would destroy you quickly. But thus shall you deal with them: you shall break down their altars, and dash in pieces their pillars, and hew down their Asherim, and burn their graven images with fire. (Deut 7:3–5 RSV)

Significant for our purposes is not only the ban on mixed marriages, but the *reason* for this in v. 4a—namely, that they (the foreign wives) will seduce their Israelite husbands into apostasy. If, however, the people remain faithful and obedient to the Lord and separated from the foreigners, then they will posses the land and be greatly blessed with fertility of body and land: "your ground, your grain (fields), your wine (vineyards) and your oil (olive groves)." All of these basic elements of the possession and settlement of the land are found in Ezra and Nehemiah, and, Naboth's "faithfulness" to his ancestral inheritance in and of the land, to his vineyard, is central to story of 1 Kgs 21.

On a theological level, in Persian-period Jehud the returnees saw themselves in the same situation as did the Israelites encamped on the Plains of Moab in the book of Deuteronomy. They saw themselves as "the true Israel" in the process of "a new conquest/settlement." They saw themselves, in their own terms, as "the Holy Seed" (זֶרַע הַקֹּדֶשׁ, Ezra 9:2) which was being planted in the Land of Promise. Mixed marriages, especially marriages with foreigners or "strangers," were seen as a particular danger to the purity, strength, and vitality of this elect "community of returnees" (קְהַל הַגּוֹלָה, Ezra 10:8). Yet, despite this perspective and danger, they even found that their rulers/leaders/officials were entering into these types of marriages:[12]

> For they have taken some of their daughters to be wives for themselves and for their sons; so that the holy race (זֶרַע הַקֹּדֶשׁ) has mixed itself with the peoples of the lands. *And in this faithlessness the hand of the officials and chief men has been foremost.* (Ezra 9:2 RSV)

Linked to the accusation of mixed marriages, we also find the direct connection being made between these marriages and the accusation of the committing "abominations" of idol worship and apostasy.[13] In Neh 13:26–27, Nehemiah

---

12. See the list in Ezra 9:16–44.
13. See Ezra 9:1, 10–15; Neh 13:26–27.

describes the danger of mixed-marriages by drawing a parallel with King Solomon, who despite being chosen and loved by God, was made to sin by his foreign wives.[14] This notion of the foreign wife/woman being a "seductress" into apostasy is key to the construction of 1 Kgs 21:1–16, 23, and 25ba, and especially to its presentation of Jezebel.[15]

When we recall the narrative outline of 1 Kgs 21, which I have argued is based upon 2 Sam 11–12, we notice that there is one element found in 1 Kgs 21 which is not found in the David and Bathsheba story. This element is an evaluative judgment (see Table 17, line 12). In the Dtr version of the David story, a much more favorable overall evaluation of David is found, a typical tendency of the Dtr Historian. David is not officially accused with the specific double charge of (1) having been "seduced by his wife," and (2) having apostatized. These two charges are unique secondary insertions into the Dtr text of 1 Kgs 21:17–29 by the anti-Jezebel author of 1 Kgs 21:1–16, and they appropriately fit his particular anti-foreign wife/woman theme. This should strike us as both ironic and unjust since in the David story Bathsheba is also presumably a foreign woman (or at least married to a foreign man, Uriah the Hittite). In the case of David the ideal king of Judah, however, this "fault" was apparently overlooked. This "generosity in judgment" will definitely not be found in the case of the most wicked of all the northern kings, Ahab, nor, in fact, for any of the northern, non-Davidic monarchs.

When we return our attention to 1 Kgs 21 and its presentation of Jezebel as the epitome of the wicked foreign wife/woman, we must eventually ask the question: Who was she? According to my analysis of the presentation of Jezebel throughout the Old Testament, we have seen that in nearly every appearance of this woman there is evidence that could indicate a secondary insertion of this material

14. See 1 Kgs 11:1–8.
15. There are many recent works discussing the issues of the return from Exile, Persian period Jehud, the foreign woman/wife, the "Peoples of the Land," and so on. See, for example: J. D. Newsome, *By the Waters of Babylon: An Introduction to the History and Theology of the Exile* (Atlanta: John Knox, 1979); T. C. Eskenazi, *In the Age of Prose: A Literary Approach to Ezra–Nehemiah* (SBLMS 36; Atlanta: Scholars Press, 1988); D. L. Smith, *The Religion of the Landless: The Social Context of the Babylonian Exile* (Bloomington, Ind.: Meyer-Stone Books, 1989); J. L. Berquist, *Judaism in Persia's Shadow: A Social and Historical Approach* (Minneapolis: Fortress, 1995); H. M. Barstad, *The Myth of the Empty Land: A Study in the History and Archaeology of Judah During the "Exilic" Period* (Symbolae Osloenses Fasc. Suppl. 28; Oslo: Scandinavian University Press, 1996); F. Gonçalves, "El 'Destierro,' Consideraciones históricas," *EstBíb* 55 (1997): 431–61. See also the contributions to *The Cambridge History of Judaism*, vol. 1, *Introduction: The Persian Period* (ed. W. D. Davies and L. Finkelstein; Cambridge: Cambridge University Press, 1984) by E. Stern, "The Persian Empire and the Political and Social History of Palestine in the Persian Period" (70–87); P. Ackroyd, "The Jewish Community in Palestine in the Persian Period" (130–61); M. Smith, "Jewish Religion in the Persian Period" (217–78), as well as the contributions to *Second Temple Studies*, vol. 2, *Temple and Community in the Persian Period* (ed. T. C. Eskenazi and Kent H. Richards; JSOTSup 175; Sheffield: JSOT Press, 1994) by D. L. Smith-Christopher, "The Mixed Marriage Crisis in Ezra 9–10 and Nehemiah 13: A Study of the Sociology of the Post-Exilic Judean Community" (243–65); T. C. Eskenazi and E. P. Judd, "Marriage to a Stranger in Ezra 9–10" (266–85); H. C. Washington, "The Strange Woman (נכריה/זרה אשה) of Proverbs 1–9 and Post-Exilic Judean Society" (217–42).

into the texts. Given these indications and the fact, as I maintain, that in 1 Kgs 21 Jezebel is presented "symbolically," it is my opinion that she may well be the literary creation of our "anti-Jezebel" author/redactor. There are only two accounts in the Old Testament where Jezebel plays any major "active" role at all: in 1 Kgs 21:1–16 and in the account of her death in 2 Kgs 9:30–37. In both of these accounts there is strong linguistic evidence to indicate that the accounts are of late, post-exilic origin. If she represents the epitome of the wicked foreign wife/woman/seductress through whose allurements the Israelites are led into apostasy, then it appears that she is, in fact, a literary figure. She is a "type" of a new "Eve," who tempted her husband, Adam, to disobey the Lord's explicit command, and to partake of the fruit of "the tree of the knowledge of good and evil" (Gen 3:6). Because of Eve's seductions, humankind was expelled from Paradise. Through Jezebel, the "new Eve," Israel's rulers and its people may once again be "seduced" into apostasy and may once again be cast out of the "Promised Land" into a new exile, unless something is done to prevent them from giving into Jezebel's temptations.

With these themes and thoughts in his mind, the author of 1 Kgs 21:1–16, the anti-Jezebel redactor, set about to create his story. This creation required that the author somehow also insert his story into the "Scriptures" as he had received them. At this time, the "Scriptures" were evidently not yet canonized, so he set about to make sure that, as much as possible, the story which he had created would integrate well into the "Bible" as it was conceived in his day. This required that he actively "borrow" from his predecessors and sources, especially the Dtr sources. He had at his disposal the Dtr History and within it he had the Dtr system of prophecy–fulfillment as well as the regnal formulas as places into which he could introduce his "Jezebel" and her dangerous "effects," together with the dangers he saw with the corrupt rulers of his time. To achieve his goal he was required to do a systematic redaction of the sources in order to establish the themes of his story and to introduce and develop his main characters in the appropriate places and in the particular forms that he desired.

With regard to Ahab, this effort was not too difficult since he already appeared in the Dtr's presentation as the epitome of the most wicked of kings. Jezebel, however, was a different situation. It is possible, though not absolutely certain, that the Dtr might have been aware of her politically motivated marriage to Ahab, and that it was he who introduced her name into the proleptic summary of Ahab's reign in 1 Kgs 16:31. This however, appears to be the only reference to her by the Dtr's own hand. All other Jezebel material comes from the hand of the anti-Jezebel redactor.

Since her presentation through the remainder of the text was basically a "creation" of this redactor, he had to do a methodical and detailed redaction of the entire Ahab Cycle (and thus the Elijah Cycle) in order to affiliate Ahab and Jezebel together throughout the entire Dtr History, both with regard to Ahab personally, and in regard to the residual effects throughout his dynasty (as well as those dynasties of Judah related to Ahab through marriages). He did this by emphasizing throughout how Ahab was totally under the control and power of his wicked foreign wife, Jezebel. She had totally seduced him. In this way, this author/redactor deliberately and systematically shifted the "blame" for Ahab's wickedness (which was the focus of the Dtr accounts) from Ahab himself to his wicked foreign wife Jezebel (the post-exilic, anti-Jezebel focus). In this, 1 Kgs 21:1–16 becomes the central or core story that proves his point.

(3) *The "vineyard" theme.* Another theme appropriate to the actual situation in Persian-period Jehud, and one which is connected to the abuses of the poor by the rulers and wealthy classes, is the theme of the "vineyard." This theme is already found in the Elijah–Naboth Fragment —a fact which allowed for the author of 1 Kgs 21:1–16 to develop another "angle of attack" against the rulers of his own day. Ownership of vineyards was a sign of stability and of possession over an extended period of time of the land upon which the vineyards were located. It is no small wonder that vineyards became symbolic of the "settlement" of the land and that they are often linked to "family inheritance." The family/tribal land allotment, which was the basis of the "ancestral inheritance," links the faithful Israelite to all his preceding generations of ancestors back to the original conquest of the Promised Land the division of the land and among the various tribes.

Taking "possession" of property belonging to another Israelite was frowned upon and considered to go against the ancient traditions "of the Fathers." This particular issue is one of the major concerns that Nehemiah was facing in Jehud. Nehemiah 5:3, 4, 5, 11, and 9:25 all directly link vineyards with the original conquest. It should not surprise us, therefore, that the unjust acquisition of a vineyard should become the central focus of the Persian-period author of the didactic parable in 1 Kgs 21:1–16, and that it is there directly linked to Naboth's ancestral inheritance.[16]

By creating the didactic parable of 1 Kgs 21:1–16, 23, and 25bα, and, by inserting it into the Dtr text of 1 Kgs 21:17–29, the author of our parable produced an excellent tool for teaching the people of his own time. His purpose was to show them that in their own ancient history there were situations very similar to their own in which their rulers, due in very large part to the seductions and negative influences of their foreign wives, abused the rights of faithful Israelites and even murdered them to achieve their wicked ends. Ultimately, these types of sins and abuses could be credited with the disastrous event of the Babylonian Exile. Unless Israel wanted to repeat its horrific past, they should heed the warning that the didactic parable of 1 Kgs 21 teaches a return to fidelity to Israel's ancient, noble, and holy traditions.

---

16. See vv. 1, 2 (×2), 6 (×3), 7, 15, 16, 18—all of which are in reference to Naboth's נַחֲלַת אֲבֹתַי ("ancestral inheritance").

# Part V

## CONCLUSION

# Chapter 17

## CONCLUSION

The history of the compilation and interpretation of 1 Kgs 21 is long and complicated. As we have seen, this text is in many ways a puzzle. Because of the
complex nature of its history of development, it has caused many difficulties for
scholars trying to discern the history of the traditions behind the text. It was often
the case that scholars were able to find ways of fitting some, or most, of the pieces
of the puzzle together, but not all of them. The text of this chapter challenges
many of the standard categories of both interpretation and of history. Because of
the complexity of its developmental history, it has especially defied the many
scholarly attempts that have been made to locate its place of origin and its time of
composition.

Scholarship over the past century and a half has read and interpreted the story
of Naboth's vineyard in 1 Kgs 21 in a rather limited variety of ways. Most
scholars have stated in one way or another at the beginning of their commentaries
or articles on this text that the story recounted in 1 Kgs 21 is not historical. However, after having said this, they have gone on to interpret the individual verses,
terms, characters, legal features, and situations in the story as if they were absolutely historical. The vast majority of scholars have interpreted the story as the
"juridical murder of Naboth," or as a justification for the destruction of the
Ahabite dynasty by Jehu's coup d'état. These have all, therefore, dated the story
either to the time of Ahab, himself, or to sometime during the dynasty of Jehu.

One of the major problems of interpretation with regard to the story has been
the fact of the major differences between vv. 1–16 and vv. 17–29. Much of
vv. 17–29 is comprised of recognizably Dtr language. This is relatively easy to
identify and to date. The major problem for scholars, however, has been with vv.
1–16, which show no evidence of standard Dtr language. This fact has given rise
to a variety of theories and opinions regarding the sources and origins of vv. 1–
16. The easiest solution, and apparently the way least fraught with danger, was to
presume that since there is no Dtr language in vv. 1–16 it must be an "ancient" or
"old" story which was placed into the text in order to give the basis for the Dtr
accusations and condemnations for Ahab and his dynasty which follow in vv.
17–29. It is my position that this is an unacceptable type of circular argument that
runs as follows:

1. Verses 17–29 obviously are linguistically and thematically of Dtr origin.
2. Since vv. 1–16 contain no obvious Dtr language, therefore, they are not
of Dtr origin.

3.    Since vv. 1–16 are not of Dtr origin, therefore, they must predate the Dtr work.

4.    Since vv. 1–16 predate the work of Dtr, therefore they don't have any Dtr language in them.

This argumentation is flawed and myopic. It is specifically this type of thinking that has misled most scholars regarding the sources and origins of 1 Kgs 21:1–16. However, there is strong evidence to show that vv. 1–16 come, not from the period prior to, or of the Dtr Historian, but rather that they come from after his time, namely, from Persian-period Jehud.

Another factor that has greatly influenced the scholarly interpretation of the story of 1 Kgs 21 has been the debate over its relationship to the account of Jehu's coup and subsequent obliteration of the Ahabite dynasty recounted in 2 Kgs 9–10. Because of the mention of Naboth in 9:21bγ, 25–26, and since many scholars consider 2 Kgs 9–10 to represent an "historical account," they have taken the position that this coup was the actual historical setting for the Naboth incident. For these scholars 1 Kgs 21 was composed *at the same time as the coup* (or at least some time during the Jehudite dynasty), and *for apologetic reasons*, namely, to give prophetic legitimization for the coup. Representative of this position is Marsha White who argues that

> a close reading of the vineyard story (1 Kings 21) together with the coup narrative (II Kings 9–10) *requires* the conclusion that they were composed at roughly the same time as two halves of a whole, and that the time of composition *could only have been after the coup exterminations*.[1]

My study has shown that here again most scholars have failed to note that 2 Kgs 9:21bγ, 25–26, what I have referred to as the "Jehu-Apologetic Redaction," is in fact a secondary insertion into the "historical account" of Jehu's coup and, that *its* very purpose was to give specific prophetic justification for Jehu's murder of Joram and for the desecration of his body. I date the Jehu-Apologetic Redaction to some time between the actual event of the coup and the end of the Jehu dynasty, but it was in no way connected to 1 Kgs 21 which, as we know it, did not even exist at that time. Neither 1 Kgs 21:1–16, nor the Dtr vv. 20–26, had been written at the historical time of the Jehu dynasty. These were, in fact, written long after the Jehu coup and long after the fall of the Northern Kingdom.

By failing to recognize the secondary nature of 2 Kgs 9:21bγ, 25–26 (and other elements of the texts of 2 Kgs 9–10), many scholars have misinterpreted the place and role of these verses vis-à-vis 1 Kgs 21. First Kings 21 begins as a "once upon a time" type of story (v. 1). As we have also seen, there is also evidence in the text of 1 Kgs 21 of some potentially very late linguistic elements and influence, especially in vv. 1–16. This contradicts any attempt to date the account to the ninth or eighth centuries B.C.E.

I have proposed a different approach and interpretation for the didactic parable found in 1 Kgs 21:1–16. Eventually, long after the destruction of Israel, the Dtr

---

1.    White, *The Elijah Legends and Jehu's Coup*, 77–78 (emphasis added).

Historian began his work of collecting, editing, and constructing his history. The first version/edition of this was most probably already begun during the reform of Josiah and was probably completed by the end of Josiah's reign. After the destruction and exile of Judah to Babylon, this original version of the Dtr History was edited, reworked, and updated during the period of the Exile. Within this Dtr History there was found the Elijah–Naboth Fragment (1 Kgs 21:17–19a, 20aα–bα) which recounted an encounter between Elijah and Ahab in which Ahab was accused and condemned for the murder of Naboth and of taking possession of the dead man's property. For this crime, Ahab was to die. This fragment was then followed by a list of Dtr accusations and condemnations of Ahab and his dynasty for all their sins recounted in 1 Kgs 17–19. These accusations and condemnations employ standardized and typical Dtr language and phrases which are also found in similar Dtr evaluations of several other kings.

The Elijah–Naboth Fragment is the remnant of an old tradition about the Naboth murder that the Dtr Historian either found in a former text of the books of Kings, or that was part of an oral tradition circulating at the time of his writing the history. He also found substantiation for this fragment in what I have referred to as the pre-Dtr "Jehu-Apologetic Redaction," which was already part of the account of the Jehu coup (2 Kgs 9:21bγ, 25–26). In this redaction, v. 26b represents, in my view, another separate and independent "Naboth Fragment." Because both referred to Naboth, and despite the significant differences between these fragments, the Dtr Historian created a prophecy–fulfillment relationship between them by means of 1 Kgs 21:27–29, in which he transfers the personal punishment from Ahab to his son Joram. Following upon vv. 20b–22, 24–26, and since Joram was the last of Ahab's line, 1 Kgs 21:27–29 also came to be understood as representative of an oracle of dynastic destruction.

Based upon linguistic, thematic, and historical evidence and indicators, I have suggested that the origins for the story in 1 Kgs 21:1–16 are to be found in post-exilic, Persian-period Jehud. A truly gifted and artistic author who was able to incorporate into his creation ancient sources and contemporary issues wrote the story. He was able to create a didactic parable that would address contemporary problems by using symbolic representations of ancient characters from Israel's past. He recreated the historical characters of the prophet Elijah and of King Ahab. He recreated the character of the faithful Israelite, Naboth the Jezreelite. Finally, he created an exemplary "negative character" in Jezebel in order to express one of his major concerns and one of the major problems facing the "community of the returnees," namely, marriage with foreign women. By creating the "extreme character," the "symbol" of Jezebel, he was able to express and address the extreme nature of the danger he saw in these marriages. By means of his parable, the author was also able to criticize the leaders and rulers, both of the initial groups of returnees, and also of the more recent returnees from Babylon, for having apostasized and for becoming abusive to the faithful Israelites under their care. The focus of his charges and the source of the problem was their marriage to foreign women who led them astray.

This didactic parable of 1 Kgs 21:1–16 was meant to teach and to warn the returnees and all future generations of the dangers which threatened to cause a repetition of history. YHWH granted the original "Chosen People" the "Promised Land" on the condition that they remain separated from the nations around them—whom the Lord would dispossess before them. Only by their fidelity to the covenant and to the ancient traditions would they, the Chosen People, remain in the land in the future. In the past, Israel and Judah had both sinned; their leaders (their kings) were the worst among them, and they received the blame for the consequent destruction of their kingdoms and the exile of their peoples. The leaders and kings of Israel sought to become like the other nations around them. They entered into treaties and alliances with other nations and sealed these alliances with marriages. They refused to remain loyal to YHWH alone, but rather were "seduced" into following after foreign gods and idols by their foreign wives. For all these things they were destroyed and expelled from the land which YHWH formerly had given them as an inheritance. In the author's mind, the very same danger threatened the returnees from Babylon.

The author of the parable in 1 Kgs 21:1–16 saw himself, and those in his "community of the returnees," as "the Holy Seed," as the true and faithful "Israel(-ites)." They saw themselves in the process of a "new conquest and settlement of the Promised Land." From this theological perspective, the "Promised Land" becomes the "vineyard" in the parable, and the author and his company become "Naboth," the true and faithful Israelites. Their vineyard was (in the event of the Exile) taken by wicked rulers (the Assyrians and Babylonians) under the influence of their even more wicked foreign wives (their pagan gods).

In the context of the difficulties faced by the returnees during the reconstruction period, the parable had practical application as well. The returnees (Naboth) find themselves once again threatened by wicked rulers and corrupt officials (Ahab), who, under the influence of their foreign wives (Jezebel), are threatening once again to take the "ancestral inheritance" (the vineyard) away from their own people. This process would naturally involve exploitation, death, and exile. This must be avoided by any and all means possible. The author of 1 Kgs 21:1–16 was bound and determined to make sure that history did not repeat itself. By means of the creation of his didactic parable, and by the related redactions that were necessary in order to insert and support his new parable, he was able to present a story that would teach and warn not only the commoner, but especially the rulers, elders, and officials—all those who had already begun to "follow in the footsteps of Ahab and Jezebel."

# APPENDICES

# Appendix 1

## THE QUESTION OF THE OLDEST LAYER OF THE TRADITION

### 1. A Review of the Scholarship

A review and classification of the scholars concerning the question of the oldest layer results in the following groupings.

#### a. Group I: 1 Kings 21 is a Complete Narrative Unity

This first group is comprised of those scholars who see the whole of 1 Kgs 21 as a narrative unity. Some belong to this group by default in the sense that they analyze the chapter as a whole and do not comment upon the individual parts. Others comment upon the parts but lean toward a unity view of the chapter. I include in this group of scholars, N. Schlögl, R. de Vaux, and N. H. Snaith.[1] A more recent scholar whom I would place partially in this group is B. O. Long. Long notes that scholars are divided in opinion as to the divisions of the text, and he concludes that "it is probably best to recognize that (1) a basic tradition has been supplemented, especially by the Dtr editor(s) in vv. 20–28 . . . (2) a clear understanding of the prior history of the text eludes us; and (3) the text is now a redacted unity."[2] Another scholar whom I would place on a bridge between those who see the chapter as a whole and those who see vv. 1–16 as the basic unit is J. T. Walsh.[3] Walsh breaks the chapter down into two separate but chiastically balanced units: vv. 1–16, "the account of the conspiracy against Naboth," and vv. 17–29, "the account of Ahab's condemnation by the prophet Elijah." He sees both parts as being connected together by means of a number of thematic and narrative linkages.[4]

#### b. Group II: Verses 1–16 Form the Basic Unit

The second group of scholars is made up of those who see the basic unit (though not necessarily the oldest part) of the chapter as comprised only of vv. 1–16. This group includes E. Würthwein, R. Bohlen, S. Timm, and W. M. Schniedewind.[5]

1. Schlögl, *Die Bücher der Könige, Die Bücher der Chronik*, 172–78; de Vaux, "Le Cycle d'Élie," 69–72; Snaith, "The First and Second Book of Kings," 172–78.
2. Long, *I Kings*, 224–25.
3. Walsh, "Methods and Meanings," 193–211, and "I Kings," 316–17, 328.
4. Walsh, "Methods and Meanings," 194–202.
5. Würthwein, "Naboth-Novelle und Elia-Wort," 375–97, and *Die Bücher der Könige: I. Kön. 17–2 Kön. 25*, 248–51; Bohlen, *Der Fall Nabot*, 96–105; Timm, *Die Dynastie Omri*, 113–14; Schniedewind, "History and Interpretation, 649–61 (653–54). Schniedewind sees vv. 17–27 as being

Würthwein maintains that vv. 1–16 are a self-contained unit which opens with Ahab wanting possession of Naboth's vineyard and ends with Ahab's taking possession of the vineyard. For him this was the original story and it called for no continuation. He holds that "speculation that the inconsistent continuation found in vv. 17ff had supplanted another original reading is absurd (or unrealistic)."[6]

c. *Group IIIa: Verses 1–20a Form the Basic Unit*
This is the largest group. There is also a sub-group to this main group who see one or more of the verses between v. 20bβ and v. 29 as part of the original story. The main group, those who hold that vv. 1–20a form the basic story and that vv. 20bβ–29 are from various later sources, is comprised of R. Kittel, H. Gressmann, G. Hölscher, A. Jepsen, J. A. Montgomery and H. S. Gehman, G. Fohrer, M. Weinfeld, H.-C Schmitt, P. Welten, H. Seebass, G. Hentschel, M. Oeming, and A. Rofé.[7] For these scholars the main reason for locating the end of the basic unit at v. 20a is that from 20bβ onward they identify various later redactional additions, most of which they attribute to various Dtr, or pre-Dtr, redactions. It is in these various analyses of vv. 20bβ–29 that we find some scholars who vary slightly with regard to the above-mentioned group and who see vv. 27–29 as part of the original story.

d. *Group IIIb: Verses 1–20a and Verses 27–29 Form the Basic Unit*
The difficulty which is the focal point of the distinction between Group IIIa and those that follow, has to do with vv. 27–29, Ahab's repentance and the postponement of the punishment. Do these three verses belong to the original story or not? Though the above-mentioned scholars recognized the difficulty with regard to the placement of these verses, they have decided that these verses were not, in fact, part of the main story (1–20a).[8] But another rather substantial group of scholars

---

from the hand of the pre-exilic and exilic redactors. Verses 28–29 were probably original but have been reworked by the exilic redactor (p. 653).

6.   Würthwein, "Naboth-Novelle und Elia-Wort," 390 (my translation).

7.   Kittel, *Die Bücher der Könige*, p. 158 (it should be noted that Kittel is unsure whether v. 27 is late or whether it belongs to the original layer of the tradition. In the end, with this reservation, he says that vv. 27–29 should be considered as later additions); Gressmann, *Die älteste Geschichtsschreibung*, 272; Hölscher, "Das Buch der Könige," 190; Jepsen, *Nabi*, 93–94; Montgomery and Gehman, *A Critical and Exegetical Commentary*, 332–33; Fohrer, *Elia*, 26; Weinfeld, *Deuteronomy and the Deuteronomic School*, 18–24 (Weinfeld holds that vv. 20bβ–26, 28–29 are from Dtr but v. 27 might be original); H.-C. Schmitt, *Elisa*, 134ff.; Welten, "Naboth's Weinberg," 26–27; Seebass, "Der Fall Naboth in 1 Reg. XXI"; Hentschel, *Die Elijaerzählungen*, 14–42; Oeming, "Naboth, der Jesreeliter" (Oeming believes v. 1–16 and vv. 17–20 were originally two separate traditions which were brought together at a certain point into their present form in which they form a unit [369]); Rofé, "The Vineyard of Naboth," 89.

8.   See, for example: Kittel, *Die Bücher der Könige*, 158; Jepsen, *Nabi*, 93, and *Die Quellen des Königsbuches*, 8 and 102; Fohrer, *Elia*, 26; Hölscher, "Das Buch der Könige," 190; Welten, "Naboth's Weinberg," 21–22; Hentschel, *Die Elijaerzählungen*, 14–43; Rofé, "The Vineyard of Naboth," 95. There are others who do *not* see the basic unit as comprised of vv. 1–20, but who also do not see vv. 27–29 as part of the original story: Steck, *Überlieferung und Zeitgeschichte*, 34; Miller, "The Fall of the House of Ahab," 310; Würthwein, "Naboth-Novelle und Elia-Wort," 382, 390, 395,

considers vv. 27–29 to be an integral part of the original tradition together with vv. 1–20a. This group includes: I. Benzinger, C. F. Burney, B. Stade and F. Schwally, A. Šanda, O. Eissfeldt, S. DeVries, Y. Zakovitch, and L. M. Barré.[9] Most of these scholars see in Ahab's repentance a natural reaction to the accusation and condemnation made by Elijah. They also see YHWH's reaction as a natural response to Ahab's repentance. DeVries, for instance, even says that vv. 27–29 form a part of the schema of the "regal self-judgment" sub-genre and are, therefore, not an attempt by redactors to change the original story.[10]

### e. *Group IV: Verses 1–19 (and Variants)*
There are a couple of scholars whose analyses of the oldest layer of the tradition do not allow them to fit well into the above-mentioned groups. One important scholar who varies slightly from the previous group is M. Noth. According to Noth, the basic story is made up of vv. 1–19 and 27–29.[11] J. Gray and K. Baltzer[12] maintain that the oldest layer is comprised of vv. 1–19, while vv. 20–29 "consists of a number of secondary statements from various sources."[13] J. M. Miller holds that the oldest unit of the tradition is found in vv. 1–19a. Verses 19b–29 he attributes to "editorial accretions."[14] Differently still is H. Schmoldt[15] who maintains that vv. 1–19aα, 21, and 24 should be seen as a complete narrative.[16]

### f. *Group V: Verses 17–20 are the Oldest Layer*
R. Bohlen sees vv. 1–9, 11–16 as a single unit ("der Kleinen Einheit"), but he differs from most in that he does not see this unit as the *earliest* part of the chapter. For him, vv. 17a–20d are the earliest layer of tradition in 1 Kgs 21 and he dates them to the period of the reign of Jeroboam II (784/83—753/52).[17] He dates vv. 1–9, 11–16 to the long period of time between the end of the Jehu dynasty (752/51) and the time of the work of DtrP[18] which ended between

---

and *Die Bücher der Könige: I. Kön. 17–2 Kön. 25*, p. 127; Dietrich, *Prophetie und Geschichte*, 47; Bohlen, *Der Fall Nabot*, 87–90, and 304–9; Oeming, "Naboth, der Jezreeliter," 381; Montgomery and Gehman, *A Critical and Exegetical Commentary*, 333, note the difficulties but do not take a position on the issue.

9.  Benzinger, *Die Bücher der Könige*, 115–16; Burney, *Notes*, 249; Stade and Schwally, *The Book of Kings*, 28; Šanda, *Das erste Buch der Könige*, 466; Eissfeldt, *Das erste Buch der Könige*, 538, also, "Die Komposition von 1 Reg. 16:29–2 Reg. 13:25," in *Das ferne und nahe Wort: Festschrift Leonhard Rost* (ed. F. Maass; BZAW 105; Berlin: de Gruyter, 1967), 49–58 (51); DeVries, *Prophet against Prophet*, 116, and, *I Kings*, 255–58; Zakovitch, "The Tale of Naboth's Vineyard," 401; Barré, *The Rhetoric of Political Persuasion*, 111.

10.  DeVries, *Prophet against Prophet*, 115, and *I Kings*, 255.

11.  Noth, *Überlieferungsgeschichtliche Studien* I, and *The Deuteronomistic History*, 112.

12.  Gray, *I & II Kings*, 435; Baltzer, "Naboths Weinberg," 73–88.

13.  Gray, *I & II Kings*, 435.

14.  Miller, "The Fall of the House of Ahab," 312. A similar point of view is found in Dietrich, *Prophetie und Geschichte*, 47.

15.  Schmoldt, "Elijas Botschaft an Ahab," 39–52.

16.  Schmoldt, "Elijas Botschaft an Ahab," 51.

17.  Bohlen, *Der Fall Nabot*, 302.

18.  His designation for a Deuteronomistic edition from a prophetic tradition.

580–560 (a period of nearly 200 years). Verses 1–9, 11–16, according to him, date from after the time of the fall of Israel, and, therefore, come from the kingdom of Judah.[19] Bohlen's interpretation appears to be an outgrowth from that of O. H. Steck. Steck also maintained that vv. 17–18a and 19–20abα were the oldest layer in the chapter.[20] Verses 1–16 and 23 belong, according to Steck, to the same later source.[21] Verses 27–29 come from the time of Joram, Ahab's son, and are therefore pre-Dtr.[22] Verses 21–22, 24–26 are assigned by Steck to the Dtr editor.[23]

## 2. Conclusions Regarding the Survey of Scholars

The first conclusion that can be drawn from the above presentation is the most obvious—there is no consensus among the scholars on what constitutes the oldest layer of the tradition. One might be able to say that generally there is agreement that there was an older layer which later underwent several redactions. There is, however, no agreement on where the oldest layer of the tradition ends or where the redactional material begins or to whom this redaction material should be assigned.

Secondly, it appears that in the last thirty years or so there has been a renewed and lively interest in 1 Kgs 21. This renewed activity in the analysis and study of the story of Naboth's Vineyard parallels, and may even be a result of, a renewed interest in biblical exegesis and in the designing and application of new approaches to the critical analysis of these ancient texts.[24]

Despite the renewed interest I have just mentioned, there is also a certain amount of consistency among scholars in the last century and a half. By this I mean that in each of the general categories (with the exception of Group II, those who see the oldest layer of tradition in vv. 1–16), there is a relatively good mixture of older and more recent scholars represented.

---

19. Bohlen, *Der Fall Nabot*, 313. I wonder at the apparent difficulty Bohlen has in dating more precisely these verses, especially given his ability to date so precisely other elements of the chapter. For example vv. 17–20 he dates to within a period of 30 years (p. 302) and vv. 25–26, which he attributes to the DtrN (a Deuteronomistic editor from a legal tradition), he dates to around 560 (p. 304).

20. Steck, *Überlieferung und Zeitgeschichte*, 43.

21. Steck, *Überlieferung und Zeitgeschichte*, 40–42.

22. Steck, *Überlieferung und Zeitgeschichte*, 34.

23. Steck, *Überlieferung und Zeitgeschichte*, 41.

24. See, for instance, Walsh, "Methods and Meanings," 193–211. See also R. Martin-Achard, "La Vigne de Naboth (1 Rois 21) d'après des Études Récentes," *ETR* 66, no. 1 (1991): 1–16.

# Appendix 2

## THE LEGALITIES INVOLVED IN NABOTH'S REFERENCE
## TO HIS VINEYARD AS נַחֲלַת אֲבֹתַי

The question of the legalities in this regard has traditionally been discussed in terms of whether Naboth "could not" or "would not" sell his vineyard. The effort to find the answer to this question has resulted in highlighting the fact that *there is no common agreement* concerning ancient Israelite legal tradition with regard to property belonging to the family or tribal inheritance (נַחֲלָה). We find scholars using a variety of terms for נַחֲלָה including "law," "legal custom," "principle," "tradition". This variation in terms indicates the diverse interpretations and the lack of agreement among scholars concerning the issue. In what follows I will give a "representative selection" of scholarly opinion in an attempt to present a summary of the wide-range of positions for these questions.

### 1. *Naboth* Could *Not Sell His Vineyard*

#### a. *C. F. Keil and F. Delitzsch*
Keil and Delitzsch, followed by Benzinger and Kittel, maintained that Naboth's rejection of Ahab's offer was "based upon religious principles . . . the sale of family inheritance was forbidden by law (see Lev 25:23–28 and Num 36:7ff.)."[1]

#### b. *M. Noth*
M. Noth held that the "ownership of land and property was the basis for economic and national life in ancient Israel. Only the landowner was considered to be a full citizen . . . [It] was a matter of honor to maintain ownership of it and not to part with it except in serious crisis."[2]

#### c. *A. Alt*
A. Alt considered Naboth's refusal to be based upon the fact that "at that time the Israelite law of the land still ruled unrestrictedly. It was guided by its rural ideal of the equal division of the Land (which was ultimately owned by YHWH), amongst all the free Israelites of the community."[3]

---

1.  Keil and Delitzsch, *Das Alte Testament*, 224. See also, Benzinger, *Die Bücher der Könige*, 114; Kittel, *Die Bücher der Könige*, 156.
2.  M. Noth, "Das Krongut der israelitischen Könige und seiner Verwaltung," *ZDPV* 50 (1927): 211–44 (211–12). More recently, Gray, *I & II Kings*, 439; DeVries, *I Kings*, 256. See also Baltzer, "Naboths Weinberg," 77–81.
3.  A. Alt, *Der Stadtstaat Samaria* (Berichte über die Verhandlungen der sächsischen Akademie der Wissenschaften zu Leipzig 101/5; Berlin: Akademie Verlag), 14. This position is similar to that

#### d. *G. Fohrer*

G. Fohrer finds both theoretical and theological bases for Naboth's refusal.[4] According to the ancient ideas, YHWH was the only owner of the land which he had given to the whole people as hereditary and inalienable property. It was divided among the whole people according to tribe and each tribe divided their portion among the clans and families. These, then, were the hereditary owners and producers of the land. Therefore, the acknowledged portion could not be optionally bought or sold. This was the theoretical and theological basis of Israelite law regarding property.[5]

#### e. *M. Rehm*

M. Rehm argued that "the offer made by Ahab actually contained nothing illegal, since even David and Omri acquired pieces of land which they desired by means of purchase (2 Sam 24:24; 1 Kgs 16:24)."[6] Rehm goes on to note that "Naboth was not inclined to accept the offer of Ahab as witnessed both by his evident affection for, or attachment to, his property and by his identification of the vineyard as נַחֲלַת אֲבֹתַי. This identification indicated his loyalty to his ancestors (1 Sam 2:33; 2 Sam 7:12–16; 1 Kgs 15:19)."[7] Rehm points out that Samuel had already warned of the possibility that the king "would take the best of the fields, vineyards and olive trees to give to his servants" (1 Sam 8:14). "His warnings must have been based upon his own observations of the surrounding nations, in

---

taken by J. Pedersen, *Israel: Its Life and Culture* (2 vols.; SFSHJ 29; Atlanta: Scholars Press, 1991), 2:68; and Snaith, "The First and Second Book of Kings," 172–73.

4. Fohrer, *Elia*, 22–27.

5. Fohrer, *Elia*, 22, 72–73. See also, Montgomery and Gehman, *A Critical and Exegetical Commentary*, 330; de Vaux, *Les livres des Rois*, 114 n. a, and "Le Cycle d'Élie", 166. Baltzer ("Naboths Weinberg," 78–79) says that "He has no free hand over the vineyard, for in a legal sense, he is not the owner but rather he is its caretaker. If he were to give up the vineyard, he would also be giving up the blessing and favor of YHWH for his children and descendents. A sale of the vineyard would be illegal both before God and man." See also Welten, "Naboth's Weinberg," 23; H. J. Boecker, *Law and the Administration of Justice in the Old Testament and Ancient East* (trans. J. Moiser; Minneapolis: Augsburg, 1980), 88–99. G. Hentschel (*I Könige* [Die Neue Echter Bibel; Würzburg: Echter Verlag, 1984], 129) maintains that Naboth held fast to his property as a sacred duty, but Ahab did not understand the land as an inheritance. Thus there is the impression that Naboth's refusal was based upon pure stubbornness. Rofé ("The Vineyard of Naboth," 90–91) states that "Naboth's refusal is categorical, deprecating the alienation of his estate. It is justified by one argument—נַחֲלַת אֲבֹתַי. This is not a law, but a principle that stands behind law." This also appears to be the way that A. Klostermann understood the situation in his reconstruction of the text, *Die Bücher Samuelis und der Könige*, 382. See also Walsh, "Methods and Meanings," 203.

6. Rehm, *Das erste Buch der Könige*, 209. However, Rehm apparently does not recognize that there is a very big difference between these two examples and the case of Ahab offering to trade or buy Naboth's vineyard. In both the cases he cites, the land being bought is not being acquired from an identified Israelite. In 2 Sam 24:24, the land is obtained from Araunah the Jebusite (see 24:16), and, in 1 Kgs 16:24, Omri bought the hill of Samaria from a certain Shemer who is not specifically identified as an Israelite, and the land involved is never specifically identified as part of the ancestral inheritance.

7. For a similar point of view, see P. Buis, *Le Livre des Rois* (Sources Bibliques; Paris: J. Gabalda, 1997), 167.

particular, of Egypt, where the entire land was considered to be the inheritance of the Pharaoh."[8] "Israelite law, however, made provision to preserve the even distribution of the land to the individual tribes and families. It did not prevent the buying of land from non-Israelites,[9] and, in rare cases, from Israelites who were in dire straits, but the purchase of these Israelite lands was strongly regulated (Lev 25:23–28) and eventually these lands were returned to the original owners/tribe (see the Jubilee Year laws, Lev 25:10–16). By these laws, even the king was bound."[10]

### f. A. Malamat

A. Malamat argues that there are parallels to the Old Testament concept of נַחֲלָה in Mari. In both Mari and in Israel, "the patrimony was conceived in basically similar terms, namely, as an essentially inalienable piece of land possessed solely by a gentilic unit, whether large or small, hence, this land could not, at least in theory, be sold to any would-be purchaser, and its transfer from one owner to another could only be effected through inheritance."[11] This principle is also found in the Old Testament, whether explicitly or implicitly stated. "Its most unequivocal expression is found in the measures taken to keep the patrimony within the tribe and to prevent it from passing into the possession of other tribes, as in the case of the daughters of Zelophehad in Num 36:7. This same principle is found in the regulations regarding the redemption of land in the Mosaic laws (Lev 25:13, 25–28)."[12]

Several scholars have suggested that the transition from a nomadic or semi-nomadic tribal system to a monarchical system would have had a wide-ranging impact on the overall life and in the laws in Israel. With the settlement and with the birth of the monarchy came also a movement toward urbanization, with collateral changes in the sociological and economic systems of the society. Particularly with the establishment of the monarchy, foreign influence would have also been increased in the areas of politics, economics, markets, trade, art, and law. Within this context there would have been inevitable clashes between the "old ways" and the "new ways," between the old tribal laws and customs and

---

8. Rehm, *Das erste Buch der Könige*, 209. This argument was strongly made earlier by I. Mendelsohn, "Samuel's Denunciation of Kingship in the Light of the Akkadian Documents from Ugarit," *BASOR* 143 (1956): 17–22. See also Sarna, "Naboth's Vineyard Revisited," 120.

9. In this regard, Timm, *Die Dynastie Omri*, 125–26, argues that when Naboth refused to trade or sell his property he was sticking to principles as formulated in Lev 25:23–34 and Num 36:1–13. He then conjectures that when, however, Ahab sought to buy economically useful land from Naboth, it must have been known from the start that nearby the inalienable נַחֲלָה there was also land that could be sold. Timm also makes the point that, in the end, this story is told more for the time of the hearers and has more to do with their specific attitudes than it does with those of the time of Ahab. By focusing upon Naboth's reasonable refusal to part with his inheritance, the author is apparently looking back at the affair which, in his own time, could no longer be possible.

10. Rehm, *Das erste Buch der Könige*, 209.

11. A. Malamat, "Mari and the Bible: Some Patterns of Tribal Organization and Institutions," *JAOS* 82 (1962): 143–50 (149); followed by F. I. Anderson, "The Socio-Juridical Background," 49.

12. Malamat, "Mari and the Bible," 150.

the new urbanized laws and customs. It is in the context of these clashes that some scholars place the story of the acquisition of the vineyard in 1 Kgs 21:1–16. W. Nowack, for instance, wrote: "a conscious shift with regard to the conditions of land ownership began in Israel in the period of the kings."[13] J. Fichtner maintained that "the king was acting based upon urban property laws."[14]

### g. *N. M. Sarna*

N. M. Sarna maintains that "it is clear from the start that even in paganized northern Israel, the monarch had no power, in the present instance, simply to impose his will by force upon its subjects."[15] The king accepted the restraint of the law and could not confiscate Naboth's vineyard merely because he desired it. For Sarna, "this remarkable limitation on crown-rights (see Deut 17:14–20; Ezek 45:8–9; 46:18) is particularly interesting in light of the contrasting arbitrary authority and personal privileges that kings could apparently assert and enjoy in Israel's neighboring states."[16]

### 2. *Naboth* Would *Not Sell His Vineyard*

A second group of scholars maintains that Naboth's refusal to sell was based less on a strong attachment to legal realities or traditions, but rather upon a lack of "desire" or "will" to trade or sell his vineyard to the king. These scholars can be grouped into three main positions.

### a. *There was no Legal Basis for Naboth's Refusal*

(1) According to R. Bohlen, as early as 1849, O. Thenius attempted to nullify the appeal to Lev 25:23–28 and Num 36:7–9 as a legal basis for Naboth's refusal to part with his property. Apparently, Thenius maintained that there was nothing in the referred-to Mosaic law which strongly forbade an Israelite from selling his ancestral inheritance, and, "at the very least, in the same references, there is nothing forbidding trade."[17]

(2) A. Šanda also attempts to nullify the validity of the references to Lev 25:23–38 and Num 36:7–9. He wrote:

> No one hangs on to ancestral property as strongly as an Easterner. Without property of their own, they would have been considered to be poor. It is for this reason that Lev

---

13. W. Nowack, *Lehrbuch der Hebräischen Archäologie* (Freiburg: J. C. B Mohr [Paul Siebeck], 1894), 351. See also Mendelsohn, "Samuel's Denunciation of Kingship," 17–22; Malamat, "Mari and the Bible," 147–50. Gray (*I & II Kings*, 435) maintains that the story in 1 Kgs 21 retains, though not literally in every detail, a true reflection of the consequences of the policy of the house of Omri to bring about a synthesis of Israelite and Canaanite traditions. See too F. I. Anderson, "The Socio-Juridical Background," 46–49; Steck, *Überlieferung und Zeitgeschichte*, 50 n. 2.

14. Fichtner, *Das erste Buch von den Königen*, 316.

15. Sarna, "Naboth's Vineyard Revisited," 119.

16. Sarna, "Naboth's Vineyard Revisited," 119–20. Somewhat similar is Zakovitch, "The Tale of Naboth's Vineyard," 384–86.

17. Bohlen, *Der Fall Nabot*, 14; referring to Thenius, *Die Bücher der Könige*, 243.

25:23–28 was written. Its purpose was to prevent poverty that the forced, or compulsory, selling of land had introduced in Israel. It applied to both the willing sale of land and the exchange of fields. Also, Num 36:7ff. could not have motivated Naboth's refusal since Ahab's family came out of Issachar, and perhaps even from Jezreel, itself.

For, Šanda, then, the motivation that led Naboth to refuse Ahab's offer was merely his affection for the inheritance from his fathers. "For this reason he uses the emphatic form, נַחֲלַת אֲבֹתַי. Naboth also uses in his response to Ahab the less-respectful form of לְךָ." Šanda concludes, therefore, that "Naboth was a distinguished (noble) man and that he spoke to Ahab as an equal."[18]

### b. *Naboth's Refusal was Based Upon his "Stubbornness"*
(1) J. Wellhausen wrote that "Naboth, the owner, was not willing to sell or trade" his vineyard.[19] J. Skinner wrote that the "tragic incident originates in a perfectly reasonable and just proposal of Ahab to his humble neighbor Naboth for the purchase of a vineyard . . . Naboth, however, true to the conservative instincts of his class, refuses on religious grounds to alienate his patrimony (see Lev 25:23ff.; Num 36:7ff.)."[20]

(2) H. Gressmann maintained that "Naboth, a stiff-necked farmer who was attached to his field, was in no way inclined to part with the inheritance of his fathers."[21] He makes no reference at all to the legal, religious, or traditional reasons why Naboth might have refused Ahab's offer.

### c. *Naboth's Refusal was a Deliberate Snub to the King*
(1) H. Seebass, focusing upon Ahab's response to Naboth's refusal, maintains that "Naboth's argument that he 'could not' sell his vineyard because it was his

18. Šanda, *Das erste Buch der Könige*, 461–62. Following Šanda is P. Fannon, "1–2 Kings," in *A New Catholic Commentary on Holy Scripture* (ed. R. C. Fuller, L. Johnson and C. Kearns; Nashville: Nelson, 1969), 375-435 (338). Fannon held that Ahab's request was not against the principles of Lev 25:23–28 since Naboth would not be left landless (he would have obtained a different vineyard). Nor would the offer have been against Num 36.7–9 since the land would not have passed from the tribe of Issachar. Fannon is of the opinion that "Naboth was obstinately conservative. It was the sharpness of the refusal which angered Ahab." Apparently following Šanda (*Das erste Buch der Könige*, 461), Fannon refers the reader in this regard to an uncertain reference, "16:16." No book reference is given for this referral and in no Old Testament book does this specific reference have anything to do with Ahab's origins, Jezreel, or Issachar. I suspect that the reference that was intended here is Josh 19:17–23, which describes the portion that fell to the tribe of Issachar, and which, in v. 18, specifically mentions Jezreel as a part of this territory. It should also be noted that the place of origin of Omri and his family, including Ahab, is never given, nor is it ever said to be specifically Jezreel or Issachar.

19. Wellhausen, *Prolegomena zur Geschichte Israels*, 301.

20. Skinner, *Kings*, 255. Despite the fact that Skinner refers to Naboth's vineyard as his patrimony, he apparently does not consider Naboth's "religious grounds" to be sufficient for the refusal of Ahab's "perfectly reasonable and just proposal." This would imply, at least, that for Skinner the reasons for Naboth's refusal were neither necessarily legal nor binding. He implies that Naboth's reasons had to do, rather, with the "conservative instincts of his class." This statement is open to various interpretations.

21. Gressmann, *Die älteste Geschichtsschreibung*, 271–72.

family inheritance does not make sense because it would make the king's angry reaction unintelligible." He argues: "if it were the case that the vineyard were inheritance and inalienable, then surely the king of all the people would have already known this, and his very offer for the vineyard would have been illegal. The only way to make sense out of the king's anger is to accept that Naboth's response to, and rejection of, the king's offer was in some way improper (unjust) or in bad form."[22]

To substantiate this interpretation, Seebass refers to F. Horst's position.[23] Horst maintained that there are distinctions to be made between various types of נַחֲלָה. First, by נַחֲלָה is meant the division of the land as it was first received by the tribes and families by means of surveys and lots during the settlement and as it was passed on from the time of the first settlement through the successive generations. In this sense, נַחֲלָה means "inherited land," the "inherited property," or the "inherited portion of the family estate." Second, in later texts of the Old Testament, נַחֲלָה usually refers to "the inheritance of the fathers, " or to the נַחֲלָה of a specific person.[24] Finally, in the Hexateuch the term נַחֲלָה refers only to the inheritance of the entire tribe or clan (i.e. not a personal or private inheritance).[25] According Horst,

> Even though the nature of land in the sphere of Canaanite life was seen as private property, it was, however, taken for granted that it could not be freely disposed of. As long as the patriarchal family structure lasted, and as long as the tribal unity, especially with its original self-evident and effective system of mutual tribal assistance, remained alive and was accepted (this was stronger in the rural areas than in the cities), there was no freedom of disposal of inherited land, since the first right to buy, and in the case of indebtedness, the right to buy it back (redeem it) went to the next authorized relative . . . . [W]hen Naboth claimed, in response to the kings offer, that he was not willing to trade or sell a part of his ancestral inheritance, it probably did not refer to the fundamental inalienability of inherited land, but rather, it probably referred to the legal custom which allowed for the sale of inherited land in cases of emergency and in consideration of the interests of the clan. This means that, fundamentally speaking, inherited land was able to be sold but that the principle remained in effect that the original owner always had the right to repurchase the property (Lev 25:23a).[26]

For Horst, then, there are two basic types of נַחֲלָה: one which is absolutely inalienable, the tribal inheritance, and one which, in certain circumstances and under certain conditions, was able to be sold (the family portion).[27]

22. Seebass, "Der Fall Naboth in 1 Reg. XXI," 475–76.

23. F. Horst, "Das Eigentum nach dem Alten Testament" (originally published in 1949), reprinted in *Gottesrecht: Gesammelte Studien zum Recht im Alten Testament* (Munich: Chr. Kaiser, 1961), 203–21.

24. See Num 27:7; 36:8, 21; Josh 19:49–50; 1 Kgs 21:3; Prov 19:14; Ruth 4:5, 6, 10; Isa 54:17; 58:14.

25. Horst, "Das Eigentum nach dem Alten Testament," 206.

26. Horst, "Das Eigentum nach dem Alten Testament," 206–7 (author's translation).

27. In a more recent article, "Zwei Begriffe für Eigentum (Besitz): נַחֲלָה und אֲחֻזָּה," in *Verbannung und Heimkehr: Beiträge zur Geschichte und Theologie Israels im 6. und 5. Jahrhundert v. Chr. Festschrift Wilhelm Rudolph* (Tübingen: J. C. B. Mohr [Paul Siebeck] 1961), 135–56, Horst distinguishes the various types or understandings of נַחֲלָה. Among these he includes: (1) נַחֲלָה of the tribes of Israel; (2) Israel's נַחֲלָה; (3) God's נַחֲלָה; (4) נַחֲלָה of the Levites; (5) the נַחֲלָה of

Seebass grasps on to Horst's position about the apparently ambiguous nature of the alienablity of inherited land and uses it to conjecture that Ahab could not accept a piece of property for his palace, which, at a later time, could be reclaimed by its former owner. He does, however, maintain that even this possible explanation is missing something.[28] The solution to the weakness which he perceives in Horst's explanation is to be found in the double-meaning of נַחֲלָה. For Seebass, there is first of all the נַחֲלָה which refers to the clan property and which is inalienable. The second type of נַחֲלָה refers to those properties which were not originally part of the tribal inheritance, but which were obtained by other means. These properties could be sold. If this were the case, and if the vineyard of Naboth was saleable, then Ahab's offer to buy the vineyard would make sense and would be legal. Furthermore, "when Naboth included such a vineyard under the category of inalienable נַחֲלָה, 'a truly shocking violation of fidelity to YHWH and the forefathers,' it also meant that this very act was a rejection of the king, something which was not legal and which must have humiliated the king. For this the king was justly angry."[29] Therefore, for vv. 1–4 to be meaningful, Seebass argues, there is no option but to maintain that "Naboth's vineyard was indeed able to be sold, but that he did not want to sell it, and thereby, his refusal was a snub to the king."[30]

(2) R. Nelson also approaches the difficulty of the story from the perspective of Ahab's response of anger. He recognizes that "we really do not understand the mechanics of land tenure and sale in ancient Israel."[31] He also maintains that in parallel cultures, land transfer was under strict control, but that there were also ways around these strictures, for example, legal fictions such as the arranging of false adoptions. Like Seebass, Nelson makes the point that if there was really no possibility for a request such as Ahab's, then why would the king have even asked in the first place? How is it possible to explain the king's sulky reaction to Naboth's refusal? For Nelson, "the real striking point is not any legal barrier, but that Naboth had put himself under an oath not to sell (v. 3)"[32] Nelson maintains that: "The plot complication is introduced by Naboth's oath. He will not have the vineyard God gave to his ancestors turned into an Egyptian-style vegetable garden (see Deut 11:10). Ahab is stymied by this adjuration in Yahweh's name and goes home to sulk, his actions being external clues to his psychological state."[33]

---

individuals, and (6) figurative נַחֲלָה. Here too, Horst places the story of 1 Kgs 21 under the category of "נַחֲלָה to individuals" and indicates that with this type of נַחֲלָה, one can add to or increase it through buying or trading land, and, these lands are open to being re-sold or traded again (see pp. 147–48). Bohlen (*Der Fall Nabot*) basically arrives at the same conclusions as Horst; see his detailed study of the issues involved on pp. 320–50.

28. Seebass, "Der Fall Naboth in 1 Reg. XXI," 476.
29. Seebass, "Der Fall Naboth in 1 Reg. XXI," 476–77.
30. Seebass, "Der Fall Naboth in 1 Reg. XXI," 478.
31. Nelson, *First and Second Kings*, 139.
32. Nelson, *First and Second Kings*, 139.
33. Nelson, *First and Second Kings*, 141.

## 3. *Conclusion*

The above review of scholarship shows that there is still no consensus as to the question of whether or not Naboth's refusal to trade or sell his vineyard was based upon proscriptions found in legal statutes, or whether it was simply a case of his unwillingness to sell. The positions taken are purely conjectural. The fact remains that we have very little knowledge of actual jurisprudence regarding inherited land in Israel (or anywhere else in the ancient Near East) in the period in which this story is supposedly set, namely, the ninth–eighth centuries B.C.E. We are, in the end, left with the story as it is found and presented in 1 Kgs 21. There, the obvious intent of the creator of this story was to present Naboth as a faithful Israelite, as one who honored, respected, and kept the traditions and customs of his forefathers regarding the preservation of his ancestral inheritance, whether or not these traditions and customs were, in fact, law.

# BIBLIOGRAPHY

Ackroyd, P. R. "The Jewish Community in Palestine in the Persian Period." Pages 130–61 in *The Cambridge History of Judaism*. Vol. 1, *Introduction: The Persian Period*. Edited by W. D. Davies and L. Finkelstein. Cambridge: Cambridge University Press, 1984.

Albright, W. F. *History, Archaeology and Christian Humanism*. New York: McGraw-Hill, 1964.

Alfrink, B. "L'Expression וַיִּשְׁכַּב עִם־אֲבֹתָיו." *Oudtestamentische Studiën* 2 (1943): 106–18.

Allen, L. C. *Psalms 101–150*. Word Biblical Commentary 21. Waco, Tex.: Word Books, 1983.

Alt, A. *Der Stadtstaat Samaria*. Berichte über die Verhandlungen der sächsischen Akademie der Wissenschaften zu Leipzig 101/5. Berlin: Akademie Verlag.

Anderson, A. A. *The Book of Psalms*. Vol. 2, *Psalms 73–150*. London: Oliphant's, 1972 [2d ed. 1977]).

Anderson, F. I. "The Socio-Juridical Background of the Naboth Incident." *Journal of Biblical Literature* 85 (1966): 46–57.

Baltzer, K. "Naboths Weinberg (I Kön. 21). Der Konflikt zwischen israelitischem und kanaanäischem Bodenrecht." *Wort und Dienst*, n.s., 8 (1965): 73–88.

Barré, L. M. *The Rhetoric of Political Persuasion*. Catholic Biblical Quarterly Monograph Series 20. Washington: Catholic Biblical Association of America, 1988.

Barstad, H. M. *The Myth of the Empty Land: A Study in the History and Archaeology of Judah During the 'Exilic' Period*. Symbolae Osloenses Fasc. Supplement 28. Oslo: Scandanavian University Press, 1996.

Barton, J. *Isaiah 1–39*. Old Testament Guides. Sheffield: Sheffield Academic Press, 1995.

Ben-Barak, Z. "The Confiscation of Land in Israel and the Ancient Near East." Pages 101–17 in *Shnaton, An Annual for Biblical and Ancient Near Eastern Studies*. Jerusalem-Tel Aviv: The Israel Bible Society, 1982 (Hebrew).

Benjamin, D. C. "An Anthropology of Prophecy." *Biblical Theology Bulletin* 21, no. 4 (1991): 135–44.

Benzinger, I. *Die Bücher der Könige*. Kurzer Hand-Kommentar zum Alten Testament 9. Freiburg: J. C. B. Mohr (Paul Siebeck), 1899.

Bernhardt, K.-H. "Prophetie und Geschichte." Pages 20–46 in *Congress Volume: Uppsala, 1971*. Supplements to Vetus Testamentum 22. Leiden: Brill, 1971.

Berquist, J. L. *Judaism in Persia's Shadow: A Social and Historical Approach*. Minneapolis: Fortress, 1995.

Blank, S. H. "The Curse, Blasphemy, the Spell, and the Oath." *Hebrew Union College Annual* 23, no. 1 (1950–51): 73–95.

Boecker, H. J. *Die Beurteilung der Anfänge des Königtums in den deuteronomistischen Abschnitten. Ein Beitrag zum Problem des "deuteronomistischen Geschichtswerks*. Wissenschaftliche Monographien zum Alten und Neuen Testament 31 Neukirchener–Vluyn Neukirchener Verlag, 1969.

—*Law and the Administration of Justice in the Old Testament and Ancient East*. Translated by J. Moiser. Minneapolis: Augsburg, 1980.

—*Redeformen des Rechtslebens im Alten Testament*. Wissenschaftliche Monographien zum Alten und Neuen Testament 14. Neukirchen–Vluyn: Neukirchener Verlag, 1964.

Bogaert, P.-M. "Le Repentir d'Achab d'après la Bible Hébraïque (I R 21) et d'après la Septante (3 Règnes 20)." Pages 39–57 in *Élie le Prophète: Bible, Tradition, Iconographie colloque des 10 et 11 novembre 1985, Bruxelles*. Edited by G. E. Willems. Publications de l'Institutum Iudaicum 6. Leuven: Peeters, 1986.

Bohlen, R. *Der Fall Nabot. Form, Hintergrund und Werdegang einer alttestamentlichen Erzählun (1 Kön 21)*. Trierer Theologische Studien 35. Trier: Paulinus-Verlag, 1978.

Borger, R. *Die Inschriften Asarhaddons Königs von Assyrien. Archiv für Orientforschung*. Beiheft 9. Graz: Im Selbstverlage des Herausgebers, 1956.

—"Die Inschriften Asarhaddons Königs von Assyrien: Nachträge und Verbesserungen." *Archiv für Orientforschung* 18 (1957–58): 113–18.

Brichto, H. C. "Background and Function of the Biblical *nāśī*." *Catholic Biblical Quarterly* 25 (1963): 111–17.

—*The Problem of "Curse" in the Hebrew Bible*. Journal of Biblical Literature Monograph Series 13. Philadelphia: Society of Biblical Literature, 1963.

Brongers, H. A. "Fasting in Israel in Biblical and Post-Biblical Times." Pages 1–21 in *Instruction and Interpretation: Studies in Hebrew Language, Palestinian Archaeology, and Biblical Exegesis*. Edited by A. S. Van Der Woude. Oudtestamentische Studiën 20. Leiden: Brill, 1977.

Buis, P. *Le Livre des Rois*. Sources Bibliques. Paris: J. Gabalda, 1997.

Burney, C. F. *Notes on the Hebrew Text of the Books of Kings*. Oxford: Oxford University Press, 1903. Reprint, New York: Ktav, 1970.

Campbell, A. F. *Of Prophets and Kings: A Late Ninth-Century Document (I Samuel 1–2 Kings 10)*. Catholic Biblical Quarterly, Monograph Series 17. Washington: Catholic Biblical Association of America, 1986.

Clements, R. E. "The Deuteronomistic Interpretations of the Founding of the Monarchy in I Sam. VIII." *Vetus Testamentum* 24 (1974): 398–410.

—*Isaiah 1–39*. The New Century Bible Commentary. Grand Rapids: Eerdmans, 1980.

Cogan, M. and H. Tadmor. *II Kings*. Anchor Bible 11. Garden City, N.Y.: Doubleday, 1988.

Daube, D. "Lex Talionis." Pages 102–53 in *Studies in Biblical Law*. Cambridge: Cambridge University Press, 1947.

Davies, W. D., and L. Finkelstein, eds. *The Cambridge History of Judaism*. Vol. 1, *Introduction: The Persian Period*. Edited by W. D. Davies and L. Finkelstein. Cambridge: Cambridge University Press, 1984.

DeVries, S. J. *I Kings*. Word Biblical Commentary 12. Waco, Tex. Word Books, 1985.

—*Prophet against Prophet: The Role of the Micaiah Narrative (I Kings 22) in the Development of Early Prophetic Tradition*. Grand Rapids: Eerdmans, 1978.

Dhorme, É. *La Bible*. Vol. 1, *L'Ancien Testament de la Bibliothèque de la Pléiade*. Bruge: La Librairie Gallimard, 1956.

Diamond, A. S. "An Eye for an Eye." *Iraq* 19 (1957): 151–55.

Dietrich, W. *Prophetie und Geschichte: Eine redaktionsgeschichtliche Untersuchung zum deuteronomistischen Geschichtswerk*. Forschungen zur Religion und Literatur des Alten und Neuen Testaments 108. Göttingen: Vandenhoeck & Ruprecht, 1972.

Doron, P. "A New Look at an Old Lex." *Journal of the Ancient Near Eastern Society of Columbia University* 1, no. 2 (1969): 21–27.

Driver, G. R., and J. C. Miles. *The Babylonian Laws*. Vol. 1, *Legal Commentary*. Oxford: Clarendon, 1952.

Driver, S. R. *An Introduction to the Literature of the Old Testament*. 5th ed.; Edinburgh: T. & T. Clark, 1894.

—*Deuteronomy*. International Critical Commentary. Edinburgh: T. & T. Clark, 1896.

Eisenbeis, W. *Die Wurzel* םלש *im Alten Testament*. Beihefte zur Zeitschrift für die alttesta-mentliche Wissenschaft 113. Berlin: de Gruyter, 1969.

Eissfeldt, O. *Das erste Buch der Könige*. Vol. 1 in E. Kautzsch *Die Heilige Schrift des Alten Testaments*. Edited by A. Bertholet. Tübingen: J. C. B. Mohr, 1922.

—"Die Komposition von 1 Reg. 16,29–2 Reg 13,25." Pages 49–58 in *Das ferne und nahe Wort: Festschrift Leonhard Rost*. Edited by F. Maass. Beihefte zur Zeitschrift für die alttestamentliche Wissenschaft 105. Berlin: de Gruyter, 1967.

Eskenazi, T. C. *In the Age of Prose: A Literary Approach to Ezra–Nehemiah*. Society of Biblical Literature Monograph Series 36. Atlanta: Scholars Press, 1988.

Eskenazi, T. C., and E. P. Judd. "Marriage to a Stranger in Ezra 9–10." Pages 266–85 in *Second Temple Studies*. Vol. 2, *Temple and Community in the Persian Period*. Edited by Tamara C. Eskenazi and Kent H. Richards. Journal for the Study of the Old Testament Supplement Series 175. Sheffield: JSOT Press, 1994.

Fannon, P. "1–2 Kings". Pages 328–51 in *A New Catholic Commentary on Holy Scripture*. Edited by R. C. Fuller, L. Johnson, and C. Kearns. Nashville: Nelson, 1969.

Fichtner, J. *Das erste Buch von den Königen*. Die Botschaft des Alten Testaments 12/1. Stuttgart: Calwer, 1972.

Finkelstein, J. J. "Ammiṣadqa's Edict and the Babylonian 'Law Codes.'" *Journal of Cuneiform Studies* 15 (1961): 98–104.

Fohrer, G. *Elia*. Abhandlungen zur Theologie des Alten und Neues Testaments 31. Zurich: Zwingli Verlag, 1957.

Fricke, K. D. *Das zweite Buch von den Königen*. Die Botschaft des Alten Testaments 12/2 Stuttgart: Calwer, 1972.

Gehman, H. S. "The Oath in the Old Testament." Pages 51–63 in *Grace upon Grace: Essays in Honor of Lester J. Kuyper*. Edited by J. I. Cook. Grand Rapids: Eerdmans, 1975.

Gerbrandt, G. E. *Kingship According to the Deuteronomistic History*. Society of Biblical Literature Dissertation Series 87. Atlanta: Scholars Press, 1986.

Gesenius, W. *Hebräisches und Aramäisches Handwörterbuch über das Alte Testament*. 17th ed. Berlin: Springer Verlag, 1961. First published 1915.

Gilbert, M. "La loi du talion." Pages 145–55 in *Il a parlé par les Prophètes: Thèmes et Figures Bibliques*. Bruxelles: Éditions Lessius, 1998. Repr. from *Christus* 31, Fasc. 121 (1984): 73–82.

Gonçalves, F. "El 'Destierro' Consideraciones Históricas." *Estudios Bíblicos* 55 (1997): 431–61.

Gray, J. *I & II Kings. A Commentary*. Old Testament Library. Philadelphia: Westminster, 1964 (3d ed. 1970).

Gressmann, H. *Die älteste Geschichtsschreibung und Prophetie Israels [von Samuel bis Amos und Hosea]*. Göttingen: Vandenhoeck & Ruprecht, 1910.

Gugler, W. *Jehu und seine Revolution: Voraussetzungen, Verlauf, Folgen*. Kampen: Kok, 1996.

Gunkel, H. *Geschichten von Elisa*. Meisterwerke hebräischer Erzählungskunst 1. Berlin: Verlag Karl Curtius, 1913.

Halpern, B. *The Constitution of the Monarchy in Israel*. Harvard Semitic Monographs 25. Chico, Calif.: Scholars Press, 1981.

Hamilton, J. M. "Caught in the Nets of Prophecy? The Death of King Ahab and the Character of God." *Catholic Biblical Quarterly* 56 (1994): 649–63.

Harris S. L., and R. L. Platzner. *The Old Testament: An Introduction to the Hebrew Bible*. Boston: McGraw-Hill, 2003.

Haupt, P. "The Hebrew term שילש." *Beiträge zur Assyriologie und Semitischen Sprachwissen-schaft* 4 (1902): 583–87.

Hentschel, G. *I Könige.* Die Neue Echter Bibel. Würzburg: Echter Verlag, 1984.

—*2 Könige.* Die Neue Echter Bibel. Würzburg: Echter Verlag, 1985.

—*Die Elijaerzählungen: Zum Verhältnis von historischen Geschehen und geschichtlicher Erfahrung.* Erfurter Theologische Studien 33. Leipzig: St.-Benno-Verlag, 1977.

Hillers, D. R. *Treaty-Curses and the Old Testament.* Biblica et orientalia 16. Rome: Pontifical Biblical Institute, 1964.

Hobbs, T. R. *2 Kings.* Word Biblical Commentary 13. Waco, Tex.: Word Books, 1985.

Hoffmann, H.-D. *Reform und Reformen: Untersuchungen zu einem Grundthema der deuteronomistischen Geschichtsschreibung.* Abhandlungen zur Theologie des Alten und Neues Testaments 66. Zurich: Theologischer Verlag, 1980.

Hölscher, G. "Das Buch der Könige, seine Quellen und seine Redaktion." Pages 158–213 in *Eucharisterion: Studien zur Religion und Literatur des Alten und Neuen Testaments; Hermann Gunkel zum 60. Geburtstage, dem 23. Mai 1922 dargebracht von seinen Schülern und Freunden.* Edited by H. Schmidt; 2 vols.; Forschungen zur Religion und Literatur des Alten und Neuen Testaments 36. Göttingen: Vandenhoeck & Ruprecht, 1923.

—*Die Profeten.* Leipzig: J.C. Hinrichs, 1914.

—*Geschichtsschreibung in Israel: Untersuchungen zum Jahvisten und Elohisten.* Lund: C. W. K. Gleerup, 1952.

Horst, F. "Das Eigentum nach dem Alten Testament." Pages 203–21 in *Gottesrecht: Gesammelte Studien zum Recht im Alten Testament.* Munich: Chr. Kaiser, 1961. Article originally published 1949.

—"Zwei Begriffe für Eigentum (Bezitz): נַחֲלָה und אֲחֻזָּה." Pages 135–56 in *Verbannung und Heimkehr: Beiträge zur Geschichte und Theologie Israels im 6. und 5. Jahrhundert v. Chr. Festschrift Wilhelm Rudolph.* Tübingen: J. C. B. Mohr (Paul Siebeck), 1961.

Hossfeld, E. L., and E. Zenger. *Die Psalmen.* Vol. 1, *Psalm 1–50.* Die Neue Echter Bibel 29. Würzburg: Echter Verlag, 1993.

Jackson, B. S. "The Problem of Exod. XXI 22–25 (*Ius Talionis*)." *Vetus Testamentum* 23 (1973): 273–304

Jensen, J., and W. H. Irwin. "Isaiah 1–39." Pages 229–48 in *The New Jerome Biblical Commentary.* Edited by R. E. Brown, J. A. Fitzmyer, and R. E. Murphy. Englewoods Cliffs, N.J.: Prentice–Hall, 1990.

Jepsen, A. "Ahabs Buße: Ein kleiner Beitrag zur Methode literar-historischer Einordnung." Pages 145–55 in *Archäologie und Altes Testament: Festschrift K. Galling.* Edited by A. Kuschke and E. Kutsch. Tübingen: J. C. B. Mohr, 1970.

—*Die Quellen des Königsbuches.* Halle: Max Niemeyer, 1953.

—*Nabi, Soziologische Studien zur alttestamentlichen Literatur und Religionsgeschichte.* Munich: Beck, 1934.

Jones, G. H. *1 Kings 17:1–2 Kings 25:30.* Vol. 2, *1 and 2 Kings.* New Century Bible Commentary. Grand Rapids: Eerdmans, 1984.

Joüon, P. *A Grammar of Biblical Hebrew.* Translated and revised by T. Muraoka. 2 vols. Subsidia biblica 14/I–II. Rome: Editrice Pontificio Istituto Biblico, 1991.

—*Notes de critique textuelle.* Mél. 5, fasc. 2. n.p.: 1912.

Kaiser, O. *Isaiah 13–39.* Translated by R. A. Wilson. Old Testament Library. Philadelphia: Westminster, 1974. Originally published as *Der Prophet Jesaja/Kap. 13–39.* Das Alte Testament Deutsch 18. Göttingen: Vandenhoeck & Ruprecht, 1973.

Keil, C. F. and F. Delitzsch, eds. *Das Alte Testament.* Zweiter Teil. *Prophetische Geschichtsbücher.* Dritter Band. *Die Bücher der Könige.* Leipzig: Dörffling & Franke, 1876.

King, L. W. *Babylonian Boundary-Stones and Memorial-Tablets in the British Museum.* 2 vols; London: The British Museum, 1912.

Kittel, R. *Die Bücher der Könige*. Handkommentar zum Alten Testament I/5. Göttingen: Vandenhoeck & Ruprecht, 1900.

Klostermann, A. *Die Bücher Samuelis und der Könige*. Kurzer Handkommentar zur Alten und Neuen Testament 3. Nördlingen Verlag der C.H. Beck'schen Buchhandlung, 1887.

Knoppers, G. N. "'There was None Like Him': Incomparability in the Book of Kings." *Catholic Biblical Quarterly* 54, no. 1 (1992): 411–31

Koehler, L., and W. Baumgartner. *Lexicon in Veteris Testamenti Libros*. Leiden: Brill, 1953.

Kutscher, E. "Mittelhebräische und Jüdaisch-Aramäisch im Neuen Köhler–Baumgartner." Pages 158–75 in *Hebräische Wortforschung: Festschrift zum 80. Geburstag von Walter Baumgartner*. Edited by B. Hartmann et al. Supplements to Vetus Testamentum 16; Leiden: Brill, 1967.

Lambdin, T. O. *Introduction to Biblical Hebrew*. 9th ed. London: Darton, Longman & Todd, 1990.

Lang, B. *Monotheism and the Prophetic Minority*. The Social World of Biblical Antiquity 1. Sheffield: Almond Press, 1983.

Lehmann, M. R. "Biblical Oaths." *Zeitschrift für die alttestamentliche Wissenschaft* 81 (1969): 74–92.

Loewenstamm, S. E., "Exodus XXI 22–25." *Vetus Testamentum* 27 (1977): 352–60.

Long, B. O. *I Kings: With an Introduction to Historical Literature*. Forms of Old Testament Literature 9. Grand Rapids: Eerdmans, 1984.

—*II Kings: With an Introduction to Historical Literature*. Forms of Old Testament Literature 10. Grand Rapids: Eerdmans, 1991.

Luckenbill, D. D. *Ancient Records of Assyria and Babylonia*. Vol. 2, *Historical Records of Assyria, from Sargon to the End*. Chicago: The University of Chicago Press, 1927.

Malamat, A. "Mari and the Bible: Some Patterns of Tribal Organization and Institutions." *Journal of the American Oriental Society* 82 (1962): 143–50

Martin-Achard, R. "La Vigne de Naboth (1 Rois 21) d'apres des Études Récentes." *Etudes Théologiques et Religieuses* 66, no. 1 (1991): 1–16.

Matthews, V. H., and D. C. Benjamin. *The Social World of Ancient Israel, 1250–857 BCE*. Peabody, Mass.: Hendrickson, 1993.

Mauchline, J. *I–II Kings*. Peakes Commentary on the Bible. Edited by M. Black and H. H. Rowley. London: Nelson, 1962.

McKenzie, S. L. *The Trouble with Kings: The Composition of the Book of Kings in the Deuteronomistic History*. Supplements to Vetus Testamentum 42. Leiden: Brill, 1991.

Mendelsohn, I. "Samuel's Denunciation of Kingship in the Light of the Akkadian Documents from Ugarit." *Bulletin of the American Schools of Oriental Research* 143 (1956): 17–22.

Miller, J. M. "The Fall of the House of Ahab." *Vetus Testamentum* 17 (1967): 307–24.

Miller, J. M., and J. H. Hayes. *A History of Ancient Israel and Judah*. Philadelphia: Westminster, 1986.

Minokami, Y. *Die Revolution des Jehu*. Göttinger Theologische Arbeiten 38. Göttingen: Vandenhoeck & Ruprecht, 1989.

Miscall, P. D. "Elijah, Ahab, and Jehu: A Prophecy Fulfilled." *Prooftexts* 9/1 (1989): 73–83.

Mitchell, H. G. "The Omission of the Interrogative Particle." Pages 113–29 in *Old Testament and Semitic Studies in Memory of W. R. Harper*. Edited by Robert Francis Harper, Francis Brown, and George Foot Moore. Chicago: University of Chicago Press, 1908.

Montgomery, J. A. "Ascetic Strains in Early Judaism." *Journal of Biblical Literature* 51 (1932): 183–213.

Montgomery, J. A., and H. S. Gehman. *A Critical and Exegetical Commentary on the Books of Kings*. International Critical Commentary. Edinburgh: T. & T. Clark, 1951.

Mulzer, M. *Jehu schlägt Joram: Text-, literar- und struckturkritische Untersuchung zu 2 Kön 8,25–10,36.* Arbeiten zu Text und Sprache im Alten Testament 37. St. Ottilien: EOS Verlag, 1992.

Muraoka, T. *Emphatic Words and Structures in Biblical Hebrew.* Jerusalem: Magnes, 1985.

Murphy-O'Connor, J. *Paul the Letter-Writer.* Good News Studies 41. Collegeville: The Liturgical Press, 1995.

Napier, B. D. "The Omrides of Jezreel." *Vetus Testamentum* 9 (1959): 366–78.

Nelson, R. D. *First and Second Kings.* Interpretations. Atlanta: John Knox, 1987.

Newsome, J. D. *By the Waters of Babylon: An Introduction to the History and Theology of the Exile.* Atlanta: John Knox, 1979.

Niccacci, A. *The Syntax of the Verb in Classical Hebrew Prose.* Translated by W. G. E. Watson. Journal for the Study of the Old Testament Supplement Series 86. Sheffield: JSOT Press, 1990.

Noth, M. "Das Krongut der israelitischen Könige und seine Verwaltung." *Zeitschrift des Deutschen Palästina-Vereins* 50 (1927): 211–44.

—"The Deuteronomistic History." 2d ed. Journal for the Study of the Old Testament Supplement Series 15. Sheffield: JSOT Press, 1991.

—*Überlieferungsgeschichtliche Studien.* Vol. 1, *Die sammelnden und bearbeiten Geschichtswerke im Alten Testament.* Schriften der Königsberger gelehrten Gesellschaft. Geistewissenschaftliche Klasse 18 Jahrgang, Heft 2; Halle (Saale): Max Niemeyer, 1943.

Nowack, W. *Lehrbuch der hebräischen Archäologie.* Freiburg: J. C. B. Mohr (Paul Siebeck), 1894.

O'Brien, M. A. *The Deuteronomistic History Hypothesis: A Reassessment.* Orbis Biblicus et Orientalis 92; Göttingen: Vandenhoeck & Ruprecht, 1989.

Oeming, M. "Naboth, der Jesreeliter: Untersuchung zu den theologischen Motiven der Überlieferungsgeschichte von 1 Reg 21." *Zeitschrift für die alttestamentliche Wissenschaft* 98 (1986): 363–82.

Olyan, S. "*Hăšālôm*: Some Literary Considerations of 2 Kings 9." *Catholic Biblical Quarterly* 46 (1984): 652–68.

Oredsson, D. "Jezreel—Its Contribution to Iron Age Chronology." *Scandinavian Journal of the Old Testament* 12 (1998): 86–101.

Parker, S. B. "Jezebel's Reception of Jehu." *A Journal for the Study of the Northwest Semitic Languages and Literature* 1/1 (1978): 67–78.

Paul, S. *Studies in the Book of the Covenant in the Light of Cuneiform and Biblical Law.* Supplements to Vetus Testamentum 18. Leiden: Brill, 1970.

Peckham, B. *The Composition of the Deuteronomistic History.* Harvard Semitic Monographs 35. Atlanta: Scholars Press, 1985.

Pedersen, J. *Israel: Its Life and Culture.* Vol. 2. South Florida Studies in the History of Judaism 29. Atlanta: Scholars Press, 1991. All volumes originally published by Oxford University Press from 1926 to 1940.

Peels, H. G. L. *The Vengeance of God: The meaning of NQM and the Function of the NQM-Texts in the Context of Divine Revelation in the Old Testament.* Oudtestamentische Studiën 31. Leiden: Brill, 1995.

Polzin, R. *Late Biblical Hebrew: Toward an Historical Typology of Biblical Hebrew Prose.* Harvard Semitic Monographs 12. Missoula, Mont.: Scholars Press, 1976.

Rad, G. von. "Die deuteronomistische Geschichtstheologie in den Königsbüchern." Pages 189–204 in *Gesammelte Studien zum Alten Testament.* Munich: Chr. Kaiser, 1971. Article originally published 1947.

—*Old Testament Theology.* Vol. 2, *The Theology of Israel's Prophetic Traditions.* Translated by D. M. G. Stalker. New York: Harper & Row, 1965.

Rehm, M. *Das erste Buch der Könige: Ein Kommentar.* Würzburg: Echter Verlag, 1979.

—*Das zweite Buch der Könige: Ein Kommentar.* Würzburg: Echter Verlag, 1982.

Riley, W. *King and Cultus in Chronicles: Worship and the Reinterpretation of History.* Journal for the Study of the Old Testament Supplement Series 160. Sheffield: JSOT Press, 1993.

Roberts, J. J. M. "In Defense of the Monarchy: The Contribution of Israelite Kingship to Biblical Theology." Pages 377–96 in *Ancient Israelite Religion: Essays in Honor of Franck Moore Cross.* Edited by P. D. Miller, Jr., P. D. Hanson, and S. D. McBride. Philadelphia: Fortress, 1987.

Robinson, B. P. *Israel's Mysterious God: An Analysis of some Old Testament Narratives.* Newcastle upon Tyne: Grevatt & Grevatt, 1986.

Rofé, A. *The Prophetical Stories. The Narratives about the Prophets in the Hebrew Bible, their Literary Types and History.* Jerusalem: Magnes, 1988.

—"The Vineyard of Naboth: The Origin and the Message of the Story." *Vetus Testamentum* 38 (1988): 89–104.

Šanda, A. *Die Bücher der Könige.* Vol. 1, *Das erste Buch der Könige.* Evangelische Handbuch zum Alten Testament 9/1. Münster, 1911.

—*Die Bücher der Könige.* Vol. 2, *Das zweite Buch der Könige.* Evangelische Handbuch zum Alten Testament 9/2. Münster, 1912.

Sarna, N. M. "Naboth's Vineyard Revisited (1 Kings 21)." Pages 119–26 in *Tehillah le Moshe, Biblical and Judaic Studies in Honor of Moshe Greenberg.* Edited by Mordechai Cogan, Barry L. Eichler, and Jeffrey H. Tigay. Winona Lake, Ind.: Eisenbrauns, 1997.

Schaack, T. *Die Ungeduld des Papiers: Studien zum alttestamentlichen Verständnis des Schreibens anhand des Verbums katab im Kontext administrativer Vorgänge.* Beihefte zur Zeitschrift für die alttestamentliche Wissenschaft 262. Berlin: de Gruyter, 1998.

Schlögl, P. N. *Die Bücher der Könige, Die Bücher der Chronik.* Kurzgefasster Wissenschaftlicher Kommentar zu den Heiligen Schriften des Alten Testamentes I, 3, II. Vienna: Verlag von Mayer, 1911.

Schmidt, W. H. "Kritik am Königtum." Pages 440–61 in *Probleme biblischer Theologie: Gerhard von Rad zum 70. Geburtstag.* Edited by H. W. Wolff. Munich: Chr. Kaiser, 1971.

Schmitt, H.-C. *Elisa: Traditionsgeschichtliche Untersuchungen zur vorklassischen nordisraelitischen Prophetie.* Gütersloh: Gütersloher Verlagshaus Gerd Mohn, 1972.

Schmoldt, H. "Elijas Bodschaft an Ahab: Überlegungen zum Werdegang von 1 Kön 21." *Biblische Notizen* 28 (1985): 39–52

Schniedewind, W. M. "History and Interpretation: The Religion of Ahab and Manasseh in the Books of Kings." *Catholic Biblical Quarterly* 55 (1993): 649–61.

Seebass, H. "Der Fall Naboth in 1 Reg. XXI." *Vetus Testamentum* 24 (1974): 474–88.

Seeligmann, I. L. "Die Auffassung von der Prophetie in der deuteronomistischen und chronistischen Geschichtsschreibung (mit einem Exkurs über das Buch Jeremia)." Pages 254–84 in *Congress Volume: Göttingen, 1977.* Supplements to Vetus Testamentum 29. Leiden: Brill, 1978.

Sekine, M. "Literatursoziologische Beobachtungen zu den Elisaerzählungen." Pages 39–62 in *The Annual of the Japanese Biblical Institute.* Edited by M. Sekine and A. Satake. Tokyo: Yamamoto Shoten, 1975.

Ska, J. L. *"Our Fathers Have Told Us": Introduction to the Analysis of Hebrew Narratives.* Subsidia biblica 13, Rome: Editrice Pontificio Istituto Biblico, 1990.

Skinner, J. *The Book of the Prophet Isaiah I–XXXIX.* Cambridge: Cambridge University Press, 1930.

—*Kings.* The Century Bible: A Modern Commentary. London: Caxton, n.d., ca. 1893.

Smend, R. "The Deuteronomistic Elijah: A Contribution to the Old Testament Portrayal of the Prophets." Translated by D. A. Knight. *Old Testament Essays* 4 (1986): 28–45.

Smith-Christopher, D. L. "The Mixed Marriage Crisis in Ezra 9–10 and Nehemiah 13: A Study of the Sociology of the Post-Exilic Judean Community." Pages 243–65 in *Second Temple Studies*. Vol. 2, *Temple and Community in the Persian Period*. Edited by Tamara C. Eskenazi and Kent H. Richards. *Journal for the Study of the Old Testament*, Supplement Series 175. Sheffield; JSOT Press, 1994.

Smith, D. L. *The Religion of the Landless: The Social Context of the Babylonian Exile*. Bloomington, Ind.: Meyer-Stone Books, 1989.

Smith, M. "Jewish Religion in the Persian Period." Pages 217–78 in *The Cambridge History of Judaism*. Vol. 1, *Introduction: The Persian Period*. Edited by W. D. Davies and L. Finkelstein. Cambridge: Cambridge University Press, 1984.

Snaith, N. H. "The First and Second Books of Kings (Introduction and Exegesis)." Pages 3–338 in vol. 3 of *The Interpreter's Bible*. Edited by G. A. Buttrick et al. 12 vols. New York, 1951–57.

—*Notes on the Hebrew Text of I Kings, XVII–XIX and XXI–XXII*. London: Epworth Press, 1954. Reprint 1965.

Soggin, J. A. *A History of Israel: From the Beginnings to the Bar Kochba Revolt, A.D. 135.* Translated by J. Bowden. London: SCM Press, 1984.

—*Introduction to the Old Testament*. Translated by J. Bowden. 3d ed. London: SCM Press, 1989.

—"Jezabel, oder die fremde Frau." Pages 453–59 in *Mélanges bibliques et orientaux en l'honneur de M. Henri Cazelles*. Edited by A. Caquot and M. Delcor. Alter Orient und Altes Testament 212. Kevelaer: Butzon & Bercker, 1981.

Speiser, E. A. "An Angelic 'Curse': Exodus 14:20." *Journal of the American Oriental Society* 80 (1960): 198–200.

Stade, B., and F. Schwally. *The Book of Kings: Critical Edition of the Hebrew Text*. Leipzig: J.C. Hinrichs, 1904.

Steck, O. H. *Bereitete Heimkehr: Jesaja 35 als redactionelle Brücke zwischen dem Ersten und Zweiten Jesaja*. Stuttgarter Bibelstudien 121. Stuttgart: Verlag Katholisches Bibelwerk, 1985.

—*Überlieferung und Zeitgeschichte in den Elia-Erzählungen*. Wissenschaftliche Monographien zum Alten und Neuen Testament 26. Neukirchen–Vluyn: Neukirchener Verlag, 1968.

Stern, E. "The Persian Empire and the Political and Social History of Palestine in the Persian Period." Pages 70–87 in *The Cambridge History of Judaism*. Vol. 1, *Introduction: The Persian Period*. Edited by W. D. Davies and L. Finkelstein. Cambridge: Cambridge University Press, 1984.

Stipp, H. -J. "Ahabs Buße und die Komposition des deuteronomistischen Geschichtswerks." *Biblica* 76 (1995): 471–97.

Thenius, O. *Die Bücher der Könige*. Kurzer Handcommentar zur Alten Testament 9. Leipzig: Weidmann, 1849. 2d. ed. 1873.

Thiel, W. "Deuteronomische Redaktionsarbeit in den Elia-Erzählungen." Pages 14–171 in *Congress Volume: Leuven, 1989.*, Supplements to Vetus Testamentum 43. Leiden: Brill, 1991.

Timm, S. *Die Dynastie Omri*. Forschungen zur Religion und Literatur des Alten und Neuen Testaments 124. Göttingen: Vandenhoeck & Ruprecht, 1982.

Tournay, R. J. "Les Affinités du Ps. XLV avec le Cantique des Cantiques et leur Interprétation Messianique." Pages 168–212 in *Congress Volume: Bonn, 1962*. Supplements Vetus Testamentum 9. Leiden: Brill, 1963.

—Recension of D. Wolfers, *Deep Things out of Darkness: The Book of Job and a New English Translation*. *Revue Biblique* 104 no. 3 (1997): 416–19.

Trebolle Barrera, J. C. *Jehú y Joás, Texto y composición literaria de 2 Reyes 9–11.* Institución San Jerónimo 17. Valencia: Institución San Jerónimo, 1984.

Uffenheimer, B. "The Deeds of Naboth the Jezreelite." Pages 47–78 in *Sefer Yosef Braslavi.* Jerusalem: Kiryat-Sepher, 1970 (Hebrew).

Ussishkin, D. and J. Woodhead. "Excavations at Tel Jezreel 1992–1993: Second Preliminary Report." The British School of Archaeology in Jerusalem. (Reprint from *Levant* XXVI [1994]: 1–71).

Van Seters, J. *In Search of History: Historiography in the Ancient World and the Origins of Biblical History.* Winona Lake, Ind.: Eisenbrauns, 1997. Originally published New Haven: Yale University Press, 1983.

Vaux, R. de. *Ancient Israel, Its Life and Institution.* Translated by J. McHugh. New York: McGraw-Hill, 1961.

—"Le Cycle d'Élie dans les Livres des Rois." Pages 53–89 in *Élie le Prophète*, Vol. 1. *Les Étude Carmélitaines.* Paris. Desclée de Brouwer, 1956.

—"Rois." Pages 375–435 in *La Bible de Jérusalem.* Edited by R. de Vaux et al. Paris: Les Éditions du Cerf, 1973.

Vaux, R. de (trans.). *Les livres des Rois.* Traduite en français sous la direction de l'École Biblique de Jérusalem. La Sainte Bible 9. Paris: Cerf, 1949.

Veijola, T. *Das Königtum in der Beurteilung der deuteronomistischen Historiographie: Eine redaktionsgeschichtliche Untersuchung.* Annales Academiae Scientiarum Fennicae 198. Helsinki: Suomalainen Tiedeakatemia, 1977.

Wallace, H. N. "The Oracles against the Israelite Dynasties in 1 and 2 Kings." *Biblica* 67 (1986): 21–40.

Walsh, J. T. *I Kings.* Edited by D. W. Cotter. Studies in Hebrew Narrative and Poetry. Collegeville: The Liturgical Press, 1996.

—"Methods and Meanings: Multiple Studies of I Kings 21." *Journal of Biblical Literature* 111, no. 2 (1992): 193–211.

Washington, H. C. "The Strange Woman (אשה זרה/נכריה) of Proverbs 1–9 and Post-Exilic Judean Society." Pages 217–42 in *Second Temple Studies.* Vol 2, *Temple and Community in the Persian Period.* Edited by Tamara C. Eskenazi and Kent H. Richards. Journal for the Study of the Old Testament Supplement Series 175. Sheffield: JSOT Press, 1994.

Watts, J. D. W. *Isaiah 34–66.* Word Biblical Commentary 25. Waco, Tex.: Word Books, 1987.

Weinfeld, M. *Deuteronomy and the Deuteronomic School.* Winona Lake, Ind.: Eisenbrauns, 1992. Originally published Oxford: Oxford University Press, 1972.

Weippert, H. "Ahab el campeador? Redaktionsgeschichtliche Untersuchungen zu 1 Kön 22." *Biblica* 69 (1988): 457–79.

Wellhausen, J. *Die Composition des Hexateuchs und der historischen Bücher des Alten Testaments.* 3d ed. Berlin: Georg Reimer, 1899.

—*Prolegomena zur Geschichte Israels.* 3d ed. Berlin: Georg Reimer, 1886.

Welten, P. "Nabot's Weinberg (I Könige 21)." *Evangelische Theologie* 33 (1973): 18–32

Westbrook, R. "Lex Talionis and Exodus 21, 22–25." *Revue Biblique* 93 (1986): 52–69.

Westermann, C. *Grundformen prophetischer Rede.* Beiträge zur evangelischen Theologie 31. Munich: Chr. Kaiser, 1960.

White, M. *The Elijah Legends and Jehu's Coup.* Brown Judaica Studies 311. Atlanta: Scholars Press, 1997.

—"Naboth's Vineyard and Jehu's Coup: The Legitimization of a Dynastic Extermination." *Vetus Testamentum* 44, no. 1 (1994): 66–76.

Whitley, C. F. "The Deuteronomic Presentation of the House of Omri." *Vetus Testamentum* 2 (1952): 137–52.

Widyapranawa, S. H. *The Lord is Savior: Faith in National Crisis: Isaiah 1–39.* International Theological Commentary. Grand Rapids: Eerdmans, 1990.

Williamson, H. G. M. "Jezreel in Biblical Texts." *Tel Aviv* 18, no.1 (1991): 72–92.

Wiseman, D. J. "The Vassal Treaties of Esarhaddon." *Iraq* 20 (1958): 1–99.

Wolfers, D. *Deep Things Out of Darkness: The Book of Job.* Grand Rapids: Eerdmans, 1995.

Wolff, H. W. " 'Die Begründungen,' der prophetischen Heils- und Unheilssprüche." *Zeitschrift für die alttestamentliche Wissenschaft* 52 (1934): 1–22.

Würthwein, E. *Die Bücher der Könige 1. Kön. 17–2 Kön. 25.* Das Alte Testament Deutsch 11/2. Göttingen: Vandenhoeck & Ruprecht, 1984.

—"Naboth-Novelle und Elia-Wort." *Zeitschrift für Theologie und Kirche* 75 (1978): 375–97.

Zakovitch, Y. "The Tale of Naboth's Vineyard: I Kings 21." Pages 379–405 in M. Weiss, *The Bible from Within: The Method of Total Interpretation.* Jerusalem: Magnes, 1984.

Zorell, F. *Lexicon Hebraicum Veteris Testamenti.* Rome: The Pontifical Biblical Institute, 1984.

## INDEX OF REFERENCES

# INDEX OF AUTHORS